PLATO'S REPUBLIC
A STUDY GUIDE

STEPHAN T. MAYO
MICHAEL S. RUSSO

SophiaOmni

Authors: Stephan T. Mayo and Michael S. Russo
Project Editor: Alexa Sussman

ISBN: 978-1475283044

SophiaOmni

Visit our website at:
www.sophiaomni.org

DEDICATION

This book would not have been possible without the committed men and women who have gone before us in the discipline of philosophy and who inspired us with their passion for wisdom and their love of the truth. This study edition is dedicted in their honor and to their memories.

CONTENTS

INTRODUCTION TO
PLATO'S REPUBLIC

Plato was born in Athens in 427 BC to a well established aristocratic family. His father, Ariston, could trace his lineage back to the old kings of Athens; his mother, Perictione, was a sister of Charmides and the cousin of Critias, two prominent figures in the Athenian oligarchy of 404-403 BC. Plato also had two brothers, Glaucon and Adeimantus, who are portrayed in his masterpiece, *The Republic*. Given this illustrious background it is almost certain that Plato, as a young man, was groomed for a life of public service.

Only a few years before Plato was born, Athens entered into a drawn-out war with Sparta (the Peloponnesian War), that eventually led to the decline of Athens' power in the Mediterranean world. Although he grew up during Athens' great experiment with democracy during the Fifth Century, it was certainly evident at this time that democracy was failing, and that some other type of political system was needed.

Around the age of twenty, he became a disciple of Socrates, the father of Western philosophy. Socrates, as you may recall from reading the *Apology,* made it his mission to examine the beliefs his fellow Athenians in order to help them and himself attain wisdom. Socrates' tenacious style of philosophical examination earned him a number of powerful enemies. In 399 BC he was tried on the charges of impiety and corruption of the city's youth, found guilty, and eventually forced to take his own life. The influence of Socrates on Plato's philosophical career cannot be understated. Plato was so taken by the character and ideas of Socrates that he used Socrates as the central figure in all his philosophical dialogues, and made considerable use of Socrates' method during his early part of his career.

Disillusioned by the manner of Socrates' death, Plato he gave up all thoughts of a political career, dedicating himself instead wholly to philosophy. He left Athens and for the next twelve years traveled around the Mediterranean, studying philosophy, geometry, religion, and other sciences. During this period, Plato was also invited to Syracuse, where he became friendly with Dion, the bother-in-law of Dionysius, the tyrant of the city. He would return to this city twice again (in 367 and 361) in a futile effort to implement some of the political ideas that he had developed in his *Republic* (Ep. 7).

Eventually Plato returned to Athens in 387 to found his Academy, the aim of which was to philosophically educate the future leaders of Greek society. The Academy has been called the first European university, since its studies included, not just philosophy, but all the known sciences. Plato himself was said to have delivered many of the lectures at the Academy, although the notes from these lectures were never published. Among the most famous students of the Academy was Aristotle, who would later go on to found his own school, the Lyceum. Plato's Academy would continue to educate Athenian noblemen for several centuries, influencing most of the major philosophical schools of the Western world. Plato died at the age of 80 in 347 BC.

THE DIALOGUES

Most of Plato's philosophical writing takes the form of dialogues. It is believed that all forty-two of the dialogues that Plato wrote have survived. These dialogues were written for educated laymen (as opposed to the elite in his academy) in order to interest them in philosophy (Taylor 10). To sum up their common characteristics, Plato's dialogues:

- are philosophical discussions between two or more participants.
- usually focus on a specific theme: i.e., justice, friendship, piety.
- are written for the most part like regular conversations, which often include digressions and frequently are inconclusive.

Plato's dialogues are not just great works of philosophy; they are also recognized as great literary works as well. He goes to much effort to carefully set the scene of each dialogue and to develop the personalities of each of the characters in them. One is frequently amazed at just how dramatic many of these dialogues are considering their lofty topics.

Plato's dialogues can be divided into three periods:

Early Dialogues	Middle Dialogues	Late Dialogues
Apology	Gorgias	Symposium
Crito	Meno	Phaedo
Laches	Euthydemus	Republic, Books 2-10
Euthyphro	Hippias I and II	Timaeus
Republic, Book 1	Cratylas	Laws

As has already been pointed out, Plato uses Socrates as the main interlocutor in his dialogues. The specific way that Plato makes use of the character of Socrates varies somewhat during the different periods in which Plato wrote.

In the early dialogues the Socrates that Plato presents to the reader is probably close to the historic Socrates. Socrates is portrayed in these dialogues as precisely what he was in real life—a gadfly, whose aim was to make people recognize that many of their beliefs are baseless. The Socrates of these early dialogues claims to be ignorant of everything except his own ignorance, and as such rarely presents his own position on the topics being discussed. Plato's aim, then, in these early dialogues primarily is critical: that is, to tear apart the inadequate moral views of others.

In the middle dialogues, Plato is coming into his own as a philosopher and is starting to develop some of his own metaphysical and epistemological positions. It is during this period that Plato begins to introduce his theory of the forms into his writings. In the late dialogues Plato uses Socrates almost exclusively to advance his own views. His approach in these dialogues is essentially constructive: that is, to develop his own mature philosophical system.

The Republic is an interesting work because in it we get the best of both the early and later dialogues. Book one is written as a traditional dialogue in which Socrates is represented in a fairly historical way, critically reacting to the views of others in the dialogue. But the rest of the text (Books 2-10) is much more of a monologue in which Socrates serves as little more than a mouth-piece for Plato's own political views.

BACKGROUND TO THE REPUBLIC

Purpose of Republic

In her *Introduction to the Republic*, Julia Annas proposes two interesting theories concerning Plato's purpose in writing the Republic. One theory is that the *Republic* can be read as a conservative reaction to the moral skepticism being taught by the Sophists. The Sophists in Athens were a group of philosophers who taught rhetoric (the art of persuasion) to those seeking a career in public life. In general they espoused a view that held that there was no objective right or wrong and that morality was merely a matter of convention. Plato's purpose in writing the *Republic*, then, may have been to refute the moral skepticism of the Sophists by demonstrating that there are indeed objective moral truths and that, therefore, moral standards are not meaningless. According to Annas, there is strong evidence within the text of the *Republic* to support this interpretation. The bulk of the work, for example, seems to be a response to the sophist Thrasymachus' view that only a sucker would behave justly, and that no one would obey moral rules if they thought they could get away with violating them. In this light, Plato can be seen in Books 2-10 as laying a foundation for conventional moral values (7-8).

But the *Republic* according to Annas can also be read as a revolutionary work as well. Some of Plato's ideas in the work are as shocking today as they certainly would have been in his own times: the ideal society that he proposes is decidedly authoritarian; he argues for rule by an educated elite who swap wives, live off the State and work without pay. According to this view, Plato's aim in the work may have been to provoke and startle his readers. He wants to force us to think and to be prepared to challenge our own unreflective views on the good life (9-10).

Dikaiosune

Whatever Plato's purpose may have been in writing the *Republic,* it is clear that his main preoccupation in the work is to give a detailed account of *dikaiosune*. According to Annas the term can be understood in two different senses. In its broad sense, *dikaiosune* can be translated as "righteousness" or simply as "morality." In this sense *The Republic* can be read as a quest for the right way to live. In its more narrow sense, *dikaiosune* can be understood for Plato as the opposite of *pleonexia* (that is, wanting more than one is entitled to). In this sense, the term could be translated simply as "justice." (11-12).

Although throughout the *Republic* Plato moves back and forth between both of these understandings of *dikaiosune*, for the sake of consistency the term will be translated throughout this commentary as "justice" in keeping with the general consensus of most contemporary translators of the work.

Outline of Republic

Book 1: What is Justice?
- Introduction (327a-328b)
- Cephalus (328b-331d)
- Polemarchus (331e-335e)
- Thrasymachus (336b-354c)

Books 2-4: Justice in the City and in the Soul
- Stating the Problem (357a-367e)
- Justice in the City (367e-434d)

- Justice in the Soul (434d-445b)

Books 5-7: Plato's Politics

- Women, Family and Warfare (445b-471c)

- The Philosopher-King (471c-541b)

Books 8-9: Injustice in the City and in the Soul

- Four Imperfect Cities and Souls (543a-576b)

- Just and Unjust Lives (576b-592b)

Book 10: Poetry and Rewards of Justice

- Critique of Poetry (595a-608b)

- Rewards of Justice (608c-621d)

ABOUT THE TRANSLATION

The translation that we have opted to use for this edition is the perennial version by Benjamin Jowett. There are many other wonderful editions of the *Republic* available in bookstores, but none, to our way of thinking, better captures the spirit of Plato's original text.

Of course even the best translation of a great work needs updating over time. We've taken the liberty, therefore, of modernizing Jowett's translation where needed and subdividing his edition of the *Republic*—with appropriate sections titles—to make it more accessible to those unfamiliar with Plato's philosophy.

SUGGESTIONS FOR FURTHER READING

Altman, William H. F. *Plato the Teacher: The Crisis of the Republic.* Lanham, MD: Lexington Books, 2012. [1-36]

Annas, Julia. *An Introduction to Plato's Republic.* Oxford: Clarendon Press, 1981. [1-15]

Copleston, Frederick. *History of Philosophy.* Vol. 1: Greece and Rome. New York: Doubleday, 1993. [127-141]

Irwin, Terence. *Plato's Ethics.* New York: Oxford UP, 1995. [3-16]

Kraut, Richard. "Introduction to the Study of Plato." *The Cambridge Companion to Plato.* Ed. Richard Kraut. Cambridge: Cambridge University Press. [1-50]

Pappas, Nickolas. *Plato and the Republic.* New York: Routledge, 1995. [3-23]

Purshouse, Luke. *Plato's Republic: A Reader's Guide.* London: Continuum, 2006. [1-15]

Rowe, Christopher. "The Literary and Philosophical Style of the *Republic*." *The Blackwell Guide to Plato's Republic.* Malden, MA: Blackwell, 2006. [7-24]

Sayers, Sean. *Plato's Republic: An Introduction.* Edinburgh: Edinburgh University Press, 1999. [1-8]

Taylor, A. E. *Plato: The Man and His Work.* Cleveland: Meridian, 1964. [1-22]

White, Nicholas P. *A Companion to Plato's Republic.* Indianapolis, Hackett, 1979. [9-60]

1

THE PROBLEM OF JUSTICE

INTRODUCTION [327A-328B]

The setting for the dialogue is the Piraeus, Athen's port located on the Aegean six miles from the city. Socrates and Glaucon (Plato's brother) are attending the festival of Bendis. This locale is appropriate for the main issue of the Republic—namely, "What is Justice?" More specifically, the topic is: what is the ideally just *polis*, or city-state, the primary political unit of the Greeks? The locale is appropriate because the discussants are outside of Athens and can figuratively look back at the City to discuss it, and also because the location is a bustling international port where the laws and customs of the Atheneans can be compared with those of foreign nations.

CEPHALUS [328B-331D]

Invited back to the home of Cephalus for supper, Socrates joins a group of young men who have gathered there. Cephalus is an elderly and wealthy *metic* (a foreign-born non-citizen) who has made a fortune as an arms manufacturer.

After greeting Cephalus, Socrates engages him in a discussion of whether the elderly are happy or not. Cephalus advances the view that his superior character (*ethos*) rather than his wealth is the secret of his successful aging and contentment. As opposed to his youth when he ignored tales of divine retribution for corrupt acts, his wealth now provides him with the means to pay his debts immediately, keep his word, and make expensive sacrifices to the demanding gods. His conventional publicly respected character, now honest and pious, protects him from the fear of divine retribution after death (328b). Note well that although *outwardly* respectable, Cephalus is still *inwardly* motivated by the selfish desire to avoid punishment, rather than by the sincere conviction that men are owed repayment and the truth and the gods should be duly worshipped.

Socrates questions Cephalus's view that justice is paying your debts and telling the truth (to men and to gods). He asks if it would be just to return borrowed weapons from a friend who, having gone insane, comes to repossess his weapons (Does the right to bear arms extend to the criminally insane?).

Here Socrates demonstrates his dialectical method: an attempt is made to define justice (paying debts) and a devastating counter-example is evoked (returning borrowed weapons to a lunatic). The definition is shown to be inadequate (too broad to exclude unjust events) and the search for the universal nature (eidos) of justice continues (331c-e).

In confronting an outwardly appearing just authority, Socrates is fulfilling the divine commandment received through the oracle of Delphi to demonstrate to those who falsely claim to have knowledge and wisdom that, like Socrates himself, they know nothing. Plato seems to tire of Socrates' sacred mission of exposing intellectual fraud by replacing it with the Theory of Forms, that is, with perfectly adequate definitions. This philosophical development is detectable in the progress from the 1st Book to Books 2-10 of the *Republic*.

POLEMARCHUS [331E-336A]

Polemarchus, Cephalus's son and heir, takes over the argument and agrees that it is not always *fitting* to return the insane man his weapons. Justice is giving what is *fitting* to people. Thus justice is giving goods to friends and harms to enemies.

Socrates challenges Polemarchus's notion that justice is giving goods to friends. He asks who, in the giving of the good of medicine, would Polemarchus utilize: the physician or the just person? In giving the good of food: the farmer or the just person? And so on. In each case, Polemarchus (rather foolishly) chooses the craftsperson. Then Socrates asks when is a just person useful and Polemarchus answers: "When goods are being stored." However, when goods are stored, they are *useless*. Socrates makes Polemarchus conclude that justice is useless when goods are useful and useful when goods are useless—in other words, an *absurdity*.

THE CRAFT ANALOGY

To fully understand this argument and others throughout The *Republic*, we should introduce an *assumption* of the ancient Greek readers of *The*

Republic: The nature of a craft (*techne*). An *assumption* is a belief (often unacknowledged) that is uncritically accepted as true. Though hidden, an assumption may serve as a premise in a line of reasoning toward a conclusion. What every 5th Century BC Athenian assumed was that every *techne* has a *telos*. *Techne* (from which we derive "technique," "technology") means craft or art in the broadest of terms—everything from carpentry to nursing to music-making. *Telos* means "goal" or "end." Arising out of the need or desire of humans for some good (*agathon*), a techne (craft) is developed to meet this need or desire. The *agathon* or good of the craft becomes the telos of the craft, that is, what the craftperson is aiming at achieving.

Techne	Telos (Agathon)
farming	crops (food for nourishment)
carpentry	furniture (sitting for comfort)

So every *techne* has a *telos*, a good internal (that is, specific to) the craft. It is peculiarly "classic" to assume that the primary *purpose* of an occupation is to produce a product or a service, rather than for the financial benefit of the practitioner.

Not everybody is good at his or her job. Some are excellent. *Arete* is the specific excellence of a craft. To become excellent at a craft, one needs to develop *specific* skills—the skills of the farmer are different than the skills of a carpenter. To gain these skills, one needs:

1.   to gain a specialized education,
2.   to emulate a model or mentor (one who possesses the desired skills), and
3.   to gain lots of experience and practice in the art (with all of the failure, hardship, trial and error that accompany real life endeavors).

If, however, the training and education are successful, the craftperson may be able to

1.   effectively achieve the *telos* of the craft,
2.   in a timely, efficient way, and
3.   in a consistent way.

When craftspersons *effectively*, *efficiently* and *consistently* achieve the *telos* of the craft, they become excellent at their craft. They obtain the virtue or *arete* that is proper to the craft. The *virtue* of a craft is the specific excellence of the craft. For example, a farmer who, year after year, produces a high yield of quality crops is an excellent farmer, that is, has the *arete* of the *techne*.

Techne	Arete	Telos (Agathon)
farming	green thumb (excellence at farming)	crops (food for nourishment)
carpentry	master craftsperson (excellence at carpentry)	furniture (e.g. sitting pretty)

The Craft as an Analogy for Life: Moral character is likened to mastery of a craft. Later Socrates will refer to moral virtue (moral excellence) as similar to the virtue of a craft. The Moral virtues of Wisdom, Courage, Justice and Moderation are necessary skills of a human life capable of achieving the *telos* or goal of human life, namely, *eudaimonia* (happiness or human flourishing).

Techne	Arete	Telos (Agathon)
Warcraft	Strength Speed Courage Judgment	Defense of Polis (peace / glory)
Life	Wisdsom Courage Justice Moderation	Eudaimonia (human flourishing / happiness)

BACK TO THE DIALOGUE

Polemarchus could accept from Socrates that a physician is more useful than a just person in the dispensing of medicine *only if* he missed altogether the *difference* between the kind of value that the moral virtue of justice would bring to you if your doctor were just, as opposed to the material value of receiving medication (there are quacks out there galore). An unjust physician could *not* be counted on to act in your best interests.

Socrates goes on to suggest that the guard who stands over the stored (useless) goods is also in the very best position to steal those goods. Polemarchus's definition of justice as giving goods to friends makes no provision as to how those goods are obtained. Thus Polemarchus has led us to the absurd position that the "just person is a kind of thief." In effect, he confuses justice with generosity.

This argument is called a *reductio ad absurdum*. When a debater can "reduce" the argument of an opponent "to an absurdity," we, the audience, will recognize it as inadequate. Socrates would also have been aware that the noble craft of the warrior in the Hellenic Age was burdened with the *assumption* that the armed man had privileges over the possessions of the citizens and ancient warfare often was indistinguishable from marauding, raping and pillaging ("To the victors go the spoils").

Socrates proceeds to question Polemarchus's notion of justice as generosity to friends. If Polemarchus has ever made a mistake between a true friend and a phony, then his justice may entail giving goods to *enemies* (false friends) and harms to *friends* (falsely accused innocents). Polemarchus is accustomed to counting people who look like him, belong to his profession, and speak his language as friends and anyone else as an enemy (the barbarian). Dehumanizing and demonizing the "enemy" often comes with military training. Polemarchus is generous to comrades, the just and unjust alike. So it is unlikely that he would go beyond the surface in defining justice.

Finally, Socrates asks whether a just person would willingly harm anyone. Polemarchus, a warrior, is understandably confused because what else does a soldier do other than wound and kill enemies? Socrates asks does a racehorse have a nature? And does that nature have a *telos*? [Another assumption of the Ancient Greek and Roman philosophers (later challenged by Darwin) was that natural species strive to realize natural goals—the acorn (unconsciously) strives to realize the form of the oak tree—the colt strives to realize the form of the thoroughbred horse.]

Now Socrates asks if harming the horse will help or hinder its fulfillment of its nature. Clearly injuring the horse will make it worse. Does the just person try to make a person just or unjust? Clearly justice seeks to produce justice. But injuring a person makes him unjust, so the just person never deliberately injures anyone, friend or enemy.

At this point we should make the distinction that Socrates fails to provide Polemarchus. Socrates, a warrior in the Peloponnesian Wars, was no pacifist, nor did he consider his own imprisonment or execution beyond the provinces of the City-State (he defends the right of the State to execute him in the *Phaedrus)*. Socrates distinguishes between harming a person *physically* and harming a person's *character*. A just person never deliberately intends to injure anyone's character. It is quite possible to promote a person's moral character *and* to injure them physically as, for example, in the case of a just war or rehabilitative retribution for wrongdoing. When we act in self-defense, we prevent another from committing an unjust act. Unless performed in a sadistic or vengeful manner, punishing a child or a wrong-doer, though physically "harming" them, could have the effect of making the child or wrong-doer more responsible and attentive to the consequences of their actions. Punishment for wrongdoing is perfectly reconcilable with the notion that the just person never deliberately harms anyone.

18   PLATO'S REPUBLIC

Suggestions for Further Reading

Altman, William H. F. *Plato the Teacher: The Crisis of the Republic.* Lanham, MD: Lexington Books, 2012. [77-87]

Annas, Julia. *An Introduction to Plato's Republic.* New York: Oxford, 1981. [16-58]

Benardete, Seth. *Socrates' Second Sailing: On Plato's* Republic. Chicago: University of Chicago Press, 1989. [9-19]

Bloom, Allan. *The Republic of Plato.* New York: Harper Collins, 1968. [310-325]

Devin, Stauffen. *Plato's Introduction to the Question of Justice.* Albany: State University of New York Press, 2001.

Irwin, Terence. *Plato's Ethics.* New York: Oxford UP, 1995. [169-180]

Lycos, Kimon. *Plato on Justice and Power.* Albany: State University of New York Press, 1987. [21-39]

Pappas, Nickolas. *Plato and the Republic.* New York: Routledge, 1995. [27-38]

Reeve, C.D.C. *Philosopher-Kings: The Argument of Plato's Republic.* Princeton, NJ: Princeton UP, 1988. [3-24]

Rosen, Stanley. *Plato's Republic: A Study.* New Haven: Yale University Press, 2005. [19-37]

Sallis, John. *Being and Logos: Reading Platonic Dialogues.* 3rd ed. Bloomington, IN: Indiana UP, 1996. [321-334]

Sesonske, Alexander. "Plato's Apology: *Republic* I." *Phronesis* 6 (1961): 29-36.

Sparshott, F. E., "Socrates and Thrasymachus." *Monist* 50 (1966): 421-459.

Tiles, J. E. "Techne and Moral Expertise." *Philosophy* 59 (1984): 49-66.

White, Nicholas P. *A Companion to Plato's Republic.* Indianapolis, Hackett, 1979. [61-73]

BOOK I

Persons of the Dialogue: *Socrates, Cephalus, Glacon, Thrasymachus, Adeimantus, Cleitophon, and Polemarchus.*

Scene: *The scene is laid in the house of Cephalus at the Piraeus; and the whole dialogue is narrated by Socrates the day after it actually took place to Timaeus Hermocrates, Critias, and a nameless person, who are introduced in the Timaeus.*

INTRODUCTION [327A-328B]

I went down yesterday to the Piraeus with Glaucon the son of Ariston, that I might offer up my prayers to the goddess (Bendis, the Thracian Artemis); and also because I wanted to see in what manner they would celebrate the festival, which was a new thing. I was delighted with the procession of the inhabitants; but that of the Thracians was equally, if not more, beautiful. When we had finished our prayers and viewed the spectacle, we turned in the direction of the city; and at that instant Polemarchus the son of Cephalus chanced to catch sight of us from a distance as we were starting on our way home, and told his servant to run and bid us wait for him. The servant took hold of me by the cloak behind, and said: Polemarchus desires you to wait.

I turned round, and asked him where his master was.

There he is, said the youth, coming after you, if you will only wait.

Certainly we will, said Glaucon; and in a few minutes Polemarchus appeared, and with him Adeimantus, Glaucon's brother, Niceratus the son of Nicias, and several others who had been at the procession.

Polemarchus said to me: I perceive, Socrates, that you and your companion are already on your way to the city.

You are not far wrong, I said.

But do you see, he rejoined, how many we are?

Of course.

And are you stronger than all these? for if not, you will have to remain where you are.

May there not be the alternative, I said, that we may persuade you to let us go?

But can you persuade us, if we refuse to listen to you? he said.

Certainly not, replied Glaucon.

Then we are not going to listen; of that you may be assured.

328   Adeimantus added: Has no one told you of the torch-race on horseback in honour of the goddess which will take place in the evening?

With horses! I replied: That is a novelty. Will horsemen carry torches and pass them one to another during the race?

Yes, said Polemarchus, and not only so, but a festival will be celebrated at night, which you certainly ought to see. Let us rise soon after supper and see this festival; there will be a gathering of

b   young men, and we will have a good talk. Stay then, and do not be perverse.

Glaucon said: I suppose, since you insist, that we must.

Very good, I replied.

CEPHALUS [328B–331D]

Accordingly we went with Polemarchus to his house; and there we found his brothers Lysias and Euthydemus, and with them Thrasymachus the Chalcedonian, Charmantides the Paeanian, and Cleitophon the son of Aristonymus. There too was Cephalus the father of

c   Polemarchus, whom I had not seen for a long time, and I thought him very much aged. He was seated on a cushioned chair, and had a garland on his head, for he had been sacrificing in the court; and there were some other chairs in the room arranged in a semicircle, upon which we sat down by him. He saluted me eagerly, and then he said:—

You don't come to see me, Socrates, as often as you ought: If I were still able to go and see you I would not ask you to come to me. But at my age I can hardly get to the city, and therefore you should

d   come oftener to the Piraeus. For let me tell you, that the more the pleasures of the body fade away, the greater to me is the pleasure and charm of conversation. Do not then deny my request, but make our house your resort and keep company with these young men; we are old friends, and you will be quite at home with us.

I replied: There is nothing which for my part I like better, Cephalus, than conversing with aged men; for I regard them as travellers who have gone a journey which I too may have to go, and of whom I ought to enquire, whether the way is smooth and easy, or rugged and difficult. And this is a question which I should like to ask of you who have arrived at that time which the poets call the 'threshold of old age'—Is life harder towards the end, or what report do you give of it?

I will tell you, Socrates, he said, what my own feeling is. Men of my age flock together; we are birds of a feather, as the old proverb says; and at our meetings the tale of my acquaintance commonly is—I cannot eat, I cannot drink; the pleasures of youth and love are fled away: there was a good time once, but now that is gone, and life is no longer life. Some complain of the slights which are put upon them by relations, and they will tell you sadly of how many evils their old age is the cause. But to me, Socrates, these complainers seem to blame that which is not really in fault. For if old age were the cause, I too being old, and every other old man, would have felt as they do. But this is not my own experience, nor that of others whom I have known. How well I remember the aged poet Sophocles, when in answer to the question, How does love suit with age, Sophocles,—are you still the man you were? Peace, he replied; most gladly have I escaped the thing of which you speak; I feel as if I had escaped from a mad and furious master. His words have often occurred to my mind since, and they seem as good to me now as at the time when he uttered them. For certainly old age has a great sense of calm and freedom; when the passions relax their hold, then, as Sophocles says, we are freed from the grasp not of one mad master only, but of many. The truth is, Socrates, that these regrets, and also the complaints about relations, are to be attributed to the same cause, which is not old age, but men's characters and tempers; for he who is of a calm and happy nature will hardly feel the pressure of age, but to him who is of an opposite disposition youth and age are equally a burden.

I listened in admiration, and wanting to draw him out, that he might go on—Yes, Cephalus, I said: but I rather suspect that people in general are not convinced by you when you speak thus; they think that old age sits lightly upon you, not because of your happy disposition, but because you are rich, and wealth is well known to be a great comforter.

You are right, he replied; they are not convinced: and there is something in what they say; not, however, so much as they imagine. I might answer them as Themistocles answered the Seriphian who was abusing him and saying that he was famous, not for his own merits but because he was an Athenian: 'If you had been a native of my country or I of yours, neither of us would have been famous.' And to those who are not rich and are impatient of old age, the same reply may be made; for to the good poor man old age cannot be a light burden, nor can a bad rich man ever have peace with himself.

May I ask, Cephalus, whether your fortune was for the most part inherited or acquired by you?

Acquired! Socrates; do you want to know how much I acquired?

In the art of making money I have been midway between my father
and grandfather: for my grandfather, whose name I bear, doubled
and trebled the value of his patrimony, that which he inherited being much what I possess now; but my father Lysanias reduced the
property below what it is at present: and I shall be satisfied if I leave
to these my sons not less but a little more than I received.

c   That was why I asked you the question, I replied, because I see
that you are indifferent about money, which is a characteristic rather
of those who have inherited their fortunes than of those who have
acquired them; the makers of fortunes have a second love of money
as a creation of their own, resembling the affection of authors for
their own poems, or of parents for their children, besides that natural
love of it for the sake of use and profit which is common to them
and all men. And hence they are very bad company, for they can talk
about nothing but the praises of wealth.

That is true, he said.

d   Yes, that is very true, but may I ask another question?—What
do you consider to be the greatest blessing which you have reaped
from your wealth?

One, he said, of which I could not expect easily to convince others. For let me tell you, Socrates, that when a man thinks himself
to be near death, fears and cares enter into his mind which he never
had before; the tales of a world below and the punishment which
is exacted there of deeds done here were once a laughing matter

e   to him, but now he is tormented with the thought that they may be
true: either from the weakness of age, or because he is now drawing
nearer to that other place, he has a clearer view of these things; suspicions and alarms crowd thickly upon him, and he begins to reflect
and consider what wrongs he has done to others. And when he finds
that the sum of his transgressions is great he will many a time like a

331   child start up in his sleep for fear, and he is filled with dark forebod-
ings. But to him who is conscious of no sin, sweet hope, as Pindar
charmingly says, is the kind nurse of his age:

'Hope,' he says, 'cherishes the soul of him who lives in justice
and holiness, and is the nurse of his age and the companion of his
journey;—hope which is mightiest to sway the restless soul of man.'

How admirable are his words! And the great blessing of riches,
b   I do not say to every man, but to a good man, is, that he has had
no occasion to deceive or to defraud others, either intentionally
or unintentionally; and when he departs to the world below he is
not in any apprehension about offerings due to the gods or debts
which he owes to men. Now to this peace of mind the possession
of wealth greatly contributes; and therefore I say, that, setting one
thing against another, of the many advantages which wealth has to
give, to a man of sense this is in my opinion the greatest.

Well said, Cephalus, I replied; but as concerning justice, what is

it?—to speak the truth and to pay your debts—no more than this? c
And even to this are there not exceptions? Suppose that a friend
when in his right mind has deposited arms with me and he asks for
them when he is not in his right mind, ought I to give them back to
him? No one would say that I ought or that I should be right in doing
so, any more than they would say that I ought always to speak the
truth to one who is in his condition.

You are quite right, he replied.

But then, I said, speaking the truth and paying your debts is not
a correct definition of justice. d

Quite correct, Socrates, if Simonides is to be believed, said
Polemarchus interposing.

I fear, said Cephalus, that I must go now, for I have to look after
the sacrifices, and I hand over the argument to Polemarchus and the
company.

Is not Polemarchus your heir? I said.

To be sure, he answered, and went away laughing to the sacrifices.

POLEMARCHUS [331E-336A]

Tell me then, O thou heir of the argument, what did Simonides say,
and according to you truly say, about justice? e

He said that the repayment of a debt is just, and in saying so he
appears to me to be right.

I should be sorry to doubt the word of such a wise and inspired
man, but his meaning, though probably clear to you, is the reverse
of clear to me. For he certainly does not mean, as we were just now
saying, that I ought to return a deposit of arms or of anything else
to one who asks for it when he is not in his right senses; and yet a
deposit cannot be denied to be a debt.

True. 332

Then when the person who asks me is not in his right mind I am
by no means to make the return?

Certainly not.

When Simonides said that the repayment of a debt was justice,
he did not mean to include that case?

Certainly not; for he thinks that a friend ought always to do good
to a friend and never evil.

You mean that the return of a deposit of gold which is to the
injury of the receiver, if the two parties are friends, is not the repayment of a debt,—that is what you would imagine him to say? b

Yes.

And are enemies also to receive what we owe to them?

To be sure, he said, they are to receive what we owe them, and
an enemy, as I take it, owes to an enemy that which is due or proper

to him—that is to say, evil.

Simonides, then, after the manner of poets, would seem to have spoken darkly of the nature of justice; for he really meant to say that justice is the giving to each man what is proper to him, and this he termed a debt.

That must have been his meaning, he said.

By heaven! I replied; and if we asked him what due or proper thing is given by medicine, and to whom, what answer do you think that he would make to us?

He would surely reply that medicine gives drugs and meat and drink to human bodies.

And what due or proper thing is given by cookery, and to what?

Seasoning to food.

And what is that which justice gives, and to whom?

If, Socrates, we are to be guided at all by the analogy of the preceding instances, then justice is the art which gives good to friends and evil to enemies.

That is his meaning then?

I think so.

And who is best able to do good to his friends and evil to his enemies in time of sickness?

The physician.

Or when they are on a voyage, amid the perils of the sea?

The pilot.

And in what sort of actions or with a view to what result is the just man most able to do harm to his enemy and good to his friend?

In going to war against the one and in making alliances with the other.

But when a man is well, my dear Polemarchus, there is no need of a physician?

No.

And he who is not on a voyage has no need of a pilot?

No.

Then in time of peace justice will be of no use?

I am very far from thinking so.

You think that justice may be of use in peace as well as in war?

Yes.

Like husbandry for the acquisition of corn?

Yes.

Or like shoemaking for the acquisition of shoes,—that is what you mean?

Yes.

And what similar use or power of acquisition has justice in time of peace?

In contracts, Socrates, justice is of use.

And by contracts you mean partnerships?

Exactly.

But is the just man or the skilful player a more useful and better partner at a game of checkers?   b

The skilful player.

And in the laying of bricks and stones is the just man a more useful or better partner than the builder?

Quite the reverse.

Then in what sort of partnership is the just man a better partner than the harp-player, as in playing the harp the harp-player is certainly a better partner than the just man?

In a money partnership.

Yes, Polemarchus, but surely not in the use of money; for you do not want a just man to be your counsellor in the purchase or sale of a horse; a man who is knowing about horses would be better for that, would he not?

Certainly.

And when you want to buy a ship, the shipwright or the pilot   c
would be better?

True.

Then what is that joint use of silver or gold in which the just man is to be preferred?

When you want a deposit to be kept safely.

You mean when money is not wanted, but allowed to lie?

Precisely.

That is to say, justice is useful when money is useless?

That is the inference.   d

And when you want to keep a pruning-hook safe, then justice is useful to the individual and to the state; but when you want to use it, then the art of the vine-dresser?

Clearly.

And when you want to keep a shield or a lyre, and not to use them, you would say that justice is useful; but when you want to use them, then the art of the soldier or of the musician?

Certainly.

And so of all other things;—justice is useful when they are useless, and useless when they are useful?

That is the inference.

Then justice is not good for much. But let us consider this further point: Is not he who can best strike a blow in a boxing match or in   e
any kind of fighting best able to ward off a blow?

Certainly.

And he who is most skilful in preventing or escaping from a disease is best able to create one?

True.

And he is the best guard of a camp who is best able to steal a march upon the enemy? [P̲SEP̲]Certainly.

334 Then he who is a good keeper of anything is also a good thief?

That, I suppose, is to be inferred.

Then if the just man is good at keeping money, he is good at stealing it.

That is implied in the argument.

Then after all the just man has turned out to be a thief. And this is a lesson which I suspect you must have learnt out of Homer; for he, speaking of Autolycus, the maternal grandfather of Odysseus, who
b is a favourite of his, affirms that 'He was excellent above all men in theft and perjury.'

And so, you and Homer and Simonides are agreed that justice is an art of theft; to be practised however 'for the good of friends and for the harm of enemies,'—that was what you were saying?

No, certainly not that, though I do not now know what I did say; but I still stand by the latter words.

Well, there is another question: By friends and enemies do we mean those who are so really, or only in seeming?
c Surely, he said, a man may be expected to love those whom he thinks good, and to hate those whom he thinks evil.

Yes, but do not persons often err about good and evil: many who are not good seem to be so, and conversely?

That is true.

Then to them the good will be enemies and the evil will be their friends? True.

And in that case they will be right in doing good to the evil and evil to the good?

Clearly.
d But the good are just and would not do an injustice?

True.

Then according to your argument it is just to injure those who do no wrong?

Nay, Socrates; the doctrine is immoral.

Then I suppose that we ought to do good to the just and harm to the unjust?

I like that better.

But see the consequence:—Many a man who is ignorant of human nature has friends who are bad friends, and in that case he ought to do harm to them; and he has good enemies whom he ought
e to benefit; but, if so, we shall be saying the very opposite of that which we affirmed to be the meaning of Simonides.

Very true, he said: and I think that we had better correct an error into which we seem to have fallen in the use of the words 'friend' and 'enemy.'

What was the error, Polemarchus? I asked.

We assumed that he is a friend who seems to be or who is thought good.

And how is the error to be corrected?

We should rather say that he is a friend who is, as well as seems, good; and that he who seems only, and is not good, only seems to be and is not a friend; and of an enemy the same may be said.

You would argue that the good are our friends and the bad our enemies?   335

Yes.

And instead of saying simply as we did at first, that it is just to do good to our friends and harm to our enemies, we should further say: It is just to do good to our friends when they are good and harm to our enemies when they are evil?

Yes, that appears to me to be the truth.

But ought the just to injure any one at all?

Undoubtedly he ought to injure those who are both wicked and   b
his enemies.

When horses are injured, are they improved or deteriorated?

The latter.

Deteriorated, that is to say, in the good qualities of horses, not of dogs?

Yes, of horses.

And dogs are deteriorated in the good qualities of dogs, and not of horses?

Of course.

And will not men who are injured be deteriorated in that which is the proper virtue of man?

Certainly.   c

And that human virtue is justice?

To be sure.

Then men who are injured are of necessity made unjust?

That is the result.

But can the musician by his art make men unmusical?

Certainly not.

Or the horseman by his art make them bad horsemen?

Impossible.

And can the just by justice make men unjust, or speaking gener-ally, can the good by virtue make them bad?

Assuredly not.   d

Any more than heat can produce cold?

It cannot.

Or drought moisture?

Clearly not.

Nor can the good harm any one?

Impossible.

And the just is the good?

Certainly.

Then to injure a friend or any one else is not the act of a just man, but of the opposite, who is the unjust?

I think that what you say is quite true, Socrates.

Then if a man says that justice consists in the repayment of debts, and that good is the debt which a just man owes to his friends, and evil the debt which he owes to his enemies,—to say this is not wise; for it is not true, if, as has been clearly shown, the injuring of another can be in no case just.

I agree with you, said Polemarchus.

Then you and I are prepared to take up arms against any one who attributes such a saying to Simonides or Bias or Pittacus, or any other wise man or seer?

I am quite ready to do battle at your side, he said.

Shall I tell you whose I believe the saying to be?

Whose?

I believe that Periander or Perdiccas or Xerxes or Ismenias the Theban, or some other rich and mighty man, who had a great opinion of his own power, was the first to say that justice is 'doing good to your friends and harm to your enemies.'

Most true, he said.

Yes, I said; but if this definition of justice also breaks down, what other can be offered?

2

THE IMMORALIST POSITION

The text of the *Republic* begins with Socrates interrogating Cephalus and his son Polemachus about the nature of justice. Neither is capable of providing Socrates with an adequate definition of justice. Just when we begin to think that there is no one in the dialogue who is capable of intellectually standing up to Socrates, Thrasymachus boisterously bursts onto the scene. Who is this Thrasymachus guy anyway?

He is a well-known Sophist, a teacher of rhetoric. Rhetoric is the art and science of persuasion; and since oratory was extremely useful in negotiating trade opportunities or for suing or defending oneself before the juries in Democratic Athens, rhetoric was a sought-after skill. Socrates' own students went on to make great fortunes in the polis, which was something Xanthippe, his wife, resented because Socrates remained poor and took no fees for his instruction. He distinguished philosophy from sophistry because the philosopher sacrificed everything, including eloquence, for the truth; whereas, he charged, the sophist sacrificed the truth for eloquence and for persuasive effectiveness. This charge is often leveled against the legal and the advertising professions (both involved in persuasion) and sophistry has a negative connotation today.

Thrasymachus presents himself as annoyed with the give and take inconclusiveness of the dialogue between Socrates and Polemarchus. He demands an answer from Socrates and a grandiloquently persuasive speech in favor of the answer.

JUSTICE AS THE ADVANTAGE OF THE STRONGEST [338C-343A]

Socrates turns over the floor to Thrasymachus who professes that justice is the advantage of the strongest (338c). By this he means that, from place to place, different political regimes rule: tyranny, aristocracy, and democracy, for example. Whoever is in power (the strongest) makes the laws and invariably they make the laws to their own financial and political advantage. Thus just rulers rule to the benefit of the strongest, namely themselves.

Socrates first tries to use the same tactics with Thrasymachus' definition of justice that he used against Polemarchus and Cephalus. He suggests that the definition is too broad. If justice is what the strongest want then what happens when the ruler makes a mistake and orders something that is not really in his interest? If justice is doing what pleases the ruler then how can it be just when he inadvertently pleases others to his own detriment? Unlike Polemarchus and Cephalus who give up their arguments after the Socratic critique, Thrasymachus is a professional rhoretician who is used to theoretical debates.

Dismissing one of the suggestions from the audience that justice is really the raw power of the ruler to enforce his will whether the ruler occasionally errs or not, Thrasymachus insists on a technical definition of rule; namely, that rulers rule to their own advantage, but, if they act inadvertently against their own interest, they cease thereby to be a ruler. This is like saying that a cobbler who puts the heal of a shoe on backwards is not a true cobbler. Since there is no clear winner yet, Socrates tries a different tack using the Craft analogy.

Socrates counters that Statecraft or rule is like any other craft, and the practitioners of any craft conduct that craft in the interest of and to the benefit of the weakest, namely their clients or customers. Physicians rule over and have authority over medicine. Between the physician and the patient, the physician is the stronger, since she has expertise and is not sick and the patient is the weaker, since he is both ignorant and sick. But the *telos* of the physician is to dispense medicine and the good of the art is the cure. The benefit, however, goes to the weaker since the patient is cured, not the physician. So in medicine the authority rules for the benefit of the weaker.

So too, if Statecraft is a craft, what is proper for the ruler is to act in the interest and to the advantage of the weakest, namely the citizens. Out of the need and the desire of the people for law and order, coordination and leadership, so that they might achieve the *telos* of their specific crafts, the ruler emerges with the expertise, strength and authority to act in the interests of each and every citizen. If rule is like any craft, then this is ideal rule. Justice is rule in the interest of the citizens.

Thrasymachus then proceeds to insult Socrates, claiming that Socrates' wet-nurse never taught him the difference between a shepherd and a sheep. Shepherds watch their flocks not for the sake of the sheep but so the sheep can be fleeced and slaughtered for their profit. So too, the relation of Ruler and citizens is that of shepherd and sheep. The citizens are like sheep to be fleeced and slaughtered for the benefit and profit of the ruler. Socrates counters by dividing the crafts of the profit-maker from that of other craft-persons like the physician. The craft of profit-making is indeed self-interested. But that craft must not be confused with that of the physician. The physician is a physician only if she cures patients. The benefit goes to the patient. Indeed the physician would only be paid if she effectively cured patients, that is, only if she achieved the advantage of the weakest. Similarly, the shepherd as shepherd must seek the advantage of the sheep, must watch them carefully, keep them from wolves, search for the stray and bring it back to the fold. If and only if the shepherd is a good shepherd does he deserve his pay. Thus the just ruler is to be compensated only if none of the advantage of the rule goes to him and all of the ruling efforts are to the advantage of the people (Socrates need not point out that the patients or citizens have higher values than sheep).

Socrates asks if Rulers rule ambitiously or reluctantly. Thrasymachus, contemplating the spoils of tyranny, suggests that rulers rule avidly. Socrates, in keeping with his notion of just rule, suggests that since none of the advantage of rule goes to the rulers, people would have to be given incentives to take on the burden of the public trust. However, the best rulers would be those who find the incentives of pay or honors distasteful. The best could be enticed to rule only to avoid the penalty of being ruled by people who are worse in character, or more unjust, than they are.

JUSTICE AS ANOTHER'S GOOD [343B-344D]

At this point, Thrasymachus drops the pretense of seeking to define justice, and now claims that, although justice is virtuous and beneficial to others, no intelligent person would adopt it because of the superior advantages of the unjust life, especially in the political arena. This position is called "immoralism," the forthright defense of immorality as the most prudent course for a life to take. Note that Socrates is able to get Thrasymachus to admit that in accord with the ordinary conventions of the day, justice is categorized among the virtues and not the vices. This admission will come back to haunt Thrasymachus later in Book I.

Thrasymachus, in a speech demonstrative of his rhetorical prowess, praises the tyrant who is unjust in a grand way. Such a man will pay far fewer taxes that the just man, receive far more benefits from contracts than the honest dupes who enter into them with him and will profit from influence peddling and the lavish gifts he is able to provide to his family and to the gods in the form of burnt offerings. Yes, the unjust man is the happiest of men.

SOCRATES: FINAL OBJECTIONS (344D-354C)

Socrates, telling Thrasymachus that he has challenged the whole conduct of living, takes up a defense of the just life:

The first argument against immoralism is a bit technical. We will follow our commentary with a more intuitively understandable version.

The just man is unwilling to get the better of another just man. The just man is willing to get the better of the unjust man. The unjust man is willing to get the better of the just man. However, the unjust man is willing to get the better of the unjust man as well. The just man does not get the better of the like, but of the unlike; whereas the unjust man gets the better of the like and the unlike.

Now Socrates shows Thrasymachus that the latter (trying to get the better of the like and the unlike) is identifiable with imprudence and ignorance. A musician doesn't try to be better than another musician but only like them. To understand this one has to realize that Plato (and classical Greece in general) believes in an Ideal Form of musicianship to which all aspire. The idea of playing in an individualistic, unique or idiosyncratic manner would not be valued by Plato or his culture. The physician would not try to take advantage of the physician who is mentoring him (his like), but would only try to get the better of quacks, amateurs or inexpert and opinionated patients. Anyone who tries to get the better of his own mentor as well as with the unlike (for example, non-musicians or non-physicians) would truly be unwise and ignorant. So the just man is like the wise and the good, but the unjust man is bad and ignorant.

The validity of this argument rests on the very loose and ambiguous definition of "like" and "unlike." It could easily fall to the objection that the terms are used in an equivocal fashion. Although Thrasymachus is caught blushing over his inability to counter Socrates' line of reasoning, this only shows his ineptitude as a debater.

A simpler version of the first argument might run as follows: To achieve knowledge of a *techne* or craft and to master the requisite skills, one must follow the direction and instruction of a mentor. One must imitate the behavior of one who has the excellence of the craft. This is the way to become like him to gain the specific excellence (*arête*) of the craft. One doesn't take short cuts, deceive, cheat or lie to the instructor. The attempt to take advantage of the like results in abject failing to learn the art. The unjust are terrible learners and this cannot be advantageous to them.

The just man does not try to get the better of other just men, but rather of unjust men who are his opposites in character. By contrast, unjust men try to get the better of both just and unjust men. The just person then follows the pattern of all craftpersons. The excellent craftperson does not try to take advantage of those who are members of his or her craft or guild but tries only to excel over amateurs.

Thrasymachus is embarrassed to find himself agreeing that justice is a human virtue. In fact, the just person's reluctance to cheat or dissemble and her willingness to cooperate with mentors allows the just person to achieve excellence in a chosen craft; whereas the consistent cheater wallows in ignorance and can only pretend at mastery.

Against Thrasymachus's contention that the most powerful city will be the most completely unjust, Socrates argues that any common course of action requires those who are engaged in it to observe justice to some degree in their dealings among themselves, for otherwise there will be dissension among them and they will accomplish nothing. Only the just cooperate, and only those who cooperate accomplish anything. Even to pull off a bank robbery, thieves must cooperate. There must be honor among thieves. But thieves tear down the accomplishments of others; and rival gangs of thieves tear each other down. Only those who are both honest and cooperate produce the accomplishments that are ample and long-lasting. "For surely Thrasymachus, it's injustice that produces factions, hatreds, and quarrels among themselves, and justice that produces unanimity and friendship. Isn't it so" (251d)?

Unjust rulers will rule a city that is unjust to its allies and neighboring nations. These will seek advantage over the citizens who will form factions; then intrigue and civil war will prevent the city from accomplishing anything. The unjust ruler will be deceitful and calculating with his closest advisors. They will turn on each other. Even within a person, when discord breaks out between one's passions and one's practical reason, a person won't stick to his or her craft and won't be able to act productively; he/she will accomplish nothing. Thus injustice is not mighty in a productive sense; it is mightily destructive. It undermines all collective enterprises, all friendship and partnerships. And injustice within a person—that is, when reason is overcome by passions such as lust, greed, or hatred—leads to a situation in which the person is either unable to accomplish anything or is destroyed.

Since Thrasymachus has admitted that justice is a virtue, Socrates uses that admission to crown his argument. A virtue is the specific excellence of a craft. It is the power to achieve the purpose or goal of a craft, its *telos*. Justice is the virtue (*arête*) of the craft of life. The human soul has the goal or *telos* of flourishing life and the management of things. The *arête* or virtue of justice is the specific excellence of the human soul; it is that which allows each life to flourish, to manage well oneself and social life. Justice allows practical reason to guide human appetites and passions. It allows us to remain loyal and faithful to friends. It allows us to keep the public promises we make as craftpersons and professionals to provide a service or product to our customers and clients. A city with just rulers who serve in the interests of the citizens accomplishes greatness as a city. Moreover a city that keeps faith with its allies accomplishes greatness as a city. The human soul cannot flourish without justice any more than the body can flourish without health. Thus a person cannot be happy without justice. The unjust person will be wretched (the opposite of flourishing humanity, perhaps "withered," "lacking maturity," "unruly"). It is not profitable to be wretched, or to become wretched as a human being; but it is profitable to be happy and to flourish humanly. Therefore, injustice is never more profitable than justice.

CONCLUSION

Socrates is pleased that Thrasymachus has been tamed and quieted by his arguments, but ultimately he has to admit dissatisfaction with the discussion. In his zeal to defend the advantages of the just life, he plumb forgot to find a definition for justice. How can he recommend the just life if he doesn't know what justice is? So ends, inconclusively, Book I of the *Republic*.

SUGGESTIONS FOR FURTHER READING

Altman, William H. F. *Plato the Teacher: The Crisis of the Republic.* Lanham, MD: Lexington Books, 2012. [87-101]

Annas, Julia. *An Introduction to Plato's Republic.* New York: Oxford, 1981. [35-57]

Barney, Rachel. "Socrates' Refutation of Thrasymachus." *The Blackwell Guide to Plato's Republic.* Malden, MA: Blackwell, 2006. [44-62]

Benardete, Seth. *Socrates' Second Sailing: On Plato's Republic.* Chicago: Univ. of Chicago, 1989. [20-32].

Bett, Richard. "Is There a Sophistic Ethics?" *Ancient Philosophy* 22 (2002): 235-262.

Bloom, Allan. *The Republic of Plato.* New York: Harper Collins, 1968. [325-337]

Chappell, Timothy. "The Virtues of Thrasymachus." *Phronesis* 38 (1993): 1-17.

Devin, Stauffen. *Plato's Introduction to the Question of Justice.* Albany: State University of New York Press, 2001.

Everson, Steven. "The Incoherence of Thrasymachus." *Oxford Studies in Ancient Philosophy* 16 (1998): 99-131.

Henderson, T.Y. "In Defense of Thrasymachus." *American Philosophical Quarterly* 7 (1970): 218-228.

Irwin, Terence. *Plato's Ethics*. New York: Oxford UP, 1995. [174-180]

Lycos, Kimon. *Plato on Justice and Power*. Albany: State University of New York Press, 1987. [40-70; 106-153]

Macguire, Jospeh P. "Thrasymachus...or Plato?" *Phronesis* 16 (1971): 142-163.

Nicholson, P.P. "Unravelling Thrasymachus' Argument in the *Republic*." *Phronesis* 16 (1974): 210-232.

O'Neill, Basil. "The Struggle for the Soul of Thrasymachus." *Ancient Philosophy* 8 (1988): 167-185.

Pappas, Nickolas. *Plato and the Republic*. New York: Routledge, 1995. [39-50]

Reeve, C.D.C. *Philosopher-Kings: The Argument of Plato's Republic*. Princeton, NJ: Princeton UP, 1988. [9-22]

Rosen, Stanley. *Plato's Republic: A Study*. New Haven: Yale University Press, 2005. [38-59]

Sallis, John. *Being and Logos: Reading Platonic Dialogues*. 3rd ed. Bloomington, IN: Indiana UP, 1996. [334-346]

Sparshott, F. E., "Socrates and Thrasymachus." *Monist* 50 (1966): 421-459.

Taylor, A.E. *Plato: The Man and His Work*. New York: Meridian, 1964. [265-270]

Tiles, J. E. "Techne and Moral Expertise." *Philosophy* 59 (1984): 49-66.

White, Nicholas P. *A Companion to Plato's Republic*. Indianapolis, Hackett, 1979. [65-73]

White, Stephen A. "Thrasymachus the Diplomat." *Classical Philology* 90 (1995): 307-327.

REPUBLIC 1.336B-354C

INTRODUCING TRASYMACHUS [336B-338C]

³³⁶
^b
Several times in the course of the discussion Thrasymachus had made an attempt to get the argument into his own hands, and had been put down by the rest of the company, who wanted to hear the end. But when Polemarchus and I had done speaking and there was a pause, he could no longer hold his peace; and, gathering himself up, he came at us like a wild beast, seeking to devour us. We were quite panic-stricken at the sight of him.

He roared out to the whole company: What folly, Socrates, has taken possession of you all? And why, fools, do you knock under to one another? I say that if you want really to know what justice is, you should not only ask but answer, and you should not seek honour to yourself from the refutation of an opponent, but have your own answer; for there is many a one who can ask and cannot answer. And now I will not have you say that justice is duty or advantage or profit or gain or interest, for this sort of nonsense will not do for me; I must have clearness and accuracy.

I was panic-stricken at his words, and could not look at him without trembling. Indeed I believe that if I had not fixed my eye upon him, I should have been struck dumb: but when I saw his fury rising, I looked at him first, and was therefore able to reply to him.

Thrasymachus, I said, with a quiver, don't be hard upon us. Polemarchus and I may have been guilty of a little mistake in the argument, but I can assure you that the error was not intentional. If we were seeking for a piece of gold, you would not imagine that we were 'knocking under to one another,' and so losing our chance of finding it. And why, when we are seeking for justice, a thing more precious than many pieces of gold, do you say that we are weakly yielding to one another and not doing our utmost to get at the truth? Nay, my good friend, we are most willing and anxious to do so, but the fact is that we cannot. And if so, you people who know all things should pity us and not be angry with us.

³³⁷

How characteristic of Socrates! he replied, with a bitter laugh;— that's your ironical style! Did I not foresee—have I not already told you, that whatever he was asked he would refuse to answer, and try irony or any other shuffle, in order that he might avoid answering?

You are a philosopher, Thrasymachus, I replied, and well know that if you ask a person what numbers make up twelve, taking care

to prohibit him whom you ask from answering twice six, or three
times four, or six times two, or four times three, 'for this sort of
nonsense will not do for me,'—then obviously, if that is your way
of putting the question, no one can answer you. But suppose that he
were to retort, 'Thrasymachus, what do you mean? If one of these
numbers which you interdict be the true answer to the question, am
I falsely to say some other number which is not the right one?—is
that your meaning?'—How would you answer him?

Just as if the two cases were at all alike! he said.

Why should they not be? I replied; and even if they are not, but
only appear to be so to the person who is asked, ought he not to say
what he thinks, whether you and I forbid him or not?

I presume then that you are going to make one of the prohibited
answers?

I dare say that I may, notwithstanding the danger, if upon reflection I approve of any of them.

But what if I give you an answer about justice other and better,
he said, than any of these? What do you deserve to have done to
you?

Done to me!—as becomes the ignorant, I must learn from the
wise—that is what I deserve to have done to me.

What, and no payment! a pleasant notion!

I will pay when I have the money, I replied.

But you have, Socrates, said Glaucon: and you, Thrasymachus,
need be under no anxiety about money, for we will all make a con-
tribution for Socrates.

Yes, he replied, and then Socrates will do as he always does—
refuse to answer himself, but take and pull to pieces the answer of
some one else.

Why, my good friend, I said, how can any one answer who
knows, and says that he knows, just nothing; and who, even if he
has some faint notions of his own, is told by a man of authority
not to utter them? The natural thing is, that the speaker should be
some one like yourself who professes to know and can tell what
he knows. Will you then kindly answer, for the edification of the
company and of myself?

Glaucon and the rest of the company joined in my request, and
Thrasymachus, as any one might see, was in reality eager to speak;
for he thought that he had an excellent answer, and would distinguish himself. But at first he affected to insist on my answering;
at length he consented to begin. Behold, he said, the wisdom of
Socrates; he refuses to teach himself, and goes about learning of
others, to whom he never even says Thank you.

That I learn of others, I replied, is quite true; but that I am un-
grateful I wholly deny. Money I have none, and therefore I pay in
praise, which is all I have; and how ready I am to praise any one

who appears to me to speak well you will very soon find out when you answer; for I expect that you will answer well.

JUSTICE AS THE ADVANTAGE OF THE STRONGER [338C-343A]

c Listen, then, he said; I proclaim that justice is nothing else than the interest of the stronger. And now why do you not praise me? But of course you won't.

Let me first understand you, I replied. Justice, as you say, is the interest of the stronger. What, Thrasymachus, is the meaning of this? You cannot mean to say that because Polydamas, the wrestler, is stronger than we are, and finds the eating of beef conducive to his bodily strength, that to eat beef is therefore equally for our good

d who are weaker than he is, and right and just for us?

That's abominable of you, Socrates; you take the words in the sense which is most damaging to the argument.

Not at all, my good sir, I said; I am trying to understand them; and I wish that you would be a little clearer.

Well, he said, have you never heard that forms of government differ; there are tyrannies, and there are democracies, and there are aristocracies?

Yes, I know.

And the government is the ruling power in each state?

Certainly.

e And the different forms of government make laws democratical, aristocratical, tyrannical, with a view to their several interests; and these laws, which are made by them for their own interests, are the justice which they deliver to their subjects, and him who transgresses them they punish as a breaker of the law, and unjust. And that is what I mean when I say that in all states there is the same principle of justice, which is the interest of the government; and as

339 the government must be supposed to have power, the only reasonable conclusion is, that everywhere there is one principle of justice, which is the interest of the stronger.

OBJECTION: RULER'S ERRORS [339A-341A]

Now I understand you, I said; and whether you are right or not I will try to discover. But let me remark, that in defining justice you have yourself used the word 'interest' which you forbade me to use. It is true, however, that in your definition the words 'of the stronger' are added.

b A small addition, you must allow, he said.

Great or small, never mind about that: we must first enquire whether what you are saying is the truth. Now we are both agreed that justice is interest of some sort, but you go on to say 'of the stronger'; about this addition I am not so sure, and must therefore consider further.

Proceed.

I will; and first tell me, Do you admit that it is just for subjects to obey their rulers?

I do.

But are the rulers of states absolutely infallible, or are they   c
sometimes liable to err?

To be sure, he replied, they are liable to err.

Then in making their laws they may sometimes make them rightly, and sometimes not?

True.

When they make them rightly, they make them agreeably to their interest; when they are mistaken, contrary to their interest; you admit that?

Yes. ⌜P⌝ And the laws which they make must be obeyed by their ⌞SEP⌟subjects,—and that is what you call justice?

Doubtless.

Then justice, according to your argument, is not only obedience to the interest of the stronger but the reverse?   d

What is that you are saying? he asked.

I am only repeating what you are saying, I believe. But let us consider: Have we not admitted that the rulers may be mistaken about their own interest in what they command, and also that to obey them is justice? Has not that been admitted?

Yes.

Then you must also have acknowledged justice not to be for the interest of the stronger, when the rulers unintentionally com-   e
mand things to be done which are to their own injury. For if, as you say, justice is the obedience which the subject renders to their commands, in that case, O wisest of men, is there any escape from the conclusion that the weaker are commanded to do, not what is for the interest, but what is for the injury of the stronger?

Nothing can be clearer, Socrates, said Polemarchus.

Yes, said Cleitophon, interposing, if you are allowed to be his   340
witness.

But there is no need of any witness, said Polemarchus, for Thrasymachus himself acknowledges that rulers may sometimes command what is not for their own interest, and that for subjects to obey them is justice.

Yes, Polemarchus,—Thrasymachus said that for subjects to do what was commanded by their rulers is just.

Yes, Cleitophon, but he also said that justice is the interest of the stronger, and, while admitting both these propositions, he further   b
acknowledged that the stronger may command the weaker who are

his subjects to do what is not for his own interest; hence it follows that justice is the injury quite as much as the interest of the stronger.

But, said Cleitophon, he meant by the interest of the stronger what the stronger thought to be his interest,—this was what the weaker had to do; and this was affirmed by him to be justice.

Those were not his words, rejoined Polemarchus.

Never mind, I replied, if he now says that they are, let us accept his statement. Tell me, Thrasymachus, I said, did you mean by justice what the stronger thought to be his interest, whether really so or not?

Certainly not, he said. Do you suppose that I call him who is mistaken the stronger at the time when he is mistaken?

Yes, I said, my impression was that you did so, when you admitted that the ruler was not infallible but might be sometimes mistaken.

You argue like an informer, Socrates. Do you mean, for example, that he who is mistaken about the sick is a physician in that he is mistaken? or that he who errs in arithmetic or grammar is an arithmetician or grammarian at the time when he is making the mistake, in respect of the mistake? True, we say that the physician or arithmetician or grammarian has made a mistake, but this is only a way of speaking; for the fact is that neither the grammarian nor any other person of skill ever makes a mistake in so far as he is what his name implies; they none of them err unless their skill fails them, and then they cease to be skilled artists. No artist or sage or ruler errs at the time when he is what his name implies; though he is commonly said to err, and I adopted the common mode of speaking. But to be perfectly accurate, since you are such a lover of accuracy, we should say that the ruler, in so far as he is a ruler, is unerring, and, being unerring, always commands that which is for his own interest; and the subject is required to execute his commands; and therefore, as I said at first and now repeat, justice is the interest of the stronger.

OBJECTION: THE OBJECT OF RULE [341A-342D]

Indeed, Thrasymachus, and do I really appear to you to argue like an informer?

Certainly, he replied.

And do you suppose that I ask these questions with any design of injuring you in the argument?

No, he replied, 'suppose' is not the word—I know it; but you will be found out, and by sheer force of argument you will never prevail.

I shall not make the attempt, my dear man; but to avoid any misunderstanding occurring between us in future, let me ask, in what sense do you speak of a ruler or stronger whose interest, as you were saying, he being the superior, it is just that the inferior should execute—is he a ruler in the popular or in the strict sense of the term?

In the strictest of all senses, he said. And now cheat and play the informer if you can; I ask no quarter at your hands. But you never will be able, never.

And do you imagine, I said, that I am such a madman as to try and cheat, Thrasymachus? I might as well shave a lion.

Why, he said, you made the attempt a minute ago, and you failed.

Enough, I said, of these civilities. It will be better that I should ask you a question: Is the physician, taken in that strict sense of which you are speaking, a healer of the sick or a maker of money? And remember that I am now speaking of the true physician.

c

A healer of the sick, he replied.

And the pilot—that is to say, the true pilot—is he a captain of sailors or a mere sailor?

A captain of sailors.

The circumstance that he sails in the ship is not to be taken into account; neither is he to be called a sailor; the name pilot by which he is distinguished has nothing to do with sailing, but is significant of his skill and of his authority over the sailors.

Very true, he said.

Now, I said, every art has an interest?

d

Certainly.

For which the art has to consider and provide?

Yes, that is the aim of art.

And the interest of any art is the perfection of it—this and nothing else?

What do you mean?

I mean what I may illustrate negatively by the example of the body. Suppose you were to ask me whether the body is self-sufficing or has wants, I should reply: Certainly the body has wants; for the body may be ill and require to be cured, and has therefore interests to which the art of medicine ministers; and this is the origin and intention of medicine, as you will acknowledge. Am I not right?

e

Quite right, he replied.

But is the art of medicine or any other art faulty or deficient in any quality in the same way that the eye may be deficient in sight or the ear fail of hearing, and therefore requires another art to provide for the interests of seeing and hearing—has art in itself, I say, any similar liability to fault or defect, and does every art require another supplementary art to provide for its interests, and that another and another without end? Or have the arts to look only after their own interests? Or have they no need either of themselves or of another?—having no faults or defects, they have no need to correct them, either by the exercise of their own art or of any other; they have only to consider the interest of their subject-matter. For every art remains pure and faultless while remaining true—that is to

342

b say, while perfect and unimpaired. Take the words in your precise sense, and tell me whether I am not right.

Yes, clearly.

Then medicine does not consider the interest of medicine, but the interest of the body?

True, he said.

Nor does the art of horsemanship consider the interests of the art of horsemanship, but the interests of the horse; neither do any other

c arts care for themselves, for they have no needs; they care only for that which is the subject of their art?

True, he said.

But surely, Thrasymachus, the arts are the superiors and rulers of their own subjects?

To this he assented with a good deal of reluctance.

Then, I said, no science or art considers or enjoins the interest of the stronger or superior, but only the interest of the subject and weaker?

He made an attempt to contest this proposition also, but finally acquiesced.

Then, I continued, no physician, in so far as he is a physician, considers his own good in what he prescribes, but the good of his

d patient; for the true physician is also a ruler having the human body as a subject, and is not a mere money-maker; that has been admitted?

Yes.

And the pilot likewise, in the strict sense of the term, is a ruler of sailors and not a mere sailor?

That has been admitted.

And such a pilot and ruler will provide and prescribe for the interest of the sailor who is under him, and not for his own or the ruler's interest?

He gave a reluctant 'Yes.'

e Then, I said, Thrasymachus, there is no one in any rule who, in so far as he is a ruler, considers or enjoins what is for his own interest, but always what is for the interest of his subject or suitable to his art; to that he looks, and that alone he considers in everything which he says and does.

JUSTICE AS ANOTHER'S GOOD [343A-344D]

When we had got to this point in the argument, and every one saw that the definition of justice had been completely upset, Thrasymachus, instead of replying to me, said: Tell me, Socrates, have you got a wet nurse?

Why do you ask such a question, I said, when you ought rather

343 to be answering?

Because she leaves you to snivel, and never wipes your nose: she has not even taught you to know the shepherd from the sheep.

What makes you say that? I replied.

Because you fancy that the shepherd or heardsman fattens or tends the sheep or oxen with a view to their own good and not to the good of himself or his master; and you further imagine that the rulers of states, if they are true rulers, never think of their subjects as sheep, and that they are not studying their own advantage day and night. Oh, no; and so entirely astray are you in your ideas about the just and unjust as not even to know that justice and the just are in reality another's good; that is to say, the interest of the ruler and stronger, and the loss of the subject and servant; and injustice the opposite; for the unjust is lord over the truly simple and just: he is the stronger, and his subjects do what is for his interest, and minister to his happiness, which is very far from being their own. Consider further, most foolish Socrates, that the just is always a loser in comparison with the unjust. First of all, in private contracts: wherever the unjust is the partner of the just you will find that, when the partnership is dissolved, the unjust man has always more and the just less. Secondly, in their dealings with the State: when there is an income-tax, the just man will pay more and the unjust less on the same amount of income; and when there is anything to be received the one gains nothing and the other much. Observe also what happens when they take an office; there is the just man neglecting his affairs and perhaps suffering other losses, and getting nothing out of the public, because he is just; moreover he is hated by his friends and acquaintance for refusing to serve them in unlawful ways. But all this is reversed in the case of the unjust man. I am speaking, as before, of injustice on a large scale in which the advantage of the unjust is most apparent; and my meaning will be most clearly seen if we turn to that highest form of injustice in which the criminal is the happiest of men, and the sufferers or those who refuse to do injustice are the most miserable—that is to say tyranny, which by fraud and force takes away the property of others, not little by little but wholesale; comprehending in one, things sacred as well as profane, private and public; for which acts of wrong, if he were detected perpetrating any one of them singly, he would be punished and incur great disgrace—they who do such wrong in particular cases are called robbers of temples, and man-stealers and burglars and swindlers and thieves. But when a man besides taking away the money of the citizens has made slaves of them, then, instead of these names of reproach, he is termed happy and blessed, not only by the citizens but by all who hear of his having achieved the consummation of injustice. For mankind censure injustice, fearing that they may be the victims of it and not because they shrink from committing it. And thus, as I have shown, Socrates, injustice, when on

b

c

d

e

344

b

c   a sufficient scale, has more strength and freedom and mastery than justice; and, as I said at first, justice is the interest of the stronger, whereas injustice is a man's own profit and interest.

OBJECTION: THE OBJECT OF RULING RECONSIDERED [344D-348B]

Thrasymachus, when he had thus spoken, having, like a bath attendant, deluged our ears with his words, had a mind to go away. But the company would not let him; they insisted that he should remain and defend his position; and I myself added my own humble request that he would not leave us. Thrasymachus, I said to him, excellent
d   man, how suggestive are your remarks! And are you going to run away before you have fairly taught or learned whether they are true or not? Is the attempt to determine the way of man's life so small a matter in your eyes—to determine how life may be passed by each one of us to the greatest advantage?

And do I differ from you, he said, as to the importance of the enquiry?

You appear rather, I replied, to have no care or thought about us, Thrasymachus—whether we live better or worse from not knowing
e   what you say you know, is to you a matter of indifference. Please, friend, do not keep your knowledge to yourself; we are a large party; and any benefit which you confer upon us will be amply rewarded. For my own part I openly declare that I am not convinced, and that I do not believe injustice to be more gainful than justice, even if
345   uncontrolled and allowed to have free play. For, granting that there may be an unjust man who is able to commit injustice either by fraud or force, still this does not convince me of the superior advantage of injustice, and there may be others who are in the same predicament with myself. Perhaps we may be wrong; if so, you in your wisdom should convince us that we are mistaken in preferring justice to injustice.

And how am I to convince you, he said, if you are not already convinced by what I have just said; what more can I do for you?
b   Would you have me put the proof bodily into your souls?

Heaven forbid! I said; I would only ask you to be consistent; or, if you change, change openly and let there be no deception. For I must remark, Thrasymachus, if you will recall what was previously said, that although you began by defining the true physician in an exact sense, you did not observe a like exactness when speaking of the shepherd; you thought that the shepherd as a shepherd tends the sheep not with a view to their own good, but like a mere diner or
c   banquetter with a view to the pleasures of the table; or, again, as a trader for sale in the market, and not as a shepherd. Yet surely the art of the shepherd is concerned only with the good of his subjects;

he has only to provide the best for them, since the perfection of the art is already ensured whenever all the requirements of it are satisfied. And that was what I was saying just now about the ruler. I conceived that the art of the ruler, considered as ruler, whether in a state or in private life, could only regard the good of his flock or subjects; whereas you seem to think that the rulers in states, that is to say, the true rulers, like being in authority.

d

Think! Nay, I am sure of it.

Then why in the case of lesser offices do men never take them willingly without payment, unless under the idea that they govern for the advantage not of themselves but of others? Let me ask you a question: Are not the several arts different, by reason of their each having a separate function? And, my dear illustrious friend, do say what you think, that we may make a little progress.

e

Yes, that is the difference, he replied.

And each art gives us a particular good and not merely a general one—medicine, for example, gives us health; navigation, safety at sea, and so on?

346

Yes, he said.

And the art of payment has the special function of giving pay: but we do not confuse this with other arts, any more than the art of the pilot is to be confused with the art of medicine, because the health of the pilot may be improved by a sea voyage. You would not be inclined to say, would you, that navigation is the art of medicine, at least if we are to adopt your exact use of language?

b

Certainly not.

Or because a man is in good health when he receives pay you would not say that the art of payment is medicine?

I should not.

Nor would you say that medicine is the art of receiving pay because a man takes fees when he is engaged in healing?

Certainly not.

And we have admitted, I said, that the good of each art is specially confined to the art?

Yes.

Then, if there be any good which all artists have in common, that is to be attributed to something of which they all have the common use?

c

True, he replied.

And when the artist is benefited by receiving pay the advantage is gained by an additional use of the art of pay, which is not the art professed by him?

He gave a reluctant assent to this.

Then the pay is not derived by the several artists from their respective arts. But the truth is, that while the art of medicine gives health, and the art of the builder builds a house, another art at-

tends them which is the art of pay. The various arts may be doing
their own business and benefiting that over which they preside, but
would the artist receive any benefit from his art unless he were paid
as well?

I suppose not.

But does he therefore confer no benefit when he works for nothing?

Certainly, he confers a benefit.

Then now, Thrasymachus, there is no longer any doubt that neither arts nor governments provide for their own interests; but, as
we were before saying, they rule and provide for the interests of
their subjects who are the weaker and not the stronger—to their
good they attend and not to the good of the superior. And this is the
reason, my dear Thrasymachus, why, as I was just now saying, no
one is willing to govern; because no one likes to take in hand the
reformation of evils which are not his concern without remunera-
tion. For, in the execution of his work, and in giving his orders to
another, the true artist does not regard his own interest, but always
that of his subjects; and therefore in order that rulers may be willing
to rule, they must be paid in one of three modes of payment, money,
or honour, or a penalty for refusing.

What do you mean, Socrates? said Glaucon. The first two modes
of payment are intelligible enough, but what the penalty is I do not
understand, or how a penalty can be a payment.

You mean that you do not understand the nature of this payment
which to the best men is the great inducement to rule? Of course
you know that ambition and avarice are held to be, as indeed they
are, a disgrace?

Very true.

And for this reason, I said, money and honour have no attraction
for them; good men do not wish to be openly demanding payment
for governing and so to get the name of hirelings, nor by secretly
helping themselves out of the public revenues to get the name of
thieves. And not being ambitious they do not care about honour.
Wherefore necessity must be laid upon them, and they must be induced to serve from the fear of punishment. And this, as I imagine,
is the reason why the forwardness to take office, instead of waiting
to be compelled, has been deemed dishonourable. Now the worst
part of the punishment is that he who refuses to rule is liable to be
ruled by one who is worse than himself. And the fear of this, as I
conceive, induces the good to take office, not because they would,
but because they cannot help—not under the idea that they are going to have any benefit or enjoyment themselves, but as a necessity,
and because they are not able to commit the task of ruling to any
one who is better than themselves, or indeed as good. For there is
reason to think that if a city were composed entirely of good men,

then to avoid office would be as much an object of contention as to obtain office is at present; then we should have plain proof that the true ruler is not meant by nature to regard his own interest, but that of his subjects; and every one who knew this would choose rather to receive a benefit from another than to have the trouble of conferring one. So far am I from agreeing with Thrasymachus that justice is the interest of the stronger. This latter question need not be further discussed at present; but when Thrasymachus says that the life of the unjust is more advantageous than that of the just, his new statement appears to me to be of a far more serious character. Which of us has spoken truly? And which sort of life, Glaucon, do you prefer?

I for my part deem the life of the just to be the more advantageous, he answered.

Did you hear all the advantages of the unjust which Thrasymachus was rehearsing?

Yes, I heard him, he replied, but he has not convinced me.

Then shall we try to find some way of convincing him, if we can, that he is saying what is not true?

Most certainly, he replied.

Objection: Injustice as Ignorance [348A-350D]

If, I said, he makes a set speech and we make another recounting all the advantages of being just, and he answers and we rejoin, there must be a numbering and measuring of the goods which are claimed on either side, and in the end we shall want judges to decide; but if we proceed in our enquiry as we lately did, by making admissions to one another, we shall unite the offices of judge and advocate in our own persons.

Very good, he said.

And which method do I understand you to prefer? I said.

That which you propose.

Well, then, Thrasymachus, I said, suppose you begin at the beginning and answer me. You say that perfect injustice is more gainful than perfect justice?

Yes, that is what I say, and I have given you my reasons.

And what is your view about them? Would you call one of them virtue and the other vice?

Certainly.

I suppose that you would call justice virtue and injustice vice?

What a charming notion! So likely too, seeing that I affirm injustice to be profitable and justice not.

What else then would you say?

The opposite, he replied.

And would you call justice vice?

No, I would rather say sublime simplicity.

Then would you call injustice malignity?

No; I would rather say discretion.

And do the unjust appear to you to be wise and good?

Yes, he said; at any rate those of them who are able to be perfectly unjust, and who have the power of subduing states and nations; but perhaps you imagine me to be talking of cutpurses. Even this profession if undetected has advantages, though they are not to be compared with those of which I was just now speaking.

I do not think that I misapprehend your meaning, Thrasymachus, I replied; but still I cannot hear without amazement that you class injustice with wisdom and virtue, and justice with the opposite.

Certainly I do so class them.

Now, I said, you are on more substantial and almost unanswerable ground; for if the injustice which you were maintaining to be profitable had been admitted by you as by others to be vice and deformity, an answer might have been given to you on received principles; but now I perceive that you will call injustice honourable and strong, and to the unjust you will attribute all the qualities which were attributed by us before to the just, seeing that you do not hesitate to rank injustice with wisdom and virtue.

You have guessed most infallibly, he replied.

Then I certainly ought not to shrink from going through with the argument so long as I have reason to think that you, Thrasymachus, are speaking your real mind; for I do believe that you are now in earnest and are not amusing yourself at our expense.

I may be in earnest or not, but what is that to you?—to refute the argument is your business.

Very true, I said; that is what I have to do: But will you be so good as answer yet one more question? Does the just man try to gain any advantage over the just?

Far otherwise; if he did he would not be the simple amusing creature which he is.

And would he try to go beyond just action?

He would not.

And how would he regard the attempt to gain an advantage over the unjust; would that be considered by him as just or unjust?

He would think it just, and would try to gain the advantage; but he would not be able.

Whether he would or would not be able, I said, is not to the point. My question is only whether the just man, while refusing to have more than another just man, would wish and claim to have more than the unjust?

Yes, he would.

And what of the unjust—does he claim to have more than the

just man and to do more than is just?

Of course, he said, for he claims to have more than all men.

And the unjust man will strive and struggle to obtain more than the unjust man or action, in order that he may have more than all?

True.

We may put the matter thus, I said—the just does not desire more than his like but more than his unlike, whereas the unjust desires more than both his like and his unlike?

Nothing, he said, can be better than that statement.

And the unjust is good and wise, and the just is neither?

Good again, he said.   d

And is not the unjust like the wise and good and the just unlike them?

Of course, he said, he who is of a certain nature, is like those who are of a certain nature; he who is not, not.

Each of them, I said, is such as his like is?

Certainly, he replied.

Very good, Thrasymachus, I said; and now to take the case of the arts: you would admit that one man is a musician and another not a musician?

Yes.

And which is wise and which is foolish?

Clearly the musician is wise, and he who is not a musician is foolish.   e

And he is good in as far as he is wise, and bad in as far as he is foolish?

Yes.

And you would say the same sort of thing of the physician?

Yes.

And do you think, my excellent friend, that a musician when he adjusts the lyre would desire or claim to exceed or go beyond a musician in the tightening and loosening the strings?

I do not think that he would.

But he would claim to exceed the non-musician?

Of course.

And what would you say of the physician? In prescribing meats and drinks would he wish to go beyond another physician or beyond the practice of medicine?

He would not.   350

But he would wish to go beyond the non-physician?

Yes.

And about knowledge and ignorance in general; see whether you think that any man who has knowledge ever would wish to have the choice of saying or doing more than another man who has knowledge. Would he not rather say or do the same as his like in the same case?

That, I suppose, can hardly be denied.

And what of the ignorant? would he not desire to have more than either the knowing or the ignorant?

I dare say.

And the knowing is wise?

b   Yes.

And the wise is good?

True.

Then the wise and good will not desire to gain more than his like, but more than his unlike and opposite?

I suppose so.

Whereas the bad and ignorant will desire to gain more than both?

Yes.

But did we not say, Thrasymachus, that the unjust goes beyond both his like and unlike? Were not these your words?

They were.

And you also said that the just will not go beyond his like but his unlike?

Yes.

c   Then the just is like the wise and good, and the unjust like the evil and ignorant?

That is the inference.

And each of them is such as his like is?

That was admitted.

Then the just has turned out to be wise and good and the unjust evil and ignorant.

OBJECTION: JUSTICE AS COOPERATION [350D-352B]

Thrasymachus made all these admissions, not fluently, as I repeat them, but with extreme reluctance; it was a hot summer's day, and the perspiration poured from him in torrents; and then I saw what d   I had never seen before, Thrasymachus blushing. As we were now agreed that justice was virtue and wisdom, and injustice vice and ignorance, I proceeded to another point:

Well, I said, Thrasymachus, that matter is now settled; but were we not also saying that injustice had strength; do you remember?

Yes, I remember, he said, but do not suppose that I approve of what you are saying or have no answer; if however I were to answer, you would be quite certain to accuse me of haranguing; therefore either permit me to have my say out, or if you would rather ask, do so, and I will answer 'Very good,' as they say to story-telling old women, and will nod 'Yes' and 'No.'

e   Certainly not, I said, if contrary to your real opinion.

Yes, he said, I will, to please you, since you will not let me speak. What else would you have?

Nothing in the world, I said; and if you are so disposed I will ask and you shall answer.

Proceed.

Then I will repeat the question which I asked before, in order that our examination of the relative nature of justice and injustice may be carried on regularly. A statement was made that injustice is stronger and more powerful than justice, but now justice, having been identified with wisdom and virtue, is easily shown to be stronger than injustice, if injustice is ignorance; this can no longer be questioned by any one. But I want to view the matter, Thrasymachus, in a different way: You would not deny that a state may be unjust and may be unjustly attempting to enslave other states, or may have already enslaved them, and may be holding many of them in subjection?

True, he replied; and I will add that the best and most perfectly unjust state will be most likely to do so.

I know, I said, that such was your position; but what I would further consider is, whether this power which is possessed by the superior state can exist or be exercised without justice or only with justice.

If you are right in your view, and justice is wisdom, then only with justice; but if I am right, then without justice.

I am delighted, Thrasymachus, to see you not only nodding assent and dissent, but making answers which are quite excellent.

That is out of civility to you, he replied.

You are very kind, I said; and would you have the goodness also to inform me, whether you think that a state, or an army, or a band of robbers and thieves, or any other gang of evil-doers could act at all if they injured one another?

No indeed, he said, they could not.

But if they abstained from injuring one another, then they might act together better?

Yes.

And this is because injustice creates divisions and hatreds and fighting, and justice imparts harmony and friendship; is not that true, Thrasymachus?

I agree, he said, because I do not wish to quarrel with you.

How good of you, I said; but I should like to know also whether injustice, having this tendency to arouse hatred, wherever existing, among slaves or among freemen, will not make them hate one another and set them at variance and render them incapable of common action?

Certainly.

And even if injustice be found in two only, will they not quarrel and fight, and become enemies to one another and to the just?

They will.

And suppose injustice abiding in a single person, would your wisdom say that she loses or that she retains her natural power?

Let us assume that she retains her power.

Yet is not the power which injustice exercises of such a nature that wherever she takes up her abode, whether in a city, in an army, in a family, or in any other body, that body is, to begin with, rendered incapable of united action by reason of sedition and distraction; and does it not become its own enemy and at variance with all that opposes it, and with the just? Is not this the case?

Yes, certainly.

And is not injustice equally fatal when existing in a single person; in the first place rendering him incapable of action because he is not at unity with himself, and in the second place making him an enemy to himself and the just? Is not that true, Thrasymachus?

Yes.

And O my friend, I said, surely the gods are just?

Granted that they are.

But if so, the unjust will be the enemy of the gods, and the just will be their friend?

Feast away in triumph, and take your fill of the argument; I will not oppose you, lest I should displease the company.

OBJECTION: JUSTICE AS HAPPINESS [352B–354C]

Well then, proceed with your answers, and let me have the remainder of my repast. For we have already shown that the just are clearly wiser and better and abler than the unjust, and that the unjust are incapable of common action; nay more, that to speak as we did of men who are evil acting at any time vigorously together, is not strictly true, for if they had been perfectly evil, they would have laid hands upon one another; but it is evident that there must have been some remnant of justice in them, which enabled them to combine; if there had not been they would have injured one another as well as their victims; they were but half-villains in their enterprises; for had they been whole villains, and utterly unjust, they would have been utterly incapable of action. That, as I believe, is the truth of the matter, and not what you said at first. But whether the just have a better and happier life than the unjust is a further question which we also proposed to consider. I think that they have, and for the reasons which I have given; but still I should like to examine further, for no light matter is at stake, nothing less than the rule of human life.

Proceed.

I will proceed by asking a question: Would you not say that a horse has some end?

I should.

And the end or use of a horse or of anything would be that which could not be accomplished, or not so well accomplished, by any other thing? e

I do not understand, he said.

Let me explain: Can you see, except with the eye?

Certainly not.

Or hear, except with the ear?

No.

These then may be truly said to be the ends of these organs?

They may.

But you can cut off a vine-branch with a dagger or with a chisel, and in many other ways?

Of course.

And yet not so well as with a pruning blade made for the pur- 353
pose?

True.

May we not say that this is the end of a pruning blade?

We may.

Then now I think you will have no difficulty in understanding my meaning when I asked the question whether the end of anything would be that which could not be accomplished, or not so well accomplished, by any other thing?

I understand your meaning, he said, and assent.

And that to which an end is appointed has also an excellence? Need I ask again whether the eye has an end?

It has. b

And has not the eye an excellence?

Yes.

And the ear has an end and an excellence also?

True.

And the same is true of all other things; they have each of them an end and a special excellence?

That is so.

Well, and can the eyes fulfil their end if they are wanting in their own proper excellence and have a defect instead?

How can they, he said, if they are blind and cannot see?

You mean to say, if they have lost their proper excellence, which c
is sight; but I have not arrived at that point yet. I would rather ask the question more generally, and only enquire whether the things which fulfil their ends fulfil them by their own proper excellence, and fail of fulfilling them by their own defect?

Certainly, he replied.

I might say the same of the ears; when deprived of their own proper excellence they cannot fulfil their end?

True.

And the same observation will apply to all other things?

I agree.

Well; and has not the soul an end which nothing else can fulfil? for example, to superintend and command and deliberate and the like. Are not these functions proper to the soul, and can they rightly be assigned to any other?

To no other.

And is not life to be reckoned among the ends of the soul?

Assuredly, he said.

And has not the soul an excellence also?

Yes.

And can she or can she not fulfil her own ends when deprived of that excellence?

She cannot.

Then an evil soul must necessarily be an evil ruler and superintendent, and the good soul a good ruler?

Yes, necessarily.

And we have admitted that justice is the excellence of the soul, and injustice the defect of the soul?

That has been admitted.

Then the just soul and the just man will live well, and the unjust man will live ill?

That is what your argument proves.

And he who lives well is blessed and happy, and he who lives ill the reverse of happy?

Certainly.

Then the just is happy, and the unjust miserable?

So be it.

But happiness and not misery is profitable.

Of course.

Then, my blessed Thrasymachus, injustice can never be more profitable than justice.

Let this, Socrates, he said, be your entertainment at the Bendidea.

For which I am indebted to you, I said, now that you have grown gentle towards me and have left off scolding. Nevertheless, I have not been well entertained; but that was my own fault and not yours. As an epicure snatches a taste of every dish which is successively brought to table, he not having allowed himself time to enjoy the one before, so have I gone from one subject to another without having discovered what I sought at first, the nature of justice. I left that enquiry and turned away to consider whether justice is virtue and wisdom or evil and folly; and when there arose a further question about the comparative advantages of justice and injustice, I could not refrain from passing on to that. And the result of the whole discussion has been that I know nothing at all. For I know not what justice is, and therefore I am not likely to know whether it is or is not a virtue, nor can I say whether the just man is happy or unhappy.

3

THE IMMORALIST POSITION RESTATED

INTRODUCTION

At the end of Book 1 Socrates has forced Thrasymachus to give up the debate on justice. This debate, however, is not over yet. Unsatisfied with the way Socrates has defeated Thrasymachus, the brothers of Plato, Glaucon and Adeimantus, press Socrates to elaborate further on the topic of justice. Glaucon and Adeimantus, like the other young men in the the room, are ambitious. The doubt brewing in their minds is that they aren't sure they couldn't get all the accolades, privileges and wealth that Socrates has just attached to the just life by merely appearing just. Do they actually have to be just? What if they put on a good show of it (like Cephalus) and prosper, all the while benefiting from backdoor secret deals and treachery? Few people are openly immoralists. Later Plato will discuss the Myth of the Cave, but here we can note that the young are still stuck on the appearance of justice rather than being out in the sun where the goodness of true justice is gleaming.

It should be pointed out that Glaucon and Adeimantus may not be devotees of Thrasymachus. What they are trying to do is to compel Socrates to offer a more satisfactory response to Thrasymachus' arguments. In a sense, they may be playing "devil's advocate" to Socrates, taking up Thrasymachus' position in order to provide Socrates with the opportunity to present a more complete account of justice. The rest of the *Republic* represents Socrates attempt to offer such an account and to prove that the life of justice is indeed "in every way better" than the life of injustice (357a).

CHALLENGE 1: IS JUSTICE GOOD IN ITSELF? [357A-362D]

Glaucon begins his challenge by positing three different types of good things (357b-358a). All good things, he argues, are desirable for one of the following reasons:

1. for their own sake, but not for their consequences (e.g., harmless pleasures)
2. for their consequences, but not for their own sake (e.g., medicine or money)
3. for their own sake and for their consequences (e.g., knowledge or health)

Glaucon then proceeds to ask Socrates where Justice fits into this scheme. According to the first position, justice would be seen to be valuable in itself, regardless of its consequences. One would choose to be just then even if the consequences of being just led to suffering or misery (the deontological position).

According to the second position, justice would seem as a good only because behaving justly produces good consequences (for example to gain the respect from other members of the community and therefore gain more gifts or contracts from them); but justice wouldn't be recognized as a good in itself (the utilitarian position).

Socrates' own position will be that justice belongs to the third class of good: something desirable for its own sake as well as for its consequences(358a) (the Platonic position).

Glaucon responds to the first part of Socrates' claim (that justice is desirable for its own sake) with an argument aimed at demonstrating that apparent justice (masking hidden unjust acts) is ultimately more advantageous to a person than justice is. He argues this point with the famous story of the Ring of Gyges (358a-360d). The shepherd Gyges finds a magic ring which renders him invisible at will, whereupon he murders the ruler, rapes the queen, enlists her cooperation, and reappears as the "just" and "generous" king of the people (a triumph of public relations). Doesn't this show that it's better to appear just than to actually be just?

The rules of justice, Glaucon maintains, arise out of convention—that is out of an agreement made by members of society. Before the *polis* emerged, the Greeks preyed upon one another and violated one another in their person and property. This led to vigilantism and vendettas. Because human beings are afraid of being harmed by others, they create laws, courts, and punish those who violate the law. [Students of political philosophy should note the striking similiarity between Glaucon's contractual origin of the state and that of Thomas Hobbes in the *Leviathan*.] Since the whole point of contracting the state is to avoid punishment, if one could safely put oneself out of its reach (via the magic ring or by the use of a secret police), one would certainly opt to behave unjustly (violate the queen, kill the king and usurp the throne). Therefore, nobody desires justice for its own sake, but only for its consequences. Human beings behave justly, in other words, not because they prefer justice to injustice, but simply because they fear the consequence of behaving unjustly.

Glaucon reinforces his point by asking Socrates which of two types of men are better off: a perfectly just man who has been viciously persecuted and falsely defamed or a perfectly unjust man, a charming charlatan who is falsely idolized by the public (360e-362d)? Wouldn't the one be living it up while the innocent accused would be lying in a prison with his eyes gouged out? If justice were desirable in itself, then we would choose it, regardless of its consequences. But no one would choose a life of justice if the consequences were as bleak as Glaucon portrays them. Therefore, nobody desires justice for its own sake, but only for its consequences.

CHALLENGE 2: DOES JUSTICE PRODUCE DESIRABLE CONSEQUENCES? [362D-367E]

Whereas Glaucon argues that justice is not desirable in itself, Adeimantus' aim is to demonstrate that it is not desirable for its consequences either. Adiemantus argues that parents don't teach children to be just because justice is good in itself, but because of its consequences. They claim that the just person receives many benefits: good marriage, public office, reputation, and rewards in the next life. But this doesn't seem to be the case. In this life, many good people suffer, and the wicked prosper. The wicked also have the opportunity to make up for their sins before they die (by offering expensive sacrifices to the gods or contributing to the church financially), thus receiving rewards in the next life as well. Therefore injustice is actually more profitable than justice is. What the two brothers are doing is challenging Socrates' claim that justice is valuable in itself and for its consequences.

By the time Glaucon and Adeimantus finish their attacks, Socrates is presented with a more viable defense of Thrasymachus' original position that justice is worthless. The burden will be placed upon him, then, to demonstrate the truth of his original claim that the life of justice is preferable to the life of injustice.

SUGGESTIONS FOR FURTHER READING

Altman, William H. F. *Plato the Teacher: The Crisis of the Republic.* Lanham, MD: Lexington Books, 2012. [101-109]

Annas, Julia. *An Introduction to Plato's Republic*. New York: Oxford, 1981. [58-71]

Benardete, Seth. *Socrates' Second Sailing: On Plato's Republic*. Chicago: University of Chicago Press, 1984. [35-44]

Bloom, Allan. *The Republic of Plato*. New York: Harper Collins, 1968. [337-344]

Irwin, Terence. *Plato's Ethics*. New York: Oxford UP, 1995. [181-202]

—. "Republic 2: Questions About Justice." *Plato 2: Ethics, Politics, Religion, and the Soul*. Ed. Gail Fine. Oxford: Oxford University Press, 1999.

Kirwin, Christopher. "Glaucon's Challenge," *Phronesis* 10 (1965): 162-173.

Pappas, Nickolas. *Plato and the Republic*. New York: Routledge, 1995. [50-57]

Reeve, C.D.C. *Philosopher-Kings: The Argument of Plato's Republic*. Princeton: Princeton University Press, 1988. [24-42]

Rice, Daryl H. *A Guide to Plato's Republic*. New York: Oxford University Press, 1998. [35-39]

Rosen, Stanley. *Plato's Republic: A Study*. New Haven: Yale University Press, 2005. [60-76]

Shields, Christopher. "Plato's Challenge: The Case Against Justice in *Republic* II." *The Blackwell Guide to Plato's Republic*. Malden, MA: Blackwell, 2006. [62-83]

White, Nicholas P. *A Companion to Plato's Republic*. Indianapolis: Hackett, 1979. [74-82]

—. "The Classification of Goods in Plato's *Republic*." *Journal of the History of Philosophy* 22 (1984): 393-421.

REPUBLIC 2.357A-367E

BOOK II

THE PROBLEM RESTATED [357A-358D]

With these words I was thinking that I had made an end of the dis-   357
cussion; but the end, in truth, proved to be only a beginning. For
Glaucon, who is always the most combative of men, was dissatisfied
at Thrasymachus' retirement; he wanted to have the battle out. So
he said to me: Socrates, do you wish really to persuade us, or only
to seem to have persuaded us, that to be just is always better than to
be unjust?   b

I should wish really to persuade you, I replied, if I could.

Then you certainly have not succeeded. Let me ask you now:—
How would you arrange goods—are there not some which we welcome for their own sakes, and independently of their consequences,
as, for example, harmless pleasures and enjoyments, which delight
us at the time, although nothing follows from them?

I agree in thinking that there is such a class, I replied.

Is there not also a second class of goods, such as knowledge,   c
sight, health, which are desirable not only in themselves, but also
for their results?

Certainly, I said.

And would you not recognize a third class, such as gymnastic,
and the care of the sick, and the physician's art; also the various
ways of money-making—these do us good but we regard them as
disagreeable; and no one would choose them for their own sakes,
but only for the sake of some reward or result which flows from
them?

There is, I said, this third class also. But why do you ask?

Because I want to know in which of the three classes you would
place justice?

In the highest class, I replied,—among those goods which he   358
who would be happy desires both for their own sake and for the sake
of their results.

Then the many are of another mind; they think that justice is to
be reckoned in the troublesome class, among goods which are to be
pursued for the sake of rewards and of reputation, but in themselves

are disagreeable and rather to be avoided.

I know, I said, that this is their manner of thinking, and that this was the thesis which Thrasymachus was maintaining just now, when he censured justice and praised injustice. But I am too stupid to be convinced by him.

b I wish, he said, that you would hear me as well as him, and then I shall see whether you and I agree. For Thrasymachus seems to me, like a snake, to have been charmed by your voice sooner than he ought to have been; but to my mind the nature of justice and injustice have not yet been made clear. Setting aside their rewards and results, I want to know what they are in themselves, and how they inwardly work in the soul. If you, please, then, I will revive c the argument of Thrasymachus. And first I will speak of the nature and origin of justice according to the common view of them. Secondly, I will show that all men who practise justice do so against their will, of necessity, but not as a good. And thirdly, I will argue that there is reason in this view, for the life of the unjust is after all better far than the life of the just—if what they say is true, Socrates, since I myself am not of their opinion. But still I acknowledge that I am perplexed when I hear the voices of Thrasymachus and myriads of others drumming in my ears; and, on the other hand, I have never yet heard the superiority of justice to injustice maintained by d any one in a satisfactory way. I want to hear justice praised in respect of itself; then I shall be satisfied, and you are the person from whom I think that I am most likely to hear this; and therefore I will praise the unjust life to the utmost of my power, and my manner of speaking will indicate the manner in which I desire to hear you too praising justice and censuring injustice. Will you say whether you approve of my proposal?

GLAUCON: THE RING OF GYGES [358D-362D]

Indeed I do; nor can I imagine any theme about which a man of sense would oftener wish to converse.

e I am delighted, he replied, to hear you say so, and shall begin by speaking, as I proposed, of the nature and origin of justice.

They say that to do injustice is, by nature, good; to suffer injustice, evil; but that the evil is greater than the good. And so when men have both done and suffered injustice and have had experience 359 of both, not being able to avoid the one and obtain the other, they think that they had better agree among themselves to have neither; hence there arise laws and mutual covenants; and that which is ordained by law is termed by them lawful and just. This they affirm to be the origin and nature of justice;—it is a mean or compromise, between the best of all, which is to do injustice and not be punished, and the worst of all, which is to suffer injustice without the power of retaliation; and justice, being at a middle point between the two, is tolerated not as a good, but as the lesser evil, and honoured by reason of the inability of men to do injustice. For no man who is worthy to be called a man would ever submit to such an agreement if he were able to resist; he would be mad if he did. Such is the received account, Socrates, of the nature and origin of justice.

Now that those who practise justice do so involuntarily and because they have not the power to be unjust will best appear if we imagine something of this kind: having given both to the just and the unjust power to do what they will, let us watch and see whither desire will lead them; then we shall discover in the very act the just and unjust man to be proceeding along the same road, following their interest, which all natures deem to be their good, and are only diverted into the path of justice by the force of law. The liberty which we are supposing may be most completely given to them in the form of such a power as is said to have been possessed by Gyges, the ancestor of Croesus the Lydian.

According to the tradition, Gyges was a shepherd in the service of the king of Lydia; there was a great storm, and an earthquake made an opening in the earth at the place where he was feeding his flock. Amazed at the sight, he descended into the opening, where, among other marvels, he beheld a hollow brass horse, having doors, at which he stooping and looking in saw a dead body of stature, as appeared to him, more than human, and having nothing on but a gold ring; this he took from the finger of the dead and reascended. Now the shepherds met together, according to custom, that they might send their monthly report about the flocks to the king; into their assembly he came having the ring on his finger, and as he was sitting among them he chanced to turn the stone of the ring inside his hand, when instantly he became invisible to the rest of the company and they began to speak of him as if he were no longer present. He was astonished at this, and again touching the ring he turned the stone outwards and reappeared; he made several trials of the ring, and always with the same result—when he turned the stone inwards he became invisible, when outwards he reappeared. Whereupon he contrived to be chosen one of the messengers who were sent to the court; whereas soon as he arrived he seduced the queen, and with her help conspired against the king and slew him, and took the kingdom.

Suppose now that there were two such magic rings, and the just put on one of them and the unjust the other; no man can be imagined to be of such an iron nature that he would stand fast in justice. No man would keep his hands off what was not his own when he could safely take what he liked out of the market, or go into houses and lie with any one at his pleasure, or kill or release from prison whom he would, and in all respects be like a God among men. Then the actions of the just would be as the actions of the unjust; they would both come at last to the same point. And this we may truly affirm to be a great proof that a man is just, not willingly or because he thinks that justice is any good to him individually, but of neces-

d   sity, for wherever any one thinks that he can safely be unjust, there he is unjust. For all men believe in their hearts that injustice is far more profitable to the individual than justice, and he who argues as I have been supposing, will say that they are right. If you could imagine any one obtaining this power of becoming invisible, and never doing any wrong or touching what was another's, he would be thought by the lookers-on to be a most wretched idiot, although they would praise him to one another's faces, and keep up appearances with one another from a fear that they too might suffer injustice. Enough of this.

e   Now, if we are to form a real judgment of the life of the just and unjust, we must isolate them; there is no other way; and how is the isolation to be effected? I answer: Let the unjust man be entirely unjust, and the just man entirely just; nothing is to be taken away from either of them, and both are to be perfectly furnished for the work of their respective lives.

First, let the unjust be like other distinguished masters of craft; like the skilful pilot or physician, who knows intuitively his own

361   powers and keeps within their limits, and who, if he fails at any point, is able to recover himself. So let the unjust make his unjust attempts in the right way, and lie hidden if he means to be great in his injustice: (he who is found out is nobody:) for the highest reach of injustice is, to be deemed just when you are not. Therefore I say that in the perfectly unjust man we must assume the most perfect injustice; there is to be no deduction, but we must allow him, while

b   doing the most unjust acts, to have acquired the greatest reputation for justice. If he have taken a false step he must be able to recover himself; he must be one who can speak with effect, if any of his deeds come to light, and who can force his way where force is required by his courage and strength, and command of money and friends.

And at his side let us place the just man in his nobleness and simplicity, wishing, as Aeschylus says, to be and not to seem good. There must be no seeming, for if he seem to be just he will be hon-

c   oured and rewarded, and then we shall not know whether he is just for the sake of justice or for the sake of honours and rewards; therefore, let him be clothed in justice only, and have no other covering; and he must be imagined in a state of life the opposite of the former. Let him be the best of men, and let him be thought the worst; then he will have been put to the proof; and we shall see whether he will be affected by the fear of infamy and its consequences. And let him

d   continue thus to the hour of death; being just and seeming to be unjust. When both have reached the uttermost extreme, the one of justice and the other of injustice, let judgment be given which of them is the happier of the two.

Heavens! my dear Glaucon, I said, how energetically you polish them up for the decision, first one and then the other, as if they were two statues.

I do my best, he said. And now that we know what they are like there is no difficulty in tracing out the sort of life which awaits either of them. This I will proceed to describe; but as you may think the description a little too coarse, I ask you to suppose, Socrates, that the words which follow are not mine.—Let me put them into the mouths of the eulogists of injustice: They will tell you that the just man who is thought unjust will be scourged, racked, bound—will have his eyes burnt out; and, at last, after suffering every kind of evil, he will be impaled: Then he will understand that he ought to seem only, and not to be, just; the words of Aeschylus may be more truly spoken of the unjust than of the just. For the unjust is pursuing a reality; he does not live with a view to appearances—he wants to be really unjust and not to seem only:—

'His mind has a soil deep and fertile, Out of which spring his prudent counsels.'

In the first place, he is thought just, and therefore bears rule in the city; he can marry whom he will, and give in marriage to whom he will; also he can trade and deal where he likes, and always to his own advantage, because he has no misgivings about injustice; and at every contest, whether in public or private, he gets the better of his antagonists, and gains at their expense, and is rich, and out of his gains he can benefit his friends, and harm his enemies; moreover, he can offer sacrifices, and dedicate gifts to the gods abundantly and magnificently, and can honour the gods or any man whom he wants to honour in a far better style than the just, and therefore he is likely to be dearer than they are to the gods. And thus, Socrates, gods and men are said to unite in making the life of the unjust better than the life of the just.

THE OBJECTION OF ADEIMANTUS [362D-367E]

I was going to say something in answer to Glaucon, when Adeimantus, his brother, interposed: Socrates, he said, you do not suppose that there is nothing more to be urged?

Why, what else is there? I answered.

The strongest point of all has not been even mentioned, he replied.

Well, then, according to the proverb, 'Let brother help brother'—if he fails in any part do you assist him; although I must confess that Glaucon has already said quite enough to lay me in the dust, and take from me the power of helping justice.

Nonsense, he replied. But let me add something more: There is another side to Glaucon's argument about the praise and censure of justiceand injustice, which is equally required in order to bring out what I believe to be his meaning. Parents and tutors are always telling their sons and their wards that they are to be just; but why? not for the sake of justice, but for the sake of character and reputation; in the hope of obtaining for him who is reputed just some of those offices, marriages,and the like which Glaucon has enumerated among the advantages accruing to the unjust from the reputation of justice. More, however, is made of appearances by this class of persons than by the others; for they throw in the good opinion of the gods, and will tell you of a shower of benefits which the heavens, as they say, rain upon the pious; and this accords with the testimony of the noble Hesiod and Homer, the first of whom says, that the gods make the oaks of the just—

'To bear acorns at their summit, and bees in the middle; And the sheep are bowed down with the weight of their fleeces,"

and many other blessings of a like kind are provided for them. And Homer has a very similar strain; for he speaks of one whose fame is—

'As the fame of some blameless king who, like a god, Maintains justice; to whom the black earth brings forth Wheat and barley, whose trees are bowed with fruit, And his sheep never fail to bear, and the sea gives him fish.'

Still grander are the gifts of heaven which Musaeus and his son vouchsafe to the just; they take them down into the world below, where they have the saints lying on couches at a feast, everlastingly drunk, crowned with garlands; their idea seems to be that an immortality of drunkenness is the highest meed of virtue. Some extend their rewards yet further; the posterity, as they say, of the faithful and just shall survive to the third and fourth generation. This is the style in which they praise justice. But about the wicked there is another strain; they bury them in a swamp in Hades, and make them carry water in a sieve; also while they are yet living they bring them to infamy, and inflict upon them the punishments which Glaucon described as the portion of the just who are reputed to be unjust; nothing else does their invention supply. Such is their manner of praising the one and censuring the other.

Once more, Socrates, I will ask you to consider another way of speaking about justice and injustice, which is not confined to the poets, but is found in prose writers. The universal voice of mankind is always declaring that justice and virtue are honourable, but grievous and toilsome; and that the pleasures of vice and injustice are easy of attainment, and are only censured by law and opinion. They say also that honesty is for the most part less profitable than dishonesty; and they are quite ready to call wicked men happy, and to honour them both in public and private when they are rich or in any other way influential, while they despise and overlook those who may be weak and poor, even though acknowledging them to be better than the others. But most extraordinary of all is their mode of speaking about virtue and the gods: they say that the gods apportion calamity and misery to many good men, and good and happiness to the wicked. And begging prophets go to rich men's doors and persuade them that they have a power committed to them by the gods of making an atonement for a man's own or his ancestor's sins by sacrifices or charms, with rejoicings and feasts; and they promise to harm an enemy, whether just or unjust, at a small cost; with magic arts and incantations binding heaven, as they say, to execute their will. And the poets are the authorities to whom they appeal, now smoothing the path of vice with the words of Hesiod;—

'Vice may be had in abundance without trouble; the way is smooth and her dwelling-place is near. But before virtue the gods have set toil,'

and a tedious and uphill road: then citing Homer as a witness that the gods may be influenced by men; for he also says:—

'The gods, too, may be turned from their purpose; and men pray to them and avert their wrath by sacrifices and soothing entreaties, and by libations and the odour of fat, when they have sinned and transgressed.'

And they produce a host of books written by Musaeus and Orpheus, who were children of the Moon and the Muses—that is what they say—according to which they perform their ritual, and persuade not only individuals, but whole cities, that expiations and atonements for sin may be made by sacrifices and amusements which fill a vacant hour, and are equally at the service of the living and the dead; the latter sort they call mysteries, and they redeem us from the pains of hell, but if we neglect them no one knows what awaits us.

He proceeded: And now when the young hear all this said about virtue and vice, and the way in which gods and men regard them, how are their minds likely to be affected, my dear Socrates,—those of them, I mean, who are quickwitted, and, like bees on the wing, light on every flower, and from all that they hear are prone to draw conclusions as to what manner of persons they should be and in what way they should walk if they would make the best of life? Probably the youth will say to himself in the words of Pindar—

'Can I by justice or by crooked ways of deceit ascend a loftier tower which may be a fortress to me all my days?'

For what men say is that, if I am really just and am not also thought just profit there is none, but the pain and loss on the other hand are unmistakeable. But if, though unjust, I acquire the reputation of justice, a heavenly life is promised to me. Since then, as philosophers prove, appearance tyrannizes over truth and is lord of happiness, to appearance I must devote myself. I will describe around me a picture and shadow of virtue to be the vestibule and exterior of my house; behind I will trail the subtle and crafty fox, as Archilochus, greatest of sages, recommends. But I hear some one exclaiming that the concealment of wickedness is often difficult; to which I answer, Nothing great is easy. Nevertheless, the argument indicates this, if we would be happy, to be the path along which we should proceed. With a view to concealment we will establish secret brotherhoods and political clubs. And there are professors of rhetoric who teach the art of persuading courts and assemblies; and so, partly by persuasion and partly by force, I shall make unlawful gains and not be punished. Still I hear a voice saying that the gods cannot be deceived, neither can they be compelled. But what if there are no gods? or, suppose them to have no care of human things—why in either case should we mind about concealment? And even if there are gods, and they do care about us, yet we know of them only from tradition and the genealogies of the poets; and these are the very persons who say that they may be influenced and turned by 'sacrifices and soothing entreaties and by offerings.' Let us be consistent then, and believe both or neither. If the poets speak truly, why then we had better be unjust, and offer of the fruits of injustice; for if we are just, although we may escape the vengeance of heaven, we shall lose the gains of injustice; but, if we are unjust, we shall keep the gains, and by our sinning and praying, and praying and sinning, the gods will be appeases, and we shall not be punished. 'But there is a world below in which either we or our posterity will suffer for our unjust deeds.' Yes, my friend, will be the reflection, but there are mysteries and atoning deities, and these have great power. That is what mighty cities declare; and the children of the gods, who were their poets and prophets, bear a like testimony.

On what principle, then, shall we any longer choose justice rather than the worst injustice? when, if we only unite the latter with a deceitful regard to appearances, we shall fare to our mind both with gods and men, in life and after death, as the most numerous and the highest authorities tell us. Knowing all this, Socrates, how can a man who has any superiority of mind or person or rank or wealth, be willing to honour justice; or indeed to refrain from laughing when he hears justice praised? And even if there should be some one who is able to disprove the truth of my words, and who is satisfied that justice is best, still he is not angry with the unjust, but is very ready to forgive them, because he also knows that men are not just of their own free will; unless, perhaps, there be some one whom the divinity within him may have inspired with a hatred of injustice, or who has attained knowledge of the truth—but no other man. He only blames injustice who, owing to cowardice or age or some weakness, has not the power of being unjust. And this is proved by the fact that when he obtains the power, he immediately becomes unjust as far as he can be.

The cause of all this, Socrates, was indicated by us at the beginning of the argument, when my brother and I told you how astonished we were to find that of all the professing praisers of justice—beginning with the ancient heroes of whom any memorial has been preserved to us, and ending with the men of our own time—no one has ever blamed injustice or praised justice except with a view to the glories, honours, and benefits which flow from them. No one has ever adequately described either in verse or prose the true essential nature of either of them abiding in the soul, and invisible to any human or divine eye; or shown that of all the things of a man's soul which he has within him, justice is the greatest good, and injustice the greatest evil. Had this been the universal strain, had you sought to persuade us of this from our youth upwards, we should not have been on the watch to keep one another from doing wrong, but every one would have been his own watchman, because afraid, if he did wrong, of harbouring in himself the greatest of evils. I dare say that Thrasymachus and others would seriously hold the language which I have been merely repeating, and words even stronger than these about justice and injustice, grossly, as I conceive, perverting their true nature. But I speak in this vehement manner, as I must frankly confess to you, because I want to hear from you the opposite side; and I would ask you to show not only the superiority which justice has over injustice, but what effect they have on the possessor of them which makes the one to be a good and the other an evil to him. And please, as Glaucon requested of you, to exclude reputations; for unless you take away from each of them his true reputation and add on the false, we shall say that you do not praise justice, but the appearance of it; we shall think that you are only exhorting us to keep injustice dark, and that you really

c   agree with Thrasymachus in thinking that justice is another's good
and the interest of the stronger, and that injustice is a man's own
profit and interest, though injurious to the weaker. Now as you have
admitted that justice is one of that highest class of goods which are
desired indeed for their results, but in a far greater degree for their
own sakes—like sight or hearing or knowledge or health, or any
other real and natural and not merely conventional good—I would
d   ask you in your praise of justice to regard one point only: I mean
the essential good and evil which justice and injustice work in the
possessors of them. Let others praise justice and censure injustice,
magnifying the rewards and honours of the one and abusing the
other; that is a manner of arguing which, coming from them, I am
ready to tolerate, but from you who have spent your whole life in
the consideration of this question, unless I hear the contrary from
e   your own lips, I expect something better. And therefore, I say, not
only prove to us that justice is better than injustice, but show what
they either of them do to the possessor of them, which makes the
one to be a good and the other an evil, whether seen or unseen by
gods and men.

4

JUSTICE IN THE CITY

SOCRATES' RESPONSE: JUSTICE IN THE CITY [367E-369B]

Socrates agrees to undertake the defense of the life of justice, but does so in a rather peculiar way. He begins with the larger task of first discussing justice in the city (*polis*); only later will he go on to describe justice in the soul. His reasons for taking this particular tact are first, that justice is the same whether in the city or in the individual soul, and second, that it is easier to analyze justice in the city than it would be to analyze it in the soul (369a), therefore, he will examine the city first (368d-434c) and then apply what he learns to the soul (434c-445e).

RISE OF THE MINIMAL CITY [369B-373A]

Socrates defines the city as an association of people based upon need (369b). A city comes into being because human beings cannot satisfy all their individual needs on their own and they need to work cooperatively with others. With the rise of the city there necessarily occurs a division of skills (e.g., farming, shoemaking, building, weaving). Before the city exists each individual has to perform all of these crafts himself, and not always satisfactorily. In his description of the primitive city, Socrates presupposes the *principle of specialization*— that within the city one person should do one job (Annas, 73-74). Following the principle leads to cooperation: everyone works on specific tasks to meet the needs of the community; each is released from the tasks taken on by the others. This leaves the specialist to develop an excellence in the craft, effectively, efficiently and consistently achieving the *telos* of the craft, supplying an abundance of high quality goods and services for the community. Specialization is natural: every person has different talents and abilities (370a). What about the person who doesn't enjoy his job (i.e., toll collector)? Socrates argues that this is a selfish attitude.

THE LUXURIOUS CITY [373A-375A]

The city that Socrates has coaxed out of Adeimantus (396b-372a) is one of simple living in the country. "Won't they make bread, wine, clothing and shoes?" Socrates asks. "And, when they have built houses, they will work in the summer, for the most part naked and without shoes, and in the winter adequately clothed and shod."

Glaucon objects, however, that such a city is fit more for pigs than for human beings (372d). Socrates reluctantly agrees that most folks wouldn't be content living in the minimal city. Not satisfied with simple comforts they would naturally desire more civilized pleasures (e.g., jewelry, plush furniture, fancy clothes, haute cuisine, entertainment). Therefore, they are going to need more specialized skills in their city (e.g., performers, barbers, prostitutes, pastry makers, etc.). Since the citizens prefer a richer, fattier diet, there will be a need for more doctors (Socrates calls the heated-up economy of the luxurious city the "feverish" city). Competition will be fiercer so there will arise a need for attorneys.

Increasing the population of the city to include all these new specialties means that people are going to need more food and hence more land to grow food. They are going to have to expand their territory through warfare (373d-e). As a consequence of that, they will need a permanent professional army. Once it is accepted that the luxurious city is a necessity, the skill of combat becomes the most important in the city. It follows that the leaders of the army—the Guardians—should also be the rulers of the city.

The minimal city is most likely Socrates' preference because its healthier cooperating citizens are satisfied with the most basic human needs and thus there will be no corruption. Moreover, larders and treasuries attract marauders from without and thieves from within, creating strife. However, Glaucon has his eye on ruling a city-state like Athens and not some Podunk, so Socrates tries to invent a city-in-speech more in tune with such glory-seeking aspirations (Pappas 63-64; Annas 77-79).

SUGGESTIONS FOR FURTHER READING

Annas, Julia. *An Introduction to Plato's Republic*. New York: Oxford, 1981. [72-79]

Benardete, Seth. *Socrates' Second Sailing: On Plato's Republic*. Chicago: University of Chicago Press. 1984 [44-54]

Bloom, Allan. *The Republic of Plato*. New York: Harper Collins, 1968. [343-349]

Pappas, Nickolas. *Plato and the Republic*. New York: Routledge, 1995. [59-64]

Rosen, Stanley. *Plato's Republic: A Study*. New Haven: Yale University Press, 2005. [79-108]

Sayers, Sean. *Plato's Republic: An Introduction*. Edinburgh: Edinburgh University Press, 1999. [20-31]

White, Nicholas P. *A Companion to Plato's Republic*. Indianapolis: Hackett, 1979. [82-91]

REPUBLIC 2.367E-375A

JUSTICE IN THE CITY [376E-396B]

I had always admired the genius of Glaucon and Adeimantus, but on hearing these words I was quite delighted, and said: Sons of an illustrious father, that was not a bad beginning of the Elegiac verses which the admirer of Glaucon made in honour of you after you had distinguished yourselves at the battle of Megara:—

368

'Sons of Ariston,' he sang, 'divine offspring of an illustrious hero.'

The epithet is very appropriate, for there is something truly divine in being able to argue as you have done for the superiority of injustice, and remaining unconvinced by your own arguments.

b

And I do believe that you are not convinced—this I infer from your general character, for had I judged only from your speeches I should have mistrusted you. But now, the greater my confidence in you, the greater is my difficulty in knowing what to say. For I am in a strait between two; on the one hand I feel that I am unequal to the task; and my inability is brought home to me by the fact that you were not satisfied with the answer which I made to Thrasymachus, proving, as I thought, the superiority which justice has over injustice. And yet I cannot refuse to help, while breath and speech remain to me;

c

I am afraid that there would be an impiety in being present when justice is evil spoken of and not lifting up a hand in her defence. And therefore I had best give such help as I can.

Glaucon and the rest entreated me by all means not to let the question drop, but to proceed in the investigation. They wanted to arrive at the truth, first, about the nature of justice and injustice, and secondly, about their relative advantages. I told them, what I really thought, that the enquiry would be of a serious nature, and

d

would require very good eyes. Seeing then, I said, that we are no great wits, I think that we had better adopt a method which I may illustrate thus; suppose that a short-sighted person had been asked by some one to read small letters from a distance; and it occurred to some one else that they might be found in another place which was larger and in which the letters were larger—if they were the same and he could read the larger letters first, and then proceed to the lesser—this would have been thought a rare piece of good fortune.

Very true, said Adeimantus; but how does the illustration apply

e

to our enquiry?

I will tell you, I replied; justice, which is the subject of our enquiry, is, as you know, sometimes spoken of as the virtue of an individual, and sometimes as the virtue of a State.

True, he replied.

And is not a State larger than an individual?

It is.

Then in the larger the quantity of justice is likely to be larger and more easily discernible. I propose therefore that we enquire into the nature of justice and injustice, first as they appear in the State, and secondly in the individual, proceeding from the greater to the lesser and comparing them.

369

That, he said, is an excellent proposal.

And if we imagine the State in process of creation, we shall see the justice and injustice of the State in process of creation also.

I dare say.

When the State is completed there may be a hope that the object of our search will be more easily discovered.

Yes, far more easily.

b

But ought we to attempt to construct one? I said; for to do so, as I am inclined to think, will be a very serious task. Reflect therefore.

I have reflected, said Adeimantus, and am anxious that you should proceed.

RISE OF THE MINIMAL CITY [369b-373a]

A State, I said, arises, as I conceive, out of the needs of mankind; no one is self-sufficing, but all of us have many wants. Can any other origin of a State be imagined?

There can be no other.

Then, as we have many wants, and many persons are needed to supply them, one takes a helper for one purpose and another for another; and when these partners and helpers are gathered together in one habitation the body of inhabitants is termed a State.

c

True, he said.

And they exchange with one another, and one gives, and another receives, under the idea that the exchange will be for their good.

Very true.

Then, I said, let us begin and create in idea a State; and yet the true creator is necessity, who is the mother of our invention.

Of course, he replied.

Now the first and greatest of necessities is food, which is the condition of life and existence.

d

Certainly.

The second is a dwelling, and the third clothing and the like.

True.

And now let us see how our city will be able to supply this

great demand: We may suppose that one man is a farmer, another a builder, some one else a weaver—shall we add to them a shoemaker, or perhaps some other purveyor to our bodily wants?

Quite right.

The barest notion of a State must include four or five men.

c   Clearly.

And how will they proceed? Will each bring the result of his labours into a common stock?—the individual farmer, for example, producing for four, and labouring four times as long and as much as he need in the provision of food with which he supplies others as well as himself; or will he have nothing to do with others and not be at the trouble of producing for them, but provide for himself alone a fourth of the food in a fourth of the time, and in the remaining three fourths of his time be employed in making a house or a coat or a pair of shoes, having no partnership with others, but supplying himself all his own wants?

370

Adeimantus thought that he should aim at producing food only and not at producing everything.

Probably, I replied, that would be the better way; and when I hear you say this, I am myself reminded that we are not all alike; b   there are diversities of natures among us which are adapted to different occupations.

Very true.

And will you have a work better done when the workman has many occupations, or when he has only one?

When he has only one.

Further, there can be no doubt that a work is spoilt when not done at the right time?

No doubt.

For business is not disposed to wait until the doer of the business is at leisure; but the doer must follow up what he is doing, and make c   the business his first object.

He must.

And if so, we must infer that all things are produced more plentifully and easily and of a better quality when one man does one thing which is natural to him and does it at the right time, and leaves other things.

Undoubtedly.

Then more than four citizens will be required; for the farmer will not make his own plow or pickaxe, or other implements of d   agriculture, if they are to be good for anything. Neither will the builder make his tools—and he too needs many; and in like manner the weaver and shoemaker.

True.

Then carpenters, and smiths, and many other artisans, will be sharers in our little State, which is already beginning to grow?

True.

Yet even if we add cowherds, shepherds, and other herdsmen, in order that our farmers may have oxen to plow with, and builders as well as farmers may have draft cattle, and leather makers and weavers fleeces and hides—still our State will not be very large.

That is true; yet neither will it be a very small State which contains all these.

Then, again, there is the situation of the city—to find a place where nothing need be imported is nearly impossible.

Impossible.

Then there must be another class of citizens who will bring the required supply from another city?

There must.

But if the trader goes empty-handed, having nothing which they require who would supply his need, he will come back empty-handed.

That is certain.

And therefore what they produce at home must be not only enough for themselves, but such both in quantity and quality as to accommodate those from whom their wants are supplied.

Very true.

Then more farmers and more artisans will be required?

They will.

Not to mention the importers and exporters, who are called merchants?

Yes.

Then we shall want merchants?

We shall.

And if merchandise is to be carried over the sea, skilful sailors will also be needed, and in considerable numbers?

Yes, in considerable numbers.

Then, again, within the city, how will they exchange their productions? To secure such an exchange was, as you will remember, one of our principal objects when we formed them into a society and constituted a State.

Clearly they will buy and sell.

Then they will need a market-place, and a money-token for purposes of exchange.

Certainly.

Suppose now that a farmer, or an artisan, brings some production to market, and he comes at a time when there is no one to exchange with him,—is he to leave his calling and sit idle in the market-place?

Not at all; he will find people there who, seeing the want, undertake the office of salesmen. In well-ordered states they are commonly those who are the weakest in bodily strength, and therefore of little use for any other purpose; their duty is to be in the market, and to give money in exchange for goods to those who desire to sell and to take money from those who desire to buy.

This want, then, creates a class of retail-traders in our State. Is not 'retailer' the term which is applied to those who sit in the market-place engaged in buying and selling, while those who wander from one city to another are called merchants?

Yes, he said.

And there is another class of servants, who are intellectually hardly on the level of companionship; still they have plenty of bodily strength for labour, which accordingly they sell, and are called, if I do not mistake, hirelings, hire being the name which is given to the price of their labour.

True.

Then hirelings will help to make up our population?

Yes.

And now, Adeimantus, is our State matured and perfected?

I think so.

Where, then, is justice, and where is injustice, and in what part of the State did they spring up?

Probably in the dealings of these citizens with one another. I cannot imagine that they are more likely to be found any where else.

I dare say that you are right in your suggestion, I said; we had better think the matter out, and not shrink from the enquiry.

Let us then consider, first of all, what will be their way of life, now that we have thus established them. Will they not produce corn, and wine, and clothes, and shoes, and build houses for themselves? And when they are housed, they will work, in summer, commonly, stripped and barefoot, but in winter substantially clothed and shod. They will feed on barley-meal and flour of wheat, baking and kneading them, making noble cakes and loaves; these they will serve up on a mat of reeds or on clean leaves, themselves reclining the while upon beds strewn with yew or myrtle. And they and their children will feast, drinking of the wine which they have made, wearing garlands on their heads, and hymning the praises of the gods, in happy converse with one another. And they will take care that their families do not exceed their means; having an eye to poverty or war.

But, said Glaucon, interposing, you have not given them a relish to their meal.

True, I replied, I had forgotten; of course they must have a relish—salt, and olives, and cheese, and they will boil roots and herbs such as country people prepare; for a dessert we shall give them figs, and peas, and beans; and they will roast myrtle-berries and acorns at the fire, drinking in moderation. And with such a diet

they may be expected to live in peace and health to a good old age,
and bequeath a similar life to their children after them.   d

Yes, Socrates, he said, and if you were providing for a city of
pigs, how else would you feed the beasts?

But what would you have, Glaucon? I replied.

Why, he said, you should give them the ordinary conveniences
of life. People who are to be comfortable are accustomed to lie on
sofas, and dine off tables, and they should have sauces and sweets
in the modern style.   e

THE LUXURIOUS CITY [373A-375A]

Yes, I said, now I understand: the question which you would have
me consider is, not only how a State, but how a luxurious State is
created; and possibly there is no harm in this, for in such a State
we shall be more likely to see how justice and injustice originate.
In my opinion the true and healthy constitution of the State is the
one which I have described. But if you wish also to see a State at
fever-heat, I have no objection. For I suspect that many will not be
satisfied with the simpler way of life. They will be for adding sofas,
and tables, and other furniture; also dainties, and perfumes, and   373
incense, and courtesans, and cakes, all these not of one sort only,
but in every variety; we must go beyond the necessaries of which
I was at first speaking, such as houses, and clothes, and shoes: the
arts of the painter and the embroiderer will have to be set in motion,
and gold and ivory and all sorts of materials must be procured.

True, he said.

Then we must enlarge our borders; for the original healthy   b
State is no longer sufficient. Now will the city have to fill and
swell with a multitude of callings which are not required by any
natural want; such as the whole tribe of hunters and actors, of
whom one large class have to do with forms and colors; another
will be the connoisseurs of music—poets and their attendant train
of rhapsodists, players, dancers, contractors; also makers of divers
kinds of articles, including women's dresses. And we shall want
more servants. Will not tutors be also in request, and nurses wet   c
and dry, maids and barbers, as well as confectioners and cooks; and
swineherds, too, who were not needed and therefore had no place
in the former edition of our State, but are needed now? They must
not be forgotten: and there will be animals of many other kinds, if
people eat them.

Certainly.

And living in this way we shall have much greater need of
physicians than before?   d

Much greater.

And the country which was enough to support the original

inhabitants will be too small now, and not enough?

Quite true.

Then a slice of our neighbours' land will be wanted by us for pasture and tillage, and they will want a slice of ours, if, like ourselves, they exceed the limit of necessity, and give themselves up to the unlimited accumulation of wealth?

That, Socrates, will be inevitable.

c   And so we shall go to war, Glaucon. Shall we not?

Most certainly, he replied.

Then without determining as yet whether war does good or harm, thus much we may affirm, that now we have discovered war to be derived from causes which are also the causes of almost all the evils in States, private as well as public.

Undoubtedly.

And our State must once more enlarge; and this time the enlargement will be nothing short of a whole army, which will have
374   to go out and fight with the invaders for all that we have, as well as for the things and persons whom we were describing above.

Why? he said; are they not capable of defending themselves?

No, I said; not if we were right in the principle which was acknowledged by all of us when we were framing the State: the principle, as you will remember, was that one man cannot practise many arts with success.

Very true, he said.

But is not war an art?

Certainly.

b   And an art requiring as much attention as shoemaking?

Quite true.

And the shoemaker was not allowed by us to be a farmer, or a weaver, or a builder—in order that we might have our shoes well made; but to him and to every other worker was assigned one work for which he was by nature fitted, and at that he was to continue working all his life long and at no other; he was not to let opportunities slip, and then he would become a good workman.
c   Now nothing can be more important than that the work of a soldier should be well done. But is war an art so easily acquired that a man may be a warrior who is also a farmer, or shoemaker, or other artisan; although no one in the world would be a good dice or checkers player who merely took up the game as a recreation, and had not from his earliest years devoted himself to this and nothing else? No tools will make a man a skilled workman, or master of defence, nor be of any use to him who has not learned how to handle them, and has never bestowed any attention upon them. How then will he who takes up a shield or other implement of war become a good fighter
d   all in a day, whether with heavy-armed or any other kind of troops?

Yes, he said, the tools which would teach men their own use

would be beyond price.

And the higher the duties of the guardian, I said, the more time, and skill, and art, and application will be needed by him?

No doubt, he replied.

Will he not also require natural aptitude for his calling?

Certainly.

Then it will be our duty to select, if we can, natures which are fitted for the task of guarding the city?

It will.

And the selection will be no easy matter, I said; but we must be brave and do our best.

We must.

5

EDUCATION OF THE GUARDIANS

THE EDUCATION OF THE GUARDIANS [375A-376D]

We have seen that, in order to provide for the protection and expansion of the luxurious city, it is necessary to have an army of guardians who will also serve as the rulers of the city. A problem arises when Socrates considers the danger that military rule could easily lead to the establishment of dictatorship. In accord with the principle of specialization, the discussants agree that it's better to have a professional class of warriors than amateurs. The problem comes in when they realize that these warriors will become the strongest, most armed, most adept killers in the City-State. Who will guard the guardians? What will prevent them from taking over the City, robbing the citizens of their freedom and property, or engaging in reckless military adventurism that puts the survival of the city at risk? Nothing physical prevents the warriors from doing this.

The solution, he maintains, will be to educate the guardians in such a way that they will become, on the one hand, gentle towards their own citizens and, on the other hand, fierce towards their enemies. In 375a, an analogy is made between the guardians and pedigree puppies. In Plato's mind, just as a "noble puppy" can be trained to be both fierce (towards strangers) and gentle (towards those it knows), so too can his guardians.

Plato's understanding of education is somewhat different than our contemporary understanding: it involves the *total training of character (ethos)* and aims at producing a morally mature individual. It is, in other words, fundamentally moral in nature. Furthermore, it strives to *connect ethics with aesthetics*. Its goal is to produce people who are attracted to the good and repulsed by evil. It attempts to combine the proper balance of both intellectual and physical training. The over-emphasis on physical training would produce a brute, the over-emphasis on the intellectual, a wimp.

CENSORSHIP OF POETRY [376D-383C]

Socrates describes the two aspects of the guardian's education: music (*mousike*) for the soul and gymnastics (*gymnastike*) for the body. White maintains that these terms are somewhat misleading and that "training in the arts" and "physical training" comes closer to the meaning that Plato has in mind (White 91). Pappas elaborates further, writing, "Music (*mousike*) means all the activities sponsored by the Muses: poetry of every stripe, dance, astronomy, history—roughly what we call in English 'the liberal arts'" (Pappas 65). The bulk of Plato's discussion in Books 2 and 3 concerns the specific types of poetry (i.e., stories) to which the young guardians will be exposed. The poetry that Plato refers to is not exactly what we usually have in mind by poetry. Poetry in ancient Greece made up an important part of a child's education, and was memorized and actually sung in unison, not read silently. The focus was mainly on the poetry of Homer—the *Iliad* and the *Odyssey*. This is extremely important, since a young child's character can easily be affected by exposure to vicious or illicit stories. Think for example about the negative effects of certain types of television programs, music or films on children in our own times, and you will understand why Plato is so concerned about this issue. Since education for Plato involves the training of one's entire character, and since certain types of poetry/stories can produce a negative impact on the child's character, it will not be surprising that Plato advocates the censorship of certain types of poems/stories (377b).

Plato first argues that all false poetry should be censored. This category would include all stories about gods and heroes which make a "bad representation" of them (377e). Since the gods are good, those stories which portray them performing indecent or immoral acts must by implication be false. Likewise heroes certainly can't be weak or undignified, so Plato will have them portrayed only in a properly heroic light. Plato does not hesitate to attack the sacred figures of Greek literature. Homer's *Iliad*, for example, would have been considered a great work even in Plato's own time. Because the gods are portrayed in Homer's work as petty, lustful, vain and vengeful (Zeus, transforming himself into a swan to commit adultery with Leda, for example) and heroes as savage, selfish and deceitful (Achilles, petulantly refusing to fight for the Achaeans because Agamemnon took away his concubine, for example), Homer's mistakes must be corrected. What Plato's guardians would be left with is a greatly sanitized version of Homer.

Plato's next move is to argue for the censorship of all *immoral poetry* (378a). Stories portraying vice of any kind, even if true, must be censored. Children must not be exposed, for example, to stories of happy tyrants, since they will eventually want to imitate these vices. Plato, as we shall see, has no problem with the rulers of his city lying to its citizens for their own good. What he is most concerned about is ensuring that the guardians grow up free of vicious influences. If that means manipulating the truth of certain tales, so be it.

THE CONTENT OF THE GUARDIAN'S POETRY [386A-392C]

In 386a-392c Plato continues with his discussion of the content of poetry that needs to be regulated in the education of the guardians. Among the specific features of poetry that should be avoided at all costs are: poetry that discourages courage by heightening the guardians' fear of death (386b-388e), poetry that encourages excessive laughter (389a-b), poetry that inspires anyone other than the rulers of the city to lie (389b-d), poetry that discourages moderation (389d-392a), poetry that teaches that injustice is profitable [only touched upon] (392a-392c).

In this section Plato deals with two of the four cardinal virtues that he will return to in Book Four. These four virtues are: courage, moderation, justice and wisdom. Plato can deal with the virtues of courage and moderation early on because he views their importance in the education of the guardians as uncontroversial. "The other two virtues are left aside, justice because its desirability in general is what is at issue, and wisdom because its role in the city will not become clear until the discussion of the rulers, which begins only in 412c" (White 96).

THE STYLE OF THE GUARDIAN'S POETRY [392C-398B]

The discussion now moves from the content of poetry to a discussion of its style. Plato distinguishes between two different types of poetry: those involving *mimesis* (e.g., drama or acting out a part) and those not involving *mimesis* (e.g., simple narrative or description). First, mimesis, which is usually translated as "imitation," always involves taking on the character of another. "In an epic poem like the *Iliad* this happens in the passages which are...'in direct speech'; a play is entirely made up of imitation. Here it helps to remember that for the Greeks all poetry was performed aloud (usually to musical accompaniment) so that reading poetry would involve taking on the role of the person represented" (Annas 95). This can be contrasted with narrative, which involves the poet describing events that happened in his own person.

Plato is suspicious of *mimesis* because it can lead to the lowering of one's character. Imitation, he believes, can induce a person to become like the character they imitate. If we imitate good people, it will elevate our characters; however if we imitate bad people, our characters can become morally worse because of a fragmentation of one's character as one adopts a variety of roles, aping the more notorious or outrageous. Plato's guardians must be focused exclusively on the task of ruling the *polis* (as per the principle of specialization); it doesn't serve them or the *polis* if their characters become dispersed (Annas 95-96).

Plato allows *mimesis* if it is confined to the imitation of good men; he limits the guardian's poetry to narratives reporting good person's speech when he is most in control of himself and avoiding the imitation of a person in love or unsteadied by drink, disease or misfortune.

Note: Plato's views on imitation strike many contemporary readers as a bit odd. Our own modern perspective is that it is healthy and good for children to identify with characters in films, novels, plays, or role-playing games because it inspires them to become more open minded and creative. Imitation from a modern perspective, then, is viewed as a catalyst for moral growth (Annas 96-97). On the other hand, while most people think it appropriate to shield children from evil or smutty depictions, the media for teens and young adults is rarely censored, because of the contemporary value of free expression and the widely accepted belief that media depictions of evil do not prompt imitation except by those who are already deranged. A steady diet of murder mysteries does not create killers. However, the more conservative Plato is concerned that if the guardians imitate vicious or immoral behavior they will lose their "guardianly" characters, hence jeopardizing the health of the entire *polis*.

CONCLUSION: IMPLICATIONS OF PLATO'S VIEWS ON POETRY

Plato's views might also strike the modern reader as dangerous and authoritarian. If one takes his arguments to their logical conclusion one would have to allow for complete state control over all the arts. Performances could not be allowed that would malign God or our national heroes or which might impart negative values. Even adults would have to be prevented from exposure to bad art because they would transmit these values to their children (381e; Pappas 69). Our own society clearly has moved in a direction that would have appalled Plato. The consensus in the developed world, however, is that whatever the negative effects of maintaining free expression of speech and press may be, the social consequences of censorship are far more dire. It is hard not to see the irony in Plato's lionization of his mentor and idol Socrates (the gadfly who stings the warhorse of State with his questions), who died as a martyr to the free exercise of philosophy and critical thinking. Yet Plato's own Guardians would be wielding the censor's ax.

MUSIC [398C-400C]

Plato's continued effort to instill courage and moderation in the guardians will now be applied to the particular type of music to which they will be exposed. Specifically, he seeks to control the content of music by eliminating "soft" music, which is ill suited for the temperaments of warriors and erratic harmony and rhythm which can cause disorder in the soul. Plato's aim is a simplicity of style that will benefit the characters of the guardians and instill in them courage and moderation. Remember: these folks have to be able to kill people in defense of the city. Plato doesn't want them to be so pumped up by music that they might harm their own citizens or so softened by it that they won't be able to fight their enemies. Through the proper use of music, Plato aims at introducing a kind of harmony and order into the young guardian's souls that corresponds to the harmony and order of the entire cosmos. Again, Plato's attempt to exercise rigid control over the arts has struck some as being somewhat authoritarian. Even Allan Bloom, who is not known for his liberal views, raises some objections: Plato, he says, "has made himself the master of poetry; he controls what it represents, how it represents, and the accompaniments which intensify its appeal. This mastery has been gained, though, only at the cost of what lovers of poetry find attractive in it" (360).

THE ARTS IN GENERAL [400C-402D]

The attempt to instill harmony and order into the young guardians' souls continues with Plato's treatment of the kind of crafts, art and architecture to which they will be exposed. He rejects all art and architecture that is "vicious, unrestrained, slavish and graceless" (401b). Plato believes that there is a connection between beauty and orderliness in the arts and the beauty and orderliness of the soul. He, therefore, wants his guardians to be exposed only to things that are beautiful, virtuous and harmonious. As Socrates says, "good speech, good harmony, good grace accompany good disposition...Mustn't the young pursue them everywhere if they are to do their work?" (400e)

SEXUAL RELATIONS [402D-403C]

Plato makes what seems to be a strange leap here when he moves from a discussion of beauty in the arts to the sexual relations among his guardians. One would think that a discussion of sexual relations would be better left for the next section on the physical training of the guardians. As we shall see, however, Plato treats sexual relations among his guardians as an aesthetic rather than a physical issue. The character that the guardians should have is incompatible with extreme sexual passion or the pursuit of physical pleasure (i.e., excesses of desire are incompatible with moderation and virtue) (402e). The kind of attraction that the guardians will feel towards one another will be founded upon the orderliness and harmony of the other's soul, not upon some sort of shallow physical attraction. Attraction, for Plato, is founded upon an appreciation of the beauty, intelligence and virtue of the other. Therefore, tender displays of affection are permitted among the guardians, but nothing more than this, lest a guardian be criticized for lacking proper aesthetic sensibility (403c).

PHYSICAL TRAINING [403C-412B]

Having finished his discussion of the guardian's training in the arts, Plato goes on to discuss their physical training. His aim here is to produce health in the body that is analogous to the harmony that he seeks to produce in the soul.

Physical Fitness (403c-404e)

His program of physical training for the guardians is actually quite sensible. In order to promote the health of their bodies, the guardians should avoid overeating, excessive indulgence in alcohol, and eating foods that are too rich (especially sweets and cakes), and should engage in a simple exercise program (gymnastics).

Medical Treatment (405a-410b)

The aim of medicine, according to Plato, is to maintain the health of the body, not to restore it in a sickly individual. Plato reserves medical treatment only for generally healthy people and only in rare situations (e.g., to heal wounds in battle or occasional illnesses). The unhealthy and unfit are a drain on the community and, therefore, must be left to die or will be permitted to kill themselves (408b; 410a). This follows from the principle of specialization which necessitates that each person fulfill his specific role in the *polis*. The sickly, however, can't fulfill their role: "in every well ordered community each man has his appointed task which he must perform; no one has leisure to spend all his life in being ill and doctoring himself" (406a).

Again, many contemporary readers find Plato's support of euthanasia problematic, but we must keep in mind that such practices were not uncommon in the ancient world. Life in ancient Greece was fairly hard, and to survive a community needed to rely on all its citizens. On the positive side, Plato is quite egalitarian insofar as he doesn't make exceptions to this rule for the wealthy or powerful (408b).

Education as a Harmony (410b-412b)

We have already seen that for Plato real education involves a delicate balance of physical and intellectual training. If we load our guardians up with too much art, music and philosophy, they will become soft. If we don't provide them with enough exposure to these arts, they will become too harsh and savage. Plato believes that the balance that he provides in the Guardian's educational program will ensure that they are cultivated and orderly, courageous and moderate. It turns out, then, that physical training is not just for the health of the body, but helps to harmonize the soul as well (410c). As Socrates puts it, "the man who makes the finest mixture of gymnastics with music and brings them to his soul in the most proper measure is the one of whom we would most correctly say that he is the most...well harmonized" (412a).

SUGGESTIONS FOR FURTHER READING

Annas, Julia. *An Introduction to Plato's Republic.* New York: Oxford, 1981. [79-101]

Benardete, Seth. *Socrates' Second Sailing: On Plato's Republic.* Chicago: University of Chicago, 1989. [54-75]

Bloom, Allan. *The Republic of Plato.* New York: Harper Collins, 1968. [348-365]

Pappas, Nickolas. *Plato and the Republic.* New York: Routledge, 1995. [64-70]

Rice, Daryl H. *A Guide to Plato's Republic.* New York: Oxford University Press, 1998. [39-55]

Sayers, Sean. Plato's Republic: An Introduction. Edinburgh: Edinburgh University Press, 1999. [32-41].

Tate, J. "Imitation' in Plato's *Republic.*" *Classical Quarterly* 26 (1928): 16-23.

—. "Plato, Socrates, and the Myths." *Classical Quarterly* 30 (1936): 142-145.

White, Nicholas P. *A Companion to Plato's Republic.* Indianapolis: Hackett, 1979. [74-94]

REPUBLIC 2.375A - 3.412B

THE EDUCATION OF THE GUARDIANS [375A-376D]

375   Is not the noble youth very like a well-bred dog in respect of guarding and watching?

What do you mean?

I mean that both of them ought to be quick to see, and swift to overtake the enemy when they see him; and strong too if, when they have caught him, they have to fight with him.

All these qualities, he replied, will certainly be required by them.

Well, and your guardian must be brave if he is to fight well?

Certainly.

And is he likely to be brave who has no spirit, whether horse or dog or any other animal? Have you never observed how invincible and unconquerable is spirit and how the presence of it makes the
b   soul of any creature to be absolutely fearless and indomitable?

I have.

Then now we have a clear notion of the bodily qualities which are required in the guardian.

True.

And also of the mental ones; his soul is to be full of spirit?

Yes.

But are not these spirited natures apt to be savage with one another, and with everybody else?

A difficulty by no means easy to overcome, he replied.

Whereas, I said, they ought to be dangerous to their enemies, and
c   gentle to their friends; if not, they will destroy themselves without waiting for their enemies to destroy them.

True, he said.

What is to be done then? I said; how shall we find a gentle nature which has also a great spirit, for the one is the contradiction of the other?

True.

He will not be a good guardian who is wanting in either of these two qualities; and yet the combination of them appears to be impossible; and hence we must infer that to be a good guardian is impossible.
d   I am afraid that what you say is true, he replied.

Here feeling perplexed I began to think over what had preceded.—
My friend, I said, no wonder that we are in a perplexity; for we have

lost sight of the image which we had before us.

What do you mean? he said.

I mean to say that there do exist natures gifted with those opposite qualities.

And where do you find them?

Many animals, I replied, furnish examples of them; our friend the dog is a very good one: you know that well-bred dogs are perfectly gentle to their familiars and acquaintances, and the reverse to strangers.

Yes, I know.

Then there is nothing impossible or out of the order of nature in our finding a guardian who has a similar combination of qualities?

Certainly not.

Would not he who is fitted to be a guardian, besides the spirited nature, need to have the qualities of a philosopher?

I do not apprehend your meaning.

The trait of which I am speaking, I replied, may be also seen in the dog, and is remarkable in the animal.

What trait?

Why, a dog, whenever he sees a stranger, is angry; when an acquaintance, he welcomes him, although the one has never done him any harm, nor the other any good. Did this never strike you as curious?

The matter never struck me before; but I quite recognise the truth of your remark.

And surely this instinct of the dog is very charming;—your dog is a true philosopher.

Why?

Why, because he distinguishes the face of a friend and of an enemy only by the criterion of knowing and not knowing. And must not an animal be a lover of learning who determines what he likes and dislikes by the test of knowledge and ignorance?

Most assuredly.

And is not the love of learning the love of wisdom, which is philosophy?

They are the same, he replied.

And may we not say confidently of man also, that he who is likely to be gentle to his friends and acquaintances, must by nature be a lover of wisdom and knowledge?

That we may safely affirm.

Then he who is to be a really good and noble guardian of the State will require to unite in himself philosophy and spirit and swiftness and strength?

Undoubtedly.

CENSORSHIP OF POETRY [376D-383C]

Then we have found the desired natures; and now that we have found them, how are they to be reared and educated? Is not this an enquiry which may be expected to throw light on the greater enquiry which is our final end—How do justice and injustice grow up in States? for we do not want either to omit what is to the point or to draw out the argument to an inconvenient length.

Adeimantus thought that the enquiry would be of great service to us.

Then, I said, my dear friend, the task must not be given up, even if somewhat long.

Certainly not.

Come then, and let us pass a leisure hour in story-telling, and our story shall be the education of our heroes.

By all means.

And what shall be their education? Can we find a better than the traditional sort?—and this has two divisions, gymnastic for the body, and music for the soul.

True.

Shall we begin education with music, and go on to gymnastic afterwards?

By all means.

And when you speak of music, do you include literature or not?

I do.

And literature may be either true or false?

Yes.

And the young should be trained in both kinds, and we begin with the false?

I do not understand your meaning, he said.

You know, I said, that we begin by telling children stories which, though not wholly destitute of truth, are in the main fictitious; and these stories are told them when they are not of an age to learn gymnastics.

Very true.

That was my meaning when I said that we must teach music before gymnastics.

Quite right, he said.

You know also that the beginning is the most important part of any work, especially in the case of a young and tender thing; for that is the time at which the character is being formed and the desired impression is more readily taken.

Quite true.

And shall we just carelessly allow children to hear any casual tales which may be devised by casual persons, and to receive into their minds ideas for the most part the very opposite of those which we should wish them to have when they are grown up?

We cannot.

Then the first thing will be to establish a censorship of the writers of fiction, and let the censors receive any tale of fiction which is good, and reject the bad; and we will desire mothers and nurses to tell their children the authorised ones only. Let them fashion the mind with such tales, even more fondly than they mould the body with their hands; but most of those which are now in use must be discarded.

Of what tales are you speaking? he said.

You may find a model of the lesser in the greater, I said; for they are necessarily of the same type, and there is the same spirit in both of them.

Very likely, he replied; but I do not as yet know what you would term the greater.

Those, I said, which are narrated by Homer and Hesiod, and the rest of the poets, who have ever been the great story-tellers of mankind.

But which stories do you mean, he said; and what fault do you find with them?

A fault which is most serious, I said; the fault of telling a lie, and, what is more, a bad lie.

But when is this fault committed?

Whenever an erroneous representation is made of the nature of gods and heroes,—as when a painter paints a portrait not having the shadow of a likeness to the original.

Yes, he said, that sort of thing is certainly very blameable; but what are the stories which you mean?

First of all, I said, there was that greatest of all lies in high places, which the poet told about Uranus, and which was a bad lie too,—I mean what Hesiod says that Uranus did, and how Cronus retaliated on him. The doings of Cronus, and the sufferings which in turn his son inflicted upon him, even if they were true, ought certainly not to be lightly told to young and thoughtless persons; if possible, they had better be buried in silence. But if there is an absolute necessity for their mention, a chosen few might hear them in a mystery, and they should sacrifice not a common (Eleusinian) pig, but some huge and unprocurable victim; and then the number of the hearers will be very few indeed.

Why, yes, said he, those stories are extremely objectionable.

Yes, Adeimantus, they are stories not to be repeated in our State; the young man should not be told that in committing the worst of crimes he is far from doing anything outrageous; and that even if he chastises his father when he does wrong, in whatever manner, he will only be following the example of the first and greatest among the gods.

I entirely agree with you, he said; in my opinion those stories are quite unfit to be repeated.

Neither, if we mean our future guardians to regard the habit of quarrelling among themselves as of all things the basest, should any word be said to them of the wars in heaven, and of the plots and fightings of the gods against one another, for they are not true. No, we shall never mention the battles of the giants, or let them be embroidered on garments; and we shall be silent about the innumerable other quarrels of gods and heroes with their friends and relatives. If they would only believe us we would tell them that quarrelling is unholy, and that never up to this time has there been any quarrel between citizens; this is what old men and old women should begin by telling children; and when they grow up, the poets also should be told to compose for them in a similar spirit. But the narrative of Hephaestus binding Here his mother, or how on another occasion Zeus sent him flying for taking her part when she was being beaten, and all the battles of the gods in Homer— these tales must not be admitted into our State, whether they are supposed to have an allegorical meaning or not. For a young person cannot judge what is allegorical and what is literal; anything that he receives into his mind at that age is likely to become indelible and unalterable; and therefore it is most important that the tales which the young first hear should be models of virtuous thoughts.

There you are right, he replied; but if any one asks where are such models to be found and of what tales are you speaking—how shall we answer him?

I said to him, You and I, Adeimantus, at this moment are not poets, but founders of a State: now the founders of a State ought to know the general forms in which poets should cast their tales, and the limits which must be observed by them, but to make the tales is not their business.

Very true, he said; but what are these forms of theology which you mean?

Something of this kind, I replied:—God is always to be represented as he truly is, whatever be the sort of poetry, epic, lyric or tragic, in which the representation is given.

Right.

And is he not truly good? and must he not be represented as such?

Certainly.

And no good thing is hurtful?

No, indeed.

And that which is not hurtful hurts not?

Certainly not.

And that which hurts not does no evil?

No.

And can that which does no evil be a cause of evil?

Impossible.

And the good is advantageous?

Yes.

And therefore the cause of well-being?

Yes.

It follows therefore that the good is not the cause of all things, but of the good only?

Assuredly.

Then God, if he be good, is not the author of all things, as the many assert, but he is the cause of a few things only, and not of most things that occur to men. For few are the goods of human life, and many are the evils, and the good is to be attributed to God alone; of the evils the causes are to be sought elsewhere, and not in him.

That appears to me to be most true, he said.

Then we must not listen to Homer or to any other poet who is guilty of the folly of saying that two casks

'Lie at the threshold of Zeus, full of lots, one of good, the other of evil lots,'

and that he to whom Zeus gives a mixture of the two

'Sometimes meets with evil fortune, at other times with good;'

but that he to whom is given the cup of unmingled ill,

'Him wild hunger drives o'er the beauteous earth.'

And again—

'Zeus, who is the dispenser of good and evil to us.'

And if any one asserts that the violation of oaths and treaties, which was really the work of Pandarus, was brought about by Athene and Zeus, or that the strife and contention of the gods was instigated by Themis and Zeus, he shall not have our approval; neither will we allow our young men to hear the words of Aeschylus, that

'God plants guilt among men when he desires utterly to destroy a house.'

And if a poet writes of the sufferings of Niobe—the subject of the tragedy in which these iambic verses occur—or of the house of Pelops, or of the Trojan war or on any similar theme, either we must not permit him to say that these are the works of God, or if they are of God, he must devise some explanation of them such as we are seeking; he must say that God did what was just and right, and they were the better for being punished; but that those who are punished are miserable, and that God is the author of their misery—the poet

b is not to be permitted to say; though he may say that the wicked are miserable because they require to be punished, and are benefited by receiving punishment from God; but that God being good is the author of evil to any one is to be strenuously denied, and not to be said or sung or heard in verse or prose by any one whether old or young in any well-ordered commonwealth. Such a fiction is suicidal, ruinous, impious.

c   I agree with you, he replied, and am ready to give my assent to the law.

Let this then be one of our rules and principles concerning the gods, to which our poets and reciters will be expected to conform,— that God is not the author of all things, but of good only.

That will do, he said.

And what do you think of a second principle? Shall I ask you whether God is a magician, and of a nature to appear insidiously

d now in one shape, and now in another—sometimes himself changing and passing into many forms, sometimes deceiving us with the semblance of such transformations; or is he one and the same immutably fixed in his own proper image?

I cannot answer you, he said, without more thought.

Well, I said; but if we suppose a change in anything, that change must be effected either by the thing itself, or by some other thing?

Most certainly.

e   And things which are at their best are also least liable to be altered or discomposed; for example, when healthiest and strongest, the human frame is least liable to be affected by meats and drinks, and the plant which is in the fullest vigour also suffers least from winds or the heat of the sun or any similar causes.

Of course.

381   And will not the bravest and wisest soul be least confused or deranged by any external influence?

True.

And the same principle, as I should suppose, applies to all composite things—furniture, houses, garments: when good and well made, they are least altered by time and circumstances.

Very true.

Then everything which is good, whether made by art or nature, or both, is least liable to suffer change from without?

b   True.

But surely God and the things of God are in every way perfect?

Of course they are.

Then he can hardly be compelled by external influence to take many shapes?

He cannot.

But may he not change and transform himself?

Clearly, he said, that must be the case if he is changed at all.

And will he then change himself for the better and fairer, or for the worse and more unsightly?

If he change at all he can only change for the worse, for we cannot suppose him to be deficient either in virtue or beauty.

Very true, Adeimantus; but then, would any one, whether God or man, desire to make himself worse?

Impossible.

Then it is impossible that God should ever be willing to change; being, as is supposed, the fairest and best that is conceivable, every God remains absolutely and for ever in his own form.

That necessarily follows, he said, in my judgment.

Then, I said, my dear friend, let none of the poets tell us that

'The gods, taking the disguise of strangers from other lands, walk up and down cities in all sorts of forms;'

and let no one slander Proteus and Thetis, neither let any one, either in tragedy or in any other kind of poetry, introduce Here disguised in the likeness of a priestess asking an alms

'For the life-giving daughters of Inachus the river of Argos;'

—let us have no more lies of that sort. Neither must we have mothers under the influence of the poets scaring their children with a bad version of these myths—telling how certain gods, as they say, 'Go about by night in the likeness of so many strangers and in divers forms;' but let them take heed lest they make cowards of their children, and at the same time speak blasphemy against the gods.

Heaven forbid, he said.

But although the gods are themselves unchangeable, still by witchcraft and deception they may make us think that they appear in various forms?

Perhaps, he replied.

Well, but can you imagine that God will be willing to lie, whether in word or deed, or to put forth a phantom of himself?

I cannot say, he replied.

Do you not know, I said, that the true lie, if such an expression may be allowed, is hated of gods and men?

What do you mean? he said.

I mean that no one is willingly deceived in that which is the truest and highest part of himself, or about the truest and highest matters; there, above all, he is most afraid of a lie having possession of him.

Still, he said, I do not comprehend you.

The reason is, I replied, that you attribute some profound meaning to my words; but I am only saying that deception, or being deceived or uninformed about the highest realities in the highest part of themselves, which is the soul, and in that part of them to have and to hold the lie, is what mankind least like;—that, I say, is what they utterly detest.

There is nothing more hateful to them.

And, as I was just now remarking, this ignorance in the soul of him who is deceived may be called the true lie; for the lie in words is only a kind of imitation and shadowy image of a previous affection of the soul, not pure unadulterated falsehood. Am I not right?

Perfectly right.

The true lie is hated not only by the gods, but also by men?

Yes.

Whereas the lie in words is in certain cases useful and not hateful; in dealing with enemies—that would be an instance; or again, when those whom we call our friends in a fit of madness or illusion are going to do some harm, then it is useful and is a sort of medicine or preventive; also in the tales of mythology, of which we were just now speaking—because we do not know the truth about ancient times, we make falsehood as much like truth as we can, and so turn it to account.

Very true, he said.

But can any of these reasons apply to God? Can we suppose that he is ignorant of antiquity, and therefore has recourse to invention?

That would be ridiculous, he said.

Then the lying poet has no place in our idea of God?

I should say not.

Or perhaps he may tell a lie because he is afraid of enemies?

That is inconceivable.

But he may have friends who are senseless or mad?

But no mad or senseless person can be a friend of God.

Then no motive can be imagined why God should lie?

None whatever.

Then the superhuman and divine is absolutely incapable of falsehood?

Yes.

Then is God perfectly simple and true both in word and deed; he changes not; he deceives not, either by sign or word, by dream or waking vision.

Your thoughts, he said, are the reflection of my own.

You agree with me then, I said, that this is the second type or

form in which we should write and speak about divine things. The
gods are not magicians who transform themselves, neither do they   383
deceive mankind in any way.

I grant that.

Then, although we are admirers of Homer, we do not admire
the lying dream which Zeus sends to Agamemnon; neither will we
praise the verses of Aeschylus in which Thetis says that Apollo at
her nuptials

> 'Was celebrating in song her fair child whose days were to
> be long, and to know no sickness. And when he had spoken
> of my lot as in all things blessed of heaven he raised a note
> of triumph and cheered my soul. And I thought that the   b
> word of Phoebus, being divine and full of prophecy, would
> not fail. And now he himself who uttered the strain, he
> who was present at the banquet, and who said this—he it
> is who has slain my son.'

These are the kind of sentiments about the gods which will arouse
our anger; and he who utters them shall be refused a chorus; neither
shall we allow teachers to make use of them in the instruction of the
young, meaning, as we do, that our guardians, as far as men can be,   c
should be true worshippers of the gods and like them.

I entirely agree, he said, in these principles, and promise to
make them my laws.

BOOK III

CONTENT OF THE GUARDIAN'S POETRY [386A-392C]

Such then, I said, are our principles of theology—some tales are
to be told, and others are not to be told to our disciples from their
youth upwards, if we mean them to honour the gods and their
parents, and to value friendship with one another.   386

Yes; and I think that our principles are right, he said.

But if they are to be courageous, must they not learn other
lessons besides these, and lessons of such a kind as will take away
the fear of death? Can any man be courageous who has the fear of
death in him?

Certainly not, he said.

And can he be fearless of death, or will he choose death in battle   b
rather than defeat and slavery, who believes the world below to be
real and terrible?

Impossible.

Then we must assume a control over the narrators of this class of tales as well as over the others, and beg them not simply to revile but rather to commend the world below, intimating to them that their descriptions are untrue, and will do harm to our future warriors.

That will be our duty, he said.

Then, I said, we shall have to obliterate many obnoxious passages, beginning with the verses,

'I would rather be a serf on the land of a poor and portionless man than rule over all the dead who have come to nothing.'

We must also expunge the verse, which tells us how Pluto feared,

'Lest the mansions grim and squalid which the gods abhor should be seen both of mortals and immortals.'

And again:—

'O heavens! Truly in the house of Hades there is soul and ghostly form but no mind at all!'

Again of Tiresias:—

'(To him even after death did Persephone grant mind,) that he alone should be wise; but the other souls are flitting shades.'

Again:—

'The soul flying from the limbs had gone to Hades, lamenting her fate, leaving manhood and youth.'

Again:—

'And the soul, with shrilling cry, passed like smoke beneath the earth.'

And,—

'As bats in hollow of mystic cavern, whenever any of them has dropped out of the string and falls from the rock, fly shrilling and cling to one another, so did they with shrilling cry hold together as they moved.'

And we must beg Homer and the other poets not to be angry

if we strike out these and similar passages, not because they are unpoetical, or unattractive to the popular ear, but because the greater the poetical charm of them, the less are they meet for the ears of boys and men who are meant to be free, and who should fear slavery more than death.

Undoubtedly.

Also we shall have to reject all the terrible and appalling names which describe the world below—Cocytus and Styx, ghosts under the earth, and sapless shades, and any similar words of which the very mention causes a shudder to pass through the inmost soul of him who hears them. I do not say that these horrible stories may not have a use of some kind; but there is a danger that the nerves of our guardians may be rendered too excitable and effeminate by them.

There is a real danger, he said.

Then we must have no more of them.

True.

Another and a nobler strain must be composed and sung by us.

Clearly.

And shall we proceed to get rid of the weepings and wailings of famous men?

They will go with the rest.

But shall we be right in getting rid of them? Reflect: our principle is that the good man will not consider death terrible to any other good man who is his comrade.

Yes; that is our principle.

And therefore he will not sorrow for his departed friend as though he had suffered anything terrible?

He will not.

Such an one, as we further maintain, is sufficient for himself and his own happiness, and therefore is least in need of other men.

True, he said.

And for this reason the loss of a son or brother, or the deprivation of fortune, is to him of all men least terrible.

Assuredly.

And therefore he will be least likely to lament, and will bear with the greatest calmness any misfortune of this sort which may befall him.

Yes, he will feel such a misfortune far less than another.

Then we shall be right in getting rid of the lamentations of famous men, and making them over to women (and not even to women who are good for anything), or to men of a baser sort, that those who are being educated by us to be the defenders of their country may scorn to do the like.

That will be very right.

Then we will once more entreat Homer and the other poets not to depict Achilles, who is the son of a goddess, first lying on his side, then on his back, and then on his face; then starting up and sailing in a frenzy along the shores of the barren sea; now taking the sooty ashes in both his hands and pouring them over his head, or weeping and wailing in the various modes which Homer has delineated. Nor should he describe Priam the kinsman of the gods as praying and beseeching,

'Rolling in the dirt, calling each man loudly by his name.'

Still more earnestly will we beg of him at all events not to introduce the gods lamenting and saying,

'Alas! my misery! Alas! that I bore the bravest to my sorrow.'

c   But if he must introduce the gods, at any rate let him not dare so completely to misrepresent the greatest of the gods, as to make him say—

'O heavens! With my eyes truly I behold a dear friend of mine chased round and round the city, and my heart is sorrowful.'

Or again:—

'Woe is me that I am fated to have Sarpedon, dearest of men to me, subdued at the hands of Patroclus the son of Menoetius.'

d   For if, my sweet Adeimantus, our youth seriously listen to such unworthy representations of the gods, instead of laughing at them as they ought, hardly will any of them deem that he himself, being but a man, can be dishonoured by similar actions; neither will he rebuke any inclination which may arise in his mind to say and do the like. And instead of having any shame or self-control, he will be always whining and lamenting on slight occasions.

Yes, he said, that is most true.

Yes, I replied; but that surely is what ought not to be, as the argument has just proved to us; and by that proof we must abide
e   until it is disproved by a better.

It ought not to be.

Neither ought our guardians to be given to laughter. For a fit of laughter which has been indulged to excess almost always produces a violent reaction.

So I believe.

Then persons of worth, even if only mortal men, must not be represented as overcome by laughter, and still less must such a representation of the gods be allowed.

Still less of the gods, as you say, he replied.

Then we shall not suffer such an expression to be used about the gods as that of Homer when he describes how   389

'Inextinguishable laughter arose among the blessed gods,
when they saw Hephaestus bustling about the mansion.'

On your views, we must not admit them.

On my views, if you like to father them on me; that we must not admit them is certain.

Again, truth should be highly valued; if, as we were saying, a lie is useless to the gods, and useful only as a medicine to men, then the use of such medicines should be restricted to physicians; private   b
individuals have no business with them.

Clearly not, he said.

Then if any one at all is to have the privilege of lying, the rulers of the State should be the persons; and they, in their dealings either with enemies or with their own citizens, may be allowed to lie for the public good. But nobody else should meddle with anything of the kind; and although the rulers have this privilege, for a private man to lie to them in return is to be deemed a more heinous fault than for the patient or the pupil of a gymnasium not to speak the truth about his own bodily illnesses to the physician or to the trainer, or for a sailor not to tell the captain what is happening about the ship and the rest of the crew, and how things are going with himself   c
or his fellow sailors.

Most true, he said.

If, then, the ruler catches anybody beside himself lying in the State,

'Any of the craftsmen, whether he be priest or physician
or carpenter,'   d

he will punish him for introducing a practice which is equally subversive and destructive of ship or State.

Most certainly, he said, if our idea of the State is ever carried out.

In the next place our youth must be temperate?

Certainly.

Are not the chief elements of temperance, speaking generally, obedience to commanders and self-control in sensual pleasures?

True.

Then we shall approve such language as that of Diomede in   e
Homer,

'Friend, sit still and obey my word,'

and the verses which follow,

'The Greeks marched breathing prowess, ...in silent awe
of their leaders,'
and other sentiments of the same kind.
We shall.
What of this line,

390

'O heavy with wine, who hast the eyes of a dog and the
heart of a stag,'

and of the words which follow? Would you say that these, or any
similar impertinences which private individuals are supposed to
address to their rulers, whether in verse or prose, are well or ill
spoken?
They are ill spoken.
They may very possibly afford some amusement, but they do
not conduce to temperance. And therefore they are likely to do
harm to our young men—you would agree with me there?
Yes.
And then, again, to make the wisest of men say that nothing in
his opinion is more glorious than

'When the tables are full of bread and meat, and the cup-
bearer carries round wine which he draws from the bowl
and pours into the cups,'

b

is it fit or conducive to temperance for a young man to hear such
words? Or the verse

'The saddest of fates is to die and meet destiny from hunger?'

What would you say again to the tale of Zeus, who, while other gods
and men were asleep and he the only person awake, lay devising
plans, but forgot them all in a moment through his lust, and was so
completely overcome at the sight of Here that he would not even
go into the hut, but wanted to lie with her on the ground, declaring
that he had never been in such a state of rapture before, even when
c   they first met one another

'Without the knowledge of their parents;'

or that other tale of how Hephaestus, because of similar goings on,
cast a chain around Ares and Aphrodite?

Indeed, he said, I am strongly of opinion that they ought not to hear that sort of thing.

But any deeds of endurance which are done or told by famous men, these they ought to see and hear; as, for example, what is said in the verses,

> 'He smote his breast, and thus reproached his heart,   d
> Endure, my heart; far worse hast thou endured!'

Certainly, he said.

In the next place, we must not let them be receivers of gifts or lovers of money.

Certainly not.

Neither must we sing to them of

> 'Gifts persuading gods, and persuading reverend kings.'   e

Neither is Phoenix, the tutor of Achilles, to be approved or deemed to have given his pupil good counsel when he told him that he should take the gifts of the Greeks and assist them; but that without a gift he should not lay aside his anger. Neither will we believe or   391 acknowledge Achilles himself to have been such a lover of money that he took Agamemnon's gifts, or that when he had received payment he restored the dead body of Hector, but that without payment he was unwilling to do so.

Undoubtedly, he said, these are not sentiments which can be approved.

Loving Homer as I do, I hardly like to say that in attributing these feelings to Achilles, or in believing that they are truly attributed to him, he is guilty of downright impiety. As little can I believe the narrative of his insolence to Apollo, where he says,

> 'You have wronged me, O far-darter, most abominable of deities. Truly I would be even with you, if I had only the power;'

or his insubordination to the river-god, on whose divinity he is ready to lay hands; or his offering to the dead Patroclus of his own hair, which had been previously dedicated to the other river-god Spercheius, and that he actually performed this vow; or that he   b dragged Hector round the tomb of Patroclus, and slaughtered the captives at the pyre; of all this I cannot believe that he was guilty, any more than I can allow our citizens to believe that he, the wise Cheiron's pupil, the son of a goddess and of Peleus who was the gentlest of men and third in descent from Zeus, was so disordered in his wits as to be at one time the slave of two seemingly inconsistent passions, meanness, not untainted by avarice, combined with   c overweening contempt of gods and men.

You are quite right, he replied.

And let us equally refuse to believe, or allow to be repeated, the tale of Theseus son of Poseidon, or of Peirithous son of Zeus, going forth as they did to perpetrate a horrid rape; or of any other hero or son of a god daring to do such impious and dreadful things as they falsely ascribe to them in our day: and let us further compel the poets to declare either that these acts were not done by them, or that they were not the sons of gods;—both in the same breath they shall not be permitted to affirm. We will not have them trying to persuade our youth that the gods are the authors of evil, and that heroes are no better than men—sentiments which, as we were saying, are neither pious nor true, for we have already proved that evil cannot come from the gods.

Assuredly not.

And further they are likely to have a bad effect on those who hear them; for everybody will begin to excuse his own vices when he is convinced that similar wickednesses are always being perpetrated by—

'The kindred of the gods, the relatives of Zeus, whose ancestral altar, the altar of Zeus, is aloft in air on the peak of Ida,'

and who have

'the blood of deities yet flowing in their veins.'

And therefore let us put an end to such tales, lest they engender laxity of morals among the young.

By all means, he replied.

But now that we are determining what classes of subjects are or are not to be spoken of, let us see whether any have been omitted by us. The manner in which gods and demigods and heroes and the world below should be treated has been already laid down.

Very true.

And what shall we say about men? That is clearly the remaining portion of our subject.

Clearly so.

But we are not in a condition to answer this question at present, my friend.

Why not?

Because, if I am not mistaken, we shall have to say that about men poets and story-tellers are guilty of making the gravest misstatements when they tell us that wicked men are often happy, and the good miserable; and that injustice is profitable when undetected, but that justice is a man's own loss and another's gain—these things we shall forbid them to utter, and command them to sing and say the opposite.

To be sure we shall, he replied.

But if you admit that I am right in this, then I shall maintain that you have implied the principle for which we have been all along contending.

I grant the truth of your inference.

That such things are or are not to be said about men is a question which we cannot determine until we have discovered what justice is, and how naturally advantageous to the possessor, whether he seem to be just or not.

Most true, he said.

STYLE OF POETRY [392C-398B]

Enough of the subjects of poetry: let us now speak of the style; and when this has been considered, both matter and manner will have been completely treated.

I do not understand what you mean, said Adeimantus.

Then I must make you understand; and perhaps I may be more intelligible if I put the matter in this way. You are aware, I suppose, that all mythology and poetry is a narration of events, either past, present, or to come?

Certainly, he replied.

And narration may be either simple narration, or imitation, or a union of the two?

That again, he said, I do not quite understand.

I fear that I must be a ridiculous teacher when I have so much difficulty in making myself apprehended. Like a bad speaker, therefore, I will not take the whole of the subject, but will break a piece off in illustration of my meaning. You know the first lines of the Iliad, in which the poet says that Chryses prayed Agamemnon to release his daughter, and that Agamemnon flew into a passion with him; whereupon Chryses, failing of his object, invoked the anger of the God against the Achaeans. Now as far as these lines,

> 'And he prayed all the Greeks, but especially the two sons
> of Atreus, the chiefs of the people,'

the poet is speaking in his own person; he never leads us to suppose that he is any one else. But in what follows he takes the person of Chryses, and then he does all that he can to make us believe that the speaker is not Homer, but the aged priest himself. And in this double form he has cast the entire narrative of the events which occurred at Troy and in Ithaca and throughout the Odyssey.

Yes.

And a narrative it remains both in the speeches which the poet recites from time to time and in the intermediate passages?

Quite true.

But when the poet speaks in the person of another, may we not say that he assimilates his style to that of the person who, as he informs you, is going to speak?

Certainly.

And this assimilation of himself to another, either by the use of voice or gesture, is the imitation of the person whose character he assumes?

Of course.

Then in this case the narrative of the poet may be said to proceed by way of imitation?

Very true.

Or, if the poet everywhere appears and never conceals himself, then again the imitation is dropped, and his poetry becomes simple narration. However, in order that I may make my meaning quite clear, and that you may no more say, 'I don't understand,' I will show how the change might be effected. If Homer had said, 'The priest came, having his daughter's ransom in his hands, supplicating the Achaeans, and above all the kings;' and then if, instead of speaking in the person of Chryses, he had continued in his own person, the words would have been, not imitation, but simple narration. The passage would have run as follows (I am no poet, and therefore I drop the metre), 'The priest came and prayed the gods on behalf of the Greeks that they might capture Troy and return safely home, but begged that they would give him back his daughter, and take the ransom which he brought, and respect the God. Thus he spoke, and the other Greeks revered the priest and assented. But Agamemnon was angry, and bade him depart and not come again, lest the staff and chaplets of the God should be of no avail to him—the daughter of Chryses should not be released, he said—she should grow old with him in Argos. And then he told him to go away and not to provoke him, if he intended to get home unscathed. And the old man went away in fear and silence, and, when he had left the camp, he called upon Apollo by his many names, reminding him of everything which he had done pleasing to him, whether in building his temples, or in offering sacrifice, and praying that his good deeds might be returned to him, and that the Achaeans might expiate his tears by the arrows of the god,'—and so on. In this way the whole becomes simple narrative.

I understand, he said.

Or you may suppose the opposite case—that the intermediate passages are omitted, and the dialogue only left.

That also, he said, I understand; you mean, for example, as in tragedy.

You have conceived my meaning perfectly; and if I mistake not, what you failed to apprehend before is now made clear to you, that poetry and mythology are, in some cases, wholly imitative— instances of this are supplied by tragedy and comedy; there is

likewise the opposite style, in which the poet is the only speaker—
of this the dithyramb affords the best example; and the combination
of both is found in epic, and in several other styles of poetry. Do I
take you with me?   c

Yes, he said; I see now what you meant.

I will ask you to remember also what I began by saying, that we
had done with the subject and might proceed to the style.

Yes, I remember.

In saying this, I intended to imply that we must come to an
understanding about the mimetic art,—whether the poets, in
narrating their stories, are to be allowed by us to imitate, and if so,
whether in whole or in part, and if the latter, in what parts; or should   d
all imitation be prohibited?

You mean, I suspect, to ask whether tragedy and comedy shall
be admitted into our State?

Yes, I said; but there may be more than this in question: I really
do not know as yet, but whither the argument may blow, thither we
go.

And go we will, he said.

Then, Adeimantus, let me ask you whether our guardians ought
to be imitators; or rather, has not this question been decided by the
rule already laid down that one man can only do one thing well,
and not many; and that if he attempt many, he will altogether fail of   e
gaining much reputation in any?

Certainly.

And this is equally true of imitation; no one man can imitate
many things as well as he would imitate a single one?

He cannot.

Then the same person will hardly be able to play a serious part
in life, and at the same time to be an imitator and imitate many other
parts as well; for even when two species of imitation are nearly
allied, the same persons cannot succeed in both, as, for example,   395
the writers of tragedy and comedy—did you not just now call them
imitations?

Yes, I did; and you are right in thinking that the same persons
cannot succeed in both.

Any more than they can be rhapsodists and actors at once?

True.

Neither are comic and tragic actors the same; yet all these things
are but imitations.

They are so.

And human nature, Adeimantus, appears to have been coined   b
into yet smaller pieces, and to be as incapable of imitating many
things well, as of performing well the actions of which the imitations
are copies.

Quite true, he replied.

If then we adhere to our original notion and bear in mind that our guardians, setting aside every other business, are to dedicate themselves wholly to the maintenance of freedom in the State, making this their craft, and engaging in no work which does not bear on this end, they ought not to practise or imitate anything else; if they imitate at all, they should imitate from youth upward only those characters which are suitable to their profession—the courageous, temperate, holy, free, and the like; but they should not depict or be skilful at imitating any kind of stinginess or baseness, lest from imitation they should come to be what they imitate. Did you never observe how imitations, beginning in early youth and continuing far into life, at length grow into habits and become a second nature, affecting body, voice, and mind?

Yes, certainly, he said.

Then, I said, we will not allow those for whom we profess a care and of whom we say that they ought to be good men, to imitate a woman, whether young or old, quarrelling with her husband, or striving and bragging against the gods in conceit of her happiness, or when she is in affliction, or sorrow, or weeping; and certainly not one who is in sickness, love, or labour.

Very right, he said.

Neither must they represent slaves, male or female, performing the offices of slaves?

They must not.

And surely not bad men, whether cowards or any others, who do the reverse of what we have just been prescribing, who scold or mock or revile one another in drink or out of drink, or who in any other manner sin against themselves and their neighbours in word or deed, as the manner of such is. Neither should they be trained to imitate the action or speech of men or women who are mad or bad; for madness, like vice, is to be known but not to be practised or imitated.

Very true, he replied.

Neither may they imitate smiths or other craftsmen, or oarsmen, or boatswains, or the like?

How can they, he said, when they are not allowed to apply their minds to the callings of any of these?

Nor may they imitate the neighing of horses, the bellowing of bulls, the murmur of rivers and roll of the ocean, thunder, and all that sort of thing?

Nay, he said, if madness be forbidden, neither may they copy the behaviour of madmen.

You mean, I said, if I understand you aright, that there is one sort of narrative style which may be employed by a truly good man when he has anything to say, and that another sort will be used by a man of an opposite character and education.

And which are these two sorts? he asked.   c

Suppose, I answered, that a just and good man in the course of a narration comes on some saying or action of another good man,—I should imagine that he will like to impersonate him, and will not be ashamed of this sort of imitation: he will be most ready to play the part of the good man when he is acting firmly and wisely; in a less degree when he is overtaken by illness or love or drink, or has met with any other disaster. But when he comes to a character which is   d unworthy of him, he will not make a study of that; he will disdain such a person, and will assume his likeness, if at all, for a moment only when he is performing some good action; at other times he will be ashamed to play a part which he has never practised, nor will he like to fashion and frame himself after the baser models; he feels the employment of such an art, unless in jest, to be beneath him, and his mind revolts at it.

So I should expect, he replied.

Then he will adopt a mode of narration such as we have illustrated   e out of Homer, that is to say, his style will be both imitative and narrative; but there will be very little of the former, and a great deal of the latter. Do you agree?

Certainly, he said; that is the model which such a speaker must necessarily take.

But there is another sort of character who will narrate anything, and, the worse he is, the more unscrupulous he will be; nothing will be too bad for him: and he will be ready to imitate anything, not as a joke, but in right good earnest, and before a large company. As I   397 was just now saying, he will attempt to represent the roll of thunder, the noise of wind and hail, or the creaking of wheels, and pulleys, and the various sounds of flutes, pipes, trumpets, and all sorts of instruments: he will bark like a dog, bleat like a sheep, or crow like a cock; his entire art will consist in imitation of voice and gesture, and there will be very little narration.

That, he said, will be his mode of speaking.

These, then, are the two kinds of style?   b

Yes.

And you would agree with me in saying that one of them is simple and has but slight changes; and if the harmony and rhythm are also chosen for their simplicity, the result is that the speaker, if he speaks correctly, is always pretty much the same in style, and he will keep within the limits of a single harmony (for the changes are not great), and in like manner he will make use of nearly the same rhythm?

That is quite true, he said.

Whereas the other requires all sorts of harmonies and all sorts of rhythms, if the music and the style are to correspond, because the   c style has all sorts of changes.

That is also perfectly true, he replied.

And do not the two styles, or the mixture of the two, comprehend all poetry, and every form of expression in words? No one can say anything except in one or other of them or in both together.

They include all, he said.

And shall we receive into our State all the three styles, or one only of the two unmixed styles? or would you include the mixed?

I should prefer only to admit the pure imitator of virtue.

Yes, I said, Adeimantus, but the mixed style is also very charming: and indeed the pantomimic, which is the opposite of the one chosen by you, is the most popular style with children and their attendants, and with the world in general.

I do not deny it.

But I suppose you would argue that such a style is unsuitable to our State, in which human nature is not twofold or manifold, for one man plays one part only?

Yes; quite unsuitable.

And this is the reason why in our State, and in our State only, we shall find a shoemaker to be a shoemaker and not a pilot also, and a farmer to be a farmer and not a dicast also, and a soldier a soldier and not a trader also, and the same throughout?

True, he said.

And therefore when any one of these pantomimic gentlemen, who are so clever that they can imitate anything, comes to us, and makes a proposal to exhibit himself and his poetry, we will fall down and worship him as a sweet and holy and wonderful being; but we must also inform him that in our State such as he are not permitted to exist; the law will not allow them. And so when we have anointed him with myrrh, and set a garland of wool upon his head, we shall send him away to another city. For we mean to employ for our souls' health the rougher and severer poet or story-teller, who will imitate the style of the virtuous only, and will follow those models which we prescribed at first when we began the education of our soldiers.

We certainly will, he said, if we have the power.

Then now, my friend, I said, that part of music or literary education which relates to the story or myth may be considered to be finished; for the matter and manner have both been discussed.

I think so too, he said.

MUSIC [398C-400C]

Next in order will follow melody and song.

That is obvious.

Every one can see already what we ought to say about them, if we are to be consistent with ourselves.

I fear, said Glaucon, laughing, that the word 'every one' hardly includes me, for I cannot at the moment say what they should be; though I may guess.

At any rate you can tell that a song or ode has three parts—the words, the melody, and the rhythm; that degree of knowledge I may presuppose?

Yes, he said; so much as that you may.

And as for the words, there will surely be no difference between words which are and which are not set to music; both will conform to the same laws, and these have been already determined by us?

Yes.

And the melody and rhythm will depend upon the words?

Certainly.

We were saying, when we spoke of the subject-matter, that we had no need of lamentation and strains of sorrow?

True.

And which are the harmonies expressive of sorrow? You are musical, and can tell me.

The harmonies which you mean are the mixed or tenor Lydian, and the full-toned or bass Lydian, and such like.

These then, I said, must be banished; even to women who have a character to maintain they are of no use, and much less to men.

Certainly.

In the next place, drunkenness and softness and indolence are utterly unbecoming the character of our guardians.

Utterly unbecoming.

And which are the soft or drinking harmonies?

The Ionian, he replied, and the Lydian; they are termed 'relaxed.'

Well, and are these of any military use?

Quite the reverse, he replied; and if so the Dorian and the Phrygian are the only ones which you have left.

I answered: Of the harmonies I know nothing, but I want to have one warlike, to sound the note or accent which a brave man utters in the hour of danger and stern resolve, or when his cause is failing, and he is going to wounds or death or is overtaken by some other evil, and at every such crisis meets the blows of fortune with firm step and a determination to endure; and another to be used by him in times of peace and freedom of action, when there is no pressure of necessity, and he is seeking to persuade God by prayer, or man by instruction and admonition, or on the other hand, when he is expressing his willingness to yield to persuasion or entreaty or admonition, and which represents him when by prudent conduct he has attained his end, not carried away by his success, but acting moderately and wisely under the circumstances, and acquiescing in the event. These two harmonies I ask you to leave; the strain of necessity and the strain of freedom, the strain of the unfortunate and the strain of the fortunate, the strain of courage, and the strain of temperance; these, I say, leave.

c

And these, he replied, are the Dorian and Phrygian harmonies of which I was just now speaking.

Then, I said, if these and these only are to be used in our songs and melodies, we shall not want multiplicity of notes or a panharmonic scale?

I suppose not.

Then we shall not maintain the makers of lyres with three corners and complex scales, or the makers of any other many-stringed curiously-harmonised instruments?

Certainly not.

But what do you say to flute-makers and flute-players? Would you admit them into our State when you reflect that in this composite use of harmony the flute is worse than all the stringed instruments put together; even the panharmonic music is only an imitation of the flute?

Clearly not.

There remain then only the lyre and the harp for use in the city,

d

and the shepherds may have a pipe in the country.

That is surely the conclusion to be drawn from the argument.

The preferring of Apollo and his instruments to Marsyas and his instruments is not at all strange, I said.

Not at all, he replied.

And so, by the dog of Egypt, we have been unconsciously

e

purging the State, which not long ago we termed luxurious.

And we have done wisely, he replied.

Then let us now finish the purgation, I said. Next in order to harmonies, rhythms will naturally follow, and they should be subject to the same rules, for we ought not to seek out complex systems of metre, or metres of every kind, but rather to discover what rhythms are the expressions of a courageous and harmonious life; and when we have found them, we shall adapt the foot and the melody to words having a like spirit, not the words to the foot and melody. To say what these rhythms are will be your duty—you must teach me them, as you have already taught me the harmonies.

400

But, indeed, he replied, I cannot tell you. I only know that there are some three principles of rhythm out of which metrical systems are framed, just as in sounds there are four notes (i.e. the four notes of the tetrachord.) out of which all the harmonies are composed; that is an observation which I have made. But of what sort of lives they are severally the imitations I am unable to say.

Then, I said, we must take Damon into our counsels; and he will tell us what rhythms are expressive of meanness, or insolence, or fury, or other unworthiness, and what are to be reserved for the

b

expression of opposite feelings. And I think that I have an indistinct

recollection of his mentioning a complex Cretic rhythm; also a
dactylic or heroic, and he arranged them in some manner which
I do not quite understand, making the rhythms equal in the rise
and fall of the foot, long and short alternating; and, unless I am
mistaken, he spoke of an iambic as well as of a trochaic rhythm,
and assigned to them short and long quantities. Also in some cases
he appeared to praise or censure the movement of the foot quite
as much as the rhythm; or perhaps a combination of the two; for
I am not certain what he meant. These matters, however, as I was
saying, had better be referred to Damon himself, for the analysis   c
of the subject would be difficult, you know? (Socrates expresses
himself carelessly in accordance with his assumed ignorance of the
details of the subject. In the first part of the sentence he appears to
be speaking of paeonic rhythms which are in the ratio of 3/2; in
the second part, of dactylic and anapaestic rhythms, which are in
the ratio of 1/1; in the last clause, of iambic and trochaic rhythms,
which are in the ratio of 1/2 or 2/1.)
     Rather so, I should say.
     But there is no difficulty in seeing that grace or the absence of
grace is an effect of good or bad rhythm.
     None at all.

ARTS IN GENERAL [400C-402D]

And also that good and bad rhythm naturally assimilate to a good
and bad style; and that harmony and discord in like manner follow
style; for our principle is that rhythm and harmony are regulated by
the words, and not the words by them.
     Just so, he said, they should follow the words.   d
     And will not the words and the character of the style depend on
the temper of the soul?
     Yes.
     And everything else on the style?
     Yes.
     Then beauty of style and harmony and grace and good rhythm
depend on simplicity,—I mean the true simplicity of a rightly and
nobly ordered mind and character, not that other simplicity which
is only an euphemism for folly?
     Very true, he replied.
     And if our youth are to do their work in life, must they not make   e
these graces and harmonies their perpetual aim?
     They must.
     And surely the art of the painter and every other creative
and constructive art are full of them,—weaving, embroidery,
architecture, and every kind of manufacture; also nature, animal
and vegetable,—in all of them there is grace or the absence of

401 grace. And ugliness and discord and inharmonious motion are
nearly allied to ill words and ill nature, as grace and harmony are
the twin sisters of goodness and virtue and bear their likeness.

That is quite true, he said.

But shall our superintendence go no further, and are the poets
only to be required by us to express the image of the good in their
works, on pain, if they do anything else, of expulsion from our
State? Or is the same control to be extended to other artists, and are
b they also to be prohibited from exhibiting the opposite forms of vice
and intemperance and meanness and indecency in sculpture and
building and the other creative arts; and is he who cannot conform
to this rule of ours to be prevented from practising his art in our
State, lest the taste of our citizens be corrupted by him? We would
not have our guardians grow up amid images of moral deformity,
as in some noxious pasture, and there browse and feed upon many a
baneful herb and flower day by day, little by little, until they silently
gather a festering mass of corruption in their own soul. Let our
c artists rather be those who are gifted to discern the true nature of the
beautiful and graceful; then will our youth dwell in a land of health,
amid fair sights and sounds, and receive the good in everything;
and beauty, the outpouring of fair works, shall flow into the eye and
ear, like a health-giving breeze from a purer region, and insensibly
draw the soul from earliest years into likeness and sympathy with
the beauty of reason.

There can be no nobler training than that, he replied.

d And therefore, I said, Glaucon, musical training is a more potent
instrument than any other, because rhythm and harmony find their
way into the inward places of the soul, on which they mightily
fasten, imparting grace, and making the soul of him who is rightly
educated graceful, or of him who is ill-educated ungraceful; and
also because he who has received this true education of the inner
being will most shrewdly perceive omissions or faults in art and
nature, and with a true taste, while he praises and rejoices over and
receives into his soul the good, and becomes noble and good, he will
e justly blame and hate the bad, now in the days of his youth, even
before he is able to know the reason why; and when reason comes
he will recognise and salute the friend with whom his education has
402 made him long familiar.

Yes, he said, I quite agree with you in thinking that our youth
should be trained in music and on the grounds which you mention.

Just as in learning to read, I said, we were satisfied when we
knew the letters of the alphabet, which are very few, in all their
recurring sizes and combinations; not slighting them as unimportant
whether they occupy a space large or small, but everywhere eager
to make them out; and not thinking ourselves perfect in the art of
reading until we recognise them wherever they are found:

True—

Or, as we recognise the reflection of letters in the water, or in a   b
mirror, only when we know the letters themselves; the same art and
study giving us the knowledge of both:

Exactly—

Even so, as I maintain, neither we nor our guardians, whom
we have to educate, can ever become musical until we and they
know the essential forms of temperance, courage, liberality,
magnificence, and their kindred, as well as the contrary forms, in
all their combinations, and can recognise them and their images   c
wherever they are found, not slighting them either in small things
or great, but believing them all to be within the sphere of one art
and study.

Most assuredly.

SEXUAL RELATIONS [402D-403C]

And when a beautiful soul harmonizes with a beautiful form, and
the two are cast in one mould, that will be the fairest of sights to
him who has an eye to see it?

The fairest indeed.

And the fairest is also the loveliest?   d

That may be assumed.

And the man who has the spirit of harmony will be most in
love with the loveliest; but he will not love him who is of an
inharmonious soul?

That is true, he replied, if the deficiency be in his soul; but if
there be any merely bodily defect in another he will be patient of it,
and will love all the same.

I perceive, I said, that you have or have had experiences of this   e
sort, and I agree. But let me ask you another question: Has excess
of pleasure any affinity to temperance?

How can that be? he replied; pleasure deprives a man of the use
of his faculties quite as much as pain.

Or any affinity to virtue in general?

None whatever.

Any affinity to wantonness and intemperance?

Yes, the greatest.

And is there any greater or keener pleasure than that of sensual
love?   403

No, nor a madder.

Whereas true love is a love of beauty and order—temperate and
harmonious?

Quite true, he said.

Then no intemperance or madness should be allowed to
approach true love?

Certainly not.

Then mad or intemperate pleasure must never be allowed to come near the lover and his beloved; neither of them can have any part in it if their love is of the right sort?

No, indeed, Socrates, it must never come near them.

b   Then I suppose that in the city which we are founding you would make a law to the effect that a friend should use no other familiarity to his love than a father would use to his son, and then only for a noble purpose, and he must first have the other's consent; and this rule is to limit him in all his intercourse, and he is never to be seen going further, or, if he exceeds, he is to be deemed guilty of coarseness and bad taste.

I quite agree, he said.

Thus much of music, which makes a fair ending; for what should
c   be the end of music if not the love of beauty?

I agree, he said.

PHYSICAL TRAINING [403C-404E]

After music comes gymnastic, in which our youth are next to be trained.

Certainly.

Gymnastic as well as music should begin in early years; the training in it should be careful and should continue through life. Now my belief is,—and this is a matter upon which I should like to have your opinion in confirmation of my own, but my own belief is,—not that the good body by any bodily excellence improves the soul, but, on the contrary, that the good soul, by her own excellence,
d   improves the body as far as this may be possible. What do you say?

Yes, I agree.

Then, to the mind when adequately trained, we shall be right in handing over the more particular care of the body; and in order to avoid talking too much we will now only give the general outlines of the subject.

Very good.

That they must abstain from intoxication has been already remarked by us; for of all persons a guardian should be the last to
e   get drunk and not know where in the world he is.

Yes, he said; that a guardian should require another guardian to take care of him is ridiculous indeed.

But next, what shall we say of their food; for the men are in training for the great contest of all—are they not?

Yes, he said.

And will the habit of body of our ordinary athletes be suited to them?

Why not?

I am afraid, I said, that a habit of body such as they have is but a sleepy sort of thing, and rather perilous to health. Do you not observe that these athletes sleep away their lives, and are liable to most dangerous illnesses if they depart, in ever so slight a degree, from their customary regimen?

Yes, I do.

Then, I said, a finer sort of training will be required for our warrior athletes, who are to be like wakeful dogs, and to see and hear with the utmost keenness; amid the many changes of water and also of food, of summer heat and winter cold, which they will have to endure when on a campaign, they must not be liable to break down in health.

That is my view.

The really excellent gymnastic is twin sister of that simple music which we were just now describing.

How so?

Why, I conceive that there is a gymnastic which, like our music, is simple and good; and especially the military gymnastic.

What do you mean?

My meaning may be learned from Homer; he, you know, feeds his heroes at their feasts, when they are campaigning, on soldiers' fare; they have no fish, although they are on the shores of the Hellespont, and they are not allowed boiled meats but only roast, which is the food most convenient for soldiers, requiring only that they should light a fire, and not involving the trouble of carrying about pots and pans.

True.

And I can hardly be mistaken in saying that sweet sauces are nowhere mentioned in Homer. In proscribing them, however, he is not singular; all professional athletes are well aware that a man who is to be in good condition should take nothing of the kind.

Yes, he said; and knowing this, they are quite right in not taking them.

Then you would not approve of Syracusan dinners, and the refinements of Sicilian cookery?

I think not.

Nor, if a man is to be in condition, would you allow him to have a Corinthian girl as his fair friend?

Certainly not.

Neither would you approve of the delicacies, as they are thought, of Athenian confectionary?

Certainly not.

All such feeding and living may be rightly compared by us to melody and song composed in the panharmonic style, and in all the rhythms.

Exactly.

There complexity engendered licence, and here disease; whereas simplicity in music was the parent of temperance in the soul; and simplicity in gymnastic of health in the body.

Most true, he said.

MEDICAL TREATMENT [405A-410B]

But when intemperance and diseases multiply in a State, halls of justice and medicine are always being opened; and the arts of the doctor and the lawyer give themselves airs, finding how keen is the interest which not only the slaves but the freemen of a city take about them.

Of course.

And yet what greater proof can there be of a bad and disgraceful state of education than this, that not only artisans and the meaner sort of people need the skill of first-rate physicians and judges, but also those who would profess to have had a liberal education? Is it not disgraceful, and a great sign of want of good-breeding, that a man should have to go abroad for his law and physic because he has none of his own at home, and must therefore surrender himself into the hands of other men whom he makes lords and judges over him?

Of all things, he said, the most disgraceful.

Would you say 'most,' I replied, when you consider that there is a further stage of the evil in which a man is not only a life-long litigant, passing all his days in the courts, either as plaintiff or defendant, but is actually led by his bad taste to pride himself on his litigiousness; he imagines that he is a master in dishonesty; able to take every crooked turn, and wriggle into and out of every hole, bending like a willow twig and getting out of the way of justice: and all for what?—in order to gain small points not worth mentioning, he not knowing that so to order his life as to be able to do without a napping judge is a far higher and nobler sort of thing. Is not that still more disgraceful?

Yes, he said, that is still more disgraceful.

Well, I said, and to require the help of medicine, not when a wound has to be cured, or on occasion of an epidemic, but just because, by indolence and a habit of life such as we have been describing, men fill themselves with waters and winds, as if their bodies were a marsh, compelling the ingenious sons of Asclepius to find more names for diseases, such as flatulence and catarrh; is not this, too, a disgrace?

Yes, he said, they do certainly give very strange and newfangled names to diseases.

Yes, I said, and I do not believe that there were any such diseases in the days of Asclepius; and this I infer from the circumstance that the hero Eurypylus, after he has been wounded in Homer, drinks a hot drink of Pramnian wine well besprinkled with barley-meal and grated cheese, which are certainly inflammatory, and yet the sons of Asclepius who were at the Trojan war do not blame the damsel who gives him the drink, or rebuke Patroclus, who is treating his case.

406

Well, he said, that was surely an extraordinary drink to be given to a person in his condition.

Not so extraordinary, I replied, if you bear in mind that in former days, as is commonly said, before the time of Herodicus, the guild of Asclepius did not practise our present system of medicine, which may be said to educate diseases. But Herodicus, being a trainer, and himself of a sickly constitution, by a combination of training and doctoring found out a way of torturing first and chiefly himself, and secondly the rest of the world.

b

How was that? he said.

By the invention of lingering death; for he had a mortal disease which he perpetually tended, and as recovery was out of the question, he passed his entire life as a hypochondriac; he could do nothing but attend upon himself, and he was in constant torment whenever he departed in anything from his usual regimen, and so dying hard, by the help of science he struggled on to old age.

A rare reward of his skill!

Yes, I said; a reward which a man might fairly expect who never understood that, if Asclepius did not instruct his descendants in hypochondriac arts, the omission arose, not from ignorance or inexperience of such a branch of medicine, but because he knew that in all well-ordered states every individual has an occupation to which he must attend, and has therefore no leisure to spend in continually being ill. This we remark in the case of the artisan, but, ludicrously enough, do not apply the same rule to people of the richer sort.

c

How do you mean? he said.

I mean this: When a carpenter is ill he asks the physician for a rough and ready cure; an emetic or a purge or a cautery or the knife,—these are his remedies. And if some one prescribes for him a course of dietetics, and tells him that he must swathe and swaddle his head, and all that sort of thing, he replies at once that he has no time to be ill, and that he sees no good in a life which is spent in nursing his disease to the neglect of his customary employment; and therefore bidding good-bye to this sort of physician, he resumes his ordinary habits, and either gets well and lives and does his business, or, if his constitution fails, he dies and has no more trouble.

d

e

Yes, he said, and a man in his condition of life ought to use the art of medicine thus far only.

Has he not, I said, an occupation; and what profit would there be in his life if he were deprived of his occupation?

407

Quite true, he said.

But with the rich man this is otherwise; of him we do not say that he has any specially appointed work which he must perform, if he would live.

He is generally supposed to have nothing to do.

Then you never heard of the saying of Phocylides, that as soon as a man has a livelihood he should practise virtue?

Nay, he said, I think that he had better begin somewhat sooner.

Let us not have a dispute with him about this, I said; but rather ask ourselves: Is the practice of virtue obligatory on the rich man, or can he live without it? And if obligatory on him, then let us raise a further question, whether this dieting of disorders, which is an impediment to the application of the mind in carpentering and the mechanical arts, does not equally stand in the way of the sentiment of Phocylides?

Of that, he replied, there can be no doubt; such excessive care of the body, when carried beyond the rules of gymnastic, is most inimical to the practice of virtue.

Yes, indeed, I replied, and equally incompatible with the management of a house, an army, or an office of state; and, what is most important of all, irreconcileable with any kind of study or thought or self-reflection—there is a constant suspicion that headache and giddiness are to be ascribed to philosophy, and hence all practising or making trial of virtue in the higher sense is absolutely stopped; for a man is always fancying that he is being made ill, and is in constant anxiety about the state of his body.

Yes, likely enough.

And therefore our politic Asclepius may be supposed to have exhibited the power of his art only to persons who, being generally of healthy constitution and habits of life, had a definite ailment; such as these he cured by purges and operations, and bade them live as usual, herein consulting the interests of the State; but bodies which disease had penetrated through and through he would not have attempted to cure by gradual processes of evacuation and infusion: he did not want to lengthen out good-for-nothing lives, or to have weak fathers begetting weaker sons;—if a man was not able to live in the ordinary way he had no business to cure him; for such a cure would have been of no use either to himself, or to the State.

Then, he said, you regard Asclepius as a statesman.

Clearly; and his character is further illustrated by his sons. Note that they were heroes in the days of old and practised the medicines of which I am speaking at the siege of Troy: You will remember how, when Pandarus wounded Menelaus, they

'Sucked the blood out of the wound, and sprinkled soothing remedies,'

but they never prescribed what the patient was afterwards to eat or drink in the case of Menelaus, any more than in the case of

Eurypylus; the remedies, as they conceived, were enough to heal any man who before he was wounded was healthy and regular in his habits; and even though he did happen to drink a cup of Pramnian wine, he might get well all the same. But they would have nothing to do with unhealthy and intemperate subjects, whose lives were of no use either to themselves or others; the art of medicine was not designed for their good, and though they were as rich as Midas, the sons of Asclepius would have declined to attend them.

They were very acute persons, those sons of Asclepius.

Naturally so, I replied. Nevertheless, the tragedians and Pindar disobeying our advice, although they acknowledge that Asclepius was the son of Apollo, say also that he was bribed into healing a rich man who was at the point of death, and for this reason he was struck by lightning. But we, in accordance with the principle already affirmed by us, will not believe them when they tell us both;—if he was the son of a god, we maintain that he was not greedy; or, if he was greedy, he was not the son of a god.

All that, Socrates, is excellent; but I should like to put a question to you: Ought there not to be good physicians in a State, and are not the best those who have treated the greatest number of constitutions good and bad? and are not the best judges in like manner those who are acquainted with all sorts of moral natures?

Yes, I said, I too would have good judges and good physicians. But do you know whom I think good?

Will you tell me?

I will, if I can. Let me however note that in the same question you join two things which are not the same.

How so? he asked.

Why, I said, you join physicians and judges. Now the most skilful physicians are those who, from their youth upwards, have combined with the knowledge of their art the greatest experience of disease; they had better not be robust in health, and should have had all manner of diseases in their own persons. For the body, as I conceive, is not the instrument with which they cure the body; in that case we could not allow them ever to be or to have been sickly; but they cure the body with the mind, and the mind which has become and is sick can cure nothing.

That is very true, he said.

But with the judge it is otherwise; since he governs mind by mind; he ought not therefore to have been trained among vicious minds, and to have associated with them from youth upwards, and to have gone through the whole calendar of crime, only in order that he may quickly infer the crimes of others as he might their bodily diseases from his own self-consciousness; the honourable mind which is to form a healthy judgment should have had no experience or contamination of evil habits when young. And this is the reason why in youth good men often appear to be simple, and are easily practised upon by the dishonest, because they have no examples of what evil is in their own souls.

Yes, he said, they are far too apt to be deceived.

Therefore, I said, the judge should not be young; he should have learned to know evil, not from his own soul, but from late and long observation of the nature of evil in others: knowledge should be his guide, not personal experience.

Yes, he said, that is the ideal of a judge.

Yes, I replied, and he will be a good man (which is my answer to your question); for he is good who has a good soul. But the cunning and suspicious nature of which we spoke,—he who has committed many crimes, and fancies himself to be a master in wickedness, when he is amongst his fellows, is wonderful in the precautions which he takes, because he judges of them by himself: but when he gets into the company of men of virtue, who have the experience of age, he appears to be a fool again, owing to his unseasonable suspicions; he cannot recognise an honest man, because he has no pattern of honesty in himself; at the same time, as the bad are more numerous than the good, and he meets with them oftener, he thinks himself, and is by others thought to be, rather wise than foolish.

Most true, he said.

Then the good and wise judge whom we are seeking is not this man, but the other; for vice cannot know virtue too, but a virtuous nature, educated by time, will acquire a knowledge both of virtue and vice: the virtuous, and not the vicious, man has wisdom—in my opinion.

And in mine also.

This is the sort of medicine, and this is the sort of law, which you will sanction in your state. They will minister to better natures, giving health both of soul and of body; but those who are diseased in their bodies they will leave to die, and the corrupt and incurable souls they will put an end to themselves.

That is clearly the best thing both for the patients and for the State.

And thus our youth, having been educated only in that simple music which, as we said, inspires temperance, will be reluctant to go to law.

Clearly.

And the musician, who, keeping to the same track, is content to practise the simple gymnastic, will have nothing to do with medicine unless in some extreme case.

That I quite believe.

EDUCATION AND HARMONY [410B–412B]

The very exercises and tolls which he undergoes are intended to stimulate the spirited element of his nature, and not to increase his strength; he will not, like common athletes, use exercise and regimen to develope his muscles.

Very right, he said.

Neither are the two arts of music and gymnastic really designed, as is often supposed, the one for the training of the soul, the other for the training of the body.

What then is the real object of them?

I believe, I said, that the teachers of both have in view chiefly the improvement of the soul.

How can that be? he asked.

Did you never observe, I said, the effect on the mind itself of exclusive devotion to gymnastic, or the opposite effect of an exclusive devotion to music?

In what way shown? he said.

The one producing a temper of hardness and ferocity, the other of softness and effeminacy, I replied.

Yes, he said, I am quite aware that the mere athlete becomes too much of a savage, and that the mere musician is melted and softened beyond what is good for him.

Yet surely, I said, this ferocity only comes from spirit, which, if rightly educated, would give courage, but, if too much intensified, is liable to become hard and brutal.

That I quite think.

On the other hand the philosopher will have the quality of gentleness. And this also, when too much indulged, will turn to softness, but, if educated rightly, will be gentle and moderate.

True.

And in our opinion the guardians ought to have both these qualities?

Assuredly.

And both should be in harmony?

Beyond question.

And the harmonious soul is both temperate and courageous?

Yes.

And the inharmonious is cowardly and boorish?

Very true.

And, when a man allows music to play upon him and to pour into his soul through the funnel of his ears those sweet and soft and melancholy airs of which we were just now speaking, and his whole life is passed in warbling and the delights of song; in the first stage of the process the passion or spirit which is in him is tempered like iron, and made useful, instead of brittle and useless. But, if he carries on the softening and soothing process, in the next stage he begins to melt and waste, until he has wasted away his spirit and cut out the sinews of his soul; and he becomes a feeble warrior.

Very true.

If the element of spirit is naturally weak in him the change is speedily accomplished, but if he have a good deal, then the power of music weakening the spirit renders him excitable;—on the least provocation he flames up at once, and is speedily extinguished; instead of having spirit he grows irritable and passionate and is quite useless.

Exactly.

And so in gymnastics, if a man takes violent exercise and is a great feeder, and the reverse of a great student of music and philosophy, at first the high condition of his body fills him with pride and spirit, and he becomes twice the man that he was.

Certainly.

And what happens? if he do nothing else, and holds no converse with the Muses, does not even that intelligence which there may be in him, having no taste of any sort of learning or enquiry or thought or culture, grow feeble and dull and blind, his mind never waking up or receiving nourishment, and his senses not being purged of their mists?

True, he said.

And he ends by becoming a hater of philosophy, uncivilized, never using the weapon of persuasion,—he is like a wild beast, all violence and fierceness, and knows no other way of dealing; and he lives in all ignorance and evil conditions, and has no sense of propriety and grace.

That is quite true, he said.

And as there are two principles of human nature, one the spirited and the other the philosophical, some God, as I should say, has given mankind two arts answering to them (and only indirectly to the soul and body), in order that these two principles (like the strings of an instrument) may be relaxed or drawn tighter until they are duly harmonized.

That appears to be the intention.

And he who mingles music with gymnastic in the fairest proportions, and best attunes them to the soul, may be rightly called the true musician and harmonist in a far higher sense than the tuner of the strings.

You are quite right, Socrates.

And such a presiding genius will be always required in our State if the government is to last.

Yes, he will be absolutely necessary.

Such, then, are our principles of nurture and education: Where would be the use of going into further details about the dances of our citizens, or about their hunting with dogs, their gymnastic and equestrian contests? For these all follow the general principle, and having found that, we shall have no difficulty in discovering them.

I dare say that there will be no difficulty.

6

LIFESTYLE OF THE GUARDIANS

DIVISION OF THE POLIS [412B-417B]

Having completed his discussion of the education of the guardians, Plato
now turns to the question of who will rule and be ruled in his *polis*. His
argument can be summed up as follows: The rulers of the city must be
the best of the best. The guardians are the best members of the society.
Therefore the rulers of Plato's city must be the "most guardianly of the
guardians."

The guardians are the best members of the society, because they are
best able to preserve the city. Therefore, an elite from among the guardians,
argues Plato, ought to be the ones who rule the city (412a-c).

Moreover, the rulers of the city ought to be those who love the city
most. If I love something I so identify with its good that I would even be
willing to sacrifice myself for its sake. The same is true with the guardians'
love for the city; they so completely identify their own good with the good
of the city that they would be willing to do whatever is necessary to ensure
its well-being (412d-e). This demands that we have rulers who are able
to retain their convictions even in the face of corrupting influences (e.g.,
the desire for pleasure or the fear of pain). Those guardians who have been
tested, and demonstrate that they can maintain their commitment to the
city in the face of corrupting forces, will become the rulers of the society
(413d-414a).

The rulers that Plato wants for his city are those that have stability of
character; they remain unchangeable in the face of dangerous internal and
external forces that threaten the good of the city (these colors will not run).
This is contrasted with the instability of rulers in a democratic society,
such as those in Plato's own Athens (White 104).

THE NOBLE LIE [414B-415D]

Plato now has three classes of citizens in his ideal *polis:* The Guardian Rulers selected from the Auxiliary Guardians or warrior class and the rest of the citizenry: the Producers or Craftsmen.

Now how does he convince the rest of the citizens to accept the leadership of the Guardian Rulers? The answer is that the rulers of the city must make them believe a myth—a "noble lie"— about their collective origins. All citizens, they will be told from very early on, were born of the same mother, the earth. Some have gold traces in their souls (the Guardian Rulers), some have silver (the Auxiliary Guardians) and some have iron or bronze (the craftsmen). The type of metal in each person determines the role that they will play in the society. This myth is told purely to gain legitimacy for the rule of the elite. The Guardian Rulers, of course, know that it is just a myth but they understand the basic principle that underlies it (i.e., the principle of specialization). The point of this myth is to encourage the kind of absolute loyalty to the city that is akin to the kind of loyalty that one feels towards family members. Plato's aim is to have all of the citizens accept the class structure of the city and to put the good of the city over their own individual good. Plato has once again offended our egalitarian sensibilities by proposing what appears to be little more than a rigid caste system. The difference between Plato's caste system and that of India, for example, is that his is based not upon wealth or birth, but purely upon ability. It's a meritocracy.

THE LIFESTYLE OF THE GUARDIANS [415D-417B]

At the end of Book 3, Plato begins a discussion of the lifestyle of the guardians that will be continued in Book 4. What we discover is that the guardians will not be allowed to possess private property or to have any dealings with money (416d-417b). Plato's aim is to prevent the guardians from having divided interests. Because they won't be allowed to accumulate wealth, they can work for the good of the city alone. This approach also allows Plato to avoid the corruption and conflicts that can occur when it is possible for rulers to place their own good above the common good. Plato's guardians, therefore, will live in common and share all of their worldly possessions. In a sense, Plato's communal/communistic approach is similar to that of religious orders during the Middle Ages. It was believed that if a monk owned nothing of his own, he would be able to devote himself totally to God. Similarly, Plato believes that guardians will be able to commit themselves totally and completely to the good of the city, because they have no material distractions.

Aristotle criticized the asceticism of Plato's Ideal City-State because if the Guardian Rulers had no dealings with money or property they would be divorced from the life of the average citizen and could not comprehend their interests. However, anyone acquainted with the problem of campaign financing and the role of funding in politics today cannot help but be sympathetic to the problem with which Plato was attempting to deal.

LIFESTYLE OF THE GUARDIANS, CONT. [419A-421C]

Book IV of the Republic begins with a challenge to Socrates' political vision. Upon hearing that the Guardian Rulers live entirely at the expense of the State working tirelessly for the interests and advantage of the citizens without a salary, property or privacy, Adeimantus interrupts: "You are hardly making the Rulers happy." At this point, Adeimantus doesn't appreciate the difference between the kind of happiness that money, pleasure and property obtain and the happiness (*eudaimonia*, human flourishing) that the virtuous life of wisdom, justice, courage and moderation obtains for the rulers. Skirting that issue, Socrates responds that the point is not to make the rulers happy, but rather to make the whole city happy.

THE DUTIES OF THE GUARDIANS [421C-427C]

Socrates suggests that the two factors that militate against a happy *polis* are wealth and poverty (since the Guardians have no wealth and the artisans have no power, this problem is resolved in the Ideal State). Adeimantus complains that a ruling party, with no wealth, will have no resources to wage war, especially against a wealthy State. Socrates observes that in the Ideal State, the Guardians will have no wealth to defend and thus their State will be of no interest to marauding enemies. Further, the Guardians will have no trouble enlisting allies against wealthier states because any spoils will be promised to the allies and not appropriated by the Guardians. Socrates claims that by virtue of the training and education provided to the Auxiliary guardians, they will defeat even the wealthiest of States (The Athenians defeated the Persians who outnumbered them two to one at Marathon).

The Rulers should contrive not to make the City too large or too small. Expansion of the population is to be curbed at that point in which the city ceases to be a functional unity. (Tyrannies, Aristocracies, Plutocracies, Democracies are divided cities because the rich are pitted against the poor or vice versa.) Guardians are to see to it that untalented children of Guardians are sent off to learn a trade and competent children among the artisan class are recruited to become Auxiliaries and Rulers, for each one must find and perform the one task most suited to him (or *her*, see Book V).

The Guardian Rulers cannot fail if they attend to the task of education and rearing the Auxiliary Guardians and continuing their own education. Plato seems to believe that acquired traits such as intelligence, wisdom, and justice are passed on genetically. In the interbreeding of the Guardians, good natures will abound among offspring, along the lines of animal husbandry. The Guardians must guard against innovations in music making (the singing of epic poetry was the principle vehicle of education in Plato's Athens). Socrates asserts that "never are the ways of music moved without the greatest political laws being moved." (Revolutionary ideas have been spread by Troubadours, student singing societies, anti-war folk singers, gangsta' rappers and Marilyn Manson groupies). If the Guardian Rulers attend to the education of their own and public education, they need not micro-manage the youth in such matters as the care of parents, hair-do's, clothing, etc. Glaucon and Socrates decide not to further speculate on specific laws or regulations for the market place, the juries, rents or the use of the harbor because well-educated Guardians will be quite competent to judge these matters for themselves. The Guardians will wisely defer to the legislation of Apollo at Delphi on the founding of temples, sacrifices and other religious matters.

SUGGESTIONS FOR FURTHER READING

Annas, Julia. *An Introduction to Plato's Republic.* New York: Oxford UP, 1981. [101-108]

Belfiore, Elizabeth. "Lie Unlike the Truth." Transactions of the *American Philological Association* 15 (1985): 45-57.

Benardette, Seth. *Socrates' Second Sailing: On Plato's Republic.* Chicago: University of Chicago, 1989. [75-82]

Bloom, Allan. *The Republic of Plato.* New York: Harper Collins, 1968. [365-372]

Pappas, Nickolas. *Plato and the Republic.* New York: Routledge, 1995. [71-74]

White, Nicholas P. *A Companion to Plato's Republic.* Indianapolis: Hackett, 1979. [102-115]

REPUBLIC 3.412B - 4.427C

DIVISION OF THE POLIS: THE NOBLE LIE [412B-415D]

Very good, I said; then what is the next question? Must we not ask who are to be rulers and who subjects?

Certainly.   c

There can be no doubt that the elder must rule the younger.

Clearly.

And that the best of these must rule.

That is also clear.

Now, are not the best farmers those who are most devoted to farming?

Yes.

And as we are to have the best of guardians for our city, must they not be those who have most the character of guardians?

Yes.

And to this end they ought to be wise and efficient, and to have a special care of the State?

True.   d

And a man will be most likely to care about that which he loves?

To be sure.

And he will be most likely to love that which he regards as having the same interests with himself, and that of which the good or evil fortune is supposed by him at any time most to affect his own?

Very true, he replied.

Then there must be a selection. Let us note among the guardians those who in their whole life show the greatest eagerness to do what   e
is for the good of their country, and the greatest repugnance to do what is against her interests.

Those are the right men.

And they will have to be watched at every age, in order that we may see whether they preserve their resolution, and never, under the influence either of force or enchantment, forget or cast off their sense of duty to the State.

How cast off? he said.

I will explain to you, I replied. A resolution may go out of a man's mind either with his will or against his will; with his will when he gets rid of a falsehood and learns better, against his will whenever he is deprived of a truth.

I understand, he said, the willing loss of a resolution; the meaning of the unwilling I have yet to learn.

Why, I said, do you not see that men are unwillingly deprived of good, and willingly of evil? Is not to have lost the truth an evil, and to possess the truth a good? and you would agree that to conceive things as they are is to possess the truth?

Yes, he replied; I agree with you in thinking that mankind are deprived of truth against their will.

And is not this involuntary deprivation caused either by theft, or force, or enchantment?

Still, he replied, I do not understand you.

I fear that I must have been talking darkly, like the tragedians. I only mean that some men are changed by persuasion and that others forget; argument steals away the hearts of one class, and time of the other; and this I call theft. Now you understand me?

Yes.

Those again who are forced, are those whom the violence of some pain or grief compels to change their opinion.

I understand, he said, and you are quite right.

And you would also acknowledge that the enchanted are those who change their minds either under the softer influence of pleasure, or the sterner influence of fear?

Yes, he said; everything that deceives may be said to enchant.

Therefore, as I was just now saying, we must enquire who are the best guardians of their own conviction that what they think the interest of the State is to be the rule of their lives. We must watch them from their youth upwards, and make them perform actions in which they are most likely to forget or to be deceived, and he who remembers and is not deceived is to be selected, and he who fails in the trial is to be rejected. That will be the way?

Yes.

And there should also be toils and pains and conflicts prescribed for them, in which they will be made to give further proof of the same qualities.

Very right, he replied.

And then, I said, we must try them with enchantments—that is the third sort of test—and see what will be their behaviour: like those who take colts amid noise and tumult to see if they are of a timid nature, so must we take our youth amid terrors of some kind, and again pass them into pleasures, and prove them more thoroughly than gold is proved in the furnace, that we may discover whether they are armed against all enchantments, and of a noble bearing always, good guardians of themselves and of the music which they have learned, and retaining under all circumstances a rhythmical and harmonious nature, such as will be most serviceable

to the individual and to the State. And he who at every age, as boy
and youth and in mature life, has come out of the trial victorious   414
and pure, shall be appointed a ruler and guardian of the State; he
shall be honoured in life and death, and shall receive sepulture and
other memorials of honour, the greatest that we have to give. But
him who fails, we must reject. I am inclined to think that this is the
sort of way in which our rulers and guardians should be chosen
and appointed. I speak generally, and not with any pretension to
exactness.

And, speaking generally, I agree with you, he said.

And perhaps the word 'guardian' in the fullest sense ought to   b
be applied to this higher class only who preserve us against foreign
enemies and maintain peace among our citizens at home, that the
one may not have the will, or the others the power, to harm us.
The young men whom we before called guardians may be more
properly designated auxiliaries and supporters of the principles of
the rulers.

I agree with you, he said.

How then may we devise one of those needful falsehoods of
which we lately spoke—just one royal lie which may deceive the
rulers, if that be possible, and at any rate the rest of the city?   c

What sort of lie? he said.

Nothing new, I replied; only an old Phoenician tale (Laws) of
what has often occurred before now in other places, (as the poets
say, and have made the world believe,) though not in our time, and
I do not know whether such an event could ever happen again, or
could now even be made probable, if it did.

How your words seem to hesitate on your lips!

You will not wonder, I replied, at my hesitation when you have
heard.

Speak, he said, and fear not.

Well then, I will speak, although I really know not how to look   d
you in the face, or in what words to utter the audacious fiction,
which I propose to communicate gradually, first to the rulers, then
to the soldiers, and lastly to the people. They are to be told that
their youth was a dream, and the education and training which they
received from us, an appearance only; in reality during all that time
they were being formed and fed in the womb of the earth, where
they themselves and their arms and equipment were manufactured;   e
when they were completed, the earth, their mother, sent them up;
and so, their country being their mother and also their nurse, they
are bound to advise for her good, and to defend her against attacks,
and her citizens they are to regard as children of the earth and their
own brothers.

You had good reason, he said, to be ashamed of the lie which
you were going to tell.

415   True, I replied, but there is more coming; I have only told you half. Citizens, we shall say to them in our tale, you are brothers, yet God has framed you differently. Some of you have the power of command, and in the composition of these he has mingled gold, wherefore also they have the greatest honour; others he has made of silver, to be auxiliaries; others again who are to be farmers and craftsmen he has composed of brass and iron; and the species will generally be preserved in the children. But as all are of the same

b   original stock, a golden parent will sometimes have a silver son, or a silver parent a golden son. And God proclaims as a first principle to the rulers, and above all else, that there is nothing which they should so anxiously guard, or of which they are to be such good guardians, as of the purity of the race. They should observe what elements mingle in their offspring; for if the son of a golden or silver parent has an admixture of brass and iron, then nature orders

c   a transposition of ranks, and the eye of the ruler must not be pitiful towards the child because he has to descend in the scale and become a farmer or artisan, just as there may be sons of artisans who having an admixture of gold or silver in them are raised to honour, and become guardians or auxiliaries. For an oracle says that when a man of brass or iron guards the State, it will be destroyed. Such is the tale; is there any possibility of making our citizens believe in it?

Not in the present generation, he replied; there is no way of

d   accomplishing this; but their sons may be made to believe in the tale, and their sons' sons, and posterity after them.

LIFESTYLE OF THE GUARDIANS I [415D-417B]

I see the difficulty, I replied; yet the fostering of such a belief will make them care more for the city and for one another. Enough, however, of the fiction, which may now fly abroad upon the wings of rumor, while we arm our earth-born heroes, and lead them forth under the command of their rulers. Let them look round and select a spot whence they can best suppress insurrection, if any prove unruly within, and also defend themselves against enemies, who

e   like wolves may come down on the fold from without; there let them encamp, and when they have encamped, let them sacrifice to the proper Gods and prepare their dwellings.

Just so, he said.

And their dwellings must be such as will shield them against the cold of winter and the heat of summer.

I suppose that you mean houses, he replied.

Yes, I said; but they must be the houses of soldiers, and not of shop-keepers.

What is the difference? he said.

416   That I will endeavour to explain, I replied. To keep watch-

dogs, who, from want of discipline or hunger, or some evil habit or other, would turn upon the sheep and worry them, and behave not like dogs but wolves, would be a foul and monstrous thing in a shepherd?

Truly monstrous, he said.

And therefore every care must be taken that our auxiliaries, being stronger than our citizens, may not grow to be too much for them and become savage tyrants instead of friends and allies?

Yes, great care should be taken.

And would not a really good education furnish the best safeguard?

But they are well-educated already, he replied.

I cannot be so confident, my dear Glaucon, I said; I am much more certain that they ought to be, and that true education, whatever that may be, will have the greatest tendency to civilize and humanize them in their relations to one another, and to those who are under their protection.

Very true, he replied.

And not only their education, but their habitations, and all that belongs to them, should be such as will neither impair their virtue as guardians, nor tempt them to prey upon the other citizens. Any man of sense must acknowledge that.

He must.

Then now let us consider what will be their way of life, if they are to realize our idea of them. In the first place, none of them should have any property of his own beyond what is absolutely necessary; neither should they have a private house or store closed against any one who has a mind to enter; their provisions should be only such as are required by trained warriors, who are men of temperance and courage; they should agree to receive from the citizens a fixed rate of pay, enough to meet the expenses of the year and no more; and they will go to mess and live together like soldiers in a camp. Gold and silver we will tell them that they have from God; the diviner metal is within them, and they have therefore no need of the dross which is current among men, and ought not to pollute the divine by any such earthly admixture; for that commoner metal has been the source of many unholy deeds, but their own is undefiled. And they alone of all the citizens may not touch or handle silver or gold, or be under the same roof with them, or wear them, or drink from them. And this will be their salvation, and they will be the saviours of the State. But should they ever acquire homes or lands or moneys of their own, they will become housekeepers and farmers instead of guardians, enemies and tyrants instead of allies of the other citizens; hating and being hated, plotting and being plotted against, they will pass their whole life in much greater terror of internal than of external enemies, and the hour of ruin, both to themselves and

to the rest of the State, will be at hand. For all which reasons may
we not say that thus shall our State be ordered, and that these shall
be the regulations appointed by us for guardians concerning their
houses and all other matters?

Yes, said Glaucon.

BOOK IV

LIFESTYLE OF THE GUARDIANS, CONT. [419A-421C]

Here Adeimantus interposed a question: How would you answer,
419   Socrates, said he, if a person were to say that you are making
these people miserable, and that they are the cause of their own
unhappiness; the city in fact belongs to them, but they are none
the better for it; whereas other men acquire lands, and build large
and handsome houses, and have everything handsome about them,
offering sacrifices to the gods on their own account, and practising
hospitality; moreover, as you were saying just now, they have gold
and silver, and all that is usual among the favourites of fortune; but
our poor citizens are no better than mercenaries who are quartered
in the city and are always mounting guard?

420   Yes, I said; and you may add that they are only fed, and not paid
in addition to their food, like other men; and therefore they cannot,
if they would, take a journey of pleasure; they have no money to
spend on a mistress or any other luxurious fancy, which, as the
world goes, is thought to be happiness; and many other accusations
of the same nature might be added.

But, said he, let us suppose all this to be included in the charge.

You mean to ask, I said, what will be our answer?

b   Yes.

If we proceed along the old path, my belief, I said, is that we
shall find the answer. And our answer will be that, even as they are,
our guardians may very likely be the happiest of men; but that our
aim in founding the State was not the disproportionate happiness of
any one class, but the greatest happiness of the whole; we thought
that in a State which is ordered with a view to the good of the whole
we should be most likely to find justice, and in the ill-ordered State
injustice: and, having found them, we might then decide which of
c   the two is the happier. At present, I take it, we are fashioning the
happy State, not piecemeal, or with a view of making a few happy
citizens, but as a whole; and by-and-by we will proceed to view
the opposite kind of State. Suppose that we were painting a statue,
and some one came up to us and said, Why do you not put the most
beautiful colours on the most beautiful parts of the body—the eyes

ought to be purple, but you have made them black—to him we
might fairly answer, Sir, you would not surely have us beautify the
eyes to such a degree that they are no longer eyes; consider rather
whether, by giving this and the other features their due proportion,
we make the whole beautiful. And so I say to you, do not compel us
to assign to the guardians a sort of happiness which will make them
anything but guardians; for we too can clothe our farmers in royal
apparel, and set crowns of gold on their heads, and bid them till the
ground as much as they like, and no more. Our potters also might
be allowed to repose on couches, and feast by the fireside, passing
round the wine cup, while their wheel is conveniently at hand, and
working at pottery only as much as they like; in this way we might
make every class happy—and then, as you imagine, the whole State
would be happy. But do not put this idea into our heads; for, if
we listen to you, the farmer will be no longer a farmer, the potter
will cease to be a potter, and no one will have the character of any
distinct class in the State. Now this is not of much consequence
where the corruption of society, and pretension to be what you are
not, is confined to cobblers; but when the guardians of the laws and
of the government are only seeming and not real guardians, then
see how they turn the State upside down; and on the other hand they
alone have the power of giving order and happiness to the State. We
mean our guardians to be true saviours and not the destroyers of the
State, whereas our opponent is thinking of peasants at a festival,
who are enjoying a life of revelry, not of citizens who are doing
their duty to the State. But, if so, we mean different things, and he
is speaking of something which is not a State. And therefore we
must consider whether in appointing our guardians we would look
to their greatest happiness individually, or whether this principle of
happiness does not rather reside in the State as a whole. But if the
latter be the truth, then the guardians and auxiliaries, and all others
equally with them, must be compelled or induced to do their own
work in the best way. And thus the whole State will grow up in a
noble order, and the several classes will receive the proportion of
happiness which nature assigns to them.

I think that you are quite right.

DUTIES OF THE GUARDIANS [421C-427C]

I wonder whether you will agree with another remark which occurs
to me.

What may that be?

There seem to be two causes of the deterioration of the arts.

What are they?

Wealth, I said, and poverty.

How do they act?

The process is as follows: When a potter becomes rich, will he, think you, any longer take the same pains with his art?

Certainly not.

He will grow more and more indolent and careless?

Very true.

And the result will be that he becomes a worse potter?

Yes; he greatly deteriorates.

But, on the other hand, if he has no money, and cannot provide himself with tools or instruments, he will not work equally well himself, nor will he teach his sons or apprentices to work equally well.

Certainly not.

Then, under the influence either of poverty or of wealth, workmen and their work are equally liable to degenerate?

That is evident.

Here, then, is a discovery of new evils, I said, against which the guardians will have to watch, or they will creep into the city unobserved.

What evils?

Wealth, I said, and poverty; the one is the parent of luxury and indolence, and the other of meanness and viciousness, and both of discontent.

That is very true, he replied; but still I should like to know, Socrates, how our city will be able to go to war, especially against an enemy who is rich and powerful, if deprived of the sinews of war.

There would certainly be a difficulty, I replied, in going to war with one such enemy; but there is no difficulty where there are two of them.

How so? he asked.

In the first place, I said, if we have to fight, our side will be trained warriors fighting against an army of rich men.

That is true, he said.

And do you not suppose, Adeimantus, that a single boxer who was perfect in his art would easily be a match for two stout and well-to-do gentlemen who were not boxers?

Hardly, if they came upon him at once.

What, now, I said, if he were able to run away and then turn and strike at the one who first came up? And supposing he were to do this several times under the heat of a scorching sun, might he not, being an expert, overturn more than one stout personage?

Certainly, he said, there would be nothing wonderful in that.

And yet rich men probably have a greater superiority in the science and practise of boxing than they have in military qualities.

Likely enough.

Then we may assume that our athletes will be able to fight with two or three times their own number?

I agree with you, for I think you right.

And suppose that, before engaging, our citizens send an embassy to one of the two cities, telling them what is the truth: Silver and gold we neither have nor are permitted to have, but you may; do you therefore come and help us in war, and take the spoils of the other city: Who, on hearing these words, would choose to fight against lean wiry dogs, rather than, with the dogs on their side, against fat and tender sheep?

That is not likely; and yet there might be a danger to the poor State if the wealth of many States were to be gathered into one.

But how simple of you to use the term State at all of any but our own!

Why so?

You ought to speak of other States in the plural number; not one of them is a city, but many cities, as they say in the game. For indeed any city, however small, is in fact divided into two, one the city of the poor, the other of the rich; these are at war with one another; and in either there are many smaller divisions, and you would be altogether beside the mark if you treated them all as a single State. But if you deal with them as many, and give the wealth or power or persons of the one to the others, you will always have a great many friends and not many enemies. And your State, while the wise order which has now been prescribed continues to prevail in her, will be the greatest of States, I do not mean to say in reputation or appearance, but in deed and truth, though she number not more than a thousand defenders. A single State which is her equal you will hardly find, either among Hellenes or barbarians, though many that appear to be as great and many times greater.

That is most true, he said.

And what, I said, will be the best limit for our rulers to fix when they are considering the size of the State and the amount of territory which they are to include, and beyond which they will not go?

What limit would you propose?

I would allow the State to increase so far as is consistent with unity; that, I think, is the proper limit.

Very good, he said.

Here then, I said, is another order which will have to be conveyed to our guardians: Let our city be accounted neither large nor small, but one and self-sufficing.

And surely, said he, this is not a very severe order which we impose upon them.

And the other, said I, of which we were speaking before is lighter still,—I mean the duty of degrading the offspring of the guardians when inferior, and of elevating into the rank of guardians the offspring of the lower classes, when naturally superior. The d   intention was, that, in the case of the citizens generally, each individual should be put to the use for which nature intended him, one to one work, and then every man would do his own business, and be one and not many; and so the whole city would be one and not many.

Yes, he said; that is not so difficult.

The regulations which we are prescribing, my good Adeimantus, are not, as might be supposed, a number of great principles, but trifles all, if care be taken, as the saying is, of the one great thing,—a thing, however, which I would rather call, not great, but sufficient
e   for our purpose.

What may that be? he asked.

Education, I said, and nurture: If our citizens are well educated, and grow into sensible men, they will easily see their way through all these, as well as other matters which I omit; such, for example, as marriage, the possession of women and the procreation of children, which will all follow the general principle that friends have all things in common, as the proverb says.

424   That will be the best way of settling them.

Also, I said, the State, if once started well, moves with accumulating force like a wheel. For good nurture and education implant good constitutions, and these good constitutions taking root in a good education improve more and more, and this improvement affects the breed in man as in other animals.
b   Very possibly, he said.

Then to sum up: This is the point to which, above all, the attention of our rulers should be directed,—that music and gymnastic be preserved in their original form, and no innovation made. They must do their utmost to maintain them intact. And when any one says that mankind most regard

'The newest song which the singers have,'

they will be afraid that he may be praising, not new songs, but a
c   new kind of song; and this ought not to be praised, or conceived to be the meaning of the poet; for any musical innovation is full of danger to the whole State, and ought to be prohibited. So Damon tells me, and I can quite believe him;—he says that when modes of music change, the fundamental laws of the State always change with them.

Yes, said Adeimantus; and you may add my vote to Damon's and your own.

Then, I said, our guardians must lay the foundations of their
d   fortress in music?

Yes, he said; the lawlessness of which you speak too easily steals in.

Yes, I replied, in the form of amusement; and at first sight it appears harmless.

Why, yes, he said, and there is no harm; were it not that little by little this spirit of licence, finding a home, imperceptibly penetrates into manners and customs; whence, issuing with greater force, it invades contracts between man and man, and from contracts goes on to laws and constitutions, in utter recklessness, ending at last, Socrates, by an overthrow of all rights, private as well as public.

Is that true? I said.

That is my belief, he replied.

Then, as I was saying, our youth should be trained from the first in a stricter system, for if amusements become lawless, and the youths themselves become lawless, they can never grow up into well-conducted and virtuous citizens.

Very true, he said.

And when they have made a good beginning in play, and by the help of music have gained the habit of good order, then this habit of order, in a manner how unlike the lawless play of the others! will accompany them in all their actions and be a principle of growth to them, and if there be any fallen places in the State will raise them up again.

Very true, he said.

Thus educated, they will invent for themselves any lesser rules which their predecessors have altogether neglected.

What do you mean?

I mean such things as these:—when the young are to be silent before their elders; how they are to show respect to them by standing and making them sit; what honour is due to parents; what garments or shoes are to be worn; the mode of dressing the hair; deportment and manners in general. You would agree with me?

Yes.

But there is, I think, small wisdom in legislating about such matters,—I doubt if it is ever done; nor are any precise written enactments about them likely to be lasting.

Impossible.

It would seem, Adeimantus, that the direction in which education starts a man, will determine his future life. Does not like always attract like?

To be sure.

Until some one rare and grand result is reached which may be good, and may be the reverse of good?

That is not to be denied.

And for this reason, I said, I shall not attempt to legislate further about them.

Naturally enough, he replied.

Well, and about the business of the agora, and the ordinary

dealings between man and man, or again about agreements with artisans; about insult and injury, or the commencement of actions, and the appointment of juries, what would you say? there may also arise questions about any impositions and exactions of market and harbour dues which may be required, and in general about the regulations of markets, police, harbours, and the like. But, oh heavens! shall we condescend to legislate on any of these particulars?

I think, he said, that there is no need to impose laws about them on good men; what regulations are necessary they will find out soon enough for themselves.

Yes, I said, my friend, if God will only preserve to them the laws which we have given them.

And without divine help, said Adeimantus, they will go on for ever making and mending their laws and their lives in the hope of attaining perfection.

You would compare them, I said, to those invalids who, having no self-restraint, will not leave off their habits of intemperance?

Exactly.

Yes, I said; and what a delightful life they lead! they are always doctoring and increasing and complicating their disorders, and always fancying that they will be cured by any nostrum which anybody advises them to try.

Such cases are very common, he said, with invalids of this sort.

Yes, I replied; and the charming thing is that they deem him their worst enemy who tells them the truth, which is simply that, unless they give up eating and drinking and wenching and idling, neither drug nor cautery nor spell nor amulet nor any other remedy will avail.

Charming! he replied. I see nothing charming in going into a passion with a man who tells you what is right.

These gentlemen, I said, do not seem to be in your good graces.

Assuredly not.

Nor would you praise the behaviour of States which act like the men whom I was just now describing. For are there not ill-ordered States in which the citizens are forbidden under pain of death to alter the constitution; and yet he who most sweetly courts those who live under this regime and indulges them and fawns upon them and is skilful in anticipating and gratifying their humours is held to be a great and good statesman—do not these States resemble the persons whom I was describing?

Yes, he said; the States are as bad as the men; and I am very far from praising them.

But do you not admire, I said, the coolness and dexterity of these ready ministers of political corruption?

Yes, he said, I do; but not of all of them, for there are some whom the applause of the multitude has deluded into the belief that they are really statesmen, and these are not much to be admired.

What do you mean? I said; you should have more feeling for them. When a man cannot measure, and a great many others who cannot measure declare that he is four cubits high, can he help believing what they say?

Nay, he said, certainly not in that case.

Well, then, do not be angry with them; for are they not as good as a play, trying their hand at paltry reforms such as I was describing; they are always fancying that by legislation they will make an end of frauds in contracts, and the other rascalities which I was mentioning, not knowing that they are in reality cutting off the heads of a hydra?

Yes, he said; that is just what they are doing.

I conceive, I said, that the true legislator will not trouble himself with this class of enactments whether concerning laws or the constitution either in an ill-ordered or in a well-ordered State; for in the former they are quite useless, and in the latter there will be no difficulty in devising them; and many of them will naturally flow out of our previous regulations.

What, then, he said, is still remaining to us of the work of legislation?

Nothing to us, I replied; but to Apollo, the God of Delphi, there remains the ordering of the greatest and noblest and chiefest things of all.

Which are they? he said.

The institution of temples and sacrifices, and the entire service of gods, demigods, and heroes; also the ordering of the repositories of the dead, and the rites which have to be observed by him who would propitiate the inhabitants of the world below. These are matters of which we are ignorant ourselves, and as founders of a city we should be unwise in trusting them to any interpreter but our ancestral deity. He is the god who sits in the centre, on the navel of the earth, and he is the interpreter of religion to all mankind.

You are right, and we will do as you propose.

7

JUSTICE IN THE CITY AND THE INDIVIDUAL

JUSTICE IN THE CITY [427D-434D]

Socrates now asks the founder of this "City in Speech," Glaucon, and all the others, where the justice in it resides. They assert that the city is perfectly good. For it to be perfectly good, it must be wise, courageous, moderate and just. Because it is assumed that there are no other virtues or excellences for a city to have, it is believed that, if the wisdom, courage and moderation of the city are defined, then by process of elimination and by highlighting these three virtues, justice will stand out in contrast. This notion derives from the Platonic theory of the unity of the virtues, that is, that the four virtues are so interrelated that a deficiency in one will imply a deficiency in or erosion of the others, and true virtue entails accomplishment in all four virtues.

The city is *wise* by virtue of a small part of it, that is, by the counsel of the Guardian Rulers. Although artisans and craftsmen know many things, their knowledge is restricted to the *telos* of their specialized craft. Statescraft, by contrast, requires knowledge of the whole city and its relation to other cities. This knowledge is found exclusively in the Guardian Rulers.

We learn in Book VII, 521c-541b, the extensive nature of the broad liberal arts education proposed for Rulers: music, gymnastics, mathematics, science (including medicine and astronomy), literature and history. If qualifying exams are passed, at the age of thirty, Auxiliary Guardians study philosophy and the dialectic for five years. They then enter positions of high command in the military for fifteen years of service. Observed in the field for courage, wisdom in the conduct of battle, for leadership abilities, for moderation and justice in the treatment of the defeated, Auxiliaries can be tapped at the age of fifty for Guardian Rule. Plato is confident that no one could mask corruption or incompetence after such a career.

The City is *courageous* because of its sterling Auxiliary Guardians. By virtue of the education the Guardians receive in music and gymnastics, they learn what is truly terrible and what is not. Thus they are able to defend the life, honor and glory of the city without cowardice or resorting to excessive violence. They combine in themselves both viciousness and gentleness. Their disciplined education prevents them from raping, rampaging or pillaging subdued enemy peoples. They are disposed to change their former enemy into an ally. Their courage, then, comes from their character, their disposition to defend the laws, and not from their ability to wreck havoc.

The city is *moderate* in a systemic way. Moderation does not reside exclusively or even predominantly in the artisan class. We know from Book II, that Socrates reluctantly accepted Glaucon's aspiration to found the "Feverish City," one dedicated to the pursuit of the unnecessary desires, namely luxuries. The artisans, far from living in moderation, are part of a feverish capitalist economy and their avocation is the amassment of wealth and acquisitions. Plato holds them in contempt as people who sadly do not desire what is most humanly desirable and also for not knowing what they really want (as opposed to the Auxiliaries and the Rulers). Unbridled acquisitiveness and hedonism would have torn the city apart. And that's why the desires of the artisan class have to be externally curbed by the impositions of Rulers, enforced by Auxiliaries.

Moderation in the ideal city comes from the recognition of every class in the society that the basest, worst and most out of control part of the society should be ruled by the better, most knowledgeable, prudent and reasonable part. Indoctrinated by the Noble Lie, the artisan class accepts the legitimacy of the Guardians to rule. They accept the prohibition against revolution or popular usurpation of power because they accept the acquired wisdom of the Guardian class as its *natural* trait (a lie). Moreover, there is no envy on the part of the populace for the ruling class because: 1. private ownership is guaranteed them by the rulers, (this should dispel once and for all the calumny of Popper and others who find in Plato a proto-communist) and 2. their rulers subsist on a far more austere standard of living than they and serve them without compensation of salary or property. The City is moderate because rulers keep their hands off the people's money and the people keep their hands off the rulers.

Auxiliaries also play their part in the city's moderation because they willingly serve as the enforcement arm of the rulers without desiring to usurp the government. Further, they are willing to defend and serve the citizens instead of abusing them and extracting tribute from the citizens (Plato knows well that the fear inspired by warriors can give them the effect of the Ring of Gyges by hiding any extortion of the citizens behind a wall of silence enforced by terror).

Now they are ready to flush out *justice*. Socrates says (with considerable surprise) that justice has been right at hand all along in the discussion ("rolling around their feet"). From his discussion with Adeimantus and the Healthy City in Book II, he extracts the principle of specialization: a person should do one function in the city and one for which s/he is particularly suited. A corollary of that principle is that a person shouldn't try to do somebody else's job or to interfere with that person when they try to do their job. This is what Plato means when he says "justice is minding your own business." He doesn't mean keeping your nose out of other people's personal lives which is the current connotation. He means exactly what Benjamin Franklin meant when he used the same phrase: attending to your craft, pursuing the *telos* of your craft (*techne*) and achieving it effectively, efficiently and consistently.

This then is justice in the city: Each class does the job for which it is best suited and no one class should meddle with the task of the other. Justice is giving and allowing each class to do what is its own. When this occurs there is a harmony in the city. Rulers rule, Auxiliary Guardians Guard, and Producers produce. The result is full productivity and employment with all the basic goods and luxuries provided; a City that is well-defended, honorable and glorious; and one in which the rulers rule in the interests and to the advantage of the citizens.

Socrates thinks that if a shoemaker wants to do a bit of carpentry this would not shatter the harmony of the city. But if a money-maker enters the class of rulers and starts to use government as a means to personal enrichment or if he enters into the military (replacing the profit motive for the defense motive), then there is political hell to pay. Also if a general or admiral took over the government and subverted the commercial sector to military purposes, the city would be lost. We too should recognize the distinct functions of public policy making, military defense and private enterprise and realize the damage that superimposing the goals of one function on the other can cause. However, what offends the modern mind is the undemocratic exclusion of whole classes from government. We accept this when it comes to the military, but not when it comes to the private sector. Plato is caught up in his rigid analogy of the State as having the same structure as the human psyche. The artisans are likened to the appetitive function of the soul. We might find it plausible that the rational soul should lord it over the baser appetites, but that this is analogous with the rulers' duty to lord it over the artisans escapes us. Plato's own psychology has it that the artisans are endowed with Reason and Spirit, as well as Appetite. More enlightened philosophers used this as a defense for universal suffrage and right of the people to govern themselves. In our view, Plato harbors an aristocratic contempt for the common man. In his opinion the artisan *could* fulfill his intellect and control his appetites but he is unlikely to do so; and it is this contempt that underlies his authoritarian and undemocratic meritocracy. In an era before the founding of universities and the scarcity of leisure time for scholarly pursuits, it is perhaps understandable why Plato had this prejudice, but it is not forgivable.

THE THREE PARTS OF THE SOUL [434D-441C]

Plato now makes the comparison between the Form of the City and the Form of the human being. We are to imagine ourselves to be complex "cities" and the crucial question is: "who's in charge?" How well are you governing this "city," that is, your *self*? The first task is to see if there are comparable factors of the soul (*psyche*) that are analogous to the Tripartite classes of the *polis*: Guardian Rulers, Auxiliary Guardians, Producers.

The human soul is complex rather than simple because different aspects of it desire different Ends:

1. Desire. The Appetitive aspect of soul desires sensual satisfaction, for example, for food, drink and sex. The appetites seek not some specific end, for example: Sam Adams Summer Ale, but rather a generic goal: anything quench-worthy (This distinguishes the appetites from the rational soul). Socrates finds in the soul conflicting tensions: one in the direction of satisfying the appetite, the other in the direction of frustrating the appetite.

2. Reason. This is the calculating part of the soul: the rational soul. There can be found in the same person the irrational desire to drink and the rational resistance to drink because of the bad consequences of drinking. An example would be the offer to a starving man of a cake the starving man knows to be poisoned. The persistent desire on the part of the appetite, in contrast to the rational part which resists it at all costs, shows the separation of these aspects of the psyche.

3. Spirit. Finally, the fact that anger sometimes makes war against the appetites reveals the third part of the tripartite soul: the spirited soul (anger, assertion, aggression).

When desire pushes a person toward an object that reason rejects as choice-worthy, reason often enlists anger to rail against and subdue the appetitive force. Once spirit vows allegiance to reason, and reason sees the worth of a political cause, any frustrations of the appetites will be accepted without anger. Spirit will docilely obey reason's dictates despite hardship.

But if reason perceives itself unjustly wronged, spirit will rear up in its defense, and appetites will be subdued even unto death for a just cause. 🔹

JUSTICE IN THE INDIVIDUAL [441C-445B]

And so the Form of the Soul is seen to have the same Form as the City. Virtue will be found in the soul in the same manner as it is found in the City. Justice in the city was found in the willingness of each class to do what it is naturally suited to do, while not interfering with the business of the other classes: Rulers rule, Auxiliary Guardians guard and Producers produce.

In the just person, each part of the complex soul does what it is natural for it to do without unduly interfering with the functions of the other parts. Thus the reasoning or calculating part rules over the appetitive and spirited parts. Spirited anger or aggression allies itself with Reason and springs to its defense. If the appetitive or spirited souls attempt to usurp and enslave reason, disaster results. Only justice among the souls, wherein each is allowed to pursue what is its own, can all human goals be effectively obtained. Thus only a wise, courageous, just and moderate soul can achieve *eudaimonia,* full human flourishment, happiness.

Tripartite Psyche	Specific Virtue (Arête)	Telos
Rational (Nous)	Wisdom	Knowledge of the True and of the Good
Spirited (Thymos)	Courage	Defense of life, honor and dignity
Appetitive (Epithumia)	Moderation	Sensual Satisfaction

Justice is not specific to a specific part of the psyche but is systemic, present in the interaction between the three parts. A harmony is achieved when each lets the other parts do their jobs and achieve their ends. Thus scholarship is not impeded by the demands of hunger or lust and anger doesn't undermine a person's health by impeding the appetites. When reason rules over the spirited and appetitive without suppressing them tyrannically, then all the parts of the psyche can achieve their *telos* (a healthy amount of food, drink, wealth, property and sex along with the honor and glory from a well-defended self and crowned with erudition and prudence). When a person achieves all the goals of each of the parts of her psyche, then, such a harmonious psyche is functioning fully. A fully flourishing human being is a *eudaimon,* a supremely happy person.

Now they test this theory of justice as *psychic harmony* against the conventional opinions about justice, that is, against the popular notion that justice is honoring parents and making acts of piety toward gods, avoiding stealing, lying, and betraying or committing acts of adultery. They see immediately that the *eudaimon*, the psychically harmonized person, is the least likely to break any of the conventional norms associated with justice. This is the triumph of an ethic of virtue over rule-based ethics. The psychically harmonized person is the least likely to injure or violate another person for they have all that they need for happiness in their own noble character. Making an analogy between virtue and health, Socrates asserts that psychic harmony is in accord with nature; but if passion overwhelms reason or spirited aggression usurps reason, such injustice between souls is as unnatural and as damaging as disease is to the body.

CONCLUSION

It should be pointed out that Plato has answered all the questions posed in Books I and II. Justice has been defined both in the City and in the person. Further, whether justice is advantageous in itself (an intrinsic value) and not only as a means to other goods, has been demonstrated in the model of the *eudaimon*, the fully flourishing, psychically harmonized person (it is never an advantage to be out of sorts spiritually). The argument for the advantage of the just life, however, is thoroughly accomplished in Books VII through IX, where Socrates compares various forms of cities and personalities in contrast with the Ideal State and individual. This is completed only after the digression on women, marriage and the philosopher-king in Books V, VI and VII.

SUGGESTIONS FOR FURTHER READING

Anagnostopoulis, Mariana. "The Divided Soul and the Desire for Good in Plato's *Republic*." *The Blackwell Guide to Plato's Republic*. Malden, MA: Blackwell, 2006. [166-188]

Annas, Julia. *An Introduction to Plato's Republic*. New York: Oxford UP, 1981. [109-152]

—. "The Psychology of Justice in Plato." *Plato's Republic: Critical Essays*. Ed. Richard Kraut. Lanham, MD: Rowman and Littlefield, 1997.

Benardete, Seth. *Socrates' Second Sailing: On Plato's* Republic. Chicago: University of Chicago Press, 1989. [82-105]

Bloom, Allan. *The Republic of Plato*. New York: Harper Collins, 1968. [372-379]

Cooper, John M. "Plato's Theory of Human Motivation." *History of*

Philosophy Quarterly 1 (1984): 3-21.

Irwin, Terence. *Plato's Ethics*. New York: Oxford University Press, 1995. [223-243]

Kenny, Anthony. "Mental Health in Plato's *Republic*." *Anatomy of the Soul*. Oxford: Blackwell, 1973. [1-27]

Lorenz, Hendrik. "The Analysis of the Soul in Plato's *Republic*." *The Blackwell Guide to Plato's Republic*. Malden, MA: Blackwell, 2006. [146-165]

—. "Desire and Reason in Plato's *Republic*." *Oxford Studies in Ancient Philosophy* 27 (2004): 83-116.

Pappas, Nickolas. *Plato and the Republic*. New York: Routledge, 1995. [81-98]

Reeve, C.D.C. *Philosopher-Kings: The Argument of Plato's Republic*. Princeton: Princeton University Press, 1988. [118-169]

Robinson, R. "Plato's Separation of Reason From Desire." *Phronesis* 16 (1971): 38-48.

Sayers, Sean. *Plato's Republic: An Introduction*. Edinburgh: Edinburgh University Press, 1999. [68-81]

Scott, Dominic. "Plato's Critique of the Democratic Character." *Phronesis* 45 (2000): 19-37.

Stalley, Richard F. "Plato's Argument for the Division of the Reasoning and Appetitive Elements within the Soul." *Phronesis* 20 (1975): 110-128.

White, Nicholas P. *A Companion to Plato's Republic*. Indianapolis: Hackett, 1979. [113-138]

Williams, Bernard. "The Analogy of City and Soul in Plato's Republic. *Plato's Republic: Critical Essays*. Ed. Richard Kraut. Lanham, MD: Rowman and Littlefield, 1997. [49-59]

Wilson, J. "The Argument of Republic 4." *Philosophical Quarterly* 26 (1976): 111-124.

Woods, Michael. "Plato's Division of the Soul." Proceedings of the British Academy 73 (1987): 23-47.

JUSTICE IN THE CITY [427D-434D]

But where, amid all this, is justice? son of Ariston, tell me where.
d   Now that our city has been made habitable, light a candle and
search, and get your brother and Polemarchus and the rest of our
friends to help, and let us see where in it we can discover justice and
where injustice, and in what they differ from one another, and which
of them the man who would be happy should have for his portion,
whether seen or unseen by gods and men.

Nonsense, said Glaucon: did you not promise to search yourself,
saying that for you not to help justice in her need would be an
e   impiety?

I do not deny that I said so, and as you remind me, I will be as
good as my word; but you must join.

We will, he replied.

Well, then, I hope to make the discovery in this way: I mean
to begin with the assumption that our State, if rightly ordered, is
perfect.

That is most certain.

And being perfect, is therefore wise and valiant and temperate
and just.

That is likewise clear.

And whichever of these qualities we find in the State, the one
which is not found will be the residue?

428   Very good.

If there were four things, and we were searching for one of them,
wherever it might be, the one sought for might be known to us from
the first, and there would be no further trouble; or we might know
the other three first, and then the fourth would clearly be the one left.

Very true, he said.

And is not a similar method to be pursued about the virtues,
which are also four in number?

Clearly.

First among the virtues found in the State, wisdom comes into
view, and in this I detect a certain peculiarity.

b   What is that?

The State which we have been describing is said to be wise as
being good in counsel?

Very true.

And good counsel is clearly a kind of knowledge, for not by ignorance, but by knowledge, do men counsel well?

Clearly.

And the kinds of knowledge in a State are many and diverse?

Of course.

There is the knowledge of the carpenter; but is that the sort of knowledge which gives a city the title of wise and good in counsel?

Certainly not; that would only give a city the reputation of skill in carpentering.

Then a city is not to be called wise because possessing a knowledge which counsels for the best about wooden implements?

Certainly not.

Nor by reason of a knowledge which advises about brass pots, I said, nor as possessing any other similar knowledge?

Not by reason of any of them, he said.

Nor yet by reason of a knowledge which cultivates the earth; that would give the city the name of agricultural?

Yes.

Well, I said, and is there any knowledge in our recently-founded State among any of the citizens which advises, not about any particular thing in the State, but about the whole, and considers how a State can best deal with itself and with other States?

There certainly is.

And what is this knowledge, and among whom is it found? I asked.

It is the knowledge of the guardians, he replied, and is found among those whom we were just now describing as perfect guardians.

And what is the name which the city derives from the possession of this sort of knowledge?

The name of good in counsel and truly wise.

And will there be in our city more of these true guardians or more smiths?

The smiths, he replied, will be far more numerous.

Will not the guardians be the smallest of all the classes who receive a name from the profession of some kind of knowledge?

Much the smallest.

And so by reason of the smallest part or class, and of the knowledge which resides in this presiding and ruling part of itself, the whole State, being thus constituted according to nature, will be wise; and this, which has the only knowledge worthy to be called wisdom, has been ordained by nature to be of all classes the least.

Most true.

Thus, then, I said, the nature and place in the State of one of the four virtues has somehow or other been discovered.

And, in my humble opinion, very satisfactorily discovered, he replied.

Again, I said, there is no difficulty in seeing the nature of courage, and in what part that quality resides which gives the name of courageous to the State.

How do you mean?

Why, I said, every one who calls any State courageous or cowardly, will be thinking of the part which fights and goes out to war on the State's behalf.

No one, he replied, would ever think of any other.

The rest of the citizens may be courageous or may be cowardly, but their courage or cowardice will not, as I conceive, have the effect of making the city either the one or the other.

Certainly not.

The city will be courageous in virtue of a portion of herself which preserves under all circumstances that opinion about the nature of things to be feared and not to be feared in which our legislator educated them; and this is what you term courage.

I should like to hear what you are saying once more, for I do not think that I perfectly understand you.

I mean that courage is a kind of salvation.

Salvation of what?

Of the opinion respecting things to be feared, what they are and of what nature, which the law implants through education; and I mean by the words 'under all circumstances' to intimate that in pleasure or in pain, or under the influence of desire or fear, a man preserves, and does not lose this opinion. Shall I give you an illustration?

If you please.

You know, I said, that dyers, when they want to dye wool for making the true sea-purple, begin by selecting their white colour first; this they prepare and dress with much care and pains, in order that the white ground may take the purple hue in full perfection. The dyeing then proceeds; and whatever is dyed in this manner becomes a fast colour, and no washing either with lyes or without them can take away the bloom. But, when the ground has not been duly prepared, you will have noticed how poor is the look either of purple or of any other colour.

Yes, he said; I know that they have a washed-out and ridiculous appearance.

Then now, I said, you will understand what our object was in selecting our soldiers, and educating them in music and gymnastic; we were contriving influences which would prepare them to take the dye of the laws in perfection, and the colour of their opinion about dangers and of every other opinion was to be indelibly fixed by their nurture and training, not to be washed away by such potent lyes as pleasure—mightier agent far in washing the soul than any soda or lye; or by sorrow, fear, and desire, the mightiest of all other solvents. And this sort of universal saving power of true opinion in conformity with law about real and false dangers I call and maintain to be courage, unless you disagree.

But I agree, he replied; for I suppose that you mean to exclude mere uninstructed courage, such as that of a wild beast or of a slave—this, in your opinion, is not the courage which the law ordains, and ought to have another name.

Most certainly.

Then I may infer courage to be such as you describe?

Why, yes, said I, you may, and if you add the words 'of a citizen,' you will not be far wrong;—hereafter, if you like, we will carry the examination further, but at present we are seeking not for courage but justice; and for the purpose of our enquiry we have said enough.

You are right, he replied.

Two virtues remain to be discovered in the State—first, temperance, and then justice which is the end of our search.

Very true.

Now, can we find justice without troubling ourselves about temperance?

I do not know how that can be accomplished, he said, nor do I desire that justice should be brought to light and temperance lost sight of; and therefore I wish that you would do me the favour of considering temperance first.

Certainly, I replied, I should not be justified in refusing your request.

Then consider, he said.

Yes, I replied; I will; and as far as I can at present see, the virtue of temperance has more of the nature of harmony and symphony than the preceding.

How so? he asked.

Temperance, I replied, is the ordering or controlling of certain pleasures and desires; this is curiously enough implied in the saying of 'a man being his own master;' and other traces of the same notion may be found in language.

No doubt, he said.

There is something ridiculous in the expression 'master of himself;' for the master is also the servant and the servant the master; and in all these modes of speaking the same person is denoted.

Certainly.

The meaning is, I believe, that in the human soul there is a better and also a worse principle; and when the better has the worse under control, then a man is said to be master of himself; and this is a term of praise: but when, owing to evil education or association, the better principle, which is also the smaller, is overwhelmed by the greater mass of the worse—in this case he is blamed and is called the slave of self and unprincipled.

Yes, there is reason in that.

b   And now, I said, look at our newly-created State, and there you will find one of these two conditions realized; for the State, as you will acknowledge, may be justly called master of itself, if the words 'temperance' and 'self-mastery' truly express the rule of the better part over the worse.

Yes, he said, I see that what you say is true.

Let me further note that the manifold and complex pleasures and desires and pains are generally found in children and women and servants, and in the freemen so called who are of the lowest and
c   more numerous class.

Certainly, he said.

Whereas the simple and moderate desires which follow reason, and are under the guidance of mind and true opinion, are to be found only in a few, and those the best born and best educated.

Very true.

These two, as you may perceive, have a place in our State; and the meaner desires of the many are held down by the virtuous desires and wisdom of the few.

That I perceive, he said.

d   Then if there be any city which may be described as master of its own pleasures and desires, and master of itself, ours may claim such a designation?

Certainly, he replied.

It may also be called temperate, and for the same reasons?

Yes.

And if there be any State in which rulers and subjects will be agreed as to the question who are to rule, that again will be our State?

e   Undoubtedly.

And the citizens being thus agreed among themselves, in which class will temperance be found—in the rulers or in the subjects?

In both, as I should imagine, he replied.

Do you observe that we were not far wrong in our guess that temperance was a sort of harmony?

Why so?

Why, because temperance is unlike courage and wisdom, each of which resides in a part only, the one making the State wise and the other valiant; not so temperance, which extends to the whole, and
432   runs through all the notes of the scale, and produces a harmony of the weaker and the stronger and the middle class, whether you suppose them to be stronger or weaker in wisdom or power or numbers or wealth, or anything else. Most truly then may we deem temperance to be the agreement of the naturally superior and inferior, as to the

right to rule of either, both in states and individuals.

I entirely agree with you.

And so, I said, we may consider three out of the four virtues to have been discovered in our State. The last of those qualities which make a state virtuous must be justice, if we only knew what that was.   b

The inference is obvious.

The time then has arrived, Glaucon, when, like huntsmen, we should surround the cover, and look sharp that justice does not steal away, and pass out of sight and escape us; for beyond a doubt she is somewhere in this country: watch therefore and strive to catch a sight of her, and if you see her first, let me know.

Would that I could! but you should regard me rather as a follower who has just eyes enough to see what you show him—that is about as much as I am good for.   c

Offer up a prayer with me and follow.

I will, but you must show me the way.

Here is no path, I said, and the wood is dark and perplexing; still we must push on.

Let us push on.

Here I saw something: Halloo! I said, I begin to perceive a track, and I believe that the quarry will not escape.   d

Good news, he said.

Truly, I said, we are stupid fellows.

Why so?

Why, my good sir, at the beginning of our enquiry, ages ago, there was justice tumbling out at our feet, and we never saw her; nothing could be more ridiculous. Like people who go about looking for what they have in their hands—that was the way with us—we looked not at what we were seeking, but at what was far off in the distance; and therefore, I suppose, we missed her.   e

What do you mean?

I mean to say that in reality for a long time past we have been talking of justice, and have failed to recognise her.

I grow impatient at the length of your introduction.

Well then, tell me, I said, whether I am right or not: You remember the original principle which we were always laying down at the foundation of the State, that one man should practise   433 one thing only, the thing to which his nature was best adapted;— now justice is this principle or a part of it.

Yes, we often said that one man should do one thing only.

Further, we affirmed that justice was doing one's own business, and not being a busybody; we said so again and again, and many others have said the same to us.

Yes, we said so.

Then to do one's own business in a certain way may be assumed   b to be justice. Can you tell me whence I derive this inference?

I cannot, but I should like to be told.

Because I think that this is the only virtue which remains in the State when the other virtues of temperance and courage and wisdom are abstracted; and, that this is the ultimate cause and condition of the existence of all of them, and while remaining in them is also their preservative; and we were saying that if the three were discovered by us, justice would be the fourth or remaining one.

That follows of necessity.

If we are asked to determine which of these four qualities by its presence contributes most to the excellence of the State, whether the agreement of rulers and subjects, or the preservation in the soldiers of the opinion which the law ordains about the true nature of dangers, or wisdom and watchfulness in the rulers, or whether this other which I am mentioning, and which is found in children and women, slave and freeman, artisan, ruler, subject,—the quality, I mean, of every one doing his own work, and not being a busybody, would claim the palm—the question is not so easily answered.

Certainly, he replied, there would be a difficulty in saying which.

Then the power of each individual in the State to do his own work appears to compete with the other political virtues, wisdom, temperance, courage.

Yes, he said.

And the virtue which enters into this competition is justice?

Exactly.

Let us look at the question from another point of view: Are not the rulers in a State those to whom you would entrust the office of determining suits at law?

Certainly.

And are suits decided on any other ground but that a man may neither take what is another's, nor be deprived of what is his own?

Yes; that is their principle.

Which is a just principle?

Yes.

Then on this view also justice will be admitted to be the having and doing what is a man's own, and belongs to him?

Very true.

Think, now, and say whether you agree with me or not. Suppose a carpenter to be doing the business of a cobbler, or a cobbler of a carpenter; and suppose them to exchange their implements or their duties, or the same person to be doing the work of both, or whatever be the change; do you think that any great harm would result to the State?

Not much.

But when the cobbler or any other man whom nature designed

to be a trader, having his heart lifted up by wealth or strength or the number of his followers, or any like advantage, attempts to force his way into the class of warriors, or a warrior into that of legislators and guardians, for which he is unfitted, and either to take the implements or the duties of the other; or when one man is trader, legislator, and warrior all in one, then I think you will agree with me in saying that this interchange and this meddling of one with another is the ruin of the State.

Most true.

Seeing then, I said, that there are three distinct classes, any meddling of one with another, or the change of one into another, is the greatest harm to the State, and may be most justly termed evil-doing?

Precisely.

And the greatest degree of evil-doing to one's own city would be termed by you injustice?

Certainly.

This then is injustice; and on the other hand when the trader, the auxiliary, and the guardian each do their own business, that is justice, and will make the city just.

I agree with you.

THREE PARTS OF THE SOUL [434D-441C]

We will not, I said, be over-positive as yet; but if, on trial, this conception of justice be verified in the individual as well as in the State, there will be no longer any room for doubt; if it be not verified, we must have a fresh enquiry. First let us complete the old investigation, which we began, as you remember, under the impression that, if we could previously examine justice on the larger scale, there would be less difficulty in discerning her in the individual. That larger example appeared to be the State, and accordingly we constructed as good a one as we could, knowing well that in the good State justice would be found. Let the discovery which we made be now applied to the individual—if they agree, we shall be satisfied; or, if there be a difference in the individual, we will come back to the State and have another trial of the theory. The friction of the two when rubbed together may possibly strike a light in which justice will shine forth, and the vision which is then revealed we will fix in our souls.

That will be in regular course; let us do as you say.

I proceeded to ask: When two things, a greater and less, are called by the same name, are they like or unlike in so far as they are called the same?

Like, he replied.

The just man then, if we regard the idea of justice only, will be like the just State?

He will.

b And a State was thought by us to be just when the three classes in the State severally did their own business; and also thought to be temperate and valiant and wise by reason of certain other affections and qualities of these same classes?

True, he said.

And so of the individual; we may assume that he has the same three principles in his own soul which are found in the State; and he may be rightly described in the same terms, because he is affected in the same manner?

c Certainly, he said.

Once more then, O my friend, we have alighted upon an easy question—whether the soul has these three principles or not?

An easy question! Nay, rather, Socrates, the proverb holds that hard is the good.

Very true, I said; and I do not think that the method which we are employing is at all adequate to the accurate solution of this question; the true method is another and a longer one. Still we may

d arrive at a solution not below the level of the previous enquiry.

May we not be satisfied with that? he said;—under the circumstances, I am quite content.

I too, I replied, shall be extremely well satisfied.

Then faint not in pursuing the speculation, he said.

Must we not acknowledge, I said, that in each of us there are the same principles and habits which there are in the State; and that from the individual they pass into the State?—how else can

e they come there? Take the quality of passion or spirit;—it would be ridiculous to imagine that this quality, when found in States, is not derived from the individuals who are supposed to possess it, e.g. the Thracians, Scythians, and in general the northern nations; and the same may be said of the love of knowledge, which is the special characteristic of our part of the world, or of the love of money, which may, with equal truth, be attributed to the Phoenicians and

436 Egyptians.

Exactly so, he said.

There is no difficulty in understanding this.

None whatever.

But the question is not quite so easy when we proceed to ask whether these principles are three or one; whether, that is to say, we learn with one part of our nature, are angry with another, and with a third part desire the satisfaction of our natural appetites; or whether the whole soul comes into play in each sort of action—to determine that is the difficulty.

Yes, he said; there lies the difficulty.

b Then let us now try and determine whether they are the same or different.

How can we? he asked.

I replied as follows: The same thing clearly cannot act or be acted upon in the same part or in relation to the same thing at the same time, in contrary ways; and therefore whenever this contradiction occurs in things apparently the same, we know that they are really not the same, but different.

Good.

For example, I said, can the same thing be at rest and in motion at the same time in the same part?

Impossible.

Still, I said, let us have a more precise statement of terms, lest we should hereafter fall out by the way. Imagine the case of a man who is standing and also moving his hands and his head, and suppose a person to say that one and the same person is in motion and at rest at the same moment—to such a mode of speech we should object, and should rather say that one part of him is in motion while another is at rest.

Very true.

And suppose the objector to refine still further, and to draw the nice distinction that not only parts of tops, but whole tops, when they spin round with their pegs fixed on the spot, are at rest and in motion at the same time (and he may say the same of anything which revolves in the same spot), his objection would not be admitted by us, because in such cases things are not at rest and in motion in the same parts of themselves; we should rather say that they have both an axis and a circumference, and that the axis stands still, for there is no deviation from the perpendicular; and that the circumference goes round. But if, while revolving, the axis inclines either to the right or left, forwards or backwards, then in no point of view can they be at rest.

That is the correct mode of describing them, he replied.

Then none of these objections will confuse us, or incline us to believe that the same thing at the same time, in the same part or in relation to the same thing, can act or be acted upon in contrary ways.

Certainly not, according to my way of thinking.

Yet, I said, that we may not be compelled to examine all such objections, and prove at length that they are untrue, let us assume their absurdity, and go forward on the understanding that hereafter, if this assumption turn out to be untrue, all the consequences which follow shall be withdrawn.

Yes, he said, that will be the best way.

Well, I said, would you not allow that assent and dissent, desire and aversion, attraction and repulsion, are all of them opposites, whether they are regarded as active or passive (for that makes no b   difference in the fact of their opposition)?

Yes, he said, they are opposites.

Well, I said, and hunger and thirst, and the desires in general, and again willing and wishing,—all these you would refer to the classes already mentioned. You would say—would you not?—that the soul of him who desires is seeking after the object of his desire; or that he is drawing to himself the thing which he wishes to possess: or

c   again, when a person wants anything to be given him, his mind, longing for the realization of his desire, intimates his wish to have it by a nod of assent, as if he had been asked a question?

Very true.

And what would you say of unwillingness and dislike and the absence of desire; should not these be referred to the opposite class of repulsion and rejection?

Certainly.

Admitting this to be true of desire generally, let us suppose a particular class of desires, and out of these we will select hunger

d   and thirst, as they are termed, which are the most obvious of them?

Let us take that class, he said.

The object of one is food, and of the other drink?

Yes.

And here comes the point: is not thirst the desire which the soul has of drink, and of drink only; not of drink qualified by anything else; for example, warm or cold, or much or little, or, in a word, drink of any particular sort: but if the thirst be accompanied by heat, then the desire is of cold drink; or, if accompanied by cold, then of warm drink; or, if the thirst be excessive, then the drink which is desired will be excessive; or, if not great, the quantity of

e   drink will also be small: but thirst pure and simple will desire drink pure and simple, which is the natural satisfaction of thirst, as food is of hunger?

Yes, he said; the simple desire is, as you say, in every case of the simple object, and the qualified desire of the qualified object.

But here a confusion may arise; and I should wish to guard against an opponent starting up and saying that no man desires drink only, but good drink, or food only, but good food; for good is the

438   universal object of desire, and thirst being a desire, will necessarily be thirst after good drink; and the same is true of every other desire.

Yes, he replied, the opponent might have something to say.

Nevertheless I should still maintain, that of relatives some have a quality attached to either term of the relation; others are simple and have their correlatives simple.

I do not know what you mean.

Well, you know of course that the greater is relative to the less?

b   Certainly.

And the much greater to the much less?

Yes.

And the sometime greater to the sometime less, and the greater that is to be to the less that is to be?

Certainly, he said.

And so of more and less, and of other correlative terms, such as the double and the half, or again, the heavier and the lighter, the swifter and the slower; and of hot and cold, and of any other relatives;—is not this true of all of them?

Yes.   c

And does not the same principle hold in the sciences? The object of science is knowledge (assuming that to be the true definition), but the object of a particular science is a particular kind of knowledge; I mean, for example, that the science of house-building is a kind of knowledge which is defined and distinguished from other kinds and is therefore termed architecture.

Certainly.

Because it has a particular quality which no other has?   d

Yes.

And it has this particular quality because it has an object of a particular kind; and this is true of the other arts and sciences?

Yes.

Now, then, if I have made myself clear, you will understand my original meaning in what I said about relatives. My meaning was, that if one term of a relation is taken alone, the other is taken alone; if one term is qualified, the other is also qualified. I do not mean to say that relatives may not be disparate, or that the science of health is healthy, or of disease necessarily diseased, or that the sciences of good and evil are therefore good and evil; but only that, when the term science is no longer used absolutely, but has a qualified object which in this case is the nature of health and disease, it becomes   e
defined, and is hence called not merely science, but the science of medicine.

I quite understand, and I think as you do.

Would you not say that thirst is one of these essentially relative terms, having clearly a relation—

Yes, thirst is relative to drink.

And a certain kind of thirst is relative to a certain kind of drink; but thirst taken alone is neither of much nor little, nor of good nor   439
bad, nor of any particular kind of drink, but of drink only?

Certainly.

Then the soul of the thirsty one, in so far as he is thirsty, desires only drink; for this he yearns and tries to obtain it?

That is plain.

And if you suppose something which pulls a thirsty soul away from drink, that must be different from the thirsty principle which draws him like a beast to drink; for, as we were saying, the same   b thing cannot at the same time with the same part of itself act in contrary ways about the same.

Impossible.

No more than you can say that the hands of the archer push and pull the bow at the same time, but what you say is that one hand pushes and the other pulls.

Exactly so, he replied.

And might a man be thirsty, and yet unwilling to drink?

Yes, he said, it constantly happens.

And in such a case what is one to say? Would you not say that there was something in the soul bidding a man to drink, and something else forbidding him, which is other and stronger than the principle which bids him?

I should say so.

And the forbidding principle is derived from reason, and that which bids and attracts proceeds from passion and disease?

Clearly.

Then we may fairly assume that they are two, and that they differ from one another; the one with which a man reasons, we may call the rational principle of the soul, the other, with which he loves and hungers and thirsts and feels the flutterings of any other desire, may be termed the irrational or appetitive, the ally of sundry pleasures and satisfactions?

Yes, he said, we may fairly assume them to be different.

Then let us finally determine that there are two principles existing in the soul. And what of passion, or spirit? Is it a third, or akin to one of the preceding?

I should be inclined to say—akin to desire.

Well, I said, there is a story which I remember to have heard, and in which I put faith. The story is, that Leontius, the son of Aglaion, coming up one day from the Piraeus, under the north wall on the outside, observed some dead bodies lying on the ground at the place of execution. He felt a desire to see them, and also a dread and abhorrence of them; for a time he struggled and covered his eyes, but at length the desire got the better of him; and forcing them open, he ran up to the dead bodies, saying, Look, ye wretches, take your fill of the fair sight.

I have heard the story myself, he said.

The moral of the tale is, that anger at times goes to war with desire, as though they were two distinct things.

Yes; that is the meaning, he said.

And are there not many other cases in which we observe that when a man's desires violently prevail over his reason, he reviles himself, and is angry at the violence within him, and that in this struggle, which is like the struggle of factions in a State, his spirit is on the side of his reason;—but for the passionate or spirited element to take part with the desires when reason decides that she should not be opposed, is a sort of thing which I believe that you never observed occurring in yourself, nor, as I should imagine, in any one else? _b

Certainly not.

Suppose that a man thinks he has done a wrong to another, the nobler he is the less able is he to feel indignant at any suffering, such as hunger, or cold, or any other pain which the injured person may inflict upon him—these he deems to be just, and, as I say, his anger refuses to be excited by them.

True, he said.

But when he thinks that he is the sufferer of the wrong, then he boils and chafes, and is on the side of what he believes to be justice; and because he suffers hunger or cold or other pain he is only the more determined to persevere and conquer. His noble spirit will not be quelled until he either slays or is slain; or until he hears the voice of the shepherd, that is, reason, bidding his dog bark no more.

The illustration is perfect, he replied; and in our State, as we were saying, the auxiliaries were to be dogs, and to hear the voice of the rulers, who are their shepherds.

I perceive, I said, that you quite understand me; there is, however, a further point which I wish you to consider.

What point?

You remember that passion or spirit appeared at first sight to be a kind of desire, but now we should say quite the contrary; for in the conflict of the soul spirit is arrayed on the side of the rational principle.

Most assuredly.

But a further question arises: Is passion different from reason also, or only a kind of reason; in which latter case, instead of three principles in the soul, there will only be two, the rational and the concupiscent; or rather, as the State was composed of three classes, traders, auxiliaries, counsellors, so may there not be in the individual soul a third element which is passion or spirit, and when not corrupted by bad education is the natural auxiliary of reason?

Yes, he said, there must be a third.

Yes, I replied, if passion, which has already been shown to be different from desire, turn out also to be different from reason.

But that is easily proved:—We may observe even in young children that they are full of spirit almost as soon as they are born, whereas some of them never seem to attain to the use of reason, and most of them late enough.

Excellent, I said, and you may see passion equally in brute animals, which is a further proof of the truth of what you are saying. And we may once more appeal to the words of Homer, which have been already quoted by us,

'He smote his breast, and thus rebuked his soul,'

for in this verse Homer has clearly supposed the power which reasons about the better and worse to be different from the unreasoning anger which is rebuked by it.

Very true, he said.

And so, after much tossing, we have reached land, and are fairly agreed that the same principles which exist in the State exist also in the individual, and that they are three in number.

Exactly.

JUSTICE IN THE INDIVIDUAL [441C-445B]

Must we not then infer that the individual is wise in the same way, and in virtue of the same quality which makes the State wise?

Certainly.

Also that the same quality which constitutes courage in the State constitutes courage in the individual, and that both the State and the individual bear the same relation to all the other virtues?

Assuredly.

And the individual will be acknowledged by us to be just in the same way in which the State is just?

That follows, of course.

We cannot but remember that the justice of the State consisted in each of the three classes doing the work of its own class?

We are not very likely to have forgotten, he said.

We must recollect that the individual in whom the several qualities of his nature do their own work will be just, and will do his own work?

Yes, he said, we must remember that too.

And ought not the rational principle, which is wise, and has the care of the whole soul, to rule, and the passionate or spirited principle to be the subject and ally?

Certainly.

And, as we were saying, the united influence of music and gymnastic will bring them into accord, nerving and sustaining the reason with noble words and lessons, and moderating and soothing and civilizing the wildness of passion by harmony and rhythm?

Quite true, he said.

And these two, thus nurtured and educated, and having learned truly to know their own functions, will rule over the appetitive, which in each of us is the largest part of the soul and by nature most insatiable of gain; over this they will keep guard, lest, waxing great and strong with the fullness of bodily pleasures, as they are termed, the appetitive soul, no longer confined to her own sphere, should attempt to enslave and rule those who are not her natural-born subjects, and overturn the whole life of man?

Very true, he said.

Both together will they not be the best defenders of the whole soul and the whole body against attacks from without; the one counselling, and the other fighting under his leader, and courageously executing his commands and counsels?

True.

And he is to be deemed courageous whose spirit retains in pleasure and in pain the commands of reason about what he ought or ought not to fear?

Right, he replied.

And him we call wise who has in him that little part which rules, and which proclaims these commands; that part too being supposed to have a knowledge of what is for the interest of each of the three parts and of the whole?

Assuredly.

And would you not say that he is temperate who has these same elements in friendly harmony, in whom the one ruling principle of reason, and the two subject ones of spirit and desire are equally agreed that reason ought to rule, and do not rebel?

Certainly, he said, that is the true account of temperance whether in the State or individual.

And surely, I said, we have explained again and again how and by virtue of what quality a man will be just.

That is very certain.

And is justice dimmer in the individual, and is her form different, or is she the same which we found her to be in the State?

There is no difference in my opinion, he said.

Because, if any doubt is still lingering in our minds, a few commonplace instances will satisfy us of the truth of what I am saying.

What sort of instances do you mean?

If the case is put to us, must we not admit that the just State, or the man who is trained in the principles of such a State, will be less likely than the unjust to make away with a deposit of gold or silver? Would any one deny this?

No one, he replied.

Will the just man or citizen ever be guilty of sacrilege or theft, or treachery either to his friends or to his country?

Never.

Neither will he ever break faith where there have been oaths or agreements?

Impossible.

No one will be less likely to commit adultery, or to dishonour his father and mother, or to fail in his religious duties?

No one.

And the reason is that each part of him is doing its own business, whether in ruling or being ruled?

Exactly so.

Are you satisfied then that the quality which makes such men
and such states is justice, or do you hope to discover some other?

Not I, indeed.

Then our dream has been realized; and the suspicion which we
entertained at the beginning of our work of construction, that some
divine power must have conducted us to a primary form of justice,
has now been verified?

Yes, certainly.

And the division of labour which required the carpenter and the
shoemaker and the rest of the citizens to be doing each his own
business, and not another's, was a shadow of justice, and for that
reason it was of use?

Clearly.

But in reality justice was such as we were describing, being
concerned however, not with the outward man, but with the inward,
which is the true self and concernment of man: for the just man
does not permit the several elements within him to interfere with
one another, or any of them to do the work of others,—he sets in
order his own inner life, and is his own master and his own law, and
at peace with himself; and when he has bound together the three
principles within him, which may be compared to the higher, lower,
and middle notes of the scale, and the intermediate intervals—when
he has bound all these together, and is no longer many, but has
become one entirely temperate and perfectly adjusted nature, then
he proceeds to act, if he has to act, whether in a matter of property,
or in the treatment of the body, or in some affair of politics or private
business; always thinking and calling that which preserves and co-
operates with this harmonious condition, just and good action, and
the knowledge which presides over it, wisdom, and that which at
any time impairs this condition, he will call unjust action, and the
opinion which presides over it ignorance.

You have said the exact truth, Socrates.

Very good; and if we were to affirm that we had discovered the
just man and the just State, and the nature of justice in each of them,
we should not be telling a falsehood?

Most certainly not.

May we say so, then?

Let us say so.

And now, I said, injustice has to be considered.

Clearly.

Must not injustice be a strife which arises among the three
principles—a meddlesomeness, and interference, and rising up
of a part of the soul against the whole, an assertion of unlawful
authority, which is made by a rebellious subject against a true

prince, of whom he is the natural vassal,—what is all this confusion   b
and delusion but injustice, and intemperance and cowardice and
ignorance, and every form of vice?

Exactly so.

And if the nature of justice and injustice be known, then the
meaning of acting unjustly and being unjust, or, again, of acting
justly, will also be perfectly clear?

What do you mean? he said.

Why, I said, they are like disease and health; being in the soul   c
just what disease and health are in the body.

How so? he said.

Why, I said, that which is healthy causes health, and that which
is unhealthy causes disease.

Yes.

And just actions cause justice, and unjust actions cause injustice?

That is certain.

And the creation of health is the institution of a natural order
and government of one by another in the parts of the body; and the
creation of disease is the production of a state of things at variance   d
with this natural order?

True.

And is not the creation of justice the institution of a natural order
and government of one by another in the parts of the soul, and the
creation of injustice the production of a state of things at variance
with the natural order?

Exactly so, he said.

Then virtue is the health and beauty and well-being of the soul,
and vice the disease and weakness and deformity of the same?

True.

And do not good practices lead to virtue, and evil practices to
vice?

Assuredly.

Still our old question of the comparative advantage of justice   e
and injustice has not been answered: Which is the more profitable,
to be just and act justly and practise virtue, whether seen or unseen
of gods and men, or to be unjust and act unjustly, if only unpunished
and unreformed?

In my judgment, Socrates, the question has now become
ridiculous. We know that, when the bodily constitution is gone, life
is no longer endurable, though pampered with all kinds of meats   445
and drinks, and having all wealth and all power; and shall we be
told that when the very essence of the vital principle is undermined
and corrupted, life is still worth having to a man, if only he be
allowed to do whatever he likes with the single exception that he
is not to acquire justice and virtue, or to escape from injustice and
vice; assuming them both to be such as we have described?

b   Yes, I said, the question is, as you say, ridiculous. Still, as we are near the spot at which we may see the truth in the clearest manner with our own eyes, let us not faint by the way.

Certainly not, he replied.

Come up hither, I said, and behold the various forms of vice, those of them, I mean, which are worth looking at.

I am following you, he replied: proceed.

I said, The argument seems to have reached a height from which, as from some tower of speculation, a man may look down and see

c   that virtue is one, but that the forms of vice are innumerable; there being four special ones which are deserving of note.

What do you mean? he said.

I mean, I replied, that there appear to be as many forms of the soul as there are distinct forms of the State.

How many?

There are five of the State, and five of the soul, I said.

What are they?

d   The first, I said, is that which we have been describing, and which may be said to have two names, monarchy and aristocracy, accordingly as rule is exercised by one distinguished man or by many.

True, he replied.

But I regard the two names as describing one form only; for

e   whether the government is in the hands of one or many, if the governors have been trained in the manner which we have supposed, the fundamental laws of the State will be maintained.

That is true, he replied.

8

Plato's Radical Politics

Introduction [449A-450C]

Book V represents something of a digression—albeit an important one—
in the argument of the *Republic*. At the end of Book IV, Socrates was
in the midst of discussing the four types of defective cities, when he is
challenged by Polemarchus to explain what he meant when he said that the
Guardian Rulers will hold women and children in common. The discussion
of defective cities will be put off until Book VIII.

Book V, then, returns to the question of the lifestyle of the guardians,
developing Plato's own radical approach to politics. What we will
discover in this book is that Plato takes very seriously the idea that the
Guardian Rulers will hold *everything* in common. It should be noted that
Plato's communalism concerns only the Guardians and not the rest of the
population. Plato believes that unity of the city can only be assured if the
Guardians, who control the city, are themselves united (465b).

The Equality of Women [450C-457B]

Women, Socrates argues, are equal to men in all ways except in strength.
They should therefore have the same responsibilities as men. If they are
to share the responsibilities of being Guardians, then they will need the
same type of education and training as male Guardians (451d). Female
guardians would therefore need to be trained in music and gymnastics as
well as the art of war alongside the male counterparts. Socrates anticipates
the objection that the sight of women exercising naked with men might
very well seem ridiculous according to conventional Greek customs. If,
however, such an arrangement is advantageous to the city as a whole, it
doesn't matter if it flies in the face of custom (452).

Socrates anticipates a conservative objection to his belief in the fundamental equality of women (253a-c). The argument that the conservatives would raise is something like the following:

Premise 1: According to the principle of specialization, each person should work according to his/her own nature. *Premise 2:* Women and men have different natures, e.g., men mount and women are mounted. *Conclusion:* Therefore they should have different functions in society e.g., men, who are aggressive by nature, should act as rulers and warriors, and women, who have nurturing natures, should act as mothers and teachers. This is the ancient "nature as destiny" argument against women's equality with men.

In his response, he needs to demonstrate that, despite their different anatomies, men and women are still capable of performing the same tasks. His argument from analogy (453e-454c) is as follows: do bald men and hairy men have the same nature? Well, no. They are of opposite natures. Yet the bald man and the hairy man can perform the same tasks. So not every distinction in physical nature means a distinction in occupational capability. Women and men are anatomically different and yet they are capable of performing the same tasks: "For example, we meant that a man and a woman whose souls are suited for the doctor's art have the same nature."

So despite their different anatomies, women and men share enough of a functional nature to be capable of practicing the physician's art. Analogously, the anatomical distinction is not essential to their abilities to do the work of ruling and protecting the *polis*. It follows then that women should be admitted into the military and receive the same education and training as male warriors. The opportunity opens up for women to become Guardian Rulers of the City-State.

The only real objection that can be raised to having women in the ranks of the guardians is that they have the possibility of having children, and raising children is a full-time job that precludes all other kinds of work. Plato's solution to this problem, as we shall see, is to devise a radically different model of child rearing that can free women to perform other kinds of work in the *polis*.

THE GUARDIAN'S FAMILY LIFE [457B-466D]

Socrates now moves to the question of family life among the guardians, which he has hinted will be completely communal in nature. If male and female guardians are working and living together, it is inevitable that there will be some degree of sexual intimacy among them. The danger of this is that sloppy interbreeding may occur (the best reproducing with those who are less desirable). The analogy that Socrates uses is that just as you wouldn't want your prize terrier reproducing with anything other then another excellent pure-bred, so too the leaders of the polis wouldn't want their best and brightest reproducing with inferior human beings (459a). The rulers of the society, therefore, will have to be diligent about arranging temporary marriages between equally suitable partners. To get everyone to go along with this, they will have to employ yet another lie: in this case, the rulers of the *polis* will tell the guardians that the selection of partners is done by lottery in order to prevent any kind of resentment from arising (459c-460a). In fact the elder Guardians will be conducting a eugenics program, husbanding the next generation of the elite guardian class.

The children who are the products of these unions will immediately be placed in a nursery and cared for by nurses. Parents, therefore, won't know who their own children are (460d). Incestuous inbreeding between close relatives will be avoided though the careful management and record-keeping of the rulers (461d-e) Children with defects and those that are products of unsanctioned unions will be left to die (460c, 461c). Plato's aim in devising the communal raising of children is to keep the city unified (462a-c). The greatest good, he maintains, is that which binds the city together and makes it one; the greatest evil is that which tears it apart. A city will be unified if its citizens feel pleasure and pain over the same things and when no one makes a distinction between what belongs to him and what belongs to others. Because they possess everything in common, there will be no dissension among the guardians, and they will better be able to keep the city together. Because they think of everyone as their brother/sister, father/mother there will no lawsuits or violence among them, nor will they be inclined to split off into factions (464d-465b).

One might find evidence here for Plato's alleged admiration of the Spartan constitution which would not have placed him in a good light during the post-Peloponnesian War restored Democracy. The Spartans never suffered a weakling neonate to live and the Spartan women were renown for their health, strength, vigor and subsequent beauty. They, unlike Athenian women, wore short dresses, exercised nude, rode horses and managed the town when the men were on the march. Plato could not however have admired the Spartans for their contempt for philosophers.

Socrates then readdresses the complaint of Adeimantus (419a) that the communal lifestyle of the guardians wouldn't seem to make them very happy (465c-466c). Even though the guardians will have to sacrifice a great deal for the good of the *polis*, Socrates is convinced that their lives will ultimately be much more satisfying than that of the craftsmen. In the first place, they won't be forced to engage in the vulgar business of supporting a household (465c), and they will have the satisfaction of knowing that, by their labors, they have preserved the good of the entire city (465e).

WAR AND PEACE [466D-471C]

Women will also share with men the task of waging warfare. So that children will gain experience in battle, they will be permitted to observe warfare—though every effort will be made to assure their security (467a-d). Soldiers who display cowardice on the battlefield will be eliminated from the ranks of the Guardians and demoted to a craftsman or farmer;

those wounded Guardians who are left alive in battle will be abandoned to the enemy. But those who demonstrate courage will be granted honors (468a-469b).

In 469b-471c Socrates discusses the standards that will be adopted in warfare. Citizens of other Greek city-states will be treated as potential friends; while non-Greeks (barbarians) will be treated as strangers and potential enemies. (This would be in contrast to the Spartans who notoriously enslaved the Greek-speaking Messeneans). Plato here is trying to broaden his conception of justice to extend beyond the walls of the individual city. Because he views all Greeks as being "related" to one another, some common practices in warfare would not apply to them (e.g., taking slaves, ravaging their lands, etc.), and warfare between Greek cities would be viewed more as a kind of discord between friends.

SUGGESTIONS FOR FURTHER READING

Annas, Julia. *An Introduction to Plato's Republic.* New York: Oxford UP, 1981. [170-189]

—. "Plato's Republic and Feminism." Philosophy 51 (1976): 307-321.

Benardete, Seth. *Socrates' Second Sailing: On Plato's* Republic. Chicago: University of Chicago Press, 1989. [109-123]

Bloom, Allan. *The Republic of Plato.* New York: Harper Collins, 1968. [379-389]

Bluestone, Natalie Harris. "Why Women Cannot Rule: Sexism in Plato's Scholarship." *Feminist Interpretations of Plato.* Ed. Nancy Tuana. University Park, PA: Pennsylvania State University Press, 1994. [109-130]

Pappas, Nickolas. *Plato and the Republic.* New York: Routledge, 1995. [99-110]

Rosen, Stanley. *Plato's Republic: A Study.* New Haven: Yale University Press, 2005. [171-197]

Saxonhouse, Arlene W. "The Philosopher and the Female in the Political Thought of Plato." *Feminist Interpretations of Plato.* Ed. Nancy Tuana. University Park, PA: Pennsylvania State University Press, 1994. [67-85]

Sayers, Sean. *Plato's Republic: An Introduction.* Edinburgh: Edinburgh University Press, 1999. [82-92]

Vlastos, Gregory. "Was Plato a Feminist?" *Plato's Republic: Critical Essays.* Ed. Richard Kraut. Lanham, MD: Rowman and Littlefield, 1997. [115-128]

White, Nicholas P. *A Companion to Plato's Republic.* Indianapolis: Hackett, 1979. [139-150]

REPUBLIC 5.449A-471C

BOOK V

INTRODUCTION [449A-450C]

Such is the good and true City or State, and the good and true man is   449
of the same pattern; and if this is right every other is wrong; and the
evil is one which affects not only the ordering of the State, but also
the regulation of the individual soul, and is exhibited in four forms.

What are they? he said.

I was proceeding to tell the order in which the four evil forms
appeared to me to succeed one another, when Polemarchus, who   b
was sitting a little way off, just beyond Adeimantus, began to
whisper to him: stretching forth his hand, he took hold of the upper
part of his coat by the shoulder, and drew him towards him, leaning
forward himself so as to be quite close and saying something in his
ear, of which I only caught the words, 'Shall we let him off, or what
shall we do?'

Certainly not, said Adeimantus, raising his voice.

Who is it, I said, whom you are refusing to let off?   c

You, he said.

I repeated, Why am I especially not to be let off?

Why, he said, we think that you are lazy, and mean to cheat us
out of a whole chapter which is a very important part of the story;
and you fancy that we shall not notice your airy way of proceeding;
as if it were self-evident to everybody, that in the matter of women
and children 'friends have all things in common.'

And was I not right, Adeimantus?

Yes, he said; but what is right in this particular case, like everything
else, requires to be explained; for community may be of many kinds.
Please, therefore, to say what sort of community you mean. We have
been long expecting that you would tell us something about the   d
family life of your citizens—how they will bring children into the
world, and rear them when they have arrived, and, in general, what
is the nature of this community of women and children—for we are
of opinion that the right or wrong management of such matters will
have a great and paramount influence on the State for good or for
evil. And now, since the question is still undetermined, and you are
taking in hand another State, we have resolved, as you heard, not to   450
let you go until you give an account of all this.

To that resolution, said Glaucon, you may regard me as saying Agreed.

And without more ado, said Thrasymachus, you may consider us all to be equally agreed.

I said, You know not what you are doing in thus assailing me: What an argument are you raising about the State! Just as I thought that I had finished, and was only too glad that I had laid this question to sleep, and was reflecting how fortunate I was in your acceptance of what I then said, you ask me to begin again at the very foundation, ignorant of what a hornet's nest of words you are stirring. Now I foresaw this gathering trouble, and avoided it.

For what purpose do you conceive that we have come here, said Thrasymachus,—to look for gold, or to hear discourse?

Yes, but discourse should have a limit.

THE EQUALITY OF WOMEN [450C-457B]

Yes, Socrates, said Glaucon, and the whole of life is the only limit which wise men assign to the hearing of such discourses. But never mind about us; take heart yourself and answer the question in your own way: What sort of community of women and children is this which is to prevail among our guardians? and how shall we manage the period between birth and education, which seems to require the greatest care? Tell us how these things will be.

Yes, my simple friend, but the answer is the reverse of easy; many more doubts arise about this than about our previous conclusions. For the practicability of what is said may be doubted; and looked at in another point of view, whether the scheme, if ever so practicable, would be for the best, is also doubtful. Hence I feel a reluctance to approach the subject, lest our aspiration, my dear friend, should turn out to be a dream only.

Fear not, he replied, for your audience will not be hard upon you; they are not sceptical or hostile.

I said: My good friend, I suppose that you mean to encourage me by these words.

Yes, he said.

Then let me tell you that you are doing just the reverse; the encouragement which you offer would have been all very well had I myself believed that I knew what I was talking about: to declare the truth about matters of high interest which a man honours and loves among wise men who love him need occasion no fear or faltering in his mind; but to carry on an argument when you are yourself only a hesitating enquirer, which is my condition, is a dangerous and slippery thing; and the danger is not that I shall be laughed at (of which the fear would be childish), but that I shall miss the truth where I have most need to be sure of my footing, and drag my friends after me in my fall. And I pray Nemesis not to visit upon me the words which I am going to utter. For I do indeed believe that to be an involuntary homicide is a less crime than to be a deceiver about beauty or goodness or justice in the matter of laws. And that is a risk which I would rather run among enemies than among friends, and therefore you do well to encourage me.   b

Glaucon laughed and said: Well then, Socrates, in case you and your argument do us any serious injury you shall be acquitted beforehand of the homicide, and shall not be held to be a deceiver; take courage then and speak.

Well, I said, the law says that when a man is acquitted he is free from guilt, and what holds at law may hold in argument.

Then why should you mind?

Well, I replied, I suppose that I must retrace my steps and say what I perhaps ought to have said before in the proper place. The   c
part of the men has been played out, and now properly enough comes the turn of the women. Of them I will proceed to speak, and the more readily since I am invited by you.

For men born and educated like our citizens, the only way, in my opinion, of arriving at a right conclusion about the possession and use of women and children is to follow the path on which we originally started, when we said that the men were to be the guardians and watchdogs of the herd.

True.

Let us further suppose the birth and education of our women to   d
be subject to similar or nearly similar regulations; then we shall see whether the result accords with our design.

What do you mean?

What I mean may be put into the form of a question, I said: Are dogs divided into hes and shes, or do they both share equally in hunting and in keeping watch and in the other duties of dogs? or do we entrust to the males the entire and exclusive care of the flocks, while we leave the females at home, under the idea that the bearing and suckling their puppies is labour enough for them?

No, he said, they share alike; the only difference between them   e
is that the males are stronger and the females weaker.

But can you use different animals for the same purpose, unless they are bred and fed in the same way?

You cannot.

Then, if women are to have the same duties as men, they must have the same nurture and education?

Yes.   452

The education which was assigned to the men was music and gymnastic.

Yes.

Then women must be taught music and gymnastic and also the

art of war, which they must practise like the men?

That is the inference, I suppose.

I should rather expect, I said, that several of our proposals, if they are carried out, being unusual, may appear ridiculous.

No doubt of it.

Yes, and the most ridiculous thing of all will be the sight of women naked in the palaestra, exercising with the men, especially when they are no longer young; they certainly will not be a vision of beauty, any more than the enthusiastic old men who in spite of wrinkles and ugliness continue to frequent the gymnasia.

Yes, indeed, he said: according to present notions the proposal would be thought ridiculous.

But then, I said, as we have determined to speak our minds, we must not fear the jests of the wits which will be directed against this sort of innovation; how they will talk of women's attainments both in music and gymnastic, and above all about their wearing armour and riding upon horseback!

Very true, he replied.

Yet having begun we must go forward to the rough places of the law; at the same time begging of these gentlemen for once in their life to be serious. Not long ago, as we shall remind them, the Hellenes were of the opinion, which is still generally received among the barbarians, that the sight of a naked man was ridiculous and improper; and when first the Cretans and then the Lacedaemonians introduced the custom, the wits of that day might equally have ridiculed the innovation.

No doubt.

But when experience showed that to let all things be uncovered was far better than to cover them up, and the ludicrous effect to the outward eye vanished before the better principle which reason asserted, then the man was perceived to be a fool who directs the shafts of his ridicule at any other sight but that of folly and vice, or seriously inclines to weigh the beautiful by any other standard but that of the good.

Very true, he replied.

First, then, whether the question is to be put in jest or in earnest, let us come to an understanding about the nature of woman: Is she capable of sharing either wholly or partially in the actions of men, or not at all? And is the art of war one of those arts in which she can or can not share? That will be the best way of commencing the enquiry, and will probably lead to the fairest conclusion.

That will be much the best way.

Shall we take the other side first and begin by arguing against ourselves; in this manner the adversary's position will not be undefended.

Why not? he said.

Then let us put a speech into the mouths of our opponents. They will say: 'Socrates and Glaucon, no adversary need convict you, for you yourselves, at the first foundation of the State, admitted the principle that everybody was to do the one work suited to his own nature.' And certainly, if I am not mistaken, such an admission was made by us. 'And do not the natures of men and women differ very much indeed?' And we shall reply: Of course they do. Then we shall be asked, 'Whether the tasks assigned to men and to women should not be different, and such as are agreeable to their different natures?' Certainly they should. 'But if so, have you not fallen into a serious inconsistency in saying that men and women, whose natures are so entirely different, ought to perform the same actions?'—What defence will you make for us, my good Sir, against any one who offers these objections?

That is not an easy question to answer when asked suddenly; and I shall and I do beg of you to draw out the case on our side.

These are the objections, Glaucon, and there are many others of a like kind, which I foresaw long ago; they made me afraid and reluctant to take in hand any law about the possession and nurture of women and children.

By Zeus, he said, the problem to be solved is anything but easy.

Why yes, I said, but the fact is that when a man is out of his depth, whether he has fallen into a little swimming bath or into mid ocean, he has to swim all the same.

Very true.

And must not we swim and try to reach the shore: we will hope that Arion's dolphin or some other miraculous help may save us?

I suppose so, he said.

Well then, let us see if any way of escape can be found. We acknowledged—did we not? that different natures ought to have different pursuits, and that men's and women's natures are different. And now what are we saying?—that different natures ought to have the same pursuits,—this is the inconsistency which is charged upon us.

Precisely.

Verily, Glaucon, I said, glorious is the power of the art of contradiction!

Why do you say so?

Because I think that many a man falls into the practice against his will. When he thinks that he is reasoning he is really disputing, just because he cannot define and divide, and so know that of which he is speaking; and he will pursue a merely verbal opposition in the spirit of contention and not of fair discussion.

Yes, he replied, such is very often the case; but what has that to do with us and our argument?

A great deal; for there is certainly a danger of our getting unintentionally into a verbal opposition.

In what way?

Why we valiantly and pugnaciously insist upon the verbal truth, that different natures ought to have different pursuits, but we never considered at all what was the meaning of sameness or difference of nature, or why we distinguished them when we assigned different pursuits to different natures and the same to the same natures.

Why, no, he said, that was never considered by us.

c
I said: Suppose that by way of illustration we were to ask the question whether there is not an opposition in nature between bald men and hairy men; and if this is admitted by us, then, if bald men are cobblers, we should forbid the hairy men to be cobblers, and conversely?

That would be a jest, he said.

Yes, I said, a jest; and why? because we never meant when we constructed the State, that the opposition of natures should extend
d
to every difference, but only to those differences which affected the pursuit in which the individual is engaged; we should have argued, for example, that a physician and one who is in mind a physician may be said to have the same nature.

True.

Whereas the physician and the carpenter have different natures?

Certainly.

And if, I said, the male and female sex appear to differ in their fitness for any art or pursuit, we should say that such pursuit or art ought to be assigned to one or the other of them; but if the difference consists only in women bearing and men begetting children, this
e
does not amount to a proof that a woman differs from a man in respect of the sort of education she should receive; and we shall therefore continue to maintain that our guardians and their wives ought to have the same pursuits.

Very true, he said.

Next, we shall ask our opponent how, in reference to any of the
455
pursuits or arts of civic life, the nature of a woman differs from that of a man?

That will be quite fair.

And perhaps he, like yourself, will reply that to give a sufficient answer on the instant is not easy; but after a little reflection there is no difficulty.

Yes, perhaps.

Suppose then that we invite him to accompany us in the argument, and then we may hope to show him that there is nothing
b
peculiar in the constitution of women which would affect them in the administration of the State.

By all means.

Let us say to him: Come now, and we will ask you a question:—

when you spoke of a nature gifted or not gifted in any respect, did you mean to say that one man will acquire a thing easily, another with difficulty; a little learning will lead the one to discover a great deal; whereas the other, after much study and application, no sooner learns than he forgets; or again, did you mean, that the one has a body which is a good servant to his mind, while the body of the other is a hindrance to him?—would not these be the sort of differences which distinguish the man gifted by nature from the one who is ungifted?

c

No one will deny that.

And can you mention any pursuit of mankind in which the male sex has not all these gifts and qualities in a higher degree than the female? Need I waste time in speaking of the art of weaving, and the management of pancakes and preserves, in which womankind does really appear to be great, and in which for her to be beaten by a man is of all things the most absurd?

d

You are quite right, he replied, in maintaining the general inferiority of the female sex: although many women are in many things superior to many men, yet on the whole what you say is true.

And if so, my friend, I said, there is no special faculty of administration in a state which a woman has because she is a woman, or which a man has by virtue of his sex, but the gifts of nature are alike diffused in both; all the pursuits of men are the pursuits of women also, but in all of them a woman is inferior to a man.

e

Very true.

Then are we to impose all our enactments on men and none of them on women?

That will never do.

One woman has a gift of healing, another not; one is a musician, and another has no music in her nature?

456

Very true.

And one woman has a turn for gymnastic and military exercises, and another is unwarlike and hates gymnastics?

Certainly.

And one woman is a philosopher, and another is an enemy of philosophy; one has spirit, and another is without spirit?

That is also true.

Then one woman will have the temper of a guardian, and another not. Was not the selection of the male guardians determined by differences of this sort?

Yes.

Men and women alike possess the qualities which make a guardian; they differ only in their comparative strength or weakness.

Obviously.

And those women who have such qualities are to be selected as b   the companions and colleagues of men who have similar qualities and whom they resemble in capacity and in character?

Very true.

And ought not the same natures to have the same pursuits?

They ought.

Then, as we were saying before, there is nothing unnatural in assigning music and gymnastic to the wives of the guardians—to that point we come round again.

Certainly not.

The law which we then enacted was agreeable to nature, and therefore not an impossibility or mere aspiration; and the contrary

c   practice, which prevails at present, is in reality a violation of nature.

That appears to be true.

We had to consider, first, whether our proposals were possible, and secondly whether they were the most beneficial?

Yes.

And the possibility has been acknowledged?

Yes.

The very great benefit has next to be established?

Quite so.

You will admit that the same education which makes a man a good guardian will make a woman a good guardian; for their original nature is the same?

Yes.

d   I should like to ask you a question.

What is it?

Would you say that all men are equal in excellence, or is one man better than another?

The latter.

And in the commonwealth which we were founding do you conceive the guardians who have been brought up on our model system to be more perfect men, or the cobblers whose education has been cobbling?

What a ridiculous question!

You have answered me, I replied: Well, and may we not further say that our guardians are the best of our citizens?

By far the best.

e   And will not their wives be the best women?

Yes, by far the best.

And can there be anything better for the interests of the State than that the men and women of a State should be as good as possible?

There can be nothing better.

And this is what the arts of music and gymnastic, when present in such manner as we have described, will accomplish?

Certainly.

457   Then we have made an enactment not only possible but in the

highest degree beneficial to the State?

True.

Then let the wives of our guardians strip, for their virtue will be their robe, and let them share in the toils of war and the defence of their country; only in the distribution of labours the lighter are to be assigned to the women, who are the weaker natures, but in other respects their duties are to be the same. And as for the man who laughs at naked women exercising their bodies from the best of motives, in his laughter he is plucking

'A fruit of unripe wisdom,'   b

and he himself is ignorant of what he is laughing at, or what he is about;—for that is, and ever will be, the best of sayings, That the useful is the noble and the hurtful is the base.

Very true.

THE GUARDIAN'S FAMILY LIFE [457B-466D]

Here, then, is one difficulty in our law about women, which we may say that we have now escaped; the wave has not swallowed us up alive for enacting that the guardians of either sex should have all their pursuits in common; to the utility and also to the possibility of this arrangement the consistency of the argument with itself bears witness.   c

Yes, that was a mighty wave which you have escaped.

Yes, I said, but a greater is coming; you will not think much of this when you see the next.

Go on; let me see.

The law, I said, which is the sequel of this and of all that has preceded, is to the following effect,—'that the wives of our guardians are to be common, and their children are to be common, and no parent is to know his own child, nor any child his parent.'

Yes, he said, that is a much greater wave than the other; and   d
the possibility as well as the utility of such a law are far more questionable.

I do not think, I said, that there can be any dispute about the very great utility of having wives and children in common; the possibility is quite another matter, and will be very much disputed.

I think that a good many doubts may be raised about both.

You imply that the two questions must be combined, I replied. Now I meant that you should admit the utility; and in this way, as   e
I thought, I should escape from one of them, and then there would remain only the possibility.

But that little attempt is detected, and therefore you will please to give a defence of both.

Well, I said, I submit to my fate. Yet grant me a little favour: let me feast my mind with the dream as day dreamers are in the

habit of feasting themselves when they are walking alone; for before
458   they have discovered any means of effecting their wishes—that is
a matter which never troubles them—they would rather not tire
themselves by thinking about possibilities; but assuming that what
they desire is already granted to them, they proceed with their plan,
and delight in detailing what they mean to do when their wish has
come true—that is a way which they have of not doing much good
to a capacity which was never good for much. Now I myself am
beginning to lose heart, and I should like, with your permission, to
b   pass over the question of possibility at present. Assuming therefore
the possibility of the proposal, I shall now proceed to enquire how
the rulers will carry out these arrangements, and I shall demonstrate
that our plan, if executed, will be of the greatest benefit to the State
and to the guardians. First of all, then, if you have no objection,
I will endeavour with your help to consider the advantages of the
measure; and hereafter the question of possibility.

I have no objection; proceed.

First, I think that if our rulers and their auxiliaries are to be worthy
of the name which they bear, there must be willingness to obey in
the one and the power of command in the other; the guardians must
c   themselves obey the laws, and they must also imitate the spirit of
them in any details which are entrusted to their care.

That is right, he said.

You, I said, who are their legislator, having selected the men, will
now select the women and give them to them;—they must be as far
as possible of like natures with them; and they must live in common
houses and meet at common meals. None of them will have anything
specially his or her own; they will be together, and will be brought
up together, and will associate at gymnastic exercises. And so they
d   will be drawn by a necessity of their natures to have intercourse with
each other—necessity is not too strong a word, I think?

Yes, he said;—necessity, not geometrical, but another sort of
necessity which lovers know, and which is far more convincing and
constraining to the mass of mankind.

True, I said; and this, Glaucon, like all the rest, must proceed
after an orderly fashion; in a city of the blessed, licentiousness is an
unholy thing which the rulers will forbid.

Yes, he said, and it ought not to be permitted.

e   Then clearly the next thing will be to make matrimony sacred
in the highest degree, and what is most beneficial will be deemed
sacred?

Exactly.

And how can marriages be made most beneficial?—that is a
question which I put to you, because I see in your house dogs for
459   hunting, and of the nobler sort of birds not a few. Now, I beseech
you, do tell me, have you ever attended to their pairing and breeding?

In what particulars?

Why, in the first place, although they are all of a good sort, are not some better than others?

True.

And do you breed from them all indifferently, or do you take care to breed from the best only?

From the best.

And do you take the oldest or the youngest, or only those of ripe age?

I choose only those of ripe age.   b

And if care was not taken in the breeding, your dogs and birds would greatly deteriorate?

Certainly.

And the same of horses and animals in general?

Undoubtedly.

Good heavens! my dear friend, I said, what consummate skill will our rulers need if the same principle holds of the human species!

Certainly, the same principle holds; but why does this involve any particular skill?

Because, I said, our rulers will often have to practise upon the body corporate with medicines. Now you know that when patients   c
do not require medicines, but have only to be put under a regimen, the inferior sort of practitioner is deemed to be good enough; but when medicine has to be given, then the doctor should be more of a man.

That is quite true, he said; but to what are you alluding?

I mean, I replied, that our rulers will find a considerable dose of falsehood and deceit necessary for the good of their subjects: we were saying that the use of all these things regarded as medicines might be of advantage.

And we were very right.

And this lawful use of them seems likely to be often needed in   d
the regulations of marriages and births.

How so?

Why, I said, the principle has been already laid down that the best of either sex should be united with the best as often, and the inferior with the inferior, as seldom as possible; and that they should rear the offspring of the one sort of union, but not of the other, if the flock is to be maintained in first-rate condition. Now these goings on must be a secret which the rulers only know, or there will be a further danger of our herd, as the guardians may be termed, breaking out into rebellion.   e

Very true.

Had we not better appoint certain festivals at which we will bring together the brides and bridegrooms, and sacrifices will be offered and suitable hymeneal songs composed by our poets: the number of weddings is a matter which must be left to the discretion of the rulers, whose aim will be to preserve the average of population? 460 There are many other things which they will have to consider, such as the effects of wars and diseases and any similar agencies, in order as far as this is possible to prevent the State from becoming either too large or too small.

Certainly, he replied.

We shall have to invent some ingenious kind of lots which the less worthy may draw on each occasion of our bringing them together, and then they will accuse their own ill-luck and not the rulers.

To be sure, he said.

And I think that our braver and better youth, besides their other honours and rewards, might have greater facilities of intercourse b with women given them; their bravery will be a reason, and such fathers ought to have as many sons as possible.

True.

And the proper officers, whether male or female or both, for offices are to be held by women as well as by men—

Yes—

The proper officers will take the offspring of the good parents to the pen or fold, and there they will deposit them with certain nurses c who dwell in a separate quarter; but the offspring of the inferior, or of the better when they chance to be deformed, will be put away in some mysterious, unknown place, as they should be.

Yes, he said, that must be done if the breed of the guardians is to be kept pure.

They will provide for their nurture, and will bring the mothers to the fold when they are full of milk, taking the greatest possible care that no mother recognises her own child; and other wet-nurses d may be engaged if more are required. Care will also be taken that the process of suckling shall not be protracted too long; and the mothers will have no getting up at night or other trouble, but will hand over all this sort of thing to the nurses and attendants.

You suppose the wives of our guardians to have a fine easy time of it when they are having children.

Why, said I, and so they ought. Let us, however, proceed with our scheme. We were saying that the parents should be in the prime of life?

Very true.

And what is the prime of life? May it not be defined as a period of about twenty years in a woman's life, and thirty in a man's? e Which years do you mean to include?

A woman, I said, at twenty years of age may begin to bear children to the State, and continue to bear them until forty; a man may begin at five-and-twenty, when he has passed the point at which the pulse of life beats quickest, and continue to beget children until he be fifty-five.

Certainly, he said, both in men and women those years are the prime of physical as well as of intellectual vigour.

Any one above or below the prescribed ages who takes part   461
in the public hymeneals shall be said to have done an unholy and unrighteous thing; the child of which he is the father, if it steals into life, will have been conceived under auspices very unlike the sacrifices and prayers, which at each hymeneal priestesses and priest and the whole city will offer, that the new generation may be better and more useful than their good and useful parents, whereas his child will be the offspring of darkness and strange lust.

Very true, he replied.

And the same law will apply to any one of those within the   b
prescribed age who forms a connection with any woman in the prime of life without the sanction of the rulers; for we shall say that he is raising up a bastard to the State, uncertified and unconsecrated.

Very true, he replied.

This applies, however, only to those who are within the specified age: after that we allow them to range at will, except that a man may not marry his daughter or his daughter's daughter, or his mother or his mother's mother; and women, on the other hand, are prohibited from marrying their sons or fathers, or son's son or father's father, and so on in either direction. And we grant all this, accompanying   c
the permission with strict orders to prevent any embryo which may come into being from seeing the light; and if any force a way to the birth, the parents must understand that the offspring of such an union cannot be maintained, and arrange accordingly.

That also, he said, is a reasonable proposition. But how will they know who are fathers and daughters, and so on?

They will never know. The way will be this:—dating from the day of the hymeneal, the bridegroom who was then married will   d
call all the male children who are born in the seventh and tenth month afterwards his sons, and the female children his daughters, and they will call him father, and he will call their children his grandchildren, and they will call the elder generation grandfathers and grandmothers. All who were begotten at the time when their fathers and mothers came together will be called their brothers and sisters, and these, as I was saying, will be forbidden to inter-marry. This, however, is not to be understood as an absolute prohibition of the marriage of brothers and sisters; if the lot favours them, and they   e
receive the sanction of the Pythian oracle, the law will allow them.

Quite right, he replied.

Such is the scheme, Glaucon, according to which the guardians of our State are to have their wives and families in common. And now you would have the argument show that this community is consistent with the rest of our polity, and also that nothing can be better—would you not?

Yes, certainly.

462   Shall we try to find a common basis by asking of ourselves what ought to be the chief aim of the legislator in making laws and in the organization of a State,—what is the greatest good, and what is the greatest evil, and then consider whether our previous description has the stamp of the good or of the evil?

By all means.

Can there be any greater evil than discord and distraction and plurality where unity ought to reign? or any greater good than the bond of unity?

b   There cannot.

And there is unity where there is community of pleasures and pains—where all the citizens are glad or grieved on the same occasions of joy and sorrow?

No doubt.

Yes; and where there is no common but only private feeling a State is disorganized—when you have one half of the world triumphing and the other plunged in grief at the same events happening to the city or the citizens?

Certainly.

c   Such differences commonly originate in a disagreement about the use of the terms 'mine' and 'not mine,' 'his' and 'not his.'

Exactly so.

And is not that the best-ordered State in which the greatest number of persons apply the terms 'mine' and 'not mine' in the same way to the same thing?

Quite true.

Or that again which most nearly approaches to the condition of the individual—as in the body, when but a finger of one of us is hurt, the whole frame, drawn towards the soul as a centre and forming one kingdom under the ruling power therein, feels the hurt and sympathizes all together with the part affected, and we say that the man has a pain in his finger; and the same expression is used about any other part of the body, which has a sensation of pain at suffering or of pleasure at the alleviation of suffering.

d

Very true, he replied; and I agree with you that in the best-ordered State there is the nearest approach to this common feeling which you describe.

Then when any one of the citizens experiences any good or evil, the whole State will make his case their own, and will either rejoice or sorrow with him?

e   Yes, he said, that is what will happen in a well-ordered State.

It will now be time, I said, for us to return to our State and see whether this or some other form is most in accordance with these fundamental principles.

Very good.

Our State like every other has rulers and subjects?

True.

All of whom will call one another citizens?   463

Of course.

But is there not another name which people give to their rulers in other States?

Generally they call them masters, but in democratic States they simply call them rulers.

And in our State what other name besides that of citizens do the people give the rulers?

They are called saviours and helpers, he replied.

And what do the rulers call the people?

Their maintainers and foster-fathers.   b

And what do they call them in other States?

Slaves.

And what do the rulers call one another in other States?

Fellow-rulers.

And what in ours?

Fellow-guardians.

Did you ever know an example in any other State of a ruler who would speak of one of his colleagues as his friend and of another as not being his friend?

Yes, very often.

And the friend he regards and describes as one in whom he has an interest, and the other as a stranger in whom he has no interest?

Exactly.

But would any of your guardians think or speak of any other   c
guardian as a stranger?

Certainly he would not; for every one whom they meet will be regarded by them either as a brother or sister, or father or mother, or son or daughter, or as the child or parent of those who are thus connected with him.

Capital, I said; but let me ask you once more: Shall they be a family in name only; or shall they in all their actions be true to the name? For example, in the use of the word 'father,' would the care of a father be implied and the filial reverence and duty and obedience to him which the law commands; and is the violator of   d
these duties to be regarded as an impious and unrighteous person who is not likely to receive much good either at the hands of God or of man? Are these to be or not to be the strains which the children will hear repeated in their ears by all the citizens about those who are intimated to them to be their parents and the rest of their kinsfolk?

These, he said, and none other; for what can be more ridiculous than for them to utter the names of family ties with the lips only and not to act in the spirit of them?   e

Then in our city the language of harmony and concord will be more often heard than in any other. As I was describing before, when any one is well or ill, the universal word will be 'with me it is well' or 'it is ill.'

Most true.

And agreeably to this mode of thinking and speaking, were we not saying that they will have their pleasures and pains in common?

464   Yes, and so they will.

And they will have a common interest in the same thing which they will alike call 'my own,' and having this common interest they will have a common feeling of pleasure and pain?

Yes, far more so than in other States.

And the reason of this, over and above the general constitution of the State, will be that the guardians will have a community of women and children?

That will be the chief reason.

And this unity of feeling we admitted to be the greatest good, as was implied in our own comparison of a well-ordered State to the relation of the body and the members, when affected by pleasure

b   or pain?

That we acknowledged, and very rightly.

Then the community of wives and children among our citizens is clearly the source of the greatest good to the State?

Certainly.

And this agrees with the other principle which we were affirming,—that the guardians were not to have houses or lands or any other property; their pay was to be their food, which they were to receive from the other citizens, and they were to have no private expenses; for we intended them to preserve their true character of

c   guardians.

Right, he replied.

Both the community of property and the community of families, as I am saying, tend to make them more truly guardians; they will not tear the city in pieces by differing about 'mine' and 'not mine;' each man dragging any acquisition which he has made into a separate house of his own, where he has a separate wife and children and private pleasures and pains; but all will be affected as far as may be by the same pleasures and pains because they are all

d   of one opinion about what is near and dear to them, and therefore they all tend towards a common end.

Certainly, he replied.

And as they have nothing but their persons which they can call their own, suits and complaints will have no existence among them; they will be delivered from all those quarrels of which money or children or relations are the occasion.

Of course they will.

Neither will trials for assault or insult ever be likely to occur   e
among them. For that equals should defend themselves against
equals we shall maintain to be honourable and right; we shall make
the protection of the person a matter of necessity.

That is good, he said.

Yes; and there is a further good in the law; viz. that if a man has
a quarrel with another he will satisfy his resentment then and there,
and not proceed to more dangerous lengths.

Certainly.   465

To the elder shall be assigned the duty of ruling and chastising
the younger.

Clearly.

Nor can there be a doubt that the younger will not strike or do
any other violence to an elder, unless the magistrates command
him; nor will he slight him in any way. For there are two guardians,
shame and fear, mighty to prevent him: shame, which makes men
refrain from laying hands on those who are to them in the relation
of parents; fear, that the injured one will be succoured by the others
who are his brothers, sons, fathers.

That is true, he replied.   b

Then in every way the laws will help the citizens to keep the
peace with one another?

Yes, there will be no want of peace.

And as the guardians will never quarrel among themselves there
will be no danger of the rest of the city being divided either against
them or against one another.

None whatever.

I hardly like even to mention the little meannesses of which
they will be rid, for they are beneath notice: such, for example,
as the flattery of the rich by the poor, and all the pains and pangs
which men experience in bringing up a family, and in finding
money to buy necessaries for their household, borrowing and then   c
repudiating, getting how they can, and giving the money into the
hands of women and slaves to keep—the many evils of so many
kinds which people suffer in this way are mean enough and obvious
enough, and not worth speaking of.

Yes, he said, a man has no need of eyes in order to perceive that.

And from all these evils they will be delivered, and their life
will be blessed as the life of Olympic victors and yet more blessed.

How so?   d

The Olympic victor, I said, is deemed happy in receiving a part
only of the blessedness which is secured to our citizens, who have
won a more glorious victory and have a more complete maintenance
at the public cost. For the victory which they have won is the
salvation of the whole State; and the crown with which they and
their children are crowned is the fullness of all that life needs; they

receive rewards from the hands of their country while living, and after death have an honourable burial.

Yes, he said, and glorious rewards they are.

Do you remember, I said, how in the course of the previous discussion some one who shall be nameless accused us of making our guardians unhappy—they had nothing and might have possessed all things—to whom we replied that, if an occasion offered, we might perhaps hereafter consider this question, but that, as at present advised, we would make our guardians truly guardians, and that we were fashioning the State with a view to the greatest happiness, not of any particular class, but of the whole?

Yes, I remember.

And what do you say, now that the life of our protectors is made out to be far better and nobler than that of Olympic victors—is the life of shoemakers, or any other artisans, or of farmers, to be compared with it?

Certainly not.

At the same time I ought here to repeat what I have said elsewhere, that if any of our guardians shall try to be happy in such a manner that he will cease to be a guardian, and is not content with this safe and harmonious life, which, in our judgment, is of all lives the best, but infatuated by some youthful conceit of happiness which gets up into his head shall seek to appropriate the whole state to himself, then he will have to learn how wisely Hesiod spoke, when he said, 'half is more than the whole.'

If he were to consult me, I should say to him: Stay where you are, when you have the offer of such a life.

WAR AND PEACE [466D-471C]

You agree then, I said, that men and women are to have a common way of life such as we have described—common education, common children; and they are to watch over the citizens in common whether abiding in the city or going out to war; they are to keep watch together, and to hunt together like dogs; and always and in all things, as far as they are able, women are to share with the men? And in so doing they will do what is best, and will not violate, but preserve the natural relation of the sexes.

I agree with you, he replied.

The enquiry, I said, has yet to be made, whether such a community be found possible—as among other animals, so also among men—and if possible, in what way possible?

You have anticipated the question which I was about to suggest.

There is no difficulty, I said, in seeing how war will be carried on by them.

How?

Why, of course they will go on expeditions together; and will take with them any of their children who are strong enough, that, after the manner of the artisan's child, they may look on at the work which they will have to do when they are grown up; and besides looking on they will have to help and be of use in war, and to wait upon their fathers and mothers. Did you never observe in the arts how the potters' boys look on and help, long before they touch the wheel?

Yes, I have.   467

And shall potters be more careful in educating their children and in giving them the opportunity of seeing and practising their duties than our guardians will be?

The idea is ridiculous, he said.

There is also the effect on the parents, with whom, as with other animals, the presence of their young ones will be the greatest incentive to valor.

That is quite true, Socrates; and yet if they are defeated, which may often happen in war, how great the danger is! the children will be lost as well as their parents, and the State will never recover.

True, I said; but would you never allow them to run any risk?   b

I am far from saying that.

Well, but if they are ever to run a risk should they not do so on some occasion when, if they escape disaster, they will be the better for it?

Clearly.

Whether the future soldiers do or do not see war in the days of their youth is a very important matter, for the sake of which some risk may fairly be incurred.

Yes, very important.

This then must be our first step,—to make our children spectators   c
of war; but we must also contrive that they shall be secured against danger; then all will be well.

True.

Their parents may be supposed not to be blind to the risks of war, but to know, as far as human foresight can, what expeditions are safe and what dangerous?

That may be assumed.

And they will take them on the safe expeditions and be cautious about the dangerous ones?   d

True.

And they will place them under the command of experienced veterans who will be their leaders and teachers?

Very properly.

Still, the dangers of war cannot be always foreseen; there is a good deal of chance about them?

True.

Then against such chances the children must be at once furnished
with wings, in order that in the hour of need they may fly away and
escape.

What do you mean? he said.

I mean that we must mount them on horses in their earliest
youth, and when they have learnt to ride, take them on horseback to
see war: the horses must not be spirited and warlike, but the most
tractable and yet the swiftest that can be had. In this way they will
get an excellent view of what is hereafter to be their own business;
and if there is danger they have only to follow their elder leaders
and escape.

I believe that you are right, he said.

Next, as to war; what are to be the relations of your soldiers to
one another and to their enemies? I should be inclined to propose
that the soldier who leaves his rank or throws away his arms, or is
guilty of any other act of cowardice, should be degraded into the
rank of a farmer or artisan. What do you think?

By all means, I should say.

And he who allows himself to be taken prisoner may as well be
made a present of to his enemies; he is their lawful prey, and let
them do what they like with him.

Certainly.

But the hero who has distinguished himself, what shall be done
to him? In the first place, he shall receive honour in the army from
his youthful comrades; every one of them in succession shall crown
him. What do you say?

I approve.

And what do you say to his receiving the right hand of fellowship?

To that too, I agree.

But you will hardly agree to my next proposal.

What is your proposal?

That he should kiss and be kissed by them.

Most certainly, and I should be disposed to go further, and say:
Let no one whom he has a mind to kiss refuse to be kissed by him
while the expedition lasts. So that if there be a lover in the army,
whether his love be youth or maiden, he may be more eager to win
the prize of valour.

Capital, I said. That the brave man is to have more wives than
others has been already determined: and he is to have first choices
in such matters more than others, in order that he may have as many
children as possible?

Agreed.

Again, there is another manner in which, according to Homer,
brave youths should be honoured; for he tells how Ajax, after he
had distinguished himself in battle, was rewarded with long chines,
which seems to be a compliment appropriate to a hero in the

flower of his age, being not only a tribute of honour but also a very strengthening thing.

Most true, he said.

Then in this, I said, Homer shall be our teacher; and we too, at sacrifices and on the like occasions, will honour the brave according to the measure of their valour, whether men or women, with hymns and those other distinctions which we were mentioning; also with

'seats of precedence, and meats and full cups;'

and in honouring them, we shall be at the same time training them.

That, he replied, is excellent.

Yes, I said; and when a man dies gloriously in war shall we not say, in the first place, that he is of the golden race?

To be sure.

Nay, have we not the authority of Hesiod for affirming that when they are dead

'They are holy angels upon the earth, authors of good, averters of evil, the guardians of speech-gifted men'?

Yes; and we accept his authority.

We must learn of the god how we are to order the burial of divine and heroic personages, and what is to be their special distinction; and we must do as he bids?

By all means.

And in ages to come we will reverence them and kneel before their sepulchres as at the graves of heroes. And not only they but any who are deemed pre-eminently good, whether they die from age, or in any other way, shall be admitted to the same honours.

That is very right, he said.

Next, how shall our soldiers treat their enemies? What about this?

In what respect do you mean?

First of all, in regard to slavery? Do you think it right that Hellenes should enslave Hellenic States, or allow others to enslave them, if they can help? Should not their custom be to spare them, considering the danger which there is that the whole race may one day fall under the yoke of the barbarians?

To spare them is infinitely better.

Then no Hellene should be owned by them as a slave; that is a rule which they will observe and advise the other Hellenes to observe.

Certainly, he said; they will in this way be united against the barbarians and will keep their hands off one another.

Next as to the slain; ought the conquerors, I said, to take anything but their armour? Does not the practice of despoiling an enemy afford an excuse for not facing the battle? Cowards skulk about the dead, pretending that they are fulfilling a duty, and many an army before now has been lost from this love of plunder.

Very true.

d   And is there not illiberality and avarice in robbing a corpse, and also a degree of meanness and womanishness in making an enemy of the dead body when the real enemy has flown away and left only his fighting gear behind him,—is not this rather like a dog who cannot get at his assailant, quarrelling with the stones which strike him instead?

Very like a dog, he said.

Then we must abstain from robbing the dead or hindering their burial?

e   Yes, he replied, we most certainly must.

Neither shall we offer up arms at the temples of the gods, least of all the arms of Hellenes, if we care to maintain good feeling with other Hellenes; and, indeed, we have reason to fear that the offering of spoils taken from kinsmen may be a pollution unless commanded by the god himself?

Very true.

Again, as to the devastation of Hellenic territory or the burning
470   of houses, what is to be the practice?

May I have the pleasure, he said, of hearing your opinion?

Both should be forbidden, in my judgment; I would take the annual produce and no more. Shall I tell you why?

Pray do.

Why, you see, there is a difference in the names 'discord' and 'war,' and I imagine that there is also a difference in their natures; the one is expressive of what is internal and domestic, the other
b   of what is external and foreign; and the first of the two is termed discord, and only the second, war.

That is a very proper distinction, he replied.

And may I not observe with equal propriety that the Hellenic race is all united together by ties of blood and friendship, and alien and strange to the barbarians?

Very good, he said.

And therefore when Hellenes fight with barbarians and barbarians
c   with Hellenes, they will be described by us as being at war when they fight, and by nature enemies, and this kind of antagonism should be called war; but when Hellenes fight with one another we shall say that Hellas is then in a state of disorder and discord, they being by nature friends; and such enmity is to be called discord.

I agree.

Consider then, I said, when that which we have acknowledged to be discord occurs, and a city is divided, if both parties destroy the lands and burn the houses of one another, how wicked does the

strife appear! No true lover of his country would bring himself to
tear in pieces his own nurse and mother: There might be reason in
the conqueror depriving the conquered of their harvest, but still they
would have the idea of peace in their hearts and would not mean to
go on fighting for ever.

Yes, he said, that is a better temper than the other.

And will not the city, which you are founding, be an Hellenic
city?

It ought to be, he replied.

Then will not the citizens be good and civilized?

Yes, very civilized.

And will they not be lovers of Hellas, and think of Hellas as their
own land, and share in the common temples?

Most certainly.

And any difference which arises among them will be regarded
by them as discord only—a quarrel among friends, which is not to
be called a war?

Certainly not.

Then they will quarrel as those who intend some day to be
reconciled?

Certainly.

They will use friendly correction, but will not enslave or destroy
their opponents; they will be correctors, not enemies?

Just so.

And as they are Hellenes themselves they will not devastate
Hellas, nor will they burn houses, nor ever suppose that the whole
population of a city—men, women, and children—are equally their
enemies, for they know that the guilt of war is always confined to
a few persons and that the many are their friends. And for all these
reasons they will be unwilling to waste their lands and raze their
houses; their enmity to them will only last until the many innocent
sufferers have compelled the guilty few to give satisfaction?

I agree, he said, that our citizens should thus deal with their
Hellenic enemies; and with barbarians as the Hellenes now deal
with one another.

Then let us enact this law also for our guardians:—that they are
neither to devastate the lands of Hellenes nor to burn their houses.

Agreed; and we may agree also in thinking that these, like all our
previous enactments, are very good.

9

THE PHILOSOPHER KINGS

PHILOSOPHERS AS KINGS [471C-474B]

Socrates has demonstrated that a just city such as the one he has described is possible *in theory*. The question remains, however, as to whether it is possible *in reality* as well. His answer is that it would be possible only if philosophers were allowed to rule, or if rulers become philosophers (473d). This surprising observation would probably have been as dubious to the average Greek as it is for contemporary readers. In order to defend his position, Socrates needs to clearly define what he means by a philosopher, why the philosopher is better suited to rule than others, and what sort of training he/she would need. This discussion would continue through the end of Book VII, and in some ways represents the heart of the *Republic*.

DEFINITION OF THE PHILOSOPHER [474A-480A]

It should be pointed out that Plato has a very specific idea of what a philosopher is. He begins his attempt to define the philosopher in the following way (474c-475c): A lover of X loves not just a certain kind of X, but all X; e.g., a lover of food loves all food, a lover of wine loves all wine. Philosophers are lovers of wisdom. Therefore the Philosopher is that person who loves all wisdom and learning, not just wisdom and learning of a certain kind.

Glaucon objects (475d-e) that according to Socrates' definition, lovers of sights and sounds (e.g., those who love festivals and spectacles) would be considered philosophers. "Glaucon here makes a somewhat complex mistake which Socrates then endeavors to combat. Part of his mistake is to take the term 'philosopher' in Plato's sense as including people with various specialized enthusiasms, such as those who ignore "serious discussions" in order to attend festivals. The other part of his mistake, which is much more important from Plato's viewpoint, is to think that the love of wisdom or learning or knowledge involves the love of information and experience of *sensible* matters rather than the intelligible ones..." (White 154-155).

The philosopher, responds Socrates, is a lover of true knowledge (475e-476d). The love of true knowledge is related to an understanding of the "forms." This is what makes a philosopher fit to rule. In response to Glaucon's objection, Socrates argues that those who love sights and sounds (476d-480a) are not philosophers (lovers of wisdom and knowledge), but are lovers of opinion.

PHILOSOPHER	NON-PHILOSOPHER
LOVES KNOWLEDGE (*Gnosis*) • infallible • concerned with "what is" • Being	LOVES OPINION (*Doxa*) • fallible • between knowledge and ignorance • between Being and Non-Being
OBJECT = FORMS • eternal and unchanging i.e., "The Beautiful"	OBJECT = The SENSIBLE • temporal and changing i.e., "a beautiful woman"
Fit to Rule	Unfit to Rule

This section represents the beginning of the heavy metaphysical portion of the *Republic*. Although Plato throws out these metaphysical concepts without much warning or support, what we have here is a general outline of his theory. Later in Book VI we will be given a more thorough treatment of the ideas that he throws out here.

THE PHILOSOPHER'S FITNESS TO RULE [484A-487A]

Book VI opens with the question, why should philosophers become the Guardian Rulers of the City? Philosophers (only) apprehend the permanent and one, whereas non-philosophers are acquainted (only) with the changing and many. Only those who can conserve the laws and practices of the City should be its guardians. Philosophers seek what is true of being—the real—and what is real is the permanent, the unchanging—that which is not susceptible to generation and decay. Philosophers love truth and hate falsehood. Since only the philosopher understands what is fine and good in the laws and practices of the City, only the philosophers should rule.

As a lover of one thing, all other desires for other things are weakened;

so too the philosopher's love for truth (wisdom) is such that other desires such as the desires for fame and glory or the desire for pleasure or wealth are weakened in him or her. A guardian should be moderate (like philosophers) so that the ruler will protect the wealth of the citizens and not covet it. The philosophic quest to apprehend the whole of the universe places individual life in cosmic perspective and death becomes insignificant to such a one (This allows us to "take hardships philosophically"). Cowards who have an inordinate fear of death are not attracted to philosophy. Philosophers, loving wisdom, courage, and moderation, are likely to be just. They learn quickly and have good memories. They are musical and harmonious. Moreover, they are led to the *idea* of each thing. Thus philosophers should rule.

OBJECTIONS TO THE NATURE OF THE PHILOSOPHER [487B-497A]

Adeimantus objects: those who are inexperienced in the art of dialogue feel that philosophers take advantage of them. When the opposite of what they initially believed is proven true by the argument, they feel like the victims of a hustler. Those who make philosophy a career turn out most eccentric and vicious, and others who are more benign end up useless to the city.

Socrates defends the philosopher with an analogy between the philosopher and a ship pilot: a certain myopic and slightly deaf ship owner is seeking a pilot for his ship. Sailors who have no understanding of the use of transept and stargazing to navigate the ship vie with the true pilot for the position. Since they do not see the importance of knowledge of astronomy and mathematics to the rule of the ship, they quarrel with one another and contrive to take over the ship. They either force, persuade or entice the owner to give them the rudder. Giving the name of "captain" and "ruler" to the one skilled in taking command, they careen off in all directions, making the one skilled in piloting useless.

The philosopher is useless in the City, not because he or she is incompetent to rule, but because those in power are so ignorant and blind as to fail to call upon the skills of the philosopher. After accounting for the charge that philosophers are useless to the City, Socrates defends them against the charge of eccentricity and viciousness (498e-493e).

The true philosopher is a lover of wisdom. Plato identifies a specific desire (*eros*) or love proper to the psyche's faculty of reason: analogous to sexual attraction or ambition for fame or glory, those characterized by the love of wisdom relentlessly pursue the truth, reject all craven rivals, adore it, commingle with it, wed it and give birth to more truth and intelligence.

Once committed, the philosopher will hate the rivals and opposers of truth, namely falsifiers. Again such a character is courageous, moderate, magnificent, intelligent, and endowed with a good memory.

So why do the many view philosophers to be so odd and so vicious? Here we find the Platonic notion that virtue is nourished in a Just and Virtuous State; but in a vicious state, every temptation contrives to corrupt and undermine the human propensity for moral excellence. In Dante's *Inferno*, the most vicious sin is the treacherous deception or betrayal of the finest natures. In Shakespeare's *The Tragedy of Othello*, the hero is incited to murder his faithful Desdemona through the vile and lying slander of Iago. Here Socrates claims that only those natures capable of magnanimous deeds for the city are capable, once corrupted, of the greatest treason. Here perhaps he is thinking of the notorious Alcibiades who was once a student of Socrates but betrayed Athens to the Spartans during the Peloponnesian Wars.

Any city other than the ideal city they are inventing is hostile to the philosophic nature, because only the ideal city is devoted to the ultimate Good, that is, to the flourishing human character in harmonious accord with the truth and a transcendent or spiritual Good (see ahead 505a). Living as he is in the restored democracy, Plato finds the values promoted by the mass of citizens to be lacking, namely the value of material pleasures and wealth and the value of military fame and glory (See *Funeral Oration* of Pericles).

Socrates puts the lion's share of blame for the corruption of the philosophic nature on the conventions and prejudices of majority opinions which are reinforced in the hearts of young people in every forum or assembly, and in every popular media. Censure, fines, punishment and the executioner enforce what is not achieved by rhetorical persuasion. (Michel Foucault recently restated the instantiation of political repression in our language, conventions, laws and modes of criminal justice. He would not, however, have thought that Plato's *Republic* or *The Laws* represent an advance in human liberation, just a replacement of one form of repression for another). Peer pressure and State coercion contrive to corrupt the philosophic nature far more than the teachings of the sophists. Sophists only teach the conventional convictions of the masses (In effect, Plato claims that the sophists found a lucrative business in reinforcing popular opinion ascertained by public opinion polls. No one ever lost money pandering to popular sentiment).

The masses will have a hard time accepting that the feature itself of things, for example, goodness itself, has being (is real), whereas the many particular aspects of particular things, for example, the specific good of a painting, the specific good of a wine, the specific good of a play, do not really exist, or, at best, exist only ephemerally, briefly, fleetingly, hovering between existence and non-existence. Thus, because of this popular skepticism about the exclusive reality of the Forms, "it's impossible for the multitude to be philosophic."

Someone with the philosophical nature who is good-looking as well is likely to gather adulators and flatterers. Filled with pretensions and conceits, such a golden one is likely to think that education should come easily. If such a one wants to adopt the philosophic life, those who enjoy her companionship will try to undermine the person's resolve. When those of true philosophical nature leave the field, pretenders and social climbers take over (replacing philosophy with rhetoric), and besmirch the good name of philosophers. So those with a truly philosophic nature, who accept the arduous education and who remain uncorrupted by the envious, wicked or narrow-minded conformists are rare indeed.

It is intriguing that Plato believes that the philosophic temperament is especially susceptible to corruption. It is noteworthy that Plato is willing to trust them with absolute power as Rulers of the City. The notion that the best of men are still susceptible to corruption is basic to the theory of popular or majority sovereignty and it also led Montesquieu and others to the view that the powers of government—executive, legislative and judiciary—ought to be separated and a balance of powers be maintained between the various branches of government.

ON THE POSSIBILITY OF PHILOSOPHIC RULE [496A-502C]

It is only the regime of the ideal state outlined previously that will (through the carefully regulated educational process) allow the philosophical nature to reach fruition. If the character of the true philosopher can be made manifest to the common people as distinct from those panderers and vicious pretenders, then it is not impossible for philosophers to be accepted as rulers.

SUGGESTIONS FOR FURTHER READING

Annas, Julia. *An Introduction to Plato's Republic.* New York: Oxford UP, 1981. [190-216]

Benardete, Seth. *Socrates' Second Sailing: On Plato's* Republic. Chicago: University of Chicago Press, 1989. [123-153]

Bloom, Allan. *The Republic of Plato.* New York: Harper Collins, 1968. [398-401]

Irwin, Terence. *Plato's Ethics.* New York: Oxford University Press, 1995. [262-271]

Pappas, Nickolas. *Plato and the Republic.* New York: Routledge, 1995. [110-116]

Rosen, Stanley. *Plato's Republic: A Study.* New Haven: Yale University Press, 2005. [201-254]

Sayers, Sean. *Plato's Republic: An Introduction.* Edinburgh: Edinburgh University Press, 1999. [93-105]

Sallis, John. *Being and Logos: Reading the Platonic Dialogues.* Bloomington: Indiana University Press, 1996. [377-401]

White, Nicholas P. *A Companion to Plato's Republic.* Indianapolis: Hackett, 1979. [150-173]

REPUBLIC 5.471C-502C

PHILOSOPHERS MUST BE KINGS [471C-474B]

But still I must say, Socrates, that if you are allowed to go on in this way you will entirely forget the other question which at the commencement of this discussion you thrust aside:—Is such an order of things possible, and how, if at all? For I am quite ready to acknowledge that the plan which you propose, if only feasible, would do all sorts of good to the State. I will add, what you have omitted, that your citizens will be the bravest of warriors, and will never leave their ranks, for they will all know one another, and each will call the other father, brother, son; and if you suppose the women to join their armies, whether in the same rank or in the rear, either as a terror to the enemy, or as auxiliaries in case of need, I know that they will then be absolutely invincible; and there are many domestic advantages which might also be mentioned and which I also fully acknowledge: but, as I admit all these advantages and as many more as you please, if only this State of yours were to come into existence, we need say no more about them; assuming then the existence of the State, let us now turn to the question of possibility and ways and means—the rest may be left.

If I loiter for a moment, you instantly make a raid upon me, I said, and have no mercy; I have hardly escaped the first and second waves, and you seem not to be aware that you are now bringing upon me the third, which is the greatest and heaviest. When you have seen and heard the third wave, I think you will be more considerate and will acknowledge that some fear and hesitation was natural respecting a proposal so extraordinary as that which I have now to state and investigate.

The more appeals of this sort which you make, he said, the more determined are we that you shall tell us how such a State is possible: speak out and at once.

Let me begin by reminding you that we found our way here in the search after justice and injustice.

True, he replied; but what of that?

I was only going to ask whether, if we have discovered them, we are to require that the just man should in nothing fail of absolute justice; or may we be satisfied with an approximation, and the attainment in him of a higher degree of justice than is to be found in other men?

The approximation will be enough.

We were enquiring into the nature of absolute justice and into the character of the perfectly just, and into injustice and the perfectly unjust, that we might have an ideal. We were to look at these in order that we might judge of our own happiness and unhappiness according to the standard which they exhibited and the degree in which we resembled them, but not with any view of showing that they could exist in fact.

True, he said.

Would a painter be any the worse because, after having delineated with consummate art an ideal of a perfectly beautiful man, he was unable to show that any such man could ever have existed?

He would be none the worse.

Well, and were we not creating an ideal of a perfect State?

To be sure.

And is our theory a worse theory because we are unable to prove the possibility of a city being ordered in the manner described?

Surely not, he replied.

That is the truth, I said. But if, at your request, I am to try and show how and under what conditions the possibility is highest, I must ask you, having this in view, to repeat your former admissions.

What admissions?

I want to know whether ideals are ever fully realized in language? Does not the word express more than the fact, and must not the actual, whatever a man may think, always, in the nature of things, fall short of the truth? What do you say?

I agree.

Then you must not insist on my proving that the actual State will in every respect coincide with the ideal: if we are only able to discover how a city may be governed nearly as we proposed, you will admit that we have discovered the possibility which you demand; and will be contented. I am sure that I should be contented—will not you?

Yes, I will.

Let me next endeavour to show what is that fault in States which is the cause of their present maladministration, and what is the least change which will enable a State to pass into the truer form; and let the change, if possible, be of one thing only, or, if not, of two; at any rate, let the changes be as few and slight as possible.

Certainly, he replied.

I think, I said, that there might be a reform of the State if only one change were made, which is not a slight or easy though still a possible one.

What is it? he said.

Now then, I said, I go to meet that which I liken to the greatest of the waves; yet shall the word be spoken, even though the wave break and drown me in laughter and dishonour; and do you mark my words.

Proceed.

I said: 'Until philosophers are kings, or the kings and princes of this world have the spirit and power of philosophy, and political greatness and wisdom meet in one, and those commoner natures who pursue either to the exclusion of the other are compelled to stand aside, cities will never have rest from their evils,—nor the human race, as I believe,—and then only will this our State have a possibility of life and behold the light of day.' Such was the thought, my dear Glaucon, which I would have gladly uttered if it had not seemed too extravagant; for to be convinced that in no other State can there be happiness private or public is indeed a hard thing.

DEFINTION OF THE PHILOSOPHER [474A-480A]

Socrates, what do you mean? I would have you consider that the word which you have uttered is one at which numerous persons, and very respectable persons too, in a figure pulling off their coats all in a moment, and seizing any weapon that comes to hand, will run at you might and main, before you know where you are, intending to do heaven knows what; and if you don't prepare an answer, and put yourself in motion, you will be 'cut down by their fine wits,' and no mistake.

You got me into the scrape, I said.

And I was quite right; however, I will do all I can to get you out of it; but I can only give you good-will and good advice, and, perhaps, I may be able to fit answers to your questions better than another—that is all. And now, having such an auxiliary, you must do your best to show the unbelievers that you are right.

I ought to try, I said, since you offer me such invaluable assistance. And I think that, if there is to be a chance of our escaping, we must explain to them whom we mean when we say that philosophers are to rule in the State; then we shall be able to defend ourselves: There will be discovered to be some natures who ought to study philosophy and to be leaders in the State; and others who are not born to be philosophers, and are meant to be followers rather than leaders.

Then now for a definition, he said.

Follow me, I said, and I hope that I may in some way or other be able to give you a satisfactory explanation.

Proceed.

I dare say that you remember, and therefore I need not remind you, that a lover, if he is worthy of the name, ought to show his love, not to some one part of that which he loves, but to the whole.

I really do not understand, and therefore beg of you to assist my memory.

Another person, I said, might fairly reply as you do; but a man of pleasure like yourself ought to know that all who are in the flower of youth do somehow or other raise a pang or emotion in a lover's breast, and are thought by him to be worthy of his affectionate regards. Is not this a way which you have with the fair: one has a snub nose, and you praise his charming face; the hook-nose of another has, you say, a royal look; while he who is neither snub nor hooked has the grace of regularity: the dark visage is manly, the fair are children of the gods; and as to the sweet 'honey pale,' as they are called, what is the very name but the invention of a lover who talks in diminutives, and is not averse to paleness if appearing on the cheek of youth? In a word, there is no excuse which you will not make, and nothing which you will not say, in order not to lose a single flower that blooms in the spring-time of youth.

If you make me an authority in matters of love, for the sake of the argument, I assent.

And what do you say of lovers of wine? Do you not see them doing the same? They are glad of any pretext of drinking any wine.

Very good.

And the same is true of ambitious men; if they cannot command an army, they are willing to command a file; and if they cannot be honoured by really great and important persons, they are glad to be honoured by lesser and meaner people,—but honour of some kind they must have.

Exactly.

Once more let me ask: Does he who desires any class of goods, desire the whole class or a part only?

The whole.

And may we not say of the philosopher that he is a lover, not of a part of wisdom only, but of the whole?

Yes, of the whole.

And he who dislikes learning, especially in youth, when he has no power of judging what is good and what is not, such an one we maintain not to be a philosopher or a lover of knowledge, just as he who refuses his food is not hungry, and may be said to have a bad appetite and not a good one?

Very true, he said.

Whereas he who has a taste for every sort of knowledge and who is curious to learn and is never satisfied, may be justly termed a philosopher? Am I not right?

Glaucon said: If curiosity makes a philosopher, you will find many a strange being will have a title to the name. All the lovers of sights have a delight in learning, and must therefore be included. Musical amateurs, too, are a folk strangely out of place among philosophers, for they are the last persons in the world who would come to anything like a philosophical discussion, if they could help, while they run about at the Dionysiac festivals as if they had let out their ears to hear every chorus; whether the performance is in town or country—that makes no difference—they are there. Now are we to maintain that all these and any who have similar tastes, as well as the professors of quite minor arts, are philosophers?

Certainly not, I replied; they are only an imitation.

He said: Who then are the true philosophers?

Those, I said, who are lovers of the vision of truth.

That is also good, he said; but I should like to know what you mean?

To another, I replied, I might have a difficulty in explaining; but I am sure that you will admit a proposition which I am about to make.

What is the proposition?

That since beauty is the opposite of ugliness, they are two?

Certainly.

And inasmuch as they are two, each of them is one?

True again.

And of just and unjust, good and evil, and of every other class, the same remark holds: taken singly, each of them is one; but from the various combinations of them with actions and things and with one another, they are seen in all sorts of lights and appear many?

Very true.

And this is the distinction which I draw between the sight-loving, art-loving, practical class and those of whom I am speaking, and who are alone worthy of the name of philosophers.

How do you distinguish them? he said.

The lovers of sounds and sights, I replied, are, as I conceive, fond of fine tones and colours and forms and all the artificial products that are made out of them, but their mind is incapable of seeing or loving absolute beauty.

True, he replied.

Few are they who are able to attain to the sight of this.

Very true.

And he who, having a sense of beautiful things has no sense of absolute beauty, or who, if another lead him to a knowledge of that beauty is unable to follow—of such an one I ask, Is he awake or in a dream only? Reflect: is not the dreamer, sleeping or waking, one who likens dissimilar things, who puts the copy in the place of the real object?

I should certainly say that such an one was dreaming.

But take the case of the other, who recognises the existence of absolute beauty and is able to distinguish the idea from the objects which participate in the idea, neither putting the objects in the place of the idea nor the idea in the place of the objects—is he a dreamer, or is he awake?

He is wide awake.

And may we not say that the mind of the one who knows has knowledge, and that the mind of the other, who opines only, has opinion?

Certainly.

But suppose that the latter should quarrel with us and dispute our statement, can we administer any soothing cordial or advice to him, without revealing to him that there is sad disorder in his wits?

e   We must certainly offer him some good advice, he replied.

Come, then, and let us think of something to say to him. Shall we begin by assuring him that he is welcome to any knowledge which he may have, and that we are rejoiced at his having it? But we should like to ask him a question: Does he who has knowledge know something or nothing? (You must answer for him.)

I answer that he knows something.

Something that is or is not?

Something that is; for how can that which is not ever be known?

And are we assured, after looking at the matter from many points

477 of view, that absolute being is or may be absolutely known, but that the utterly non-existent is utterly unknown?

Nothing can be more certain.

Good. But if there be anything which is of such a nature as to be and not to be, that will have a place intermediate between pure being and the absolute negation of being?

Yes, between them.

And, as knowledge corresponded to being and ignorance of necessity to not-being, for that intermediate between being and not-being there has to be discovered a corresponding intermediate between ignorance and knowledge, if there be such?

b   Certainly.

Do we admit the existence of opinion?

Undoubtedly.

As being the same with knowledge, or another faculty?

Another faculty.

Then opinion and knowledge have to do with different kinds of matter corresponding to this difference of faculties?

Yes.

And knowledge is relative to being and knows being. But before I proceed further I will make a division.

What division?

I will begin by placing faculties in a class by themselves: they are powers in us, and in all other things, by which we do as we

c   do. Sight and hearing, for example, I should call faculties. Have I clearly explained the class which I mean?

Yes, I quite understand.

Then let me tell you my view about them. I do not see them,

and therefore the distinctions of figure, colour, and the like, which enable me to discern the differences of some things, do not apply to them. In speaking of a faculty I think only of its sphere and its result; and that which has the same sphere and the same result I call the same faculty, but that which has another sphere and another result I call different. Would that be your way of speaking?

Yes.

And will you be so very good as to answer one more question? Would you say that knowledge is a faculty, or in what class would you place it?

Certainly knowledge is a faculty, and the mightiest of all faculties.

And is opinion also a faculty?

Certainly, he said; for opinion is that with which we are able to form an opinion.

And yet you were acknowledging a little while ago that knowledge is not the same as opinion?

Why, yes, he said: how can any reasonable being ever identify that which is infallible with that which errs?

An excellent answer, proving, I said, that we are quite conscious of a distinction between them.

Yes.

Then knowledge and opinion having distinct powers have also distinct spheres or subject-matters?

That is certain.

Being is the sphere or subject-matter of knowledge, and knowledge is to know the nature of being?

Yes.

And opinion is to have an opinion?

Yes.

And do we know what we opine? or is the subject-matter of opinion the same as the subject-matter of knowledge?

Nay, he replied, that has been already disproven; if difference in faculty implies difference in the sphere or subject-matter, and if, as we were saying, opinion and knowledge are distinct faculties, then the sphere of knowledge and of opinion cannot be the same.

Then if being is the subject-matter of knowledge, something else must be the subject-matter of opinion?

Yes, something else.

Well then, is not-being the subject-matter of opinion? or, rather, how can there be an opinion at all about not-being? Reflect: when a man has an opinion, has he not an opinion about something? Can he have an opinion which is an opinion about nothing?

Impossible.

He who has an opinion has an opinion about some one thing?

Yes.

And not-being is not one thing but, properly speaking, nothing?

True.

Of not-being, ignorance was assumed to be the necessary correlative; of being, knowledge?

True, he said.

Then opinion is not concerned either with being or with not-being?

Not with either.

And can therefore neither be ignorance nor knowledge?

That seems to be true.

But is opinion to be sought without and beyond either of them, in a greater clearness than knowledge, or in a greater darkness than ignorance?

In neither.

Then I suppose that opinion appears to you to be darker than knowledge, but lighter than ignorance?

Both; and in no small degree.

And also to be within and between them?

Yes.

Then you would infer that opinion is intermediate?

No question.

But were we not saying before, that if anything appeared to be of a sort which is and is not at the same time, that sort of thing would appear also to lie in the interval between pure being and absolute not-being; and that the corresponding faculty is neither knowledge nor ignorance, but will be found in the interval between them?

True.

And in that interval there has now been discovered something which we call opinion?

There has.

Then what remains to be discovered is the object which partakes equally of the nature of being and not-being, and cannot rightly be termed either, pure and simple; this unknown term, when discovered, we may truly call the subject of opinion, and assign each to their proper faculty,—the extremes to the faculties of the extremes and the mean to the faculty of the mean.

True.

This being premised, I would ask the gentleman who is of opinion that there is no absolute or unchangeable idea of beauty— in whose opinion the beautiful is the manifold—he, I say, your lover of beautiful sights, who cannot bear to be told that the beautiful is one, and the just is one, or that anything is one—to him I would appeal, saying, Will you be so very kind, sir, as to tell us whether, of all these beautiful things, there is one which will not be found ugly; or of the just, which will not be found unjust; or of the holy, which will not also be unholy?

No, he replied; the beautiful will in some point of view be found ugly; and the same is true of the rest.

And may not the many which are doubles be also halves?— doubles, that is, of one thing, and halves of another?   b

Quite true.

And things great and small, heavy and light, as they are termed, will not be denoted by these any more than by the opposite names?

True; both these and the opposite names will always attach to all of them.

And can any one of those many things which are called by particular names be said to be this rather than not to be this?

He replied: They are like the punning riddles which are asked at feasts or the children's puzzle about the eunuch aiming at the bat, with what he hit him, as they say in the puzzle, and upon what the bat was sitting. The individual objects of which I am speaking are also a riddle, and have a double sense: nor can you fix them in your   c mind, either as being or not-being, or both, or neither.

Then what will you do with them? I said. Can they have a better place than between being and not-being? For they are clearly not in greater darkness or negation than not-being, or more full of light and existence than being.

That is quite true, he said.

Thus then we seem to have discovered that the many ideas which the multitude entertain about the beautiful and about all other things   d are tossing about in some region which is half-way between pure being and pure not-being?

We have.

Yes; and we had before agreed that anything of this kind which we might find was to be described as matter of opinion, and not as matter of knowledge; being the intermediate flux which is caught and detained by the intermediate faculty.

Quite true.

Then those who see the many beautiful, and who yet neither see absolute beauty, nor can follow any guide who points the way thither; who see the many just, and not absolute justice, and the   e like,—such persons may be said to have opinion but not knowledge?

That is certain.

But those who see the absolute and eternal and immutable may be said to know, and not to have opinion only?

Neither can that be denied.

The one love and embrace the subjects of knowledge, the other those of opinion? The latter are the same, as I dare say you will remember, who listened to sweet sounds and gazed upon fair colours, but would not tolerate the existence of absolute beauty.   480

Yes, I remember.

Shall we then be guilty of any impropriety in calling them lovers of opinion rather than lovers of wisdom, and will they be very angry with us for thus describing them?

I shall tell them not to be angry; no man should be angry at what is true.

But those who love the truth in each thing are to be called lovers of wisdom and not lovers of opinion.

Assuredly.

BOOK VI

The Philosophers Fitness to Rule [484A-487A]

And thus, Glaucon, after the argument has gone a weary way, the true and the false philosophers have at length appeared in view.

I do not think, he said, that the way could have been shortened.

484   I suppose not, I said; and yet I believe that we might have had a better view of both of them if the discussion could have been confined to this one subject and if there were not many other questions awaiting us, which he who desires to see in what respect the life of the just differs from that of the unjust must consider.

And what is the next question? he asked.

b   Surely, I said, the one which follows next in order. Inasmuch as philosophers only are able to grasp the eternal and unchangeable, and those who wander in the region of the many and variable are not philosophers, I must ask you which of the two classes should be the rulers of our State?

And how can we rightly answer that question?

Whichever of the two are best able to guard the laws and institutions of our State—let them be our guardians.

Very good.

c   Neither, I said, can there be any question that the guardian who is to keep anything should have eyes rather than no eyes?

There can be no question of that.

And are not those who are verily and indeed wanting in the knowledge of the true being of each thing, and who have in their souls no clear pattern, and are unable as with a painter's eye to look at the absolute truth and to that original to repair, and having perfect vision of the other world to order the laws about beauty, goodness,

d   justice in this, if not already ordered, and to guard and preserve the order of them—are not such persons, I ask, simply blind?

Truly, he replied, they are much in that condition.

And shall they be our guardians when there are others who, besides being their equals in experience and falling short of them in no particular of virtue, also know the very truth of each thing?

There can be no reason, he said, for rejecting those who have this greatest of all great qualities; they must always have the first place unless they fail in some other respect.

Suppose then, I said, that we determine how far they can unite this and the other excellences.

By all means.

In the first place, as we began by observing, the nature of the philosopher has to be ascertained. We must come to an understanding about him, and, when we have done so, then, if I am not mistaken, we shall also acknowledge that such an union of qualities is possible, and that those in whom they are united, and those only, should be rulers in the State.

What do you mean?

Let us suppose that philosophical minds always love knowledge of a sort which shows them the eternal nature not varying from generation and corruption.

Agreed.

And further, I said, let us agree that they are lovers of all true being; there is no part whether greater or less, or more or less honourable, which they are willing to renounce; as we said before of the lover and the man of ambition.

True.

And if they are to be what we were describing, is there not another quality which they should also possess?

What quality?

Truthfulness: they will never intentionally receive into their mind falsehood, which is their detestation, and they will love the truth.

Yes, that may be safely affirmed of them.

'May be,' my friend, I replied, is not the word; say rather 'must be affirmed:' for he whose nature is amorous of anything cannot help loving all that belongs or is akin to the object of his affections.

Right, he said.

And is there anything more akin to wisdom than truth?

How can there be?

Can the same nature be a lover of wisdom and a lover of falsehood?

Never.

The true lover of learning then must from his earliest youth, as far as in him lies, desire all truth?

Assuredly.

But then again, as we know by experience, he whose desires are strong in one direction will have them weaker in others; they will be like a stream which has been drawn off into another channel.

True.

He whose desires are drawn towards knowledge in every form will be absorbed in the pleasures of the soul, and will hardly feel bodily pleasure—I mean, if he be a true philosopher and not a sham one.

That is most certain.

e   Such an one is sure to be temperate and the reverse of covetous; for the motives which make another man desirous of having and spending, have no place in his character.

Very true.

Another criterion of the philosophical nature has also to be considered.

What is that?

486   There should be no secret corner of stinginess; nothing can be more antagonistic than meanness to a soul which is ever longing after the whole of things both divine and human.

Most true, he replied.

Then how can he who has magnificence of mind and is the spectator of all time and all existence, think much of human life?

He cannot.

Or can such an one account death fearful?

No indeed.

Then the cowardly and mean nature has no part in true
b   philosophy?

Certainly not.

Or again: can he who is harmoniously constituted, who is not covetous or mean, or a boaster, or a coward—can he, I say, ever be unjust or hard in his dealings?

Impossible.

Then you will soon observe whether a man is just and gentle, or rude and unsociable; these are the signs which distinguish even in youth the philosophical nature from the unphilosophical.

True.

There is another point which should be remarked.

What point?

Whether he has or has not a pleasure in learning; for no one will
c   love that which gives him pain, and in which after much toil he makes little progress.

Certainly not.

And again, if he is forgetful and retains nothing of what he learns, will he not be an empty vessel?

That is certain.

Labouring in vain, he must end in hating himself and his fruitless occupation? Yes.

Then a soul which forgets cannot be ranked among genuine philosophic natures; we must insist that the philosopher should have a good memory?

d   Certainly.

And once more, the inharmonious and unseemly nature can only tend to disproportion?

Undoubtedly.

And do you consider truth to be akin to proportion or to disproportion?

To proportion.

Then, besides other qualities, we must try to find a naturally well-proportioned and gracious mind, which will move spontaneously towards the true being of everything.

Certainly.

Well, and do not all these qualities, which we have been enumerating, go together, and are they not, in a manner, necessary to a soul, which is to have a full and perfect participation of being?

They are absolutely necessary, he replied.   c

And must not that be a blameless study which he only can pursue who has the gift of a good memory, and is quick to learn,—noble, gracious, the friend of truth, justice, courage, temperance, who are   487 his kindred?

The god of jealousy himself, he said, could find no fault with such a study.

And to men like him, I said, when perfected by years and education, and to these only you will entrust the State.

Corruption of Philosophical Natures [487a–497a]

Here Adeimantus interposed and said: To these statements, Socrates, no one can offer a reply; but when you talk in this way, a strange feeling passes over the minds of your hearers: They fancy that they are led astray a little at each step in the argument, owing to their own want of skill in asking and answering questions; these littles   b accumulate, and at the end of the discussion they are found to have sustained a mighty overthrow and all their former notions appear to be turned upside down. And as unskillful players of checkers are at last shut up by their more skilful adversaries and have no piece to move, so they too find themselves shut up at last; for they have nothing to say in this new game of which words are the pieces; and yet all the time they are in the right. The observation is suggested to me by what is now occurring. For any one of us might say, that   c although in words he is not able to meet you at each step of the argument, he sees as a fact that the advocates of philosophy, when they carry on the study, not only in youth as a part of education, but as the pursuit of their maturer years, most of them become strange monsters, not to say utter rogues, and that those who may be considered the best of them are made useless to the world by the very study which you extol.   d

Well, and do you think that those who say so are wrong?

I cannot tell, he replied; but I should like to know what is your opinion.

Hear my answer; I am of opinion that they are quite right.

Then how can you be justified in saying that cities will not cease from evil until philosophers rule in them, when philosophers are acknowledged by us to be of no use to them?

You ask a question, I said, to which a reply can only be given in a parable.

Yes, Socrates; and that is a way of speaking to which you are not at all accustomed, I suppose.

I perceive, I said, that you are vastly amused at having plunged me into such a hopeless discussion; but now hear the parable, and then you will be still more amused at the meagreness of my imagination: for the manner in which the best men are treated in their own States is so grievous that no single thing on earth is comparable to it; and therefore, if I am to plead their cause, I must have recourse to fiction, and put together a figure made up of many things, like the fabulous unions of goats and stags which are found in pictures. Imagine then a fleet or a ship in which there is a captain who is taller and stronger than any of the crew, but he is a little deaf and has a similar infirmity in sight, and his knowledge of navigation is not much better. The sailors are quarrelling with one another about the steering—every one is of opinion that he has a right to steer, though he has never learned the art of navigation and cannot tell who taught him or when he learned, and will further assert that it cannot be taught, and they are ready to cut in pieces any one who says the contrary. They throng about the captain, begging and praying him to commit the helm to them; and if at any time they do not prevail, but others are preferred to them, they kill the others or throw them overboard, and having first chained up the noble captain's senses with drink or some narcotic drug, they mutiny and take possession of the ship and make free with the stores; thus, eating and drinking, they proceed on their voyage in such manner as might be expected of them. Him who is their partisan and cleverly aids them in their plot for getting the ship out of the captain's hands into their own whether by force or persuasion, they compliment with the name of sailor, pilot, able seaman, and abuse the other sort of man, whom they call a good-for-nothing; but that the true pilot must pay attention to the year and seasons and sky and stars and winds, and whatever else belongs to his art, if he intends to be really qualified for the command of a ship, and that he must and will be the steerer, whether other people like or not—the possibility of this union of authority with the steerer's art has never seriously entered into their thoughts or been made part of their calling. Now in vessels which are in a state of mutiny and by sailors who are mutineers, how will the true pilot be regarded? Will he not be called by them a babbler, a star-gazer, a good-for-nothing?

Of course, said Adeimantus.

Then you will hardly need, I said, to hear the interpretation of

the figure, which describes the true philosopher in his relation to the   489
State; for you understand already.

Certainly.

Then suppose you now take this parable to the gentleman who is
surprised at finding that philosophers have no honour in their cities;
explain it to him and try to convince him that their having honour
would be far more extraordinary.

I will.

Say to him, that, in deeming the best advocatess of philosophy
to be useless to the rest of the world, he is right; but also tell him
to attribute their uselessness to the fault of those who will not use   b
them, and not to themselves. The pilot should not humbly beg the
sailors to be commanded by him—that is not the order of nature;
neither are 'the wise to go to the doors of the rich'—the ingenious
author of this saying told a lie—but the truth is, that, when a man is
ill, whether he be rich or poor, to the physician he must go, and he
who wants to be governed, to him who is able to govern. The ruler
who is good for anything ought not to beg his subjects to be ruled
by him; although the present governors of mankind are of a different
stamp; they may be justly compared to the mutinous sailors, and the   c
true helmsmen to those who are called by them good-for-nothings
and star-gazers.

Precisely so, he said.

For these reasons, and among men like these, philosophy, the
noblest pursuit of all, is not likely to be much esteemed by those of
the opposite faction; not that the greatest and most lasting injury is
done to her by her opponents, but by her own professing followers,
the same of whom you suppose the accuser to say, that the greater
number of them are complete villains, and the best are useless; in
which opinion I agreed.   d

Yes.

And the reason why the good are useless has now been explained?
True.

Then shall we proceed to show that the corruption of the majority
is also unavoidable, and that this is not to be laid to the charge of
philosophy any more than the other?

By all means.

And let us ask and answer in turn, first going back to the description
of the gentle and noble nature. Truth, as you will remember, was his
leader, whom he followed always and in all things; failing in this, he   e
was an impostor, and had no part or lot in true philosophy.

Yes, that was said.

Well, and is not this one quality, to mention no others, greatly at
variance with present notions of him?

Certainly, he said.   490

And have we not a right to say in his defence, that the true lover of knowledge is always striving after being—that is his nature; he will not rest in the multiplicity of individuals which is an appearance only, but will go on—the keen edge will not be blunted, nor the force of his desire abate until he have attained the knowledge of the true nature of every essence by a sympathetic and kindred power in the soul, and by that power drawing near and mingling and becoming incorporate with very being, having begotten mind and truth, he will have knowledge and will live and grow truly, and then, and not till then, will he cease from his travail.

Nothing, he said, can be more just than such a description of him.

And will the love of a lie be any part of a philosopher's nature? Will he not utterly hate a lie?

He will.

And when truth is the captain, we cannot suspect any evil of the band which he leads?

Impossible.

Justice and health of mind will be of the company, and temperance will follow after?

True, he replied.

Neither is there any reason why I should again set in array the philosopher's virtues, as you will doubtless remember that courage, magnificence, apprehension, memory, were his natural gifts. And you objected that, although no one could deny what I then said, still, if you leave words and look at facts, the persons who are thus described are some of them manifestly useless, and the greater number utterly depraved; we were then led to enquire into the grounds of these accusations, and have now arrived at the point of asking why are the majority bad, which question of necessity brought us back to the examination and definition of the true philosopher.

Exactly.

And we have next to consider the corruptions of the philosophic nature, why so many are spoiled and so few escape spoiling—I am speaking of those who were said to be useless but not wicked— and, when we have done with them, we will speak of the imitators of philosophy, what manner of men are they who aspire after a profession which is above them and of which they are unworthy, and then, by their manifold inconsistencies, bring upon philosophy, and upon all philosophers, that universal reprobation of which we speak.

What are these corruptions? he said.

I will see if I can explain them to you. Every one will admit that a nature having in perfection all the qualities which we required in a philosopher, is a rare plant which is seldom seen among men.

Rare indeed.

And what numberless and powerful causes tend to destroy these rare natures!

What causes?

In the first place there are their own virtues, their courage, temperance, and the rest of them, every one of which praiseworthy qualities (and this is a most singular circumstance) destroys and distracts from philosophy the soul which is the possessor of them. b

That is very singular, he replied.

Then there are all the ordinary goods of life—beauty, wealth, strength, rank, and great connections in the State—you understand the sort of things—these also have a corrupting and distracting effect.

I understand; but I should like to know more precisely what you mean about them.

Grasp the truth as a whole, I said, and in the right way; you will then have no difficulty in apprehending the preceding remarks, and they will no longer appear strange to you. c

And how am I to do so? he asked.

Why, I said, we know that all germs or seeds, whether vegetable or animal, when they fail to meet with proper nutriment or climate or soil, in proportion to their vigour, are all the more sensitive to the want of a suitable environment, for evil is a greater enemy to what is good than to what is not.

Very true.

There is reason in supposing that the finest natures, when under alien conditions, receive more injury than the inferior, because the contrast is greater. d

Certainly.

And may we not say, Adeimantus, that the most gifted minds, when they are ill-educated, become pre-eminently bad? Do not great crimes and the spirit of pure evil spring out of a fulness of nature ruined by education rather than from any inferiority, whereas weak natures are scarcely capable of any very great good or very great evil?

There I think that you are right. e

And our philosopher follows the same analogy—he is like a plant which, having proper nurture, must necessarily grow and mature into all virtue, but, if sown and planted in an alien soil, becomes the most noxious of all weeds, unless he be preserved by some divine power. Do you really think, as people so often say, that our youth are corrupted by Sophists, or that private teachers of the art corrupt them in any degree worth speaking of? Are not the public who say 492 these things the greatest of all Sophists? And do they not educate to perfection young and old, men and women alike, and fashion them after their own hearts?

When is this accomplished? he said.

When they meet together, and the world sits down at an assembly, or in a court of law, or a theatre, or a camp, or in any other popular

b resort, and there is a great uproar, and they praise some things which
are being said or done, and blame other things, equally exaggerating
both, shouting and clapping their hands, and the echo of the rocks
and the place in which they are assembled redoubles the sound of
the praise or blame—at such a time will not a young man's heart,
as they say, leap within him? Will any private training enable him
to stand firm against the overwhelming flood of popular opinion? or
will he be carried away by the stream? Will he not have the notions
of good and evil which the public in general have—he will do as
c they do, and as they are, such will he be?

Yes, Socrates; necessity will compel him.

And yet, I said, there is a still greater necessity, which has not
been mentioned.

What is that?

The gentle force of condemnation or confiscation or death,
which, as you are aware, these new Sophists and educators, who are
d the public, apply when their words are powerless.

Indeed they do; and in right good earnest.

Now what opinion of any other Sophist, or of any private person,
can be expected to overcome in such an unequal contest?

None, he replied.

No, indeed, I said, even to make the attempt is a great piece of
folly; there neither is, nor has been, nor is ever likely to be, any
different type of character which has had no other training in virtue
but that which is supplied by public opinion—I speak, my friend, of
human virtue only; what is more than human, as the proverb says, is
e not included: for I would not have you ignorant that, in the present
evil state of governments, whatever is saved and comes to good is
saved by the power of God, as we may truly say.

I quite assent, he replied.

Then let me crave your assent also to a further observation.

What are you going to say?

Why, that all those mercenary individuals, whom the many call
493 Sophists and whom they deem to be their adversaries, do, in fact,
teach nothing but the opinion of the many, that is to say, the opinions
of their assemblies; and this is their wisdom. I might compare them
to a man who should study the tempers and desires of a mighty
strong beast who is fed by him—he would learn how to approach and
handle him, also at what times and from what causes he is dangerous
or the reverse, and what is the meaning of his several cries, and by
what sounds, when another utters them, he is soothed or infuriated;
and you may suppose further, that when, by continually attending
upon him, he has become perfect in all this, he calls his knowledge
wisdom, and makes of it a system or art, which he proceeds to teach,
b although he has no real notion of what he means by the principles or
passions of which he is speaking, but calls this honourable and that

dishonourable, or good or evil, or just or unjust, all in accordance with the tastes and tempers of the great brute. Good he pronounces to be that in which the beast delights and evil to be that which he dislikes; and he can give no other account of them except that the just and noble are the necessary, having never himself seen, and having no power of explaining to others the nature of either, or the difference between them, which is immense. By heaven, would not such an one be a rare educator?

Indeed he would.

And in what way does he who thinks that wisdom is the discernment of the tempers and tastes of the motley multitude, whether in painting or music, or, finally, in politics, differ from him whom I have been describing? For when a man consorts with the many, and exhibits to them his poem or other work of art or the service which he has done the State, making them his judges when he is not obliged, the so-called necessity of Diomede will oblige him to produce whatever they praise. And yet the reasons are utterly ludicrous which they give in confirmation of their own notions about the honourable and good. Did you ever hear any of them which were not?

No, nor am I likely to hear.

You recognise the truth of what I have been saying? Then let me ask you to consider further whether the world will ever be induced to believe in the existence of absolute beauty rather than of the many beautiful, or of the absolute in each kind rather than of the many in each kind?

Certainly not.

Then the world cannot possibly be a philosopher?

Impossible.

And therefore philosophers must inevitably fall under the censure of the world?

They must.

And of individuals who consort with the mob and seek to please them?

That is evident.

Then, do you see any way in which the philosopher can be preserved in his calling to the end? and remember what we were saying of him, that he was to have quickness and memory and courage and magnificence—these were admitted by us to be the true philosopher's gifts.

Yes.

Will not such an one from his early childhood be in all things first among all, especially if his bodily endowments are like his mental ones?

Certainly, he said.

And his friends and fellow-citizens will want to use him as he gets older for their own purposes?

No question.

Falling at his feet, they will make requests to him and do him honour and flatter him, because they want to get into their hands now, the power which he will one day possess.

That often happens, he said.

And what will a man such as he is be likely to do under such circumstances, especially if he be a citizen of a great city, rich and noble, and a tall proper youth? Will he not be full of boundless aspirations, and fancy himself able to manage the affairs of Hellenes and of barbarians, and having got such notions into his head will he not dilate and elevate himself in the fulness of vain pomp and senseless pride?

To be sure he will.

Now, when he is in this state of mind, if some one gently comes to him and tells him that he is a fool and must get understanding, which can only be got by slaving for it, do you think that, under such adverse circumstances, he will be easily induced to listen?

Far otherwise.

And even if there be some one who through inherent goodness or natural reasonableness has had his eyes opened a little and is humbled and taken captive by philosophy, how will his friends behave when they think that they are likely to lose the advantage which they were hoping to reap from his companionship? Will they not do and say anything to prevent him from yielding to his better nature and to render his teacher powerless, using to this end private intrigues as well as public prosecutions?

There can be no doubt of it.

And how can one who is thus circumstanced ever become a philosopher?

Impossible.

Then were we not right in saying that even the very qualities which make a man a philosopher may, if he be ill-educated, divert him from philosophy, no less than riches and their accompaniments and the other so-called goods of life?

We were quite right.

Thus, my excellent friend, is brought about all that ruin and failure which I have been describing of the natures best adapted to the best of all pursuits; they are natures which we maintain to be rare at any time; this being the class out of which come the men who are the authors of the greatest evil to States and individuals; and also of the greatest good when the tide carries them in that direction; but a small man never was the doer of any great thing either to individuals or to States.

That is most true, he said.

And so philosophy is left desolate, with her marriage rite

incomplete: for her own have fallen away and forsaken her, and while they are leading a false and unbecoming life, other unworthy persons, seeing that she has no kinsmen to be her protectors, enter in and dishonour her; and fasten upon her the reproaches which, as you say, her reprovers utter, who affirm of her advocates that some are good for nothing, and that the greater number deserve the severest punishment.

c

That is certainly what people say.

Yes; and what else would you expect, I said, when you think of the puny creatures who, seeing this land open to them—a land well stocked with fair names and showy titles—like prisoners running out of prison into a sanctuary, take a leap out of their trades into philosophy; those who do so being probably the cleverest hands at their own miserable crafts? For, although philosophy be in this evil case, still there remains a dignity about her which is not to be found in the arts. And many are thus attracted by her whose natures are imperfect and whose souls are maimed and disfigured by their meannesses, as their bodies are by their trades and crafts. Is not this unavoidable?

d

Yes.

Are they not exactly like a bald little tinker who has just got out of prison and come into a fortune; he takes a bath and puts on a new coat, and is decked out as a bridegroom going to marry his master's daughter, who is left poor and desolate?

e

A most exact parallel.

What will be the issue of such marriages? Will they not be vile and bastard?

There can be no question of it.

And when persons who are unworthy of education approach philosophy and make an alliance with her who is in a rank above them what sort of ideas and opinions are likely to be generated? Will they not be sophisms captivating to the ear, having nothing in them genuine, or worthy of or akin to true wisdom?

496

No doubt, he said.

ON THE POSSIBILITY OF PHILOSOPHICAL RULE
[496A-502C]

Then, Adeimantus, I said, the worthy disciples of philosophy will be but a small remnant: perchance some noble and well-educated person, detained by exile in her service, who in the absence of corrupting influences remains devoted to her; or some lofty soul born in a mean city, the politics of which he condemns and neglects; and there may be a gifted few who leave the arts, which they justly despise, and come to her;—or perhaps there are some who are restrained by our friend Theages' bridle; for everything in the life

b

of Theages conspired to divert him from philosophy; but ill-health kept him away from politics. My own case of the internal sign is hardly worth mentioning, for rarely, if ever, has such a monitor been given to any other man. Those who belong to this small class have tasted how sweet and blessed a possession philosophy is, and have also seen enough of the madness of the multitude; and they know that no politician is honest, nor is there any champion of justice at whose side they may fight and be saved. Such an one may be compared to a man who has fallen among wild beasts—he will not join in the wickedness of his fellows, but neither is he able singly to resist all their fierce natures, and therefore seeing that he would be of no use to the State or to his friends, and reflecting that he would have to throw away his life without doing any good either to himself or others, he holds his peace, and goes his own way. He is like one who, in the storm of dust and sleet which the driving wind hurries along, retires under the shelter of a wall; and seeing the rest of mankind full of wickedness, he is content, if only he can live his own life and be pure from evil or unrighteousness, and depart in peace and good-will, with bright hopes.

Yes, he said, and he will have done a great work before he departs.

A great work—yes; but not the greatest, unless he find a State suitable to him; for in a State which is suitable to him, he will have a larger growth and be the saviour of his country, as well as of himself.

The causes why philosophy is in such an evil name have now been sufficiently explained: the injustice of the charges against her has been shown—is there anything more which you wish to say?

Nothing more on that subject, he replied; but I should like to know which of the governments now existing is in your opinion the one adapted to her.

Not any of them, I said; and that is precisely the accusation which I bring against them—not one of them is worthy of the philosophic nature, and hence that nature is warped and estranged;—as the exotic seed which is sown in a foreign land becomes denaturalized, and is likely to be overpowered and to lose itself in the new soil, even so this growth of philosophy, instead of persisting, degenerates and receives another character. But if philosophy ever finds in the State that perfection which she herself is, then will be seen that she is in truth divine, and that all other things, whether natures of men or institutions, are but human;—and now, I know, that you are going to ask, What that State is:

No, he said; there you are wrong, for I was going to ask another question—whether it is the State of which we are the founders and inventors, or some other?

Yes, I replied, ours in most respects; but you may remember my saying before, that some living authority would always be required in the State having the same idea of the constitution which guided you when as legislator you were laying down the laws.

That was said, he replied.

Yes, but not in a satisfactory manner; you frightened us by interposing objections, which certainly showed that the discussion would be long and difficult; and what still remains is the reverse of easy.

What is there remaining?

The question how the study of philosophy may be so ordered as   d
not to be the ruin of the State: All great attempts are attended with risk; 'hard is the good,' as men say.

Still, he said, let the point be cleared up, and the enquiry will then be complete.

I shall not be hindered, I said, by any want of will, but, if at all, by a want of power: my zeal you may see for yourselves; and please to remark in what I am about to say how boldly and unhesitatingly I declare that States should pursue philosophy, not as they do now, but in a different spirit.

In what manner?

At present, I said, the students of philosophy are quite young;   e
beginning when they are hardly past childhood, they devote only the time saved from moneymaking and housekeeping to such pursuits; and even those of them who are reputed to have most of the philosophic spirit, when they come within sight of the great difficulty of the subject, I mean dialectic, take themselves off. In after life when invited by some one else, they may, perhaps, go and hear a lecture, and about this they make much ado, for philosophy is not considered by them to be their proper business: at last, when they grow old, in most cases they are extinguished more truly than Heracleitus' sun, inasmuch as they never light up again. (Heraclitus   498 said that the sun was extinguished every evening and relighted every morning.)

But what ought to be their course?

Just the opposite. In childhood and youth their study, and what philosophy they learn, should be suited to their tender years: during this period while they are growing up towards manhood, the chief and special care should be given to their bodies that they may have them to use in the service of philosophy; as life advances and the   b
intellect begins to mature, let them increase the gymnastics of the soul; but when the strength of our citizens fails and is past civil and military duties, then let them range at will and engage in no serious labour, as we intend them to live happily here, and to crown this life with a similar happiness in another.

How truly in earnest you are, Socrates! he said; I am sure of that; and yet most of your hearers, if I am not mistaken, are likely to be still more earnest in their opposition to you, and will never be convinced; Thrasymachus least of all.

Do not make a quarrel, I said, between Thrasymachus and me, who have recently become friends, although, indeed, we were never enemies; for I shall go on striving to the utmost until I either convert him and other men, or do something which may profit them against the day when they live again, and hold the like discourse in another state of existence.

You are speaking of a time which is not very near.

Rather, I replied, of a time which is as nothing in comparison with eternity. Nevertheless, I do not wonder that the many refuse to believe; for they have never seen that of which we are now speaking realized; they have seen only a conventional imitation of philosophy, consisting of words artificially brought together, not like these of ours having a natural unity. But a human being who in word and work is perfectly moulded, as far as he can be, into the proportion and likeness of virtue—such a man ruling in a city which bears the same image, they have never yet seen, neither one nor many of them—do you think that they ever did?

No indeed.

No, my friend, and they have seldom, if ever, heard free and noble sentiments; such as men utter when they are earnestly and by every means in their power seeking after truth for the sake of knowledge, while they look coldly on the subtleties of controversy, of which the end is opinion and strife, whether they meet with them in the courts of law or in society.

They are strangers, he said, to the words of which you speak.

And this was what we foresaw, and this was the reason why truth forced us to admit, not without fear and hesitation, that neither cities nor States nor individuals will ever attain perfection until the small class of philosophers whom we termed useless but not corrupt are providentially compelled, whether they will or not, to take care of the State, and until a like necessity be laid on the State to obey them; or until kings, or if not kings, the sons of kings or princes, are divinely inspired with a true love of true philosophy. That either or both of these alternatives are impossible, I see no reason to affirm: if they were so, we might indeed be justly ridiculed as dreamers and visionaries. Am I not right?

Quite right.

If then, in the countless ages of the past, or at the present hour in some foreign clime which is far away and beyond our ken, the perfected philosopher is or has been or hereafter shall be compelled by a superior power to have the charge of the State, we are ready to assert to the death, that this our constitution has been, and is—yea, and will be whenever the Muse of Philosophy is queen. There is no impossibility in all this; that there is a difficulty, we acknowledge ourselves.

My opinion agrees with yours, he said.

But do you mean to say that this is not the opinion of the multitude?   d

I should imagine not, he replied.

O my friend, I said, do not attack the multitude: they will change their minds, if, not in an aggressive spirit, but gently and with the view of soothing them and removing their dislike of over-education, you show them your philosophers as they really are and describe as you were just now doing their character and profession, and then mankind will see that he of whom you are speaking is not such as they supposed—if they view him in this new light, they will surely change their notion of him, and answer in another strain. Who can be at enmity with one who loves them, who that is himself gentle and free from envy will be jealous of one in whom there is no jealousy?   e
Nay, let me answer for you, that in a few this harsh temper may be found but not in the majority of mankind.

I quite agree with you, he said.

And do you not also think, as I do, that the harsh feeling which   500
the many entertain towards philosophy originates in the pretenders, who rush in uninvited, and are always abusing them, and finding fault with them, who make persons instead of things the theme of their conversation? and nothing can be more unbecoming in philosophers than this.

It is most unbecoming.

For he, Adeimantus, whose mind is fixed upon true being, has surely no time to look down upon the affairs of earth, or to   b
be filled with malice and envy, contending against men; his eye is ever directed towards things fixed and immutable, which he sees neither injuring nor injured by one another, but all in order moving according to reason; these he imitates, and to these he will, as far as he can, conform himself. Can a man help imitating that with which he holds reverential converse?

Impossible.

And the philosopher holding converse with the divine order, becomes orderly and divine, as far as the nature of man allows; but   c
like every one else, he will suffer from detraction.

Of course.

And if a necessity be laid upon him of fashioning, not only himself, but human nature generally, whether in States or individuals, into that which he beholds elsewhere, will he, think you, be an unskilful artificer of justice, temperance, and every civil virtue?

Anything but unskilful.   d

And if the world perceives that what we are saying about him is the truth, will they be angry with philosophy? Will they disbelieve us, when we tell them that no State can be happy which is not designed by artists who imitate the heavenly pattern?

They will not be angry if they understand, he said. But how will they draw out the plan of which you are speaking?

They will begin by taking the State and the manners of men, from which, as from a tablet, they will rub out the picture, and leave a clean surface. This is no easy task. But whether easy or not, herein will lie the difference between them and every other legislator,— they will have nothing to do either with individual or State, and will inscribe no laws, until they have either found, or themselves made, a clean surface.

They will be very right, he said.

Having effected this, they will proceed to trace an outline of the constitution?

No doubt.

And when they are filling in the work, as I conceive, they will often turn their eyes upwards and downwards: I mean that they will first look at absolute justice and beauty and temperance, and again at the human copy; and will mingle and temper the various elements of life into the image of a man; and this they will conceive according to that other image, which, when existing among men, Homer calls the form and likeness of God.

Very true, he said.

And one feature they will erase, and another they will put in, until they have made the ways of men, as far as possible, agreeable to the ways of God?

Indeed, he said, in no way could they make a fairer picture.

And now, I said, are we beginning to persuade those whom you described as rushing at us with might and main, that the painter of constitutions is such an one as we are praising; at whom they were so very indignant because to his hands we committed the State; and are they growing a little calmer at what they have just heard?

Much calmer, if there is any sense in them.

Why, where can they still find any ground for objection? Will they doubt that the philosopher is a lover of truth and being?

They would not be so unreasonable.

Or that his nature, being such as we have delineated, is akin to the highest good?

Neither can they doubt this.

But again, will they tell us that such a nature, placed under favorable circumstances, will not be perfectly good and wise if any ever was? Or will they prefer those whom we have rejected?

Surely not.

Then will they still be angry at our saying, that, until philosophers bear rule, States and individuals will have no rest from evil, nor will this our imaginary State ever be realized?

I think that they will be less angry.

Shall we assume that they are not only less angry but quite gentle, and that they have been converted and for very shame, if for no other reason, cannot refuse to come to terms?

By all means, he said.

Then let us suppose that the reconciliation has been effected. Will any one deny the other point, that there may be sons of kings or princes who are by nature philosophers?

Surely no man, he said.

And when they have come into being will any one say that they must of necessity be destroyed; that they can hardly be saved is not denied even by us; but that in the whole course of ages no single one of them can escape—who will venture to affirm this?

Who indeed!

But, said I, one is enough; let there be one man who has a city obedient to his will, and he might bring into existence the ideal polity about which the world is so incredulous.

Yes, one is enough.

The ruler may impose the laws and institutions which we have been describing, and the citizens may possibly be willing to obey them?

Certainly.

And that others should approve, of what we approve, is no miracle or impossibility?

I think not.

But we have sufficiently shown, in what has preceded, that all this, if only possible, is assuredly for the best.

We have.

And now we say not only that our laws, if they could be enacted, would be for the best, but also that the enactment of them, though difficult, is not impossible.

Very good.

10

PLATO'S METAPHYSICS

THE EIDOS OF THE GOOD [502C-509C]

Socrates now raises the level of the conversation. The philosopher who is best to rule the city must not only know what justice is, for justice is but one specific instance of the good. The greatest study of all is the study of the idea—The Form (*Eidos*) of the good—Goodness Itself (505a). Plato believes that the Good which is real (has being) as opposed to that which only seems good is the Feature Itself—The Form (*eidos*) that is Goodness Itself. He believes that specific goods like justice, health, and wisdom are good only to the extent that they participate in the Form of Goodness Itself.

The philosopher cannot know whether a specific good (for example, a good law) is really good or only apparently good, if she does not know what Goodness itself is. No one is satisfied with the obtainment of the seeming good; everyone seeks the genuine article. Plato assumes that if we do not know the entirely adequate definition of Goodness Itself we cannot know (only opine) that some particular thing is good. (Those who find this claim highly suspect call the claim the Socratic fallacy).Since the ruler must be able to know what is fine and good among the laws and practices of the City, the ruler must seek knowledge of Goodness Itself. Every aspect of the tripartite soul is desirous of some particular Good or End. Each of those particular goods is good in so far as it participates in Goodness Itself (share the feature of goodness). Goodness Itself then is the ultimate End of human life—the ultimate fulfillment of all human desiring. Human flourishing, the achievement of excellence as a human being, is possible only when the rational psyche apprehends the Form of the Good. Only then can it provide itself with the object of its desire—

the true Good, and can recognize the Ends of fulfilling the goods of the Spirited and appetitive souls as well. This commingling and identification of the rational desire for the Good and the object of knowledge: the Form of the Good, is a kind of secular beatitude—a life fulfilling consummation.

But what is The Good? Socrates must distinguish the Form of the Good from the particular goods that participate in it, for example: must distinguish between Goodness Itself and the goodness of (some types) of pleasure or the goodness of prudence. Socrates claims not to have knowledge of the Form of the Good. However, something that is a child of the Good and looks like it can be described.

THE ANALOGY OF THE SUN [507A-509C]

Socrates suggests that of the many fine and good things, the feature that unites them is the Idea of the Good. This one idea must be real, for otherwise there would be no particular thing that would be good. Between the visible and sight there must be a third thing which allows the visible to come out of the darkness and be seen; and that third thing is light. The god that supplies light is Apollo, the sun.

After the 5th Century BC, Apollo, the son of Zeus and Leto, was identified with Helios, the sun god. Phoebus Apollo, the god of light, was a moral god concerned with prophecy, medicine, music, poetry, archery and various bucolic arts. He was responsible for law, philosophy and the arts. He, along with Athena, was a patron god of Athens and his Oracle at his shrine in Delphi inspired Socrates to carry out his sacred mission of exposing intellectual fraud wherever he found it.

Just as the sun provides the light that makes the eye aware of color and the colored thing visible, so too The Good provides the idea (enlightenment) that allows the rational mind to know the Forms of things. The Good is that whereby we grasp the universal and eternal Features (*eide*) of particular things. Just as the sun, through the emanation of its heat energy and light causes the generation of living things, so too the Good causes the being of the things it makes knowable. And finally, just as the sun causes generation but is not itself generation (is eternally beyond generation or corruption), so too The Good is not itself a being like those it causes, is not itself a thing, but is beyond beings.

INTERPRETATION OF THE ANALOGY OF THE SUN

What is this all about? This passage is perhaps one of the most obscure and mysterious in all of Plato's writings. Plato is offering his cryptic answer to life's most fundamental mystery: why reality? why is there anything at all? Nothingness would have been so much simpler. The analogy with the sun god suggests that Plato's explanation for the universe is a move beyond polytheism to a monotheism. However, the transcendent source of all the beings and all of the forms is not a personal god. It is a real, transcendent, eternal, unchanging, universal source of existence; but Goodness Itself has no personality (*although* Glaucon thinks Socrates owes us a narrative on the Father of the sun-god, and Socrates described Apollo as the "child" of the Good). That the Form of the Good is the ultimate cause of the Forms makes sense in light of the fact that:

1. Forms make things *what* they are and thus are the origin of beings.
2. Forms are universal, permanent, eternal and thus more real (and real making) than particular things which are fleeting, changing, hovering between being and non-being.
3. Forms are united by the Good—when we apprehend an apple, we understand it as participating in the universal and eternal Form (Idea) of Appleness Itself—Appleness itself is ideal, it is perfection without flaws, without corruption. Thus the Good in the apple, Ideal Appleness, allows us to know the thing as an apple.

Goodness Itself is a good candidate for ultimate reality since it unites all the Forms of things and the apprehension of the good in things is the same as grasping the thing in its essence, making it known to us.

Why is the Good the most important study of the lover of wisdom? Reason will not achieve its End—absolute knowledge of the totality of being—unless it has an appetite (*eros*) of its own. The Faustian quest for complete and absolute knowledge must be driven by a yearning. Since every yearning has its proper object, the ultimate cause of reality (which is mysteriously beyond reality, that is, beyond particular beings) must be an object of intellectual desire. So ultimate Being must also be ultimate Good, the End of all desiring. The consummation of human life is in knowledge of Goodness Itself.

THE DIVIDED LINE [509C-511E]

Once Socrates has divided up the visible natural world (sun lit) and the intelligible invisible world of the Forms (Good sent), he further illustrates the venture of the philosopher's life with the Divided Line. A line A-E is divided in unequal measures: AC-CE. Then each section is divided by an equal amount so that the following proportions are produced:

[AB:BC::CD:DE]::AC:CE.

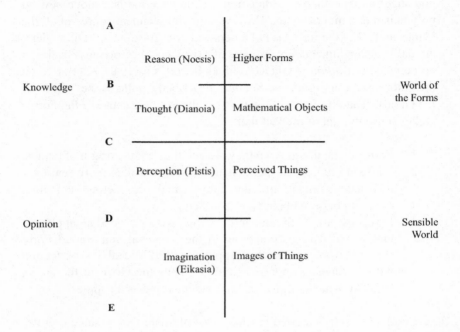

CE represents the visible world and includes the categories of visible thing (CD) and the images and shadows (DE) that emanate from them. AC represents the intellected world of the Forms including the categories of mathematical entities and scientific Forms (BC) and the Higher Forms of Wisdom, Justice, Courage, Moderation and the Form of the Good (AB). The line suggests two progressions, one epistemological, another metaphysical.

Epistemological progression: Starting with the minimal evidence of images and first impressions, the young Guardian gains a tenuous grasp of reality through the images of Homer and Hesiod, the poetic content of musical education. Ordinary perception of the changing particulars (trees, flowers, Spartans, the agora) provides acquaintance with their universal essences without a full grasping or understanding of them. A child may perceive clearly the flowers in the garden she is skipping through without a botanist's understanding of what is there. The child's awareness is one of opinion not knowledge.

Only on the intellectual level of CB, apprehension of the Forms of mathematics and scientific natures, can the Guardian student obtain knowledge. A circle is an enclosed arc every point along which is equidistant from a central point. This essence of Circleness applies to the quadrillions of particular circles and wheels that participate in it. This essence of Circle is eternal, universal, and unchanging. These Forms (e.g. of the Isosceles triangle) are imperceptible (because they are ideal, universal and eternal) and thus only apprehended by reason alone. A visible line is not really a mathematical line, because as the shortest distance between two points, the line has no width. Mathematical points have no dimensions at all, and so cannot be apprehended by the senses.

Finally, ultimate knowledge is knowledge of Forms which are matters of pure intellection, reasoning not from hypotheses, as in the case of the scientific generalizations from particular observations or from the use of visual illustration as in the case of geometrical proofs, but rather purely from the use of reason alone, e.g., understanding the Form of the Good. Understanding the Higher Forms results from the method of the dialectic which discovers first principles from which conclusions about particulars are deduced.

In terms of the progression of knowledge, Plato is saying that knowledge of the higher Forms is comparable to knowledge derived from Math and Science as knowledge of visible things is to knowledge derived from images and shadows, as knowledge of intellectual Forms is to the opinions derived from perception and imagination. Knowing the Form of the Good then makes knowledge of anything else possible, whereas opinion formed and restricted to political propaganda, popular media and societal conventions guarantees ignorance of the true, the real and the good.

Metaphysically the line represents a progression from the most ephemeral, changing, multiple, unstable and particular to the more enduring, unified, eternal, universal, stable, permanent and ideal. So from the unreality and derivative nature of shadows, we progress up the scale of reality to the eternal source of being, the Form of the Good. Math and natural Forms are as real compared to the Higher Forms, as shadows are to perceived things as the entities dwelling in the world of opinion are to the intellected Forms in the World of Knowledge. The philosopher grasps this great chain of being and accepts the unconventional notion that ideal Forms are real and perceived particulars are not (as real). Because of her knowledge of the true Good, only the philosopher can apprehend the fine and the good in the laws and practices of the City.

THE MYTH OF THE CAVE [514A-517A]

In an attempt to explain why philosophers should rule or guardians should be philosophers, Socrates, at the beginning of Book VII, attempts to show why the philosopher's quest for knowledge of the Good itself demands the sacrifice of the greater good of a life of contemplation in favor of a lesser, more particular, political good of Just Rule. The evocative Myth of the Cave is a pictorial analogy designed to explain the sacrifice demanded of State leaders (and by analogy, the beneficence demanded of the wise and just rational part of an individual's psyche).

Socrates likens those who are uneducated to people who from the time of their infancy have been chained hand and foot and forced to sit on benches staring at the back wall of a deep cave. Neck braces prevent them from seeing one another. Behind the captives is a parapet where people parade statues of men, animals, and artifacts of all kinds carved from stone or wood.

When these bearers talk as they go by, it is the shadows of these replicas that seem to be talking. The captives try to predict which will appear next in what order; which are in more or less constant conjunction. Behind the statue bearers is a fire. The light from the fire casts the shadows of the moving statues onto to the back wall of the cave and the shadows are observed by the captives. These prisoners are like us, says Socrates, for their whole world of conscious experience is of the shadows of things rather than of the true things and yet they would claim that they know best what daily appears before their eyes. The captives discuss and name the things they experience.

If one of the captives is released and forced to stand up and look at the bonfire, her eyes would sting painfully and she would flee back to the shadow world. If dragged up the steep upward way out of the cave and into the light of the sun, she would be dazzled and temporarily blinded. She would not be able to make out the sunlit clouds, meadows and streams of the world outside the cave. At first, she would look at the shadows of things and the reflections of things in water. But eventually her eyes would adjust, allowing her to gaze on the things themselves: nature, human society, the moon, the stars and finally the sun in the middle of the sky.

The former captive would realize that the sun is the source of the seasons and the years. The Sun is the "steward" of all things in the visible place. It directs and manages the natural world and it is the cause of all the things, not only in the world outside the cave, but also the bonfire, the statues and the shadows that she formally took to be the whole of reality. Comparing her life above to that lived before with her fellow prisoners she would consider herself happy and pity those she left behind. Any honors, praises or prizes the captives would bestow upon one another would be devalued by the escapee, who would much rather live without those accolades and live free and unsung in the sunlit upper region.

Socrates ponders what would happen if the liberated one returned to the cave and took her seat among the captives. Unable to adjust her eyes to the dim light, she couldn't enter into the chatter about the shadows; and her failure to form expected judgments or opinions about the shadows would make her laughable. And if she tries to explain her difficulties with the shadows by describing her escape from the cave and her experience of the world above, the other captives would conclude that such a trip was useless and vicious: useless because it ruins your ability to make practical judgments about shadows and vicious because getting the captives to doubt is socially disruptive. Any liberator who would try likewise to release them from their chains and lead them to the higher region would be killed if they could get their hands on such a one.

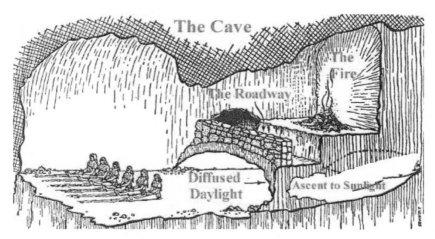

THE CAVE, THE SUN AND THE LINE [517B-517C]

Socrates insists that the Myth of the Cave must be compared with the Analogy of the Sun and the Divided Line in Book VI. The fire is likened to our earthly sun and the statues and puppets lit up by the fire are the objects of ordinary perception. The shadows on the walls are derivative copies mixed up with the imaginings of ordinary people as their opinions are manipulated and misled by government propagandists, poets, media merchants, Sophists and indoctrinating teachers. If the cave represents the lower region of the divided line (World of Opinion), then outside the cave represents the World of the Forms, the intelligible World. The Forms have real being as opposed to perceived material particulars and the Highest Form (represented by the Sun) is the Idea of Goodness Itself. Just as the Sun above is the source and cause of all visible things (all the way down to the shadows), so too the cause of all that is right and fair is Goodness Itself. It provides truth and intelligence to all the Forms and to all the particulars that participate in the Forms.

Commentators are left to speculate about the region of Mathematical entities. Are they symbolized by the statues and puppets used to represent real natural things to the captives? Are they found in the arduous climb out of the cave, symbolizing their intermediate role between opinion and the knowledge of pure conceptual formality outside the cave? Are they the shadows and reflections seen outside the cave just before the liberated one grasps the pure Species Forms and higher Forms of Justice, Moderation, Courage, Wisdom and above all Goodness?

Socrates suggests that the Myth of the Cave is not only to be conceived as a political contrast between unjust, rancorous States and the Ideal State, but primarily as the journey of the soul from childhood ignorance, through education, to knowledge and the happiness (*eudaimonia*) that comes from fulfilling the desire of the Rational psyche for Wisdom through apprehension of the Forms (Of course, it is only the special education accorded the Auxiliary Guardian that provides the possibility of obtaining wisdom and *eudaimonia*) .

THE TURNING [517D]

We can now discern the development of lovers of opinion into lovers of wisdom: Once out of the cave, seeing the real things and becoming enlightened about the Forms and grasping Goodness Itself, the liberated one would never want to return to the Cave. This is in keeping with what was claimed in Book I against Thrasymachus that the best Rulers are those who are most reluctant to rule.

In leisure, soaking in the sun at the beach and watching the clouds drift by and the waves roll in, we're often reluctant to return to the grind of our work. Not only philosophers but all academicians prefer reveling in their subject matter rather than making practical applications or attending committee meetings. Here is a great paradox of the *Republic*: just at the moment of Beatitude or Nirvana, when the lover of wisdom has in her arms the object of her deepest longing, she must sacrifice it to return to the cave and its shadows. The philosopher must become a warrior and then a ruler over citizens who prefer their familiar chains and ignorance.

It is a lot easier for tyrants operating behind a wall of respectability (as though they held the Ring of Gyges) to rule over the oppressed by keeping them amused with shows and propaganda (the shadow show) than any claim the philosopher makes to rule. If a person raised in popular prejudices, opinion, crass materialism and crude pleasure turns from this darkness into the light of conceptual understanding, then they will be painfully dazzled and will have difficulty adjusting. Equally the person who is thrust from intellectual enlightenment into the darkness of practical matters and popular culture will also find it difficult to adjust. One who is unaware or unable to kibitz about the usual prejudices will seem like a fool to the uneducated person.

NATURE VS NURTURE [518A 519A]

The capacity for enlightenment is in the soul of each captive. Education is not a matter of native ability but of a turning that is a choice of objects to focus on: either shadows or sunlight, opinions or knowledge, from material particulars or Ideal Forms, from generating things to eternally actual things. It is important to note that Plato doesn't pity the uneducated because they are, by nature, incapable of knowledge or wisdom. Their souls have the capacity for *eudaimonia* (full human flourishing) simply because they all share a human Form or nature. But not every person has the opportunity or willingness to turn from ignorant opinion and popular prejudice to take the arduous educational climb out of the cave to the light of the true and the good.

Many have commented that there is an air of contempt on the part of Plato's Socrates for the uneducated, but his target seems to be those who claim that those uninformed opinions are to be promoted as true or are the equal of truth or at least are valuable tools in the arsenal of panderers for promoting their own selfish advantage. Many who today decry the crass commercialization of the holidays, the use of sex and violence on TV, movies or advertisements, the tabloid sensationalism of the news, or the perpetuation of popular prejudice, have no trouble distinguishing between their contempt of such views with their respect for the intrinsic worth of those who hold them. Whether or not Plato always managed that distinction is an interesting question.

THE SACRIFICE EXPLAINED [519A - 521B]

Some who exercise their reason and who awake from the delusion of the shadow world of popular opinion still have their souls turned to the lower levels of pleasure and material sensuality. They cannot fully detach themselves and ascend to the full light of the cerebral heavens. They turn to lives of vice and tyranny. Here Plato may be referring to the tyrants who perform the shadow show from behind the scene. It should be noted that regardless of the amusement they enjoy by oppressing and controlling others, they spend their entire lives in the caves along with the captives.

As the sun is the steward of the stars and planets, so too the philosopher Kings and Queens will be ideal stewards of the City. They see the fine and the good in everything they see or do, because the source of everything fine and good is Goodness Itself. Non-philosophers are not fit to rule because they have no vision of the Common Good, but only of a multitude of particular goods. Thus, for example, one who seeks wealth rules in the interest of the wealthy to the detriment of other classes and to the threatened neighboring City-States. Something similar is in store when ambitious rulers seek pleasure, fame or glory. Those eager to rule in the mistaken belief that they can obtain some precious material value for themselves are more likely to stir up factions and fracture the City. Philosophers, however, who are only philosophers, are not fit to rule because they are mesmerized by their meditations and revelations. But the enlightened ones must be compelled to take over the stewardship of the City. They reluctantly but willingly do so because they have a Vision of a Transcendent Good; they recognize a Good for All beyond what benefits them individually, and part of the Good they love is Justice for all and thus they develop a sense of duty to achieve justice in the City.

This public burden is not an injustice to the philosopher king or queen because, having seen the goodness of cosmic order, they see that their own good is bound up with a harmonious city. For the sake of harmony, the citizens sacrifice some of their material aspirations for lawful order in the City. For the same reason the Rulers pass up the time they desire for intellectual pursuits to manage the affairs of the City. One's highest Good is bound up with a Universal Good for All. Thus the Best City is ruled by those least eager to rule.

SUGGESTIONS FOR FURTHER READING

Altman, William H. F. *Plato the Teacher: The Crisis of the Republic.* Lanham, MD: Lexington Books, 2012. [181-236]

Annas, Julia. *An Introduction to Plato's Republic.* New York: Oxford, 1981. [217-271]

Benardete, Seth. *Socrates' Second Sailing: On Plato's Republic.* Chicago: University of Chicago Press, 1989. [153-181]

Blackburn, Simon. *Plato's Republic: A Biography.* New York: Atlantic Monthly Press, 2006. [94-129]

Bloom, Allan. *The Republic of Plato.* New York: Harper Collins, 1968. [397-414]

Cherniss, Harold. "The Philosophical Economy of the Theory of Ideas." *American Journal of Philology* 57 (1936): 445-456.

Ferejohn, Michael T. "Knowledge, Recollection, and the Forms in *Republic* VII." *The Blackwell Guide to Plato's Republic*. Malden, MA: Blackwell, 2006. [214-233]

Irwin, Terence. *Plato's Ethics*. New York: Oxford University Press, 1995. [271-280]

Malcolm, J. "The Line and the Cave." *Phronesis* 7 (1962): 38-45.

Morrison, J. "Two Unresolved Difficulties in the Line and the Cave." *Phronesis* 22 (1977): 212-231.

Nemas, Alexander. "Plato on the Imperfection of the Sensible World." *American Philosophical Quarterly* 12 (1975): 105-117.

Pappas, Nickolas. *Plato and the Republic*. New York: Routledge, 1995. [125-155]

Penner, Terry. "The Forms in the *Republic*." *The Blackwell Guide to Plato's Republic*. Malden, MA: Blackwell, 2006. [234-262]

Raven, J.E. "Sun, Divided Line, and Cave." *Classical Quarterly* 3 (1953): 22-32.

Reeve, C.D.C. Philosopher-Kings: The Argument of Plato's Republic. Princeton: Princeton University Press, 1988. [43-117]

Rice, Daryl H. *A Guide to Plato's Republic*. Oxford: Oxford University Press, 1998. [65-91]

Rosen, Stanley. *Plato's Republic: A Study*. New Haven: Yale University Press, 2005. [255-301]

Sallis, John. *Being and Logos: Reading the Platonic Dialogues*. 3rd ed. Bloomington, IN: Indiana University Press, 1996. [396-412]

Santas, Gerasimos. "The Socratic Fallacy." *Journal of the History of Philosophy* 10 (1972): 17-41.

—. "The Form of the Good in Plato's Republic." *Plato I: Metaphysics and Epistemology*. Ed. Gail Fine. Oxford: Oxford University Press, 1999.

Sayers, Sean. *Plato's Republic: An Introduction*. Edinburgh: Edinburgh University Press, 1999. [106-130]

White, Nicholas P. *A Companion to Plato's Republic*. Indianapolis: Hackett, 1979. [174-196]

Wilson, J. "The Contents of the Cave." *Canadian Journal of Philosophy*. Supplement II (1976): 117-129.

REPUBLIC 6.502c-7.521b

THE EIDOS OF THE GOOD [502C-509C]

And so with pain and toil we have reached the end of one subject, but more remains to be discussed;—how and by what studies and pursuits will the saviours of the constitution be created, and at what ages are they to apply themselves to their several studies?

Certainly.

I omitted the troublesome business of the possession of women, and the procreation of children, and the appointment of the rulers, because I knew that the perfect State would be eyed with jealousy and was difficult of attainment; but that piece of cleverness was not of much service to me, for I had to discuss them all the same. The women and children are now disposed of, but the other question of the rulers must be investigated from the very beginning. We were saying, as you will remember, that they were to be lovers of their country, tried by the test of pleasures and pains, and neither in hardships, nor in dangers, nor at any other critical moment were to lose their patriotism—he was to be rejected who failed, but he who always came forth pure, like gold tried in the refiner's fire, was to be made a ruler, and to receive honours and rewards in life and after death. This was the sort of thing which was being said, and then the argument turned aside and veiled her face; not liking to stir the question which has now arisen.

I perfectly remember, he said.

Yes, my friend, I said, and I then shrank from hazarding the bold word; but now let me dare to say—that the perfect guardian must be a philosopher.

Yes, he said, let that be affirmed.

And do not suppose that there will be many of them; for the gifts which were deemed by us to be essential rarely grow together; they are mostly found in shreds and patches.

What do you mean? he said.

You are aware, I replied, that quick intelligence, memory, sagacity, cleverness, and similar qualities, do not often grow together, and that persons who possess them and are at the same time high-spirited and magnanimous are not so constituted by nature as to live orderly and in a peaceful and settled manner; they are driven any way by their impulses, and all solid principle goes out of them.

Very true, he said.

On the other hand, those steadfast natures which can better be depended upon, which in a battle are impregnable to fear and immovable, are equally immovable when there is anything to be learned; they are always in a torpid state, and are apt to yawn and go to sleep over any intellectual toil.

Quite true.

And yet we were saying that both qualities were necessary in those to whom the higher education is to be imparted, and who are to share in any office or command.

Certainly, he said.

And will they be a class which is rarely found?

Yes, indeed.

Then the aspirant must not only be tested in those labours and dangers and pleasures which we mentioned before, but there is another kind of probation which we did not mention—he must be exercised also in many kinds of knowledge, to see whether the soul will be able to endure the highest of all, or will faint under them, as in any other studies and exercises.

Yes, he said, you are quite right in testing him. But what do you mean by the highest of all knowledge?

You may remember, I said, that we divided the soul into three parts; and distinguished the several natures of justice, temperance, courage, and wisdom?

Indeed, he said, if I had forgotten, I should not deserve to hear more.

And do you remember the word of caution which preceded the discussion of them?

To what do you refer?

We were saying, if I am not mistaken, that he who wanted to see them in their perfect beauty must take a longer and more circuitous way, at the end of which they would appear; but that we could add on a popular exposition of them on a level with the discussion which had preceded. And you replied that such an exposition would be enough for you, and so the enquiry was continued in what to me seemed to be a very inaccurate manner; whether you were satisfied or not, it is for you to say.

Yes, he said, I thought and the others thought that you gave us a fair measure of truth.

But, my friend, I said, a measure of such things which in any degree falls short of the whole truth is not fair measure; for nothing imperfect is the measure of anything, although persons are too apt to be contented and think that they need search no further.

Not an uncommon case when people are lazy.

Yes, I said; and there cannot be any worse fault in a guardian of the State and of the laws.

True.

The guardian then, I said, must be required to take the longer circuit, and toil at learning as well as at gymnastics, or he will never reach the highest knowledge of all which, as we were just now saying, is his proper calling.

What, he said, is there a knowledge still higher than this—higher than justice and the other virtues?

Yes, I said, there is. And of the virtues too we must behold not the outline merely, as at present—nothing short of the most finished picture should satisfy us. When little things are elaborated with an infinity of pains, in order that they may appear in their full beauty and utmost clearness, how ridiculous that we should not think the highest truths worthy of attaining the highest accuracy!

A right noble thought; but do you suppose that we shall refrain from asking you what is this highest knowledge?

Nay, I said, ask if you will; but I am certain that you have heard the answer many times, and now you either do not understand me or, as I rather think, you are disposed to be troublesome; for you have often been told that the idea of good is the highest knowledge, and that all other things become useful and advantageous only by their use of this. You can hardly be ignorant that of this I was about to speak, concerning which, as you have often heard me say, we know so little; and, without which, any other knowledge or possession of any kind will profit us nothing. Do you think that the possession of all other things is of any value if we do not possess the good? or the knowledge of all other things if we have no knowledge of beauty and goodness?

Assuredly not.

You are further aware that most people affirm pleasure to be the good, but the finer sort of wits say it is knowledge?

Yes.

And you are aware too that the latter cannot explain what they mean by knowledge, but are obliged after all to say knowledge of the good?

How ridiculous!

Yes, I said, that they should begin by reproaching us with our ignorance of the good, and then presume our knowledge of it—for the good they define to be knowledge of the good, just as if we understood them when they use the term 'good'—this is of course ridiculous.

Most true, he said.

And those who make pleasure their good are in equal perplexity; for they are compelled to admit that there are bad pleasures as well as good.

Certainly.

And therefore to acknowledge that bad and good are the same?

True.

There can be no doubt about the numerous difficulties in which   d
this question is involved.

There can be none.

Further, do we not see that many are willing to do or to have or
to seem to be what is just and honourable without the reality; but
no one is satisfied with the appearance of good—the reality is what
they seek; in the case of the good, appearance is despised by every
one.

Very true, he said.

Of this then, which every soul of man pursues and makes the end
of all his actions, having a presentiment that there is such an end,
and yet hesitating because neither knowing the nature nor having   e
the same assurance of this as of other things, and therefore losing
whatever good there is in other things,—of a principle such and so
great as this ought the best men in our State, to whom everything is
entrusted, to be in the darkness of ignorance?   506

Certainly not, he said.

I am sure, I said, that he who does not know how the beautiful
and the just are likewise good will be but a sorry guardian of them;
and I suspect that no one who is ignorant of the good will have a true
knowledge of them.

That, he said, is a shrewd suspicion of yours.

And if we only have a guardian who has this knowledge our
State will be perfectly ordered?   b

Of course, he replied; but I wish that you would tell me whether
you conceive this supreme principle of the good to be knowledge or
pleasure, or different from either?

Aye, I said, I knew all along that a fastidious gentleman like you
would not be contented with the thoughts of other people about
these matters.

True, Socrates; but I must say that one who like you has passed
a lifetime in the study of philosophy should not be always repeating
the opinions of others, and never telling his own.

Well, but has any one a right to say positively what he does not   c
know?

Not, he said, with the assurance of positive certainty; he has
no right to do that: but he may say what he thinks, as a matter of
opinion.

And do you not know, I said, that all mere opinions are bad, and
the best of them blind? You would not deny that those who have any
true notion without intelligence are only like blind men who feel
their way along the road?

Very true.

And do you wish to behold what is blind and crooked and base,
when others will tell you of brightness and beauty?

Still, I must implore you, Socrates, said Glaucon, not to turn   d away just as you are reaching the goal; if you will only give such an explanation of the good as you have already given of justice and temperance and the other virtues, we shall be satisfied.

Yes, my friend, and I shall be at least equally satisfied, but I cannot help fearing that I shall fail, and that my indiscreet zeal will bring ridicule upon me. No, sweet sirs, let us not at present ask what is the actual nature of the good, for to reach what is now in my thoughts would be an effort too great for me. But of the child of the good who is likest him, I would fain speak, if I could be sure that you wished to hear—otherwise, not.

By all means, he said, tell us about the child, and you shall remain in our debt for the account of the parent.

I do indeed wish, I replied, that I could pay, and you receive, the account of the parent, and not, as now, of the offspring only; take, however, this latter by way of interest, and at the same time have a care that I do not render a false account, although I have no intention of deceiving you.

Yes, we will take all the care that we can: proceed.

THE ANALOGY OF THE SUN [507A-509C]

Yes, I said, but I must first come to an understanding with you, and remind you of what I have mentioned in the course of this discussion, and at many other times.

What?

The old story, that there is a many beautiful and a many good, and so of other things which we describe and define; to all of them the term 'many' is applied.

True, he said.

And there is an absolute beauty and an absolute good, and of other things to which the term 'many' is applied there is an absolute; for they may be brought under a single idea, which is called the essence of each.

Very true.

The many, as we say, are seen but not known, and the ideas are known but not seen.

Exactly.

And what is the organ with which we see the visible things?

The sight, he said.

And with the hearing, I said, we hear, and with the other senses perceive the other objects of sense?

True.

But have you remarked that sight is by far the most costly and complex piece of workmanship which the artificer of the senses ever contrived?

No, I never have, he said.

Then reflect; has the ear or voice need of any third or additional nature in order that the one may be able to hear and the other to be heard?

Nothing of the sort.

No, indeed, I replied; and the same is true of most, if not all, the other senses—you would not say that any of them requires such an addition?   d

Certainly not.

But you see that without the addition of some other nature there is no seeing or being seen?

How do you mean?

Sight being, as I conceive, in the eyes, and he who has eyes wanting to see; colour being also present in them, still unless there be a third nature specially adapted to the purpose, the owner of the eyes will see nothing and the colours will be invisible.   e

Of what nature are you speaking?

Of that which you term light, I replied.

True, he said.

Noble, then, is the bond which links together sight and visibility, and great beyond other bonds by no small difference of nature; for light is their bond, and light is no ignoble thing?   508

Nay, he said, the reverse of ignoble.

And which, I said, of the gods in heaven would you say was the lord of this element? Whose is that light which makes the eye to see perfectly and the visible to appear?

You mean the sun, as you and all mankind say.

May not the relation of sight to this deity be described as follows?

How?

Neither sight nor the eye in which sight resides is the sun?

No.

Yet of all the organs of sense the eye is the most like the sun?   b

By far the most like.

And the power which the eye possesses is a sort of effluence which is dispensed from the sun?

Exactly.

Then the sun is not sight, but the author of sight who is recognised by sight?

True, he said.

And this is he whom I call the child of the good, whom the good begat in his own likeness, to be in the visible world, in relation to sight and the things of sight, what the good is in the intellectual world in relation to mind and the things of mind:

Will you be a little more explicit? he said.   c

Why, you know, I said, that the eyes, when a person directs them towards objects on which the light of day is no longer shining, but the moon and stars only, see dimly, and are nearly blind; they seem to have no clearness of vision in them?

Very true.

But when they are directed towards objects on which the sun shines, they see clearly and there is sight in them?

Certainly.

And the soul is like the eye: when resting upon that on which truth and being shine, the soul perceives and understands, and is radiant with intelligence; but when turned towards the twilight of becoming and perishing, then she has opinion only, and goes blinking about, and is first of one opinion and then of another, and seems to have no intelligence?

Just so.

Now, that which imparts truth to the known and the power of knowing to the knower is what I would have you term the idea of good, and this you will deem to be the cause of science, and of truth in so far as the latter becomes the subject of knowledge; beautiful too, as are both truth and knowledge, you will be right in esteeming this other nature as more beautiful than either; and, as in the previous instance, light and sight may be truly said to be like the sun, and yet not to be the sun, so in this other sphere, science and truth may be deemed to be like the good, but not the good; the good has a place of honour yet higher.

What a wonder of beauty that must be, he said, which is the author of science and truth, and yet surpasses them in beauty; for you surely cannot mean to say that pleasure is the good?

God forbid, I replied; but may I ask you to consider the image in another point of view?

In what point of view?

You would say, would you not, that the sun is not only the author of visibility in all visible things, but of generation and nourishment and growth, though he himself is not generation?

Certainly.

In like manner the good may be said to be not only the author of knowledge to all things known, but of their being and essence, and yet the good is not essence, but far exceeds essence in dignity and power.

Glaucon said, with a ludicrous earnestness: By the light of heaven, how amazing!

Yes, I said, and the exaggeration may be set down to you; for you made me utter my fancies.

And pray continue to utter them; at any rate let us hear if there is anything more to be said about the similitude of the sun.

Yes, I said, there is a great deal more.

Then omit nothing, however slight.

I will do my best, I said; but I should think that a great deal will have to be omitted.

I hope not, he said.

THE DIVIDED LINE [509C-511E]

You have to imagine, then, that there are two ruling powers, and
that one of them is set over the intellectual world, the other over the
visible. I do not say heaven, lest you should fancy that I am playing   d
upon the name ('ourhanoz, orhatoz'). May I suppose that you have
this distinction of the visible and intelligible fixed in your mind?
   I have.
   Now take a line which has been cut into two unequal parts, and
divide each of them again in the same proportion, and suppose the
two main divisions to answer, one to the visible and the other to
the intelligible, and then compare the subdivisions in respect of
their clearness and want of clearness, and you will find that the
first section in the sphere of the visible consists of images. And by
images I mean, in the first place, shadows, and in the second place,
reflections in water and in solid, smooth and polished bodies and the   e
like: Do you understand?
   Yes, I understand.   510
   Imagine, now, the other section, of which this is only the
resemblance, to include the animals which we see, and everything
that grows or is made.
   Very good.
   Would you not admit that both the sections of this division have
different degrees of truth, and that the copy is to the original as the
sphere of opinion is to the sphere of knowledge?
   Most undoubtedly.
   Next proceed to consider the manner in which the sphere of the
intellectual is to be divided.   b
   In what manner?
   Thus:—There are two subdivisions, in the lower of which the
soul uses the figures given by the former division as images; the
enquiry can only be hypothetical, and instead of going upwards to
a principle descends to the other end; in the higher of the two, the
soul passes out of hypotheses, and goes up to a principle which is
above hypotheses, making no use of images as in the former case,
but proceeding only in and through the ideas themselves.
   I do not quite understand your meaning, he said.
   Then I will try again; you will understand me better when I have
made some preliminary remarks. You are aware that students of
geometry, arithmetic, and the kindred sciences assume the odd and   c
the even and the figures and three kinds of angles and the like in
their several branches of science; these are their hypotheses, which
they and every body are supposed to know, and therefore they do
not deign to give any account of them either to themselves or others;

but they begin with them, and go on until they arrive at last, and in a consistent manner, at their conclusion?

d

Yes, he said, I know.

And do you not know also that although they make use of the visible forms and reason about them, they are thinking not of these, but of the ideals which they resemble; not of the figures which they draw, but of the absolute square and the absolute diameter, and so on—the forms which they draw or make, and which have shadows and reflections in water of their own, are converted by them into

e

images, but they are really seeking to behold the things themselves, which can only be seen with the eye of the mind?

That is true.

511

And of this kind I spoke as the intelligible, although in the search after it the soul is compelled to use hypotheses; not ascending to a first principle, because she is unable to rise above the region of hypothesis, but employing the objects of which the shadows below are resemblances in their turn as images, they having in relation to the shadows and reflections of them a greater distinctness, and therefore a higher value.

I understand, he said, that you are speaking of the province of geometry and the sister arts.

b

And when I speak of the other division of the intelligible, you will understand me to speak of that other sort of knowledge which reason herself attains by the power of dialectic, using the hypotheses not as first principles, but only as hypotheses—that is to say, as steps and points of departure into a world which is above hypotheses, in order that she may soar beyond them to the first principle of the whole; and clinging to this and then to that which depends on this, by successive steps she descends again without the aid of any sensible object, from ideas, through ideas, and in ideas she ends.

c

I understand you, he replied; not perfectly, for you seem to me to be describing a task which is really tremendous; but, at any rate, I understand you to say that knowledge and being, which the science of dialectic contemplates, are clearer than the notions of the arts, as they are termed, which proceed from hypotheses only: these are also contemplated by the understanding, and not by the senses: yet, because they start from hypotheses and do not ascend to a principle, those who contemplate them appear to you not to exercise the higher reason upon them, although when a first principle is added to them

d

they are cognizable by the higher reason. And the habit which is concerned with geometry and the cognate sciences I suppose that you would term understanding and not reason, as being intermediate between opinion and reason.

You have quite conceived my meaning, I said; and now, corresponding to these four divisions, let there be four faculties in the soul—reason answering to the highest, understanding to the second, faith (or conviction) to the third, and perception of shadows to the last—and let there be a scale of them, and let us suppose that the several faculties have clearness in the same degree that their objects have truth.

I understand, he replied, and give my assent, and accept your arrangement.

BOOK VII

THE MYTH OF THE CAVE [514A-521B]

And now, I said, let me show in a figure how far our nature is enlightened or unenlightened:—Behold! human beings living in a underground den, which has a mouth open towards the light and reaching all along the den; here they have been from their childhood, and have their legs and necks chained so that they cannot move, and can only see before them, being prevented by the chains from turning round their heads. Above and behind them a fire is blazing at a distance, and between the fire and the prisoners there is a raised way; and you will see, if you look, a low wall built along the way, like the screen which marionette players have in front of them, over which they show the puppets.

I see.

And do you see, I said, men passing along the wall carrying all sorts of vessels, and statues and figures of animals made of wood and stone and various materials, which appear over the wall? Some of them are talking, others silent.

You have shown me a strange image, and they are strange prisoners.

Like ourselves, I replied; and they see only their own shadows, or the shadows of one another, which the fire throws on the opposite wall of the cave?

True, he said; how could they see anything but the shadows if they were never allowed to move their heads?

And of the objects which are being carried in like manner they would only see the shadows?

Yes, he said.

And if they were able to converse with one another, would they not suppose that they were naming what was actually before them?

Very true.

And suppose further that the prison had an echo which came

from the other side, would they not be sure to fancy when one of the passers-by spoke that the voice which they heard came from the passing shadow?

No question, he replied.

To them, I said, the truth would be literally nothing but the shadows of the images.

c

That is certain.

And now look again, and see what will naturally follow if the prisoners are released and disabused of their error. At first, when any of them is liberated and compelled suddenly to stand up and turn his neck round and walk and look towards the light, he will suffer sharp pains; the glare will distress him, and he will be unable to see the realities of which in his former state he had seen the shadows; and then conceive some one saying to him, that what he saw before was an illusion, but that now, when he is approaching nearer to being

d

and his eye is turned towards more real existence, he has a clearer vision,—what will be his reply? And you may further imagine that his instructor is pointing to the objects as they pass and requiring him to name them,—will he not be perplexed? Will he not fancy that the shadows which he formerly saw are truer than the objects which are now shown to him?

Far truer.

And if he is compelled to look straight at the light, will he not have a pain in his eyes which will make him turn away to take

e

refuge in the objects of vision which he can see, and which he will conceive to be in reality clearer than the things which are now being shown to him?

True, he said.

And suppose once more, that he is reluctantly dragged up a steep and rugged ascent, and held fast until he is forced into the presence of the sun himself, is he not likely to be pained and irritated? When he approaches the light his eyes will be dazzled, and he will not be able to see anything at all of what are now called realities.

516

Not all in a moment, he said.

He will require to grow accustomed to the sight of the upper world. And first he will see the shadows best, next the reflections of men and other objects in the water, and then the objects themselves; then he will gaze upon the light of the moon and the stars and the spangled heaven; and he will see the sky and the stars by night better than the sun or the light of the sun by day?

Certainly.

b

Last of all he will be able to see the sun, and not mere reflections of him in the water, but he will see him in his own proper place, and not in another; and he will contemplate him as he is.

Certainly.

He will then proceed to argue that this is he who gives the season and the years, and is the guardian of all that is in the visible world, and in a certain way the cause of all things which he and his fellows have been accustomed to behold?

Clearly, he said, he would first see the sun and then reason about him.

And when he remembered his old habitation, and the wisdom of the den and his fellow-prisoners, do you not suppose that he would congratulate himself on the change, and pity them?

Certainly, he would.

And if they were in the habit of conferring honours among themselves on those who were quickest to observe the passing shadows and to remark which of them went before, and which followed after, and which were together; and who were therefore best able to draw conclusions as to the future, do you think that he would care for such honours and glories, or envy the possessors of them? Would he not say with Homer,

'Better to be the poor servant of a poor master,'

and to endure anything, rather than think as they do and live after their manner?

Yes, he said, I think that he would rather suffer anything than entertain these false notions and live in this miserable manner.

Imagine once more, I said, such an one coming suddenly out of the sun to be replaced in his old situation; would he not be certain to have his eyes full of darkness?

To be sure, he said.

And if there were a contest, and he had to compete in measuring the shadows with the prisoners who had never moved out of the den, while his sight was still weak, and before his eyes had become steady (and the time which would be needed to acquire this new habit of sight might be very considerable), would he not be ridiculous? Men would say of him that up he went and down he came without his eyes; and that it was better not even to think of ascending; and if any one tried to loose another and lead him up to the light, let them only catch the offender, and they would put him to death.

No question, he said.

This entire allegory, I said, you may now append, dear Glaucon, to the previous argument; the prison-house is the world of sight, the light of the fire is the sun, and you will not misapprehend me if you interpret the journey upwards to be the ascent of the soul into the intellectual world according to my poor belief, which, at your desire, I have expressed—whether rightly or wrongly God knows. But, whether true or false, my opinion is that in the world of knowledge the idea of good appears last of all, and is seen only with an effort; and, when seen, is also inferred to be the universal author of all things beautiful and right, parent of light and of the lord of light in this visible world, and the immediate source of reason and truth in the intellectual; and that this is the power upon which he who would act rationally either in public or private life must have his eye fixed.

I agree, he said, as far as I am able to understand you.

Moreover, I said, you must not wonder that those who attain to this beatific vision are unwilling to descend to human affairs; for their souls are ever hastening into the upper world where they desire to dwell; which desire of theirs is very natural, if our allegory may be trusted.

Yes, very natural.

And is there anything surprising in one who passes from divine contemplations to the evil state of man, misbehaving himself in a ridiculous manner; if, while his eyes are blinking and before he has become accustomed to the surrounding darkness, he is compelled to fight in courts of law, or in other places, about the images or the shadows of images of justice, and is endeavouring to meet the conceptions of those who have never yet seen absolute justice?

Anything but surprising, he replied.

Any one who has common sense will remember that the bewilderments of the eyes are of two kinds, and arise from two causes, either from coming out of the light or from going into the light, which is true of the mind's eye, quite as much as of the bodily eye; and he who remembers this when he sees any one whose vision is perplexed and weak, will not be too ready to laugh; he will first ask whether that soul of man has come out of the brighter life, and is unable to see because unaccustomed to the dark, or having turned from darkness to the day is dazzled by excess of light. And he will count the one happy in his condition and state of being, and he will pity the other; or, if he have a mind to laugh at the soul which comes from below into the light, there will be more reason in this than in the laugh which greets him who returns from above out of the light into the den.

That, he said, is a very just distinction.

But then, if I am right, certain professors of education must be wrong when they say that they can put a knowledge into the soul which was not there before, like sight into blind eyes.

They undoubtedly say this, he replied.   c

Whereas, our argument shows that the power and capacity of learning exists in the soul already; and that just as the eye was unable to turn from darkness to light without the whole body, so too the instrument of knowledge can only by the movement of the whole soul be turned from the world of becoming into that of being, and learn by degrees to endure the sight of being, and of the brightest and best of being, or in other words, of the good.

Very true.

And must there not be some art which will effect conversion in   d
the easiest and quickest manner; not implanting the faculty of sight, for that exists already, but has been turned in the wrong direction, and is looking away from the truth?

Yes, he said, such an art may be presumed.

And whereas the other so-called virtues of the soul seem to be akin to bodily qualities, for even when they are not originally innate they can be implanted later by habit and exercise, the virtue of wisdom more than anything else contains a divine element which always remains, and by this conversion is rendered useful   e
and profitable; or, on the other hand, hurtful and useless. Did you never observe the narrow intelligence flashing from the keen eye of a clever rogue—how eager he is, how clearly his paltry soul sees the way to his end; he is the reverse of blind, but his keen eye-sight is   519
forced into the service of evil, and he is mischievous in proportion to his cleverness?

Very true, he said.

But what if there had been a circumcision of such natures in the days of their youth; and they had been severed from those sensual pleasures, such as eating and drinking, which, like leaden weights, were attached to them at their birth, and which drag them down and turn the vision of their souls upon the things that are below—if, I say, they had been released from these impediments and turned in   b
the opposite direction, the very same faculty in them would have seen the truth as keenly as they see what their eyes are turned to now.

Very likely.

Yes, I said; and there is another thing which is likely, or rather a necessary inference from what has preceded, that neither the uneducated and uninformed of the truth, nor yet those who never make an end of their education, will be able ministers of State; not the former, because they have no single aim of duty which is the rule

c   of all their actions, private as well as public; nor the latter, because they will not act at all except upon compulsion, fancying that they are already dwelling apart in the islands of the blest.

Very true, he replied.

Then, I said, the business of us who are the founders of the State will be to compel the best minds to attain that knowledge which we have already shown to be the greatest of all—they must continue to ascend until they arrive at the good; but when they have ascended and seen enough we must not allow them to do as they do now.

d   What do you mean?

I mean that they remain in the upper world: but this must not be allowed; they must be made to descend again among the prisoners in the den, and partake of their labours and honours, whether they are worth having or not.

But is not this unjust? he said; ought we to give them a worse life, when they might have a better?

You have again forgotten, my friend, I said, the intention of the legislator, who did not aim at making any one class in the State happy

e   above the rest; the happiness was to be in the whole State, and he held the citizens together by persuasion and necessity, making them

520 benefactors of the State, and therefore benefactors of one another; to this end he created them, not to please themselves, but to be his instruments in binding up the State.

True, he said, I had forgotten.

Observe, Glaucon, that there will be no injustice in compelling our philosophers to have a care and providence of others; we shall explain to them that in other States, men of their class are not obliged to share in the toils of politics: and this is reasonable, for they grow up at their own sweet will, and the government would rather not have them. Being self-taught, they cannot be expected to

b   show any gratitude for a culture which they have never received. But we have brought you into the world to be rulers of the hive, kings of yourselves and of the other citizens, and have educated you far better and more perfectly than they have been educated, and you are better able to share in the double duty. Wherefore each of you, when his turn comes, must go down to the general underground abode,

c   and get the habit of seeing in the dark. When you have acquired the habit, you will see ten thousand times better than the inhabitants of the den, and you will know what the several images are, and what they represent, because you have seen the beautiful and just and good in their truth. And thus our State, which is also yours, will be a reality, and not a dream only, and will be administered in a spirit unlike that of other States, in which men fight with one another about shadows only and are distracted in the struggle for power, which in their eyes is a great good. Whereas the truth is that the State in which the rulers are most reluctant to govern is always the best and most quietly governed, and the State in which they are most eager, the worst.

Quite true, he replied.

And will our pupils, when they hear this, refuse to take their turn at the toils of State, when they are allowed to spend the greater part of their time with one another in the heavenly light?

Impossible, he answered; for they are just men, and the commands which we impose upon them are just; there can be no doubt that every one of them will take office as a stern necessity, and not after the fashion of our present rulers of State.

Yes, my friend, I said; and there lies the point. You must contrive for your future rulers another and a better life than that of a ruler, and then you may have a well-ordered State; for only in the State which offers this, will they rule who are truly rich, not in silver and gold, but in virtue and wisdom, which are the true blessings of life. Whereas if they go to the administration of public affairs, poor and hungering after their own private advantage, thinking that hence they are to snatch the chief good, order there can never be; for they will be fighting about office, and the civil and domestic broils which thus arise will be the ruin of the rulers themselves and of the whole State.

Most true, he replied.

And the only life which looks down upon the life of political ambition is that of true philosophy. Do you know of any other?

Indeed, I do not, he said.

And those who govern ought not to be lovers of the task? For, if they are, there will be rival lovers, and they will fight.

No question.

Who then are those whom we shall compel to be guardians? Surely they will be the men who are wisest about affairs of State, and by whom the State is best administered, and who at the same time have other honours and another and a better life than that of politics?

They are the men, and I will choose them, he replied.

11

EDUCATION OF THE PHILOSOPHER-KINGS

THE EDUCATION OF GUARDIAN RULERS (521C-540C)

In this section of the text, Socrates describes in detail the curriculum for the Guardian Rulers. It begins with the education of the Auxiliaries and accordingly with music and gymnastics (the arts and humanities). This can be related to the shadow world of the Cave and the lowest section of the Divided Line. Then they study mathematics, considered very useful to a general or admiral in war. Mathematics, as the third level of the Divided Line, is touted as the intermediary way to higher intellection of the Pure Forms, "to draw men toward being." Socrates illustrates the studies that draw the mind higher by contrasting the mind's apprehension of the Form of the finger (Fingerness Itself) as universal, eternal, perfect, common to all particular fingers—three fingers: middle, ring and forefinger—held before one's eyes. Each visible finger is shaped and sized differently and positioned differently and, depending on the type of work one engages in, soft or rough. But each, the mind perceives, participates in the one unchanging Form of the Finger. Mathematics thus can lead the philosopher warrior from practical application to pure formal entities and relationships. These will bring her closer to eternal truth.

Geometry is added on, and solid geometry would be if more headway can be made in it. Astronomy is the next study. Here the position and movement of the planets are useful for navigation and also generalship. Socrates is reluctant to say that the study of astronomy has led souls to higher intellection, because stargazing without understanding cosmic laws of motions is as ignorant as shadow gazing. One has to understand the lightning fast motion of the sphere of the fixed stars and how it imports motion to the ethereal spheres and their planets below [Aristotle and Ptolemy describe these motions in more depth, but here they are mentioned in the *Republic*. Accordingly the fixed stars were imbedded in a crystalline sphere consisting of the heavenly element of aether. Aristotle thought that the movement of the outer sphere was capable of generating all the mechanical energy for the universe because it was so fast. The farthest out sphere of the universe made a complete revolution every twenty-four hours. Today, that phenomenal speed is accounted for by the heliocentric model of the universe and, instead of the stars rotating, it's the earth rotating on its axis every twenty-four hours.]. Motions in depth are the true subject of astronomy. One can only guess what Plato thought of the mythology and astrology associated with the planets and the stars.

True astronomy leads you to the Demiurge who rationally crafts the universe and sets it on a harmonious continuous direction. That there is a rational cosmic order inspires the philosopher to suspend her contemplation of it and work in public life to establish a civic order that reflects it. The discusants add the study of musical harmony as it relates to astrological harmony (The Music of the Spheres).

After qualifying exams, the most proficient enter into five years of philosophy and the study of dialectic. Socrates names the sectors of the Divided Line from the top down:

- Knowledge
- Thought
- Trust
- Imagination

The guardians picked to enter philosophy must be virtuous and their education should not be forced upon them. "The free man ought not to learn any study slavishly" (536d). Study must be integrated and multi-disciplinary. A capstone course providing an overview of the studies is recommended. They begin the study of dialectic at the age of thirty. Dialectic can destroy belief in conventional norms and religious myths and tradition. The neophyte philosopher can have her head turned by Sophists toward self-serving acquisitiveness or vicious aggression. But the philosopher should be able to refocus the dialectic back to the eternal Forms and to the form of the Good which the myths represented about as well as a shadow represents the thing that casts it. Then after five years of philosophy they "return to the cave." At the age of thirty-five they take command of the military and conduct war for fifteen years. They are observed to see who disgraces themselves in the field out of greed, cowardice, or concupiscence. Those who are best at everything take up the rule of the City at age 50 (540a).

IS THE IDEAL CITY POSSIBLE? [540C-541B]

If they kidnap and march off to the country all the children under ten to be resocialized away from their parents and the corrupting culture of the City, then they have a shot at producing the Ideally Just City. (Horrible images of the depopulation of the city by Pol Pot and the Khmer Rouge in Cambodia, the resocialization of children in rural settings during the Stalin era and even the presumed kidnapping and chaining of infants in the Cave, intrude upon our reflections).

Can Plato be serious? Commentators are divided on this. If the Ideal State is practical only if all the children below ten are resocialized in a rural setting, then the Ideal State, for some, is not a serious proposal. What then is this all about?

The State is a metaphor for the individual soul and the individual can be home-schooled at ten apart from popular conventions and prejudices and taught the Cardinal Virtues (Jean Jacques Rousseau would agree). That is possible. This view downplays the notion that the *Republic* is a political treatise at all and is instead primarily a vehicle for teaching virtue. For that camp, Plato's last work *The Laws* alone represents his political philosophy. For those who find it implausible that Plato is offering no practical political advice in the *Republic,* Plato is interpreted as sincere in his belief that radical educational reform, especially on the collegiate level of the auxiliaries and guardians, is essential if the ideal State is to be approached, no less achieved.

SUGGESTIONS FOR FURTHER READING

Annas, Julia. *An Introduction to Plato's Republic*. New York: Oxford, 1981. [272-293]

Benardete, Seth. *Socrates' Second Sailing: On Plato's Republic*. Chicago: University of Chicago Press, 1989. [181-185].

Bloom, Allan. *The Republic of Plato*. New York: Harper Collins, 1968. [401-412]

Pappas, Nickolas. *Plato and the Republic*. New York: Routledge, 1995. [148-151]

Sayers, Sean. *Plato's Republic: An Introduction.* Edinburgh: Edinburgh University Press, 1999. [106-130]

White, Nicholas P. *A Companion to Plato's Republic.* Indianapolis: Hackett, 1979. [196-204]

REPUBLIC 7.521C-7.541B

THE EDUCATION OF THE GUARDIANS [521C-540C]

And now shall we consider in what way such guardians will be   c
produced, and how they are to be brought from darkness to light,—
as some are said to have ascended from the world below to the gods?

By all means, he replied.

The process, I said, is not the turning over of an oyster-shell (In
allusion to a game in which two parties fled or pursued according as
an oyster-shell which was thrown into the air fell with the dark or
light side uppermost.), but the turning round of a soul passing from
a day which is little better than night to the true day of being, that
is, the ascent from below, which we affirm to be true philosophy?

Quite so.

And should we not enquire what sort of knowledge has the power
of effecting such a change?   d

Certainly.

What sort of knowledge is there which would draw the soul from
becoming to being? And another consideration has just occurred
to me: You will remember that our young men are to be warrior
athletes?

Yes, that was said.

Then this new kind of knowledge must have an additional
quality?

What quality?

Usefulness in war.

Yes, if possible.

There were two parts in our former scheme of education, were   e
there not?

Just so.

There was gymnastic which presided over the growth and decay
of the body, and may therefore be regarded as having to do with
generation and corruption?

True.

Then that is not the knowledge which we are seeking to discover?

No.

522   But what do you say of music, which also entered to a certain extent into our former scheme?

Music, he said, as you will remember, was the counterpart of gymnastic, and trained the guardians by the influences of habit, by harmony making them harmonious, by rhythm rhythmical, but not giving them science; and the words, whether fabulous or possibly true, had kindred elements of rhythm and harmony in them. But in music there was nothing which tended to that good which you are now seeking.

b   You are most accurate, I said, in your recollection; in music there certainly was nothing of the kind. But what branch of knowledge is there, my dear Glaucon, which is of the desired nature; since all the useful arts were judged to be lowly by us?

Undoubtedly; and yet if music and gymnastic are excluded, and the arts are also excluded, what remains?

Well, I said, there may be nothing left of our special subjects; and then we shall have to take something which is not special, but of universal application.

What may that be?

A something which all arts and sciences and intelligences use in
c   common, and which every one first has to learn among the elements of education.

What is that?

The little matter of distinguishing one, two, and three—in a word, number and calculation:—do not all arts and sciences necessarily partake of them?

Yes.

Then the art of war partakes of them?

To be sure.

Then Palamedes, whenever he appears in tragedy, proves
d   Agamemnon ridiculously unfit to be a general. Did you never remark how he declares that he had invented number, and had numbered the ships and set in array the ranks of the army at Troy; which implies that they had never been numbered before, and Agamemnon must be supposed literally to have been incapable of counting his own feet—how could he if he was ignorant of number? And if that is true, what sort of general must he have been?

I should say a very strange one, if this was as you say.

Can we deny that a warrior should have a knowledge of
e   arithmetic?

Certainly he should, if he is to have the smallest understanding of military tactics, or indeed, I should rather say, if he is to be a man at all.

I should like to know whether you have the same notion which I have of this study?

What is your notion?

It appears to me to be a study of the kind which we are seeking, and which leads naturally to reflection, but never to have been rightly used; for the true use of it is simply to draw the soul towards being.

Will you explain your meaning? he said.

I will try, I said; and I wish you would share the enquiry with me, and say 'yes' or 'no' when I attempt to distinguish in my own mind what branches of knowledge have this attracting power, in order that we may have clearer proof that arithmetic is, as I suspect, one of them.

Explain, he said.

I mean to say that objects of sense are of two kinds; some of them do not invite thought because the sense is an adequate judge of them; while in the case of other objects sense is so untrustworthy that further enquiry is imperatively demanded.

You are clearly referring, he said, to the manner in which the senses are imposed upon by distance, and by painting in light and shade.

No, I said, that is not at all my meaning.

Then what is your meaning?

When speaking of uninviting objects, I mean those which do not pass from one sensation to the opposite; inviting objects are those which do; in this latter case the sense coming upon the object, whether at a distance or near, gives no more vivid idea of anything in particular than of its opposite. An illustration will make my meaning clearer:—here are three fingers—a little finger, a second finger, and a middle finger.

Very good.

You may suppose that they are seen quite close: And here comes the point.

What is it?

Each of them equally appears a finger, whether seen in the middle or at the extremity, whether white or black, or thick or thin— it makes no difference; a finger is a finger all the same. In these cases a man is not compelled to ask of thought the question what is a finger? for the sight never intimates to the mind that a finger is other than a finger.

True.

And therefore, I said, as we might expect, there is nothing here e   which invites or excites intelligence.

There is not, he said.

But is this equally true of the greatness and smallness of the fingers? Can sight adequately perceive them? and is no difference made by the circumstance that one of the fingers is in the middle and another at the extremity? And in like manner does the touch adequately perceive the qualities of thickness or thinness, of softness or hardness? And so of the other senses; do they give perfect intimations of such matters? Is not their mode of operation on this
524   wise—the sense which is concerned with the quality of hardness is necessarily concerned also with the quality of softness, and only intimates to the soul that the same thing is felt to be both hard and soft?

You are quite right, he said.

And must not the soul be perplexed at this intimation which the sense gives of a hard which is also soft? What, again, is the meaning of light and heavy, if that which is light is also heavy, and that which is heavy, light?

b   Yes, he said, these intimations which the soul receives are very curious and require to be explained.

Yes, I said, and in these perplexities the soul naturally summons to her aid calculation and intelligence, that she may see whether the several objects announced to her are one or two.

True.

And if they turn out to be two, is not each of them one and different?

Certainly.

And if each is one, and both are two, she will conceive the two
c   as in a state of division, for if there were undivided they could only be conceived of as one?

True.

The eye certainly did see both small and great, but only in a confused manner; they were not distinguished.

Yes.

Whereas the thinking mind, intending to light up the chaos, was compelled to reverse the process, and look at small and great as separate and not confused.

Very true.

Was not this the beginning of the enquiry 'What is great?' and 'What is small?'

Exactly so.

And thus arose the distinction of the visible and the intelligible.

Most true.   d

This was what I meant when I spoke of impressions which invited the intellect, or the reverse—those which are simultaneous with opposite impressions, invite thought; those which are not simultaneous do not.

I understand, he said, and agree with you.

And to which class do unity and number belong?

I do not know, he replied.

Think a little and you will see that what has preceded will supply the answer; for if simple unity could be adequately perceived by the sight or by any other sense, then, as we were saying in the case of   e the finger, there would be nothing to attract towards being; but when there is some contradiction always present, and one is the reverse of one and involves the conception of plurality, then thought begins to be aroused within us, and the soul perplexed and wanting to arrive at a decision asks 'What is absolute unity?' This is the way in which   525 the study of the one has a power of drawing and converting the mind to the contemplation of true being.

And surely, he said, this occurs notably in the case of one; for we see the same thing to be both one and infinite in multitude?

Yes, I said; and this being true of one must be equally true of all number?

Certainly.

And all arithmetic and calculation have to do with number?

Yes.

And they appear to lead the mind towards truth?   b

Yes, in a very remarkable manner.

Then this is knowledge of the kind for which we are seeking, having a double use, military and philosophical; for the man of war must learn the art of number or he will not know how to array his troops, and the philosopher also, because he has to rise out of the sea of change and lay hold of true being, and therefore he must be an arithmetician.

That is true.

And our guardian is both warrior and philosopher?

Certainly.

Then this is a kind of knowledge which legislation may fitly prescribe; and we must endeavour to persuade those who are to be the principal men of our State to go and learn arithmetic, not as   c amateurs, but they must carry on the study until they see the nature of numbers with the mind only; nor again, like merchants or retail-traders, with a view to buying or selling, but for the sake of their military use, and of the soul herself; and because this will be the easiest way for her to pass from becoming to truth and being.

That is excellent, he said.

d   Yes, I said, and now having spoken of it, I must add how charming the science is! and in how many ways it conduces to our desired end, if pursued in the spirit of a philosopher, and not of a shopkeeper!

How do you mean?

I mean, as I was saying, that arithmetic has a very great and elevating effect, compelling the soul to reason about abstract number, and rebelling against the introduction of visible or tangible

e   objects into the argument. You know how steadily the masters of the art repel and ridicule any one who attempts to divide absolute unity when he is calculating, and if you divide, they multiply (Meaning either (1) that they integrate the number because they deny the possibility of fractions; or (2) that division is regarded by them as a process of multiplication, for the fractions of one continue to be units.), taking care that one shall continue one and not become lost in fractions.

526   That is very true.

Now, suppose a person were to say to them: O my friends, what are these wonderful numbers about which you are reasoning, in which, as you say, there is a unity such as you demand, and each unit is equal, invariable, indivisible,—what would they answer?

They would answer, as I should conceive, that they were speaking of those numbers which can only be realized in thought.

b   Then you see that this knowledge may be truly called necessary, necessitating as it clearly does the use of the pure intelligence in the attainment of pure truth?

Yes; that is a marked characteristic of it.

And have you further observed, that those who have a natural talent for calculation are generally quick at every other kind of knowledge; and even the dull, if they have had an arithmetical training, although they may derive no other advantage from it, always become much quicker than they would otherwise have been.

c   Very true, he said.

And indeed, you will not easily find a more difficult study, and not many as difficult.

You will not.

And, for all these reasons, arithmetic is a kind of knowledge in which the best natures should be trained, and which must not be given up.

I agree.

Let this then be made one of our subjects of education. And next, shall we enquire whether the kindred science also concerns us?

You mean geometry?

Exactly so.   d

Clearly, he said, we are concerned with that part of geometry which relates to war; for in pitching a camp, or taking up a position, or closing or extending the lines of an army, or any other military manoeuvre, whether in actual battle or on a march, it will make all the difference whether a general is or is not a geometrician.

Yes, I said, but for that purpose a very little of either geometry or calculation will be enough; the question relates rather to the greater and more advanced part of geometry—whether that tends in any degree to make more easy the vision of the idea of good; and thither,   e as I was saying, all things tend which compel the soul to turn her gaze towards that place, where is the full perfection of being, which she ought, by all means, to behold.

True, he said.

Then if geometry compels us to view being, it concerns us; if becoming only, it does not concern us?

Yes, that is what we assert.   527

Yet anybody who has the least acquaintance with geometry will not deny that such a conception of the science is in flat contradiction to the ordinary language of geometricians.

How so?

They have in view practice only, and are always speaking, in a narrow and ridiculous manner, of squaring and extending and applying and the like—they confuse the necessities of geometry with those of daily life; whereas knowledge is the real object of the   b whole science.

Certainly, he said.

Then must not a further admission be made?

What admission?

That the knowledge at which geometry aims is knowledge of the eternal, and not at all about perishing and transience.

That, he replied, may be readily allowed, and is true.

Then, my noble friend, geometry will draw the soul towards truth, and create the spirit of philosophy, and raise up that which is now unhappily allowed to fall down.

Nothing will be more likely to have such an effect.   c

Then nothing should be more sternly laid down than that the inhabitants of your fair city should by all means learn geometry.

Moreover the science has indirect effects, which are not small.

Of what kind? he said.

There are the military advantages of which you spoke, I said; and in all departments of knowledge, as experience proves, any one who has studied geometry is infinitely quicker of apprehension than one who has not.

Yes indeed, he said, there is an infinite difference between them.

Then shall we propose this as a second branch of knowledge which our youth will study?

Let us do so, he replied.

d   And suppose we make astronomy the third—what do you say?

I am strongly inclined to it, he said; the observation of the seasons and of months and years is as essential to the general as it is to the farmer or sailor.

I am amused, I said, at your fear of the world, which makes you guard against the appearance of insisting upon useless studies; and I quite admit the difficulty of believing that in every man there is an eye of the soul which, when by other pursuits lost and dimmed,

e   is by these purified and re-illumined; and is more precious far than ten thousand bodily eyes, for by it alone is truth seen. Now there are two classes of persons: one class of those who will agree with you and will take your words as a revelation; another class to whom they will be utterly unmeaning, and who will naturally deem them to be idle tales, for they see no sort of profit which is to be obtained from them. And therefore you had better decide at once with which

528   of the two you are proposing to argue. You will very likely say with neither, and that your chief aim in carrying on the argument is your own improvement; at the same time you do not grudge to others any benefit which they may receive.

I think that I should prefer to carry on the argument mainly on my own behalf.

Then take a step backward, for we have gone wrong in the order of the sciences.

What was the mistake? he said.

After plane geometry, I said, we proceeded at once to solids in

c   revolution, instead of taking solids in themselves; whereas after the second dimension the third, which is concerned with cubes and dimensions of depth, ought to have followed.

That is true, Socrates; but so little seems to be known as yet about these subjects.

Why, yes, I said, and for two reasons:—in the first place, no government patronises them; this leads to a want of energy in the pursuit of them, and they are difficult; in the second place, students cannot learn them unless they have a director. But then a director can hardly be found, and even if he could, as matters now stand, the students, who are very conceited, would not attend to him. That, however, would be otherwise if the whole State became the director of these studies and gave honour to them; then disciples would want to come, and there would be continuous and earnest search, and discoveries would be made; since even now, disregarded as they are by the world, and maimed of their fair proportions, and although none of their votaries can tell the use of them, still these studies force their way by their natural charm, and very likely, if they had the help of the State, they would some day emerge into light.

Yes, he said, there is a remarkable charm in them. But I do not clearly understand the change in the order. First you began with a geometry of plane surfaces?

Yes, I said.

And you placed astronomy next, and then you made a step backward?

Yes, and I have delayed you by my hurry; the ludicrous state of solid geometry, which, in natural order, should have followed, made me pass over this branch and go on to astronomy, or motion of solids.

True, he said.

Then assuming that the science now omitted would come into existence if encouraged by the State, let us go on to astronomy, which will be fourth.

The right order, he replied. And now, Socrates, as you rebuked the vulgar manner in which I praised astronomy before, my praise shall be given in your own spirit. For every one, as I think, must see that astronomy compels the soul to look upwards and leads us from this world to another.

Every one but myself, I said; to every one else this may be clear, but not to me.

And what then would you say?

I should rather say that those who elevate astronomy into philosophy appear to me to make us look downwards and not upwards.

What do you mean? he asked.

You, I replied, have in your mind a truly sublime conception of our knowledge of the things above. And I dare say that if a person were to throw his head back and study the carved ceiling, you would still think that his mind was the percipient, and not his eyes. And you are very likely right, and I may be a simpleton: but, in my opinion, that knowledge only which is of being and of the unseen can make the soul look upwards, and whether a man gapes at the heavens or blinks on the ground, seeking to learn some particular of sense, I would deny that he can learn, for nothing of that sort is matter of science; his soul is looking downwards, not upwards, whether his way to knowledge is by water or by land, whether he floats, or only lies on his back.

I acknowledge, he said, the justice of your rebuke. Still, I should like to ascertain how astronomy can be learned in any manner more conducive to that knowledge of which we are speaking?

I will tell you, I said: The starry heaven which we behold is molded upon a visible ground, and therefore, although the fairest and most perfect of visible things, must necessarily be deemed inferior far to the true motions of absolute swiftness and absolute slowness, which are relative to each other, and carry with them that which is contained in them, in the true number and in every true figure. Now, these are to be apprehended by reason and intelligence, but not by sight.

True, he replied.

The spangled heavens should be used as a pattern and with a view to that higher knowledge; their beauty is like the beauty of figures or pictures excellently wrought by the hand of Daedalus, or some other great artist, which we may chance to behold; any geometrician who saw them would appreciate the exquisiteness of their workmanship, but he would never dream of thinking that in them he could find the true equal or the true double, or the truth of any other proportion.

No, he replied, such an idea would be ridiculous.

And will not a true astronomer have the same feeling when he looks at the movements of the stars? Will he not think that heaven and the things in heaven are framed by the Creator of them in the most perfect manner? But he will never imagine that the proportions of night and day, or of both to the month, or of the month to the year, or of the stars to these and to one another, and any other things that are material and visible can also be eternal and subject to no deviation—that would be absurd; and it is equally absurd to take so much pains in investigating their exact truth.

I quite agree, though I never thought of this before.

Then, I said, in astronomy, as in geometry, we should employ problems, and let the heavens alone if we would approach the subject in the right way and so make the natural gift of reason to be of any real use.

That, he said, is a work infinitely beyond our present astronomers.

Yes, I said; and there are many other things which must also have a similar extension given to them, if our legislation is to be of any value. But can you tell me of any other suitable study?

No, he said, not without thinking.

Motion, I said, has many forms, and not one only; two of them are obvious enough even to wits no better than ours; and there are others, as I imagine, which may be left to wiser persons.

But where are the two?   d

There is a second, I said, which is the counterpart of the one already named.

And what may that be?

The second, I said, would seem relatively to the ears to be what the first is to the eyes; for I conceive that as the eyes are designed to look up at the stars, so are the ears to hear harmonious motions; and these are sister sciences—as the Pythagoreans say, and we, Glaucon, agree with them?

Yes, he replied.

But this, I said, is a laborious study, and therefore we had better go and learn of them; and they will tell us whether there are any other applications of these sciences. At the same time, we must not lose sight of our own higher object.   e

What is that?

There is a perfection which all knowledge ought to reach, and which our pupils ought also to attain, and not to fall short of, as I was saying that they did in astronomy. For in the science of harmony, as you probably know, the same thing happens. The teachers of harmony compare the sounds and consonances which are heard only, and their labour, like that of the astronomers, is in vain.   531

Yes, by heaven! he said; and 'tis as good as a play to hear them talking about their condensed notes, as they call them; they put their ears close alongside of the strings like persons catching a sound from their neighbour's wall—one set of them declaring that they distinguish an intermediate note and have found the least interval which should be the unit of measurement; the others insisting that the two sounds have passed into the same—either party setting their ears before their understanding.   b

You mean, I said, those gentlemen who tease and torture the strings and rack them on the pegs of the instrument: I might carry on the metaphor and speak after their manner of the blows which the plectrum gives, and make accusations against the strings, both of backwardness and forwardness to sound; but this would be tedious, and therefore I will only say that these are not the men, and that I am referring to the Pythagoreans, of whom I was just now proposing to enquire about harmony. For they too are in error, like the astronomers; they investigate the numbers of the harmonies which are heard, but they never attain to problems—that is to say, they never reach the natural harmonies of number, or reflect why some numbers are harmonious and others not.

That, he said, is a thing of more than mortal knowledge.

A thing, I replied, which I would rather call useful; that is, if sought after with a view to the beautiful and good; but if pursued in any other spirit, useless.

Very true, he said.

Now, when all these studies reach the point of inter-communion and connection with one another, and come to be considered in their mutual affinities, then, I think, but not till then, will the pursuit of them have a value for our objects; otherwise there is no profit in them.

I suspect so; but you are speaking, Socrates, of a vast work.

What do you mean? I said; the prelude or what? Do you not know that all this is but the prelude to the actual strain which we have to learn? For you surely would not regard the skilled mathematician as a dialectician?

Assuredly not, he said; I have hardly ever known a mathematician who was capable of reasoning.

But do you imagine that men who are unable to give and take a reason will have the knowledge which we require of them?

Neither can this be supposed.

And so, Glaucon, I said, we have at last arrived at the hymn of dialectic. This is that strain which is of the intellect only, but which the faculty of sight will nevertheless be found to imitate; for sight, as you may remember, was imagined by us after a while to behold the real animals and stars, and last of all the sun himself. And so with dialectic; when a person starts on the discovery of the absolute by the light of reason only, and without any assistance of sense, and perseveres until by pure intelligence he arrives at the perception of the absolute good, he at last finds himself at the end of the intellectual world, as in the case of sight at the end of the visible.

Exactly, he said.

Then this is the progress which you call dialectic?

True.

But the release of the prisoners from chains, and their translation from the shadows to the images and to the light, and the ascent from the underground den to the sun, while in his presence they are vainly trying to look on animals and plants and the light of the sun, but are able to perceive even with their weak eyes the images in the water (which are divine), and are the shadows of true existence (not shadows of images cast by a light of fire, which compared with the sun is only an image)—this power of elevating the highest principle in the soul to the contemplation of that which is best in existence, with which we may compare the raising of that faculty which is the very light of the body to the sight of that which is brightest in the material and visible world—this power is given, as I was saying, by all that study and pursuit of the arts which has been described.

I agree in what you are saying, he replied, which may be hard to believe, yet, from another point of view, is harder still to deny. This, however, is not a theme to be treated of in passing only, but will have to be discussed again and again. And so, whether our conclusion be true or false, let us assume all this, and proceed at once from the prelude or preamble to the chief strain (A play upon the Greek word, which means both 'law' and 'strain.'), and describe that in like manner. Say, then, what is the nature and what are the divisions of dialectic, and what are the paths which lead thither; for these paths will also lead to our final rest.

Dear Glaucon, I said, you will not be able to follow me here, though I would do my best, and you should behold not an image only but the absolute truth, according to my notion. Whether what I told you would or would not have been a reality I cannot venture to say; but you would have seen something like reality; of that I am confident.

Doubtless, he replied.

But I must also remind you, that the power of dialectic alone can reveal this, and only to one who is a disciple of the previous sciences.

Of that assertion you may be as confident as of the last.

And assuredly no one will argue that there is any other method of comprehending by any regular process all true existence or of ascertaining what each thing is in its own nature; for the arts in general are concerned with the desires or opinions of men, or are cultivated with a view to production and construction, or for the preservation of such productions and constructions; and as to the mathematical sciences which, as we were saying, have some apprehension of true being—geometry and the like—they only dream about being, but never can they behold the waking reality so long as they leave the hypotheses which they use unexamined, and are unable to give an account of them. For when a man knows not

c his own first principle, and when the conclusion and intermediate steps are also constructed out of he knows not what, how can he imagine that such a fabric of convention can ever become science?

Impossible, he said.

Then dialectic, and dialectic alone, goes directly to the first principle and is the only science which does away with hypotheses in order to make her ground secure; the eye of the soul, which is

d literally buried in an outlandish slough, is by her gentle aid lifted upwards; and she uses as handmaids and helpers in the work of conversion, the sciences which we have been discussing. Custom terms them sciences, but they ought to have some other name, implying greater clearness than opinion and less clearness than science: and this, in our previous sketch, was called understanding. But why should we dispute about names when we have realities of

e such importance to consider?

Why indeed, he said, when any name will do which expresses the thought of the mind with clearness?

At any rate, we are satisfied, as before, to have four divisions; two for intellect and two for opinion, and to call the first division science, the second understanding, the third belief, and the fourth perception of shadows, opinion being concerned with becoming,

534 and intellect with being; and so to make a proportion:—

As being is to becoming, so is pure intellect to opinion. And as intellect is to opinion, so is science to belief, and understanding to the perception of shadows.

But let us defer the further correlation and subdivision of the subjects of opinion and of intellect, for it will be a long enquiry, many times longer than this has been.

As far as I understand, he said, I agree.

b And do you also agree, I said, in describing the dialectician as one who attains a conception of the essence of each thing? And he who does not possess and is therefore unable to impart this conception, in whatever degree he fails, may in that degree also be said to fail in intelligence? Will you admit so much?

Yes, he said; how can I deny it?

And you would say the same of the conception of the good? Until the person is able to abstract and define rationally the idea of good, and unless he can run the gauntlet of all objections, and is

c ready to disprove them, not by appeals to opinion, but to absolute truth, never faltering at any step of the argument—unless he can do all this, you would say that he knows neither the idea of good nor any other good; he apprehends only a shadow, if anything at all, which is given by opinion and not by science;—dreaming and slumbering in this life, before he is well awake here, he arrives at the world below, and has his final quietus.

In all that I should most certainly agree with you.

And surely you would not have the children of your ideal State, whom you are nurturing and educating—if the ideal ever becomes a reality—you would not allow the future rulers to be like posts (Literally 'lines,' probably the starting-point of a race-course.), having no reason in them, and yet to be set in authority over the highest matters?

Certainly not.

Then you will make a law that they shall have such an education as will enable them to attain the greatest skill in asking and answering questions?

Yes, he said, you and I together will make it.

Dialectic, then, as you will agree, is the coping-stone of the sciences, and is set over them; no other science can be placed higher—the nature of knowledge can no further go?

I agree, he said.

But to whom we are to assign these studies, and in what way they are to be assigned, are questions which remain to be considered.

Yes, clearly.

You remember, I said, how the rulers were chosen before?

Certainly, he said.

The same natures must still be chosen, and the preference again given to the surest and the bravest, and, if possible, to the fairest; and, having noble and generous tempers, they should also have the natural gifts which will facilitate their education.

And what are these?

Such gifts as keenness and ready powers of acquisition; for the mind more often faints from the severity of study than from the severity of gymnastics: the toil is more entirely the mind's own, and is not shared with the body.

Very true, he replied.

Further, he of whom we are in search should have a good memory, and be an unwearied solid man who is a lover of labour in any line; or he will never be able to endure the great amount of bodily exercise and to go through all the intellectual discipline and study which we require of him.

Certainly, he said; he must have natural gifts.

The mistake at present is, that those who study philosophy have no vocation, and this, as I was before saying, is the reason why she has fallen into disrepute: her true sons should take her by the hand and not bastards.

What do you mean?

d   In the first place, her devoted advocate should not have a lame or halting industry—I mean, that he should not be half industrious and half idle: as, for example, when a man is a lover of gymnastic and hunting, and all other bodily exercises, but a hater rather than a lover of the labour of learning or listening or enquiring. Or the occupation to which he devotes himself may be of an opposite kind, and he may have the other sort of lameness.

Certainly, he said.

e   And as to truth, I said, is not a soul equally to be deemed halt and lame which hates voluntary falsehood and is extremely indignant at herself and others when they tell lies, but is patient of involuntary falsehood, and does not mind wallowing like a swinish beast in the mire of ignorance, and has no shame at being detected?

To be sure.

536   And, again, in respect of temperance, courage, magnificence, and every other virtue, should we not carefully distinguish between the true son and the bastard? for where there is no discernment of such qualities states and individuals unconsciously err; and the state makes a ruler, and the individual a friend, of one who, being defective in some part of virtue, is in a figure lame or a bastard.

That is very true, he said.

b   All these things, then, will have to be carefully considered by us; and if only those whom we introduce to this vast system of education and training are sound in body and mind, justice herself will have nothing to say against us, and we shall be the saviours of the constitution and of the State; but, if our pupils are men of another stamp, the reverse will happen, and we shall pour a still greater flood of ridicule on philosophy than she has to endure at present.

That would not be creditable.

Certainly not, I said; and yet perhaps, in thus turning jest into earnest I am equally ridiculous.

In what respect?

c   I had forgotten, I said, that we were not serious, and spoke with too much excitement. For when I saw philosophy so undeservedly trampled under foot of men I could not help feeling a sort of indignation at the authors of her disgrace: and my anger made me too vehement.

Indeed! I was listening, and did not think so.

But I, who am the speaker, felt that I was. And now let me remind you that, although in our former selection we chose old men, we must not do so in this. Solon was under a delusion when he said that a man when he grows old may learn many things—for he can no more learn much than he can run much; youth is the time for any extraordinary toil.

d

Of course.

And, therefore, calculation and geometry and all the other elements of instruction, which are a preparation for dialectic, should be presented to the mind in childhood; not, however, under any notion of forcing our system of education.

Why not?

Because a freeman ought not to be a slave in the acquisition of knowledge of any kind. Bodily exercise, when compulsory, does no harm to the body; but knowledge which is acquired under compulsion obtains no hold on the mind.

e

Very true.

Then, my good friend, I said, do not use compulsion, but let early education be a sort of amusement; you will then be better able to find out the natural bent.

537

That is a very rational notion, he said.

Do you remember that the children, too, were to be taken to see the battle on horseback; and that if there were no danger they were to be brought close up and, like young hounds, have a taste of blood given them?

Yes, I remember.

The same practice may be followed, I said, in all these things— labours, lessons, dangers—and he who is most at home in all of them ought to be enrolled in a select number.

At what age?

At the age when the necessary gymnastics are over: the period whether of two or three years which passes in this sort of training is useless for any other purpose; for sleep and exercise are unconducive to learning; and the trial of who is first in gymnastic exercises is one of the most important tests to which our youth are subjected.

b

Certainly, he replied.

After that time those who are selected from the class of twenty years old will be promoted to higher honour, and the sciences which they learned without any order in their early education will now be brought together, and they will be able to see the natural relationship of them to one another and to true being.

c

Yes, he said, that is the only kind of knowledge which takes lasting root.

Yes, I said; and the capacity for such knowledge is the great criterion of dialectical talent: the comprehensive mind is always the dialectical.

I agree with you, he said.

These, I said, are the points which you must consider; and those who have most of this comprehension, and who are most steadfast in their learning, and in their military and other appointed duties, when they have arrived at the age of thirty have to be chosen by you out of the select class, and elevated to higher honour; and you will have to prove them by the help of dialectic, in order to learn which of them is able to give up the use of sight and the other senses, and in company with truth to attain absolute being: And here, my friend, great caution is required.

Why great caution?

Do you not remark, I said, how great is the evil which dialectic has introduced?

What evil? he said.

The students of the art are filled with lawlessness.

Quite true, he said.

Do you think that there is anything so very unnatural or inexcusable in their case? or will you make allowance for them?

In what way make allowance?

I want you, I said, by way of parallel, to imagine a hypothetical son who is brought up in great wealth; he is one of a great and numerous family, and has many flatterers. When he grows up to manhood, he learns that his alleged are not his real parents; but who the real are he is unable to discover. Can you guess how he will be likely to behave towards his flatterers and his supposed parents, first of all during the period when he is ignorant of the false relation, and then again when he knows? Or shall I guess for you?

If you please.

Then I should say, that while he is ignorant of the truth he will be likely to honour his father and his mother and his supposed relations more than the flatterers; he will be less inclined to neglect them when in need, or to do or say anything against them; and he will be less willing to disobey them in any important matter.

He will.

But when he has made the discovery, I should imagine that he would diminish his honour and regard for them, and would become more devoted to the flatterers; their influence over him would greatly

increase; he would now live after their ways, and openly associate
with them, and, unless he were of an unusually good disposition, he
would trouble himself no more about his supposed parents or other   c
relations.

Well, all that is very probable. But how is the image applicable
to the disciples of philosophy?

In this way: you know that there are certain principles about
justice and honour, which were taught us in childhood, and under
their parental authority we have been brought up, obeying and
honouring them.

That is true.

There are also opposite maxims and habits of pleasure which
flatter and attract the soul, but do not influence those of us who   d
have any sense of right, and they continue to obey and honour the
maxims of their fathers.

True.

Now, when a man is in this state, and the questioning spirit asks
what is fair or honourable, and he answers as the legislator has
taught him, and then arguments many and diverse refute his words,
until he is driven into believing that nothing is honourable any more
than dishonourable, or just and good any more than the reverse, and
so of all the notions which he most valued, do you think that he will   e
still honour and obey them as before?

Impossible.

And when he ceases to think them honourable and natural as
heretofore, and he fails to discover the true, can he be expected to
pursue any life other than that which flatters his desires?

He cannot.   539

And from being a keeper of the law he is converted into a breaker
of it?

Unquestionably.

Now all this is very natural in students of philosophy such as I
have described, and also, as I was just now saying, most excusable.

Yes, he said; and, I may add, pitiable.

Therefore, that your feelings may not be moved to pity about our
citizens who are now thirty years of age, every care must be taken in
introducing them to dialectic.

Certainly.

There is a danger lest they should taste the dear delight too
early; for youngsters, as you may have observed, when they first   b
get the taste in their mouths, argue for amusement, and are always
contradicting and refuting others in imitation of those who refute

them; like puppy-dogs, they rejoice in pulling and tearing at all who come near them.

Yes, he said, there is nothing which they like better.

c   And when they have made many conquests and received defeats at the hands of many, they violently and speedily get into a way of not believing anything which they believed before, and hence, not only they, but philosophy and all that relates to it is apt to have a bad name with the rest of the world.

Too true, he said.

But when a man begins to get older, he will no longer be guilty of such insanity; he will imitate the dialectician who is seeking for truth, and not the eristic, who is contradicting for the sake of amusement; and the greater moderation of his character will increase instead of diminishing the honour of the pursuit.

d

Very true, he said.

And did we not make special provision for this, when we said that the disciples of philosophy were to be orderly and steadfast, not, as now, any chance aspirant or intruder?

Very true.

Suppose, I said, the study of philosophy to take the place of gymnastics and to be continued diligently and earnestly and exclusively for twice the number of years which were passed in bodily exercise—will that be enough?

Would you say six or four years? he asked.

e   Say five years, I replied; at the end of the time they must be sent down again into the den and compelled to hold any military or other office which young men are qualified to hold: in this way they will get their experience of life, and there will be an opportunity of trying whether, when they are drawn all manner of ways by temptation, they will stand firm or flinch.

540   And how long is this stage of their lives to last?

Fifteen years, I answered; and when they have reached fifty years of age, then let those who still survive and have distinguished themselves in every action of their lives and in every branch of knowledge come at last to their consummation: the time has now arrived at which they must raise the eye of the soul to the universal light which lightens all things, and behold the absolute good; for that is the pattern according to which they are to order the State and the lives of individuals, and the remainder of their own lives also;

b   making philosophy their chief pursuit, but, when their turn comes, toiling also at politics and ruling for the public good, not as though they were performing some heroic action, but simply as a matter of duty; and when they have brought up in each generation others like themselves and left them in their place to be governors of the State, then they will depart to the Islands of the Blest and dwell there; and the city will give them public memorials and sacrifices and honour them, if the Pythian oracle consent, as demigods, but if not, as in any case blessed and divine.   c

You are a sculptor, Socrates, and have made statues of our governors faultless in beauty.

Yes, I said, Glaucon, and of our governesses too; for you must not suppose that what I have been saying applies to men only and not to women as far as their natures can go.

There you are right, he said, since we have made them to share in all things like the men.

Is the Ideal City Possible? [540C-541B]

Well, I said, and you would agree (would you not?) that what has been said about the State and the government is not a mere dream,   d and although difficult not impossible, but only possible in the way which has been supposed; that is to say, when the true philosopher kings are born in a State, one or more of them, despising the honours of this present world which they deem mean and worthless, esteeming above all things right and the honour that springs from right, and regarding justice as the greatest and most necessary of all things, whose ministers they are, and whose principles will be   e exalted by them when they set in order their own city?

How will they proceed?

They will begin by sending out into the country all the inhabitants of the city who are more than ten years old, and will take possession of their children, who will be unaffected by the habits of their parents; these they will train in their own habits and laws, I mean in   541 the laws which we have given them: and in this way the State and constitution of which we were speaking will soonest and most easily attain happiness, and the nation which has such a constitution will gain most.

Yes, that will be the best way. And I think, Socrates, that you have very well described how, if ever, such a constitution might come into being.

Enough then of the perfect State, and of the man who bears its   b image—there is no difficulty in seeing how we shall describe him.

There is no difficulty, he replied; and I agree with you in thinking that nothing more need be said.

12

IMPERFECT JUSTICE

A quick review of the Craft analogy from Book I might be helpful here. The Ideal State consists of three crafts or *techne*: On top are the Guardian Rulers (Philosopher-Kings/Queens) endowed with the virtue (arête) of Wisdom; subordinate to them are the Auxiliary Guardians or warrior class endowed with the virtue of courage; and beneath them are the Producers or craftsmen. The Ideal City is just and moderate since these virtues are systemic throughout (each minds its own business and the Guardian Rulers temper the aggression of the Auxiliary class and the avarice and sensuality of the Producers). The Craft analogy then applies to the psyche of the best most fully flourishing Person in the Ideal City (The Philosopher King/Queen or the *Eudaimon*). Corresponding to the tripartite City is the tripartite psyche of Reason, Spirit and Appetites. Endowed with the virtues of wisdom, courage, moderation and justice the *Eudaimon* (the fully flourishing individual) is the *megalopsuchos* or great-souled individual. This one sees that the good of the individual is universal Goodness itself and willingly sacrifices pleasure and contemplation for the sake of the citizens.

This best of all Cities is now compared with four degenerate City constitutions. Ranging from the best, most just, to the worst, least just, we have: 1. The Ideal State, 2.Timocracy (Spartan-like), 3. Oligarchy of Wealth or Plutocracy, 4. Democracy, and 5. Tyranny. In accord with the Craft Analogy, there are five types of characters that are associated with the rulers of each respective government: 1. The Philosopher-King, 2. the Timocrat, 3. the Plutocrat, 4. the Democrat, and 5. the Tyrant.

The procedure Plato follows here is to describe how the better government degenerates into the inferior. Then he describes the character of the degenerate State, followed by the character of the degenerate ruler of the state.

FROM IDEAL STATE TO TIMOCRACY [543A-550B]

Plato has in mind the government of Sparta. Many people in Athens admired the Spartans for their authoritarian discipline, their healthy physiques, and the beauty of their athletic women. However, having experienced a humiliating defeat by them in the Peloponnesian Wars and recently recovering from the tyrannical rule of the Thirty Tyrants, a puppet government set up in Athens by the Spartans, it was politically dangerous in the restored Athenian democracy to openly praise them. Plato's family connections with two of the disgraced (Thirty) Tyrants cost him a political career.

The term Timocracy comes from the words *time* and *kratia*. *Time* means honor and *kratia* means rule. The two kings of Sparta were military rulers and the militant have a large capacity of *thymos* or spiritedness (anger, aggression, assertion). The Spirited man is one who is a lover of honor, fame or glory. Clearly in these militant societies this is best achieved in the arenas or on the battlefield although others gained fame in other ways. The vices associated with the Spirited man are vainglory and rashness. Since the warrior is the best trained, the strongest, swiftest, most heavily armed and most adept at killing, he is the most dangerous person in the City. Only philosophy can make such a one obedient to the Rule of the Wise and moderate in his appetites.

According to Socrates, the cause of the degeneration of the Ideal State to the Timocratic lies in the failure of the eugenics program of the Guardian Rulers. In a highly controversial passage, Plato seems to believe that astrology can be utilized by the Guardian elders in picking the perfect time for the Guardian Rulers to have intercourse. If the elders do not master this eugenic science or neglect to use it, then inferior offspring will be produced and raised in the commune. The supply of the best stock for guardianship and eventually rule will not become easy or automatic. The elders will have to recognize the less intelligent and crude among the students and demote them to the "silver" or "bronze" classes. They also may have to resort to recruiting talented prospects from the Producer class (remember the Noble Lie is a lie!) and that would entail a great deal of explaining to the folks.

The failure of the eugenics program would mean that some very inferior stock may be promoted to the Guardian Rulers. The vices of the lesser character types would then pollute the ranks of the aristocrats of knowledge such as avarice and the lust for glory. Although admired for their spirit and self-discipline, the Athenians believed themselves to be superior in intellectual achievements and the arts. Spartans, although personally abstemious, were considered ruthless marauders and pillagers of neighboring territories. The laconic phrases of the Laconians ("Come back with your shield, or on it") were inelegant because of an alleged disinterest in higher education or philosophy. The boys of Sparta were educated through force rather than the liberal way of the Athenians and so the boys grew up with no great love of learning or understanding of the delight it brings.

Because of the impurity of the genetic stock of the ruling elite, factions emerge in the guardian class. War ensues between the parties. Provisions of the Ideal State are abandoned. Guardian rulers insist on raising their own offspring and demand estates and private incomes. Since rulers of 'bronze" and "iron" are mixed in with rulers of "gold" and "silver" the avaricious pull the State in the direction of an Oligarchy of wealth while the best pull the State in the direction of Justice and Goodness. The State ends up in the middle, that is, as a Timocracy. Land is distributed to the warrior class and the producers are enslaved. The government is reoriented toward maintaining control over the slave class while preparing for aggressive wars for expanded territory. Historically the Spartans, having enslaved the near-by Meccenians, ruled them by terror; and the ruling warrior class was constantly on alert for war.

Socrates now speculates on the emergence of a Timocrat out of an Aristocratic family. The wife (do we detect a bias here) of an aristocratic father resents his disinterest in wealth or renown. The father is not part of the ruling class so she resents the lack of status and the wealth that goes with office-holding. The father doesn't busy himself with others' affairs, doesn't sue his debtors in court, and isn't hungry for money or fame (he's a regular Socrates). The wife complains to the son that her husband is neither ambitious nor bold. He avoids politics because of cowardice. Even the house servants murmer to the boy that the father is a push-over and a slacker.

The son grows up with a sense of shame and he resolves to gain renown and glory for himself when he can. His psyche is a compromise between his father's wisdom and his mother's avarice. He will temper his appetites and sacrifice his pleasure for the sake of honor, but he will not dedicate himself to reason. Thus he becomes the personally moderate but rash Timocrat.

FROM TIMOCRACY TO PLUTOCRACY [550C-556E]

"Plutus" became an alternate name for "Hades" in the 5th century B.C. Plutus was the god of the underworld, wealth, and death, and he was a blind god. Thus the worshippers of money, the Plutocrats, were worshippers of a blind god. If money is a means to an end, i.e., a means to what money can buy, then pursuing it for its own sake is a blind pursuit. Most people, when asked, want to be millionaires; but when you ask them "why?" they often return an incredulous but blank look.

Since the Timocrats neglect reason and seek honor through war, their treasuries become stocked with the spoils hauled back from the battlefields. Enriched by slave labor, the Timocracy becomes thoroughly corrupt by money, wealth and property. Wealth plus power creates a huge gap between the rich and the poor. The rich rulers find themselves feeling above the law; love of honor and virtue diminish in their souls. The producers become more and more despised by and are exploited by the wealthy oligarchs. The selling of office, bribery and influence-peddling becomes commonplace. The producers sell their land for money, fall into debt, and many lose their freedom by selling themselves into slavery. Landless debtors populate the City: some ("the winged drones") become beggars; others ("the drones with stingers") become cutthroats and thieves.

Now only the wealthy are in power. Poor philosophers, like Socrates, who Plato considered the best the City has to offer, are the least favored, while those whose appetites and avarice are out of control are in power. We recall the scene in Book I when the warrior son of the rich Cephalus threatens to force Socrates into remaining in the Piraeus. The theme of power versus reason and the need to combine them was set out early in the dialogue.

The Oligarchs pervert the Auxiliary class whose *telos* is to defend the lives, honor and glory of the citizens. Now the warriors are used to pillage not only the property of the surrounding territories but the property of the people as well; and the troops are used to enforce a reign of terror so that the Oligarchs can operate with impunity (giving themselves the Ring of Gyges). The State itself obtains a reputation for ignorance, intemperance and injustice. Its honor is besmirched.

Socrates speculates that the son of a Timocrat experiences first hand how fleeting are fame and honor. Unlike the wisdom and the other virtues which once habituated cannot be taken from the *Eudaimon*, fame, honor and glory depend upon the recognition of others; and if the fickle crowd demurs, the values associated with the Spirited Psyche disappear. *Sic transit Gloria munde*. The Timocratic father may have been a general or warrior ruler in the Timocratic State, but then is accused of treason and is exiled or executed. The subsequent stigma and disgrace permanently kills any love of honor in the son and the poverty which he is now subject to endure makes him long for more favorable material well-being. Growing up having saved and scrimped for every drachma, he becomes excessively self-centered and greedy. He lives a dissipated life of pleasure and dedicates himself to acquisition. Rather than using his appetites to gain the health necessary to expand his reason, he subordinates his reason to his appetites and thinks only of ways of expanding the horizons of his desires. Reason becomes the slave of the passions.

The oligarchic man has so many diverse desires in himself that they are like political factions vying for power over him. He will go to war like an oligarch, sending in too few troops and losing them to the dishonor of the City. The sons of the rich will be indulged and they will grow soft, fat and lazy. When ranged beside a "lean tanned poor man" in a military phalanx then the poor will make the comparisons. They will murmer among themselves: "Those men are ours. They are nothing."

FROM OLIGARCHY OF WEALTH TO DEMOCRACY [557A-563E]

The Plutocrats create the circumstances which are rife for a democratic revolution. They weaken the luxury or sumptuary laws and thus create envy by their conspicuous consumption. The capitalism they foster promotes usury, which entices the young to take out loans for property and luxuries. The social drift is toward a sensate materialistic culture and it's every man for himself. The high interest rates and predator loan-sharks bring many noble citizens to bankruptcy and poverty. Some sell themselves into slavery to pay their debts.

The debt-ridden poor and middle class begin to see that the capitalist system is rigged against them and the wealthy arrogantly display their political and material privileges. The wealthy young men are fops: spoiled, greedy, cowardly and indolent. The wealthy scions become flabby, pale, weak and dissipated. In battle the healthy strong grunts whisper about their out-of-shape, phlegmatic, plutocratic officers. The conscripts then begin plotting revolution.

The feverish City, devoted to money making and luxuries, so desired by Glaucon, is sickly and likely to be brought down by the disease of democratic revolution. Commoners steeped in debt rise up against the oligarchs and disperse them and redistribute their land and property. They then share the offices on an equal basis. Selections are often by lottery.

At first sight the Democratic City appears to be delightful and beautiful. It is filled with freedom. People do and say pretty much what they want. There is great diversity tolerated in the City. Everyone is treated as of equal worth from philosopher to oarsman. Children would be raised without the virtues of the *Eudaimon* held up as a model to emulate. There would be a multiplicity of life-styles in the City.

Such a City would not be anarchic but multi-archic. There would be a plethora of contradicting laws and constitutions to follow. Enforcement of the law would be haphazard as the frequent release of criminals in democracies attests. Beneath its pretty surface lies disorder, disharmony, faction and chaos. The unchecked appetites of the producers lead to competitive markets that constantly seek to undermine, cheat or take over rivals. The radical democracy of Plato's day (radical because even the unpropertied males could vote, sit on the juries and hold office) was a recipe for disaster, disorder and dishonor. It pushes aside the elite class of learned aristocrats for the sake of rule by the rabble. This is like throwing the skilled pilot overboard and putting the roughest, loudest, most aggressive seaman in charge of the ship. A ship of fools.

In the democratic state, fathers fear their children and try to imitate them (and their hair styles?). Metics or alien residents take themselves to be the equal of the citizens. Teachers fear their students and pander to them. Pupils disrespect their teachers and give them lip (and surf the web and text in class). Plato is suggesting that it was not Socrates whohad corrupted the young as was charged by the Athenians, but rather the democracy had done so.

The democratic man is the son of an Oligarch of wealth. Like so many self-made men, the old man is tight with his money and it's hard for the son to get him to part with it. Unencumbered from the need to work, the son falls in with roustabouts and revelers. The boy is swept up into the quest for unbridled pleasure though feasting, wine-binges, orgies and gambling. He rejects the penny-pinching probity of the Wealthy scion in favor of working-class hedonism and license. Clearly the education of the Auxiliaries, which fosters the rule of reason over the passions and appetites, would have saved the young man from this dissipated life.

The Oligarchs' materialistic values thoroughly corrupt the son and then the son loses all respect for the father. The son switches allegiance from the Plutocrats to the democrats and a democratic revolution takes place. These farmers, merchants, sailors, and craftsmen consider themselves to be the equal of their wealthy masters and they resent any government restrictions or regulations on their petty businesses, labor or lifestyles—restrictions which they consider forms of tyranny. Debts are forgiven, land redistributed and popular orators are established as rulers.

THE DEMOCRATIC STATE

The democratic state opens the vote to all male citizens and adopts an egalitarian and tolerant politic. Rule now is by the most unruly and libidinous sector of the society: the Producers. The absence of moderation, justice, wisdom and courage of democratic rulers leads to a breakdown of the rule of law.

With the loss of authority by the ruling class, a cascade of weakened authority ensues: fathers have no authority over sons, foreign inhabitants become the equal of Athenians, teachers pander to their students (afraid of course evaluations, I suppose) and the unruly students disrupt the class. Even women consider themselves to be the equal to men. Slaves will be treated as the equal of male citizens and even animals will run about in the city like they do in the country. So we can see that the end state of democracy is really anarchy and this is due to the licentiousness and appetitiveness of the common folk.

The contempt that Plato heaps on the ordinary people is precisely what has led modern critics such as Popper and I.M. Stone to condemn him as a proto-totalitarian, an enemy of the "open" society. The last part of Book XIII and Book IX should put to rest any sense that Plato was a secret admirer of the tyrant. His beloved mentor Socrates hailed from the working class, having been born of a day laborer and a mid-wife, having fought as a foot-soldier and having as a profession stonecutting. If Plato was indeed an aristocratic snob he wouldn't have made an exception for the poverty-stricken street-philosopher. And if the Letters are authentic, Plato had first-hand knowledge of the respect tyrants had for philosophers when Dionysus I of Syracuse had Plato sold as a slave. Still the democrats who took over after the rule of the Thirty Tyrants put Socrates on trial and had him executed. Plato had no love for democracy.

So we will suggest two reasons drawn from the dialogue to explain his distrust of the people:

1. Although even humble Athenians were taught how to read, do simple math, to write and to memorize the epics of Homer and writings of Hesiod, Plato believed that the values taught through the common texts were flawed: the gods were not good and the heroes were not heroic. Indeed Socrates was condemned because he told the Athenians that it was they and not he that was corrupting the youth. This complaint against the arts is explored in Book 10. It is only those with the superior education provided by the philosophers that know the truth of the Forms; and clearly such an education is reserved for an elite and not available to the ordinary folk (It was Jefferson who claimed that a democracy will work only if the electorate is educated and he established the University of Virginia to begin the process).

2. The Craft analogy and the symmetry it imposes clearly works against the Producers. Plato has little respect for the unbridled appetites. They are the lowest sector of the psyche shared with the creatures that crawl and swim. He's portrayed them as a many-headed gryphon, a monster who, if one cuts off one head, another grows in its place. They're a wild team of flying horses carrying the charioteer away from his goal of Goodness/ the Sun. Once they raid the citadel of the Rational Soul and take over (as in the case of the tyrant, see Book IX) chaos will rule in the person and excessive pleasure will bring on disease and early death. Since Plato needs an analogy for the appetites in his tripartite City-State the role is performed by the Producers, the suppliers of both the necessary desires (needs) and the unnecessary desires (luxuries). Similar to Freud's notion of the blind drive of the Libido for sensual satisfaction, Plato believed that the appetites, without rational intervention, would seek unlimited gratification anywhere, anyway. To form symmetry with this psychology, Plato envisions the Producers as sensual, rapacious, greedy, gluttonous, promiscuous, slovenly and inebriated. Clearly if this is their habituated predisposition, they are in general vicious and hardly the equal to the *Eudaimon*. Plato may be playing the amateur sociologist pointing out the pathology of poverty but, as advocates of Democracy, we can point out that he makes the common mistake of taking the consequences of a prejudice as a reason for the prejudice: People existing on a subsistence level, spending their waking hours in hard physical labor, may exhibit pragmatic law-bending means to stay afloat. But there is nothing natural about that, no criminal mind among the working class. That is not analogous to the

first-born nature of the appetitive psyche. The Producers are as capable of delayed gratification as the Guardians. They are just less fortunate. Plato himself, in the myth of the cave, accounts for the enlightenment of the escapee as a "turning" toward the light and not native talent since the escapee is chosen at random from the chained people in the cave. The Noble Lie told to establish the legitimacy of the Guardian rulers is a "LIE." That their moral and political superiority is created by battle-tested education, not nature and the recruitment from the Producing class (by artificially claiming gold in the recruit) suggest that there is talent there to be exploited. Plato needed a Jean Jacques Rousseau to point out that the common man was often more noble than the aristocrats. Here the Craft Analogy limps.

THE TAKEOVER OF THE TYRANT FROM THE DEMOCRACY [563E-557A]

The Democratic leadership cancels debts, enraging the lenders. The people are overjoyed by the confiscation of the property of the Rich and of its redistribution to them. This leads to class warfare as the rich hire mercenaries to retake the government. The poor themselves turn to a mercenary: a fast-talking ruthless "man-of-the-people," to protect themselves and preserve their hold on government.

This is a man who has committed murder and thus has no qualms about killing again, or of killing even his own supporters (Hitler's orders to murder the leaders of the Brown Shirts and Stalin's murder of the generals and his closest colleagues come to mind). No lover of truth, the strongman convinces the democrats that he needs protection to champion their cause and thus is in need of a private army, which he recruits from the beggarly class. Seduced by extravagant promises of even more debt reduction and confiscations from the wealthy, the democrats provide him with military personnel and materiel. With this army, he storms the citadel and takes over from the democrats. Immediately appropriating the property of the Rich for himself, he rewards his army and body guards with the spoils thus guaranteeing their loyalty. The strongman then purges the city of all freethinking dissenters. He eliminates from his cabinet all who would criticize his opinions or actions. Thus he purges his true friends and rewards his false friends (sycophants). This is exactly what Socrates accused Polemarchus of doing in Book. I (Polemarchus: Justice is giving goods to friends and harm to enemies. Socrates: Have you ever mistaken a friend for an enemy?).

Too late the people discover that the Ruler is ruling in his own interest and to his own advantage (See Book I, Thrasymachus' definition of the just ruler) and not in the interest of the weakest. Though soon hated by the people, the Tyrant commands tributes and paeans. To free associate we are reminded of the master/bondsman dialectic in Hegel's *Phenomenology of Spirit* where physical mastery is not sufficient for the usurper; rather recognition as the Master by the subordinates is required for the self-consciousness of the Tyrant. Behind the Mask of the Noble King lies the tyrant with the Ring of Gyges since no one dares to call him out. Rather than the protection and liberation of the people from the predations of the rich, the people have put into place the worst, most unjust of rulers since he has made them all slaves. Now they produce not for the Polis but for the tyrant.

TRANSITION TO BOOK IX [571A-575D]

Book IX completes the task of comparing the *ethos* of the rulers in the various constitutions discussed in the order from the best to the worst: The Philosopher King/Queen, the Timocrat, Plutocrat, Democrat and Tyrant. Socrates will finally demonstrate to Glaucon just how far away and inferior in character is the Tyrant from the Philosopher King/Queen and in so doing finish what he began in Book II by demonstrating that the life of injustice is never to the advantage of the tyrant. He will convince Glaucon once and for all, that becoming a tyrant, although extremely tempting to a man of Glaucon's talents, would be a colossal mistake.

Socrates is now intent on discussing the origin of the tyrant from a democratic household. He distinguishes between our "necessary" desires, i.e., those that are needed to be quenched in order to survive and the "unnecessary" desires, i.e., the luxuries. Among the latter are those that would be considered unlawful and shameful.

Raised by democrats, the budding tyrant is not taught the virtue of restraint or of the superiority of the goods of the soul over the goods of the body (reason and the virtues over sensory satisfaction).

Plato then describes in lurid and shocking detail the passionate beasts that lurk in the souls of men. After an evening of feasting and besotted with drink, a man is awakened out of a deep sleep by desire. While his reason slumbers on, the man impulsively seeks someone or something to satisfy his lust, not stopping himself from raping his own mother or a nearby animal. Afterwards he raids the refrigerator and gorges himself with food. Out he goes in the middle of the night to murder his neighbors.

Now a *eudaimon* with a psychically harmonized soul would act quite differently when his own demons awaken him in the middle of the night. 1. He snaps his thinking cap on, 2. He neither represses his desires nor overindulges them (he makes a sandwich and drinks a glass of milk or he makes love to his lawfully wedded wife) and thereby calms his passions, and 3. He keeps his anger under control so he can get a good night's sleep.

Now we know the kind of education that would produce the *eudaimon* but the would-be tyrant grows up in a household of a leveler who sneers at the better educated and the virtuous, much like the prisoners in the cave treated the enlightened escapee. Without a decent role model to teach him the virtues, the would-be tyrant browbeats and threatens his parents and goes through their money. He perpetually needs money to pay for his revelries, girlfriends and boyfriends. He and his carousing buddies rob temples, extort money from the citizens, bear false witness and take bribes. The criminal youth of dictators has been noted throughout history.

The future authoritarian is a slavish personality in youth showing excessive deference to those who are stronger or more powerful than he. Excessively sycophantic in the ascendancy, once in power, the tyrant expects slavish deference in return. The fawning and ingratiation brings him to the head of a criminal faction on the brink of a popular uprising to place him on the throne.

Once in charge, the young tyrant drops the mask of populism and banishes all democratic consultation from the city.

GLAUCON'S MASTER CLASS [575D-580D]

Ever since Book II we have wondered whether Glaucon is really convinced that the life of a tyrant isn't a viable option. After all, once the tyrant is in power and surrounded by loyal well-compensated bodyguards he can satisfy his lascivious propensities with impunity. Libido meets heaven.

Socrates now shows Glaucon that, not only is the city ruled by the tyrant the most wretched, but so is the tyrant.

Once the people learn that it is not only the wealthy whose property is controlled by the tyrant but their own as well, the tyrant soon earns the hatred of the populace. Assassination plots spring up and the tyrant is a constant target. Uneasy sits the head that wears the crown (especially, as Machiavelli would later note, if the duke is not only feared but hated). The tyrant who enslaves the population can never leave the city for fear of being usurped during his absence. He is like the oppressors who manipulate the shadows in the Cave. They spend as well their whole lives in the Cave with the prisoners.

Further, in a Good City, the private man can rely on the entire polis to guard him against harm and suffering. However, the man who sets himself against his neighbors is like a man transported to a hostile territory alone with his servants and family. He will live in fear for his life and health and will turn to his own slaves, flattering them and freeing them, so that he might protect himself. The turning to one's slave is analogous to the inharmonious soul who turns to his slavish appetites and makes them into the master of his reason. When reason steers a course in which it loses the friendships and honor needed for a happy and peaceful life, it turns to its own rage and passions to unleash the dogs of war against all.

Also such a man will recruit the most sycophantic flatterers and most ruthless and vicious of people as bodyguards and advisers. These are the least trustworthy, least sincere people in the City and as such no true friends to the tyrant. Just like Polemarchus in Book I, the tyrant has a big problem telling the difference between a true friend and a false one; and thus the tyrant lives without friendship, incapable of both gaining friendship and being a friend. Clearly friendship is one of the most valuable things both in itself and for the good consequences it brings in life and an essential contributor of human flourishing and happiness.

Socrates piles on the attributes of the tyrant—envious, faithless, unjust, friendless, impious and a host and nurse for all vice (580a). And so ends the first proof that the tyrant is the most wretched of men.

RETURN TO THE TRIPARTITE SOUL [580D-585E]

Before hiring a herald to trumpet Glaucon's acceptance of the Philosopher King as the happiest of persons and the tyrant as the most wretched, Socrates suggests that they dig deeper into the psyche of the tyrant to reveal the psychological turmoil that make his life miserable rather than happy.

Here we find an extensive recapitulation of the Tripartite Psyche and of Platonic psychology that we outlined in the commentary on Book I and again in Book IV.

Each of the souls, rational, spirited and appetitive, has separate Ends: For Reason, knowledge of the True Forms and the Form of Goodness itself. For the Spirited soul, defense of the life, honor and glory of the individual, and for the appetites, sensory satisfaction.

Each end is accompanied by a different pleasure. For the rational soul, contemplation and delight in the Forms; For the Spirited soul, the recognition that comes with honors and fame; For the appetites, immediate sensory satisfaction.

In the Platonic psychology, each human aspect is owed a measure of each specific pleasure, contemplative, honorific and physical satisfaction. Psychic disorder occurs when any one of the souls tries to unjustly interfere with the rightful attaining of the specific satisfaction by each of the other souls.

There are lovers of wisdom, of honor and of sensation. Which of these personality types is in the best position to judge the happiness of the others? This discussion is reminiscent of the Judges' argument in Kierkegaard's *Either/Or* that the man of reason is in the best position to judge the life of the hedonist since only the judge knows the goods of the flesh (in moderation) and the goods of the law.

The person who is wise has the pleasure not only of the Forms and of Goodness itself; but also of the pleasures of honor, as well as the pleasures (in moderation) of the appetites. The wise person knows all the goods of humanity.

The lover of honor does not know the pleasure that comes from the contemplation of the Forms. Worst off, the lover of money and sensual satisfaction knows only the one kind of pleasure and is ignorant of honor, knowledge and wisdom. Consequently his belief that the life of unbridled sensation is superior to that of the noble king is ignorant. He is simply in no position to judge.

Socrates then distinguishes two kinds of pleasures: 1. Pleasures that are not derived from the absence of pain and 2. Pleasure that is derived from the relieving of pain.

Ceasing to contemplate leaves no pain in its wake. The delight of a pleasant aroma leaves no pain when the smell dissipates.

On the contrary, the sensory pleasures result from slaking painful states: hunger, thirst, craving for alcohol, tobacco or drugs, sexual yearning, envy for the property and the honor of others. Once sated, especially in the intemperate person who sees no reason to moderate or delay these appetites, the pain of absence from these sensations quickly rears up again and gnaws away and maddens the lover of passion.

Storming the Citadel [586A-592B]

Reason is properly the ruling part of the person. The appetites properly should be the slaves of the rational soul. However, when the appetitive soul usurps the legitimate authority of Reason, it perverts Reason's natural End. The passions use reason to calculate means for slaking its desires, thus preventing it from peacefully pursuing its quest for the Truth and the Good.

The proper End of the Spirited Soul is to defend and secure the honor and glory of the whole person. However when the appetitive soul storms the citadel displacing reason from the throne of rule, the Spirited soul gets perverted as well. The vengeful and ruthless tyrant violates the citizens, persecutes dissenters and engages in military adventurism for the spoils of war. These bring disgrace, dishonor and infamy upon the tyrant and his City. Neither the Ends of the rational soul or of the Spirited soul are obtained by the lover of passion.

With reason enslaved by passion, the untamed appetites are cranked up to such excessive levels that they cannot ever be satisfied. Thus ironically even the End or goal of the appetitive soul is perverted since its specific End is sensory satisfaction. Debauched indulgence leads, like a heroin addiction, to greater and greater levels of sensation and the accompanying dissipation threatens and ruins the health of the intemperate person's body. Unfulfilling any of the three separate ends of the human soul and by placing the lowest psyche in charge of the highest, the sick, paranoid, ignorant, desperate, enraged, distraught tyrant becomes the most wretched of men.

By contrast the Philosopher King/Queen is the most blessed because she can quietly contemplate the Truth and the Good, can defend her honor and glory through a tempered response to adversity, and can moderately satisfy her appetites in a way that gives her peace, health and time for contemplation and friendship.

In a characteristic attempt to discover the mathematical foundations that underlay the fleeting appearances of the sensory world, Plato has Socrates calculating the degree to which the tyrant falls below the Philosopher King/Queen in human flourishing. Down the scale from the King, Timocrat,

Plutocrat, Democrat to the tyrant, Socrates calculates that the tyrant is 729 degrees below the King/Queen in human flourishing...729 times more humanly wretched than the King/Queen.

In one of those memorable and vivid images that Plato is known for, Book IX ends with the contemplation of a man trapped in a room with a savage lion and a many-headed gryphon. The gryphon is a mythological creature with the body of a dragon with a multitude of heads. When a gryphon's head is cut off, several more take its place. Here the man symbolizes the rational soul, the lion the spirited soul and the gryphon the appetites. Socrates imagines a god placing all three creatures in a single body. Clearly the man can be devoured by the savage lion or the gryphon ,and he is wise not to attempt to slay them outright since this would mean the death of the organism that contains them. His work is to tame them, giving each his due so that he might go about his business in peace and harmony. Clearly the Philosopher King/Queen has mastered the craft of life, achieving *eudaimonia*—fully flourishing humanity; whereas the tyrant is being attacked and gnawed on by the gryphon and the lion inside him.

SUGGESTIONS FOR FURTHER READING

Annas, Julia. *An Introduction to Plato's* Republic. New York: Oxford, 1981. [294-320]

Bernadete, Seth. *Socrates' Second Sailing: On Plato's* Republic. Chicago: University of Chicago Press, 1989. [189-213]

Bloom, Allan. *The Republic of Plato.* New York: Harper Collins, 1968. [372-426]

Irwin, Terence. Plato's Ethics. Oxford: Oxford University Press, 1995. [281-302]

Pappas, Nickolas. *Plato and the Republic.* New York: Routledge, 1995. [157-171]

Rice, Daryl. *A Guide to Plato's Republic.* Oxford: Oxford University Press, 1998. [93-131]

Rosen, Stanley. *Plato's Republic: A Study.* New Haven: Yale University Press, 2005. [305-351]

Sayers, Sean. *Plato's Republic: An Introductiuon.* Edinburgh: Edinburgh University Press, 1999. [135-147]

White, Nicholas P. *A Companion to Plato's Republic.* Indianapolis, Hackett, 1979. [205-245]

REPUBLIC 8.543A-9.592B

BOOK VIII

FROM IDEAL STATE TO TIMOCRACY [543A-550B]

543   And so, Glaucon, we have arrived at the conclusion that in the perfect State wives and children are to be in common; and that all education and the pursuits of war and peace are also to be common, and the best philosophers and the bravest warriors are to be their kings?

That, replied Glaucon, has been acknowledged.

b   Yes, I said; and we have further acknowledged that the governors, when appointed themselves, will take their soldiers and place them in houses such as we were describing, which are common to all, and contain nothing private, or individual; and about their property, you remember what we agreed?

Yes, I remember that no one was to have any of the ordinary possessions of mankind; they were to be warrior athletes and

c   guardians, receiving from the other citizens, in lieu of annual payment, only their maintenance, and they were to take care of themselves and of the whole State.

True, I said; and now that this division of our task is concluded, let us find the point at which we digressed, that we may return into the old path.

There is no difficulty in returning; you implied, then as now, that you had finished the description of the State: you said that such a State was good, and that the man was good who answered to it,

c   although, as now appears, you had more excellent things to relate
544   both of State and man. And you said further, that if this was the true form, then the others were false; and of the false forms, you said, as I remember, that there were four principal ones, and that their defects, and the defects of the individuals corresponding to them, were worth examining. When we had seen all the individuals, and finally agreed as to who was the best and who was the worst of them, we were to consider whether the best was not also the happiest,

and the worst the most miserable. I asked you what were the four forms of government of which you spoke, and then Polemarchus and Adeimantus put in their word; and you began again, and have found your way to the point at which we have now arrived.

Your recollection, I said, is most exact.

Then, like a wrestler, he replied, you must put yourself again in the same position; and let me ask the same questions, and do you give me the same answer which you were about to give me then.

Yes, if I can, I will, I said.

I shall particularly wish to hear what were the four constitutions of which you were speaking.

That question, I said, is easily answered: the four governments of which I spoke, so far as they have distinct names, are, first, those of Crete and Sparta, which are generally applauded; what is termed oligarchy comes next; this is not equally approved, and is a form of government which teems with evils: thirdly, democracy, which naturally follows oligarchy, although very different: and lastly comes tyranny, great and famous, which differs from them all, and is the fourth and worst disorder of a State. I do not know, do you? of any other constitution which can be said to have a distinct character. There are lordships and principalities which are bought and sold, and some other intermediate forms of government. But these are nondescripts and may be found equally among Hellenes and among barbarians.

Yes, he replied, we certainly hear of many curious forms of government which exist among them.

Do you know, I said, that governments vary as the dispositions of men vary, and that there must be as many of the one as there are of the other? For we cannot suppose that States are made of 'oak and rock,' and not out of the human natures which are in them, and which in a figure turn the scale and draw other things after them?

Yes, he said, the States are as the men are; they grow out of human characters.

Then if the constitutions of States are five, the dispositions of individual minds will also be five?

Certainly.

Him who answers to aristocracy, and whom we rightly call just and good, we have already described.

We have.

Then let us now proceed to describe the inferior sort of natures, being the contentious and ambitious, who answer to the Spartan polity; also the oligarchical, democratical, and tyrannical. Let us place the most just by the side of the most unjust, and when we see them we shall be able to compare the relative happiness or unhappiness of him who leads a life of pure justice or pure injustice. The enquiry will then be completed. And we shall know whether we ought to pursue injustice, as Thrasymachus advises, or in accordance with the conclusions of the argument to prefer justice.

Certainly, he replied, we must do as you say.

Shall we follow our old plan, which we adopted with a view to clearness, of taking the State first and then proceeding to the individual, and begin with the government of honour?—I know of no name for such a government other than timocracy, or perhaps timarchy. We will compare with this the like character in the individual; and, after that, consider oligarchy and the oligarchical man; and then again we will turn our attention to democracy and the democratical man; and lastly, we will go and view the city of tyranny, and once more take a look into the tyrant's soul, and try to arrive at a satisfactory decision.

That way of viewing and judging of the matter will be very suitable.

First, then, I said, let us enquire how timocracy (the government of honour) arises out of aristocracy (the government of the best). Clearly, all political changes originate in divisions of the actual governing power; a government which is united, however small, cannot be moved.

Very true, he said.

In what way, then, will our city be moved, and in what manner will the two classes of auxiliaries and rulers disagree among themselves or with one another? Shall we, after the manner of Homer, pray the Muses to tell us 'how discord first arose'? Shall we imagine them in solemn mockery, to play and jest with us as if we were children, and to address us in a lofty tragic vein, making believe to be in earnest?

How would they address us?

After this manner:—A city which is thus constituted can hardly be shaken; but, seeing that everything which has a beginning has also an end, even a constitution such as yours will not last for ever, but will in time be dissolved. And this is the dissolution:—In plants that grow in the earth, as well as in animals that move on the earth's surface, fertility and sterility of soul and body occur when the circumferences of the circles of each are completed, which in short-lived existences pass over a short space, and in long-lived ones over a long space. But to the knowledge of human fertility and sterility all the wisdom and education of your rulers will not attain; the laws which regulate them will not be discovered by an intelligence which is alloyed with sense, but will escape them, and they will bring children into the world when they ought not. Now that which is of divine birth has a period which is contained in a perfect number (i.e. a cyclical number, such as 6, which is equal to the sum of its divisors 1, 2, 3, so that when the circle or time represented by 6 is completed, the lesser times or rotations represented by 1, 2, 3 are also completed.), but the period of human birth is comprehended in a number in which first increments by involution and evolution (or squared and cubed) obtaining three intervals and four terms of like and unlike, waxing and waning numbers, make all the terms commensurable and agreeable to one another. (Probably the numbers 3, 4, 5, 6 of which the three first = the sides of the Pythagorean triangle. The terms will then be 3 cubed, 4 cubed, 5 cubed, which together = 6 cubed = 216.) The base of these (3) with a third added (4) when combined with five (20) and raised to the third power furnishes two harmonies; the first a square which is a hundred times as great (400 = 4 x 100) (Or the first a square which is 100 x 100 = 10,000. The whole number will then be 17,500 = a square of 100, and an oblong of 100 by 75.), and the other a figure having one side equal to the former, but oblong, consisting of a hundred numbers squared upon rational diameters of a square (i.e. omitting fractions), the side of which is five (7 x 7 = 49 x 100 = 4900), each of them being less by one (than the perfect square which includes the fractions, sc. 50) or less by (Or, 'consisting of two numbers squared upon irrational diameters,' etc. = 100. For other explanations of the passage see Introduction.) two perfect squares of irrational diameters (of a square the side of which is five = 50 + 50 = 100); and a hundred cubes of three (27 x 100 = 2700 + 4900 + 400 = 8000). Now this number represents a geometrical figure which has control over the good and evil of births. For when your guardians are ignorant of the law of births, and unite bride and bridegroom out of season, the children will not be goodly or fortunate. And though only the best of them will be appointed by their predecessors, still they will be unworthy to hold their fathers' places, and when they come into power as guardians, they will soon be found to fail in taking care of us, the Muses, first by under-valuing music; which neglect will soon extend to gymnastic; and hence the young men of your State will be less cultivated. In the succeeding generation rulers will be appointed who have lost the guardian power of testing the metal of your different races, which, like Hesiod's, are of gold and silver and brass and iron. And so iron will be mingled with silver, and brass with gold, and hence there will arise dissimilarity and inequality and irregularity, which always and in all places are causes of hatred and war. This the Muses affirm to be the stock from which discord has sprung, wherever arising; and this is their answer to us.

Yes, and we may assume that they answer truly.

Why, yes, I said, of course they answer truly; how can the Muses speak falsely?

And what do the Muses say next?

When discord arose, then the two races were drawn different ways: the iron and brass fell to acquiring money and land and houses and gold and silver; but the gold and silver races, not wanting money but having the true riches in their own nature, inclined towards virtue and the ancient order of things. There was a battle between them, and at last they agreed to distribute their land and houses among individual owners; and they enslaved their friends and maintainers, whom they had formerly protected in the condition of freemen, and made of them subjects and servants; and they themselves were engaged in war and in keeping a watch against them.

I believe that you have rightly conceived the origin of the change.

And the new government which thus arises will be of a form intermediate between oligarchy and aristocracy?

Very true.

Such will be the change, and after the change has been made, how will they proceed? Clearly, the new State, being in a mean between oligarchy and the perfect State, will partly follow one and partly the other, and will also have some peculiarities.

True, he said.

In the honour given to rulers, in the abstinence of the warrior class from agriculture, handicrafts, and trade in general, in the institution of common meals, and in the attention paid to gymnastics and military training—in all these respects this State will resemble the former.

True.

But in the fear of admitting philosophers to power, because they are no longer to be had simple and earnest, but are made up of mixed elements; and in turning from them to passionate and less complex characters, who are by nature fitted for war rather than peace; and in the value set by them upon military stratagems and contrivances, and in the waging of everlasting wars—this State will be for the most part peculiar.

Yes.

Yes, I said; and men of this stamp will be covetous of money, like those who live in oligarchies; they will have, a fierce secret longing after gold and silver, which they will hoard in dark places, having magazines and treasuries of their own for the deposit and concealment of them; also castles which are just nests for their eggs, and in which they will spend large sums on their wives, or on any others whom they please.

That is most true, he said.

And they are miserly because they have no means of openly acquiring the money which they prize; they will spend that which is another man's on the gratification of their desires, stealing their pleasures and running away like children from the law, their father: they have been schooled not by gentle influences but by force, for they have neglected her who is the true Muse, the companion of reason and philosophy, and have honoured gymnastic more than music.

Undoubtedly, he said, the form of government which you describe is a mixture of good and evil.

Why, there is a mixture, I said; but one thing, and one thing only, is predominantly seen,—the spirit of contention and ambition; and these are due to the prevalence of the passionate or spirited element.

Assuredly, he said.

Such is the origin and such the character of this State, which has been described in outline only; the more perfect execution was not required, for a sketch is enough to show the type of the most perfectly just and most perfectly unjust; and to go through all the States and all the characters of men, omitting none of them, would be an interminable labour.

Very true, he replied.

Now what man answers to this form of government-how did he come into being, and what is he like?

I think, said Adeimantus, that in the spirit of contention which characterises him, he is not unlike our friend Glaucon.

Perhaps, I said, he may be like him in that one point; but there are other respects in which he is very different.

In what respects?

He should have more of self-assertion and be less cultivated, and yet a friend of culture; and he should be a good listener, but no speaker. Such a person is apt to be rough with slaves, unlike the educated man, who is too proud for that; and he will also be courteous to freemen, and remarkably obedient to authority; he is a lover of power and a lover of honour; claiming to be a ruler, not because he is eloquent, or on any ground of that sort, but because he is a soldier and has performed feats of arms; he is also a lover of gymnastic exercises and of the chase.

Yes, that is the type of character which answers to timocracy.

Such an one will despise riches only when he is young; but as he gets older he will be more and more attracted to them, because he has a piece of the avaricious nature in him, and is not single-minded towards virtue, having lost his best guardian.

Who was that? said Adeimantus.

Philosophy, I said, tempered with music, who comes and takes up her abode in a man, and is the only saviour of his virtue throughout life.

Good, he said.

Such, I said, is the timocratical youth, and he is like the timocratical State.

Exactly.

His origin is as follows:—He is often the young son of a brave father, who dwells in an ill-governed city, of which he declines the honours and offices, and will not go to law, or exert himself in any way, but is ready to waive his rights in order that he may escape trouble.

And how does the son come into being?

The character of the son begins to develope when he hears his mother complaining that her husband has no place in the government, of which the consequence is that she has no precedence among other women. Further, when she sees her husband not very eager about money, and instead of battling and railing in the law courts or assembly, taking whatever happens to him quietly; and when she observes that his thoughts always centre in himself, while he treats her with very considerable indifference, she is annoyed, and says to her son that his father is only half a man and far too easy-going: adding all the other complaints about her own ill-treatment which women are so fond of rehearsing.

Yes, said Adeimantus, they give us plenty of them, and their complaints are so like themselves.

And you know, I said, that the old servants also, who are supposed to be attached to the family, from time to time talk privately in the same strain to the son; and if they see any one who owes money to his father, or is wronging him in any way, and he fails to prosecute them, they tell the youth that when he grows up he must retaliate upon people of this sort, and be more of a man than his father. He has only to walk abroad and he hears and sees

the same sort of thing: those who do their own business in the   550
city are called simpletons, and held in no esteem, while the busy-
bodies are honoured and applauded. The result is that the young
man, hearing and seeing all these things—hearing, too, the words of
his father, and having a nearer view of his way of life, and making
comparisons of him and others—is drawn opposite ways: while his
father is watering and nourishing the rational principle in his soul,
the others are encouraging the passionate and appetitive; and he   b
being not originally of a bad nature, but having kept bad company,
is at last brought by their joint influence to a middle point, and
gives up the kingdom which is within him to the middle principle of
contentiousness and passion, and becomes arrogant and ambitious.

You seem to me to have described his origin perfectly.

Then we have now, I said, the second form of government and
the second type of character?   c

We have.

FROM TIMOCRACY TO PLUTOCRACY [550C-557A]

Next, let us look at another man who, as Aeschylus says, 'Is set
over against another State;'

or rather, as our plan requires, begin with the State.

By all means.

I believe that oligarchy follows next in order.

And what manner of government do you term oligarchy?

A government resting on a valuation of property, in which the
rich have power and the poor man is deprived of it.

I understand, he replied.   d

Ought I not to begin by describing how the change from
timocracy to oligarchy arises?

Yes.

Well, I said, no eyes are required in order to see how the one
passes into the other.

How?

The accumulation of gold in the treasury of private individuals is
the ruin of timocracy; they invent illegal modes of expenditure; for
what do they or their wives care about the law?

Yes, indeed.

And then one, seeing another grow rich, seeks to rival him, and
thus the great mass of the citizens become lovers of money.   e

Likely enough.

And so they grow richer and richer, and the more they think

of making a fortune the less they think of virtue; for when riches
and virtue are placed together in the scales of the balance, the one
always rises as the other falls.

True.

And in proportion as riches and rich men are honoured in the
551 State, virtue and the virtuous are dishonoured.

Clearly.

And what is honoured is cultivated, and that which has no honour
is neglected.

That is obvious.

And so at last, instead of loving contention and glory, men
become lovers of trade and money; they honour and look up to the
rich man, and make a ruler of him, and dishonour the poor man.

They do so.

They next proceed to make a law which fixes a sum of money as
the qualification of citizenship; the sum is higher in one place and
b   lower in another, as the oligarchy is more or less exclusive; and they
allow no one whose property falls below the amount fixed to have
any share in the government. These changes in the constitution they
effect by force of arms, if intimidation has not already done their
work.

Very true.

And this, speaking generally, is the way in which oligarchy is
established.

Yes, he said; but what are the characteristics of this form of
government, and what are the defects of which we were speaking?

c   First of all, I said, consider the nature of the qualification. Just
think what would happen if pilots were to be chosen according to
their property, and a poor man were refused permission to steer,
even though he were a better pilot?

You mean that they would shipwreck?

Yes; and is not this true of the government of anything?

I should imagine so.

Except a city?—or would you include a city?

Nay, he said, the case of a city is the strongest of all, inasmuch as
the rule of a city is the greatest and most difficult of all.

This, then, will be the first great defect of oligarchy?

d   Clearly.

And here is another defect which is quite as bad.

What defect?

The inevitable division: such a State is not one, but two States,
the one of poor, the other of rich men; and they are living on the

same spot and always conspiring against one another.

That, surely, is at least as bad.

Another discreditable feature is, that, for a like reason, they are incapable of carrying on any war. Either they arm the multitude, and then they are more afraid of them than of the enemy; or, if they do not call them out in the hour of battle, they are oligarchs indeed, few to fight as they are few to rule. And at the same time their fondness for money makes them unwilling to pay taxes.

c

How discreditable!

And, as we said before, under such a constitution the same persons have too many callings—they are farmers, tradesmen, warriors, all in one. Does that look well?

552

Anything but well.

There is another evil which is, perhaps, the greatest of all, and to which this State first begins to be liable.

What evil?

A man may sell all that he has, and another may acquire his property; yet after the sale he may dwell in the city of which he is no longer a part, being neither trader, nor artisan, nor horseman, nor hoplite, but only a poor, helpless creature.

Yes, that is an evil which also first begins in this State.

The evil is certainly not prevented there; for oligarchies have both the extremes of great wealth and utter poverty.

b

True.

But think again: In his wealthy days, while he was spending his money, was a man of this sort a whit more good to the State for the purposes of citizenship? Or did he only seem to be a member of the ruling body, although in truth he was neither ruler nor subject, but just a spendthrift?

As you say, he seemed to be a ruler, but was only a spendthrift.

May we not say that this is the drone in the house who is like the drone in the honeycomb, and that the one is the plague of the city as the other is of the hive?

c

Just so, Socrates.

And God has made the flying drones, Adeimantus, all without stings, whereas of the walking drones he has made some without stings but others have dreadful stings; of the stingless class are those who in their old age end as paupers; of the stingers come all the criminal class, as they are termed.

Most true, he said.

d

Clearly then, whenever you see paupers in a State, somewhere in that neighborhood there are hidden away thieves, and cut-purses and robbers of temples, and all sorts of evil-doers.

Clearly.

Well, I said, and in oligarchical States do you not find paupers?

Yes, he said; nearly everybody is a pauper who is not a ruler.

e And may we be so bold as to affirm that there are also many criminals to be found in them, rogues who have stings, and whom the authorities are careful to restrain by force?

Certainly, we may be so bold.

The existence of such persons is to be attributed to want of education, ill-training, and an evil constitution of the State?

True.

Such, then, is the form and such are the evils of oligarchy; and there may be many other evils.

Very likely.

553 Then oligarchy, or the form of government in which the rulers are elected for their wealth, may now be dismissed. Let us next proceed to consider the nature and origin of the individual who answers to this State.

By all means.

Does not the timocratical man change into the oligarchical in this way?

How?

A time arrives when the representative of timocracy has a son: at first he begins by emulating his father and walking in his footsteps, but presently he sees him of a sudden foundering against the State b as upon a sunken reef, and he and all that he has is lost; he may have been a general or some other high officer who is brought to trial under a prejudice raised by informers, and either put to death, or exiled, or deprived of the privileges of a citizen, and all his property taken from him.

Nothing more likely.

And the son has seen and known all this—he is a ruined man, and his fear has taught him to knock ambition and passion headforemost from his bosom's throne; humbled by poverty he takes to money-c making and by mean and miserly savings and hard work gets a fortune together. Is not such an one likely to seat the concupiscent and covetous element on the vacant throne and to suffer it to play the great king within him, girt with tiara and chain and scimitar?

Most true, he replied.

And when he has made reason and spirit sit down on the ground d obediently on either side of their sovereign, and taught them to know their place, he compels the one to think only of how lesser sums may be turned into larger ones, and will not allow the other to worship and admire anything but riches and rich men, or to be ambitious of anything so much as the acquisition of wealth and the means of acquiring it.

Of all changes, he said, there is none so speedy or so sure as the conversion of the ambitious youth into the greedy one.

And the greedy, I said, is the oligarchical youth?

Yes, he said; at any rate the individual out of whom he came is   e
like the State out of which oligarchy came.

Let us then consider whether there is any likeness between them.

Very good.

First, then, they resemble one another in the value which they set upon wealth?   554

Certainly.

Also in their poverty-striken, laborious character; the individual only satisfies his necessary appetites, and confines his expenditure to them; his other desires he subdues, under the idea that they are unprofitable.

True.

He is a shabby fellow, who saves something out of everything and makes a purse for himself; and this is the sort of man whom the vulgar applaud. Is he not a true image of the State which he represents?

He appears to me to be so; at any rate money is highly valued by   b
him as well as by the State.

You see that he is not a man of cultivation, I said.

I imagine not, he said; had he been educated he would never have made a blind god director of his chorus, or given him chief honour.

Excellent! I said. Yet consider: Must we not further admit that owing to this want of cultivation there will be found in him dronelike desires as of pauper and rogue, which are forcibly kept down by his general habit of life?

True.

Do you know where you will have to look if you want to discover   c
his rogueries?

Where must I look?

You should see him where he has some great opportunity of acting dishonestly, as in the guardianship of an orphan.

Aye.

It will be clear enough then that in his ordinary dealings which give him a reputation for honesty he coerces his bad passions by an enforced virtue; not making them see that they are wrong, or taming them by reason, but by necessity and fear constraining them, and because he trembles for his possessions.

d   To be sure.

Yes, indeed, my dear friend, but you will find that the natural desires of the drone commonly exist in him all the same whenever he has to spend what is not his own.

Yes, and they will be strong in him too.

The man, then, will be at war with himself; he will be two men, and not one; but, in general, his better desires will be found to prevail over his inferior ones.

True.

For these reasons such an one will be more respectable than most
e   people; yet the true virtue of a unanimous and harmonious soul will flee far away and never come near him.

I should expect so.

And surely, the miser individually will be an ignoble competitor in a State for any prize of victory, or other object of honourable ambition; he will not spend his money in the contest for glory; so afraid is he of awakening his expensive appetites and inviting them
555   to help and join in the struggle; in true oligarchical fashion he fights with a small part only of his resources, and the result commonly is that he loses the prize and saves his money.

Very true.

Can we any longer doubt, then, that the miser and money-maker answers to the oligarchical State?

There can be no doubt.

Next comes democracy; of this the origin and nature have still to
b   be considered by us; and then we will enquire into the ways of the democratic man, and bring him up for judgment.

That, he said, is our method.

Well, I said, and how does the change from oligarchy into democracy arise? Is it not in this way?—The good at which such a State aims is to become as rich as possible, a desire which is insatiable?

What then?

The rulers, being aware that their power rests upon their wealth, refuse to curtail by law the extravagance of the spendthrift youth because they gain by their ruin; they take interest from them and buy
c   up their estates and thus increase their own wealth and importance?

To be sure.

There can be no doubt that the love of wealth and the spirit of moderation cannot exist together in citizens of the same state to any considerable extent; one or the other will be disregarded.

That is tolerably clear.

And in oligarchical States, from the general spread of carelessness and extravagance, men of good family have often been reduced to beggary?

Yes, often.

And still they remain in the city; there they are, ready to sting and fully armed, and some of them owe money, some have forfeited their citizenship; a third class are in both predicaments; and they hate and conspire against those who have got their property, and against everybody else, and are eager for revolution.

That is true.

On the other hand, the men of business, stooping as they walk, and pretending not even to see those whom they have already ruined, insert their sting—that is, their money—into some one else who is not on his guard against them, and recover the parent sum many times over multiplied into a family of children: and so they make drone and pauper to abound in the State.

Yes, he said, there are plenty of them—that is certain.

The evil blazes up like a fire; and they will not extinguish it, either by restricting a man's use of his own property, or by another remedy:

What other?

One which is the next best, and has the advantage of compelling the citizens to look to their characters:—Let there be a general rule that every one shall enter into voluntary contracts at his own risk, and there will be less of this scandalous money-making, and the evils of which we were speaking will be greatly lessened in the State.

Yes, they will be greatly lessened.

At present the governors, induced by the motives which I have named, treat their subjects badly; while they and their adherents, especially the young men of the governing class, are habituated to lead a life of luxury and idleness both of body and mind; they do nothing, and are incapable of resisting either pleasure or pain.

Very true.

They themselves care only for making money, and are as indifferent as the pauper to the cultivation of virtue.

Yes, quite as indifferent.

Such is the state of affairs which prevails among them. And often rulers and their subjects may come in one another's way, whether on a journey or on some other occasion of meeting, on a pilgrimage or a march, as fellow-soldiers or fellow-sailors; yes and they may observe the behaviour of each other in the very moment of danger— for where danger is, there is no fear that the poor will be despised by the rich—and very likely the wiry sunburnt poor man may be placed in battle at the side of a wealthy one who has never spoilt his complexion and has plenty of superfluous flesh—when he sees such an one puffing and at his wits'-end, how can he avoid drawing the conclusion that men like him are only rich because no one has the courage to despoil them? And when they meet in private will not people be saying to one another 'Our warriors are not good for much'?

Yes, he said, I am quite aware that this is their way of talking.

And, as in a body which is diseased the addition of a touch from without may bring on illness, and sometimes even when there is no external provocation a commotion may arise within—in the same way wherever there is weakness in the State there is also likely to be illness, of which the occasion may be very slight, the one party introducing from without their oligarchical, the other their democratical allies, and then the State falls sick, and is at war with herself; and may be at times distracted, even when there is no external cause.

Yes, surely.

And then democracy comes into being after the poor have conquered their opponents, slaughtering some and banishing some, while to the remainder they give an equal share of freedom and power; and this is the form of government in which the magistrates are commonly elected by lot.

Yes, he said, that is the nature of democracy, whether the revolution has been effected by arms, or whether fear has caused the opposite party to withdraw.

FROM OLIGARCHY OF WEALTH TO DEMOCRACY [557A-563E]

And now what is their manner of life, and what sort of a government have they? for as the government is, such will be the man.

Clearly, he said.

In the first place, are they not free; and is not the city full of freedom and frankness—a man may say and do what he likes?

'Tis said so, he replied.

And where freedom is, the individual is clearly able to order for himself his own life as he pleases?

Clearly.

Then in this kind of State there will be the greatest variety of human natures?

There will.   c

This, then, seems likely to be the fairest of States, being like an embroidered robe which is spangled with every sort of flower. And just as women and children think a variety of colours to be of all things most charming, so there are many men to whom this State, which is spangled with the manners and characters of mankind, will appear to be the fairest of States.

Yes.

Yes, my good Sir, and there will be no better in which to look for a government.

Why?   d

Because of the liberty which reigns there—they have a complete assortment of constitutions; and he who has a mind to establish a State, as we have been doing, must go to a democracy as he would to a bazaar at which they sell them, and pick out the one that suits him; then, when he has made his choice, he may found his State.

He will be sure to have patterns enough.

And there being no necessity, I said, for you to govern in this State, even if you have the capacity, or to be governed, unless you   e like, or go to war when the rest go to war, or to be at peace when others are at peace, unless you are so disposed—there being no necessity also, because some law forbids you to hold office or be a juror, that you should not hold office or be a juror, if you have a fancy—is not this a way of life which for the moment is supremely delightful?

For the moment, yes.   558

And is not their humanity to the condemned in some cases quite charming? Have you not observed how, in a democracy, many persons, although they have been sentenced to death or exile, just stay where they are and walk about the world—the gentleman parades like a hero, and nobody sees or cares?

Yes, he replied, many and many a one.

See too, I said, the forgiving spirit of democracy, and the 'don't care' about trifles, and the disregard which she shows of all the fine principles which we solemnly laid down at the foundation of   b the city—as when we said that, except in the case of some rarely gifted nature, there never will be a good man who has not from his childhood been used to play amid things of beauty and make of them a joy and a study—how grandly does she trample all these fine notions of ours under her feet, never giving a thought to the pursuits which make a statesman, and promoting to honour any one who professes to be the people's friend.

c   Yes, she is of a noble spirit.

These and other kindred characteristics are proper to democracy, which is a charming form of government, full of variety and disorder, and dispensing a sort of equality to equals and unequals alike.

We know her well.

Consider now, I said, what manner of man the individual is, or rather consider, as in the case of the State, how he comes into being.

Very good, he said.

Is not this the way—he is the son of the miserly and oligarchical father who has trained him in his own habits?

Exactly.

And, like his father, he keeps under by force the pleasures which

d   are of the spending and not of the getting sort, being those which are called unnecessary?

Obviously.

Would you like, for the sake of clearness, to distinguish which are the necessary and which are the unnecessary pleasures?

I should.

Are not necessary pleasures those of which we cannot get rid, and of which the satisfaction is a benefit to us? And they are rightly called so, because we are framed by nature to desire both what is

e   beneficial and what is necessary, and cannot help it.

True.

We are not wrong therefore in calling them necessary?

We are not.

And the desires of which a man may get rid, if he takes pains

559   from his youth upwards—of which the presence, moreover, does no good, and in some cases the reverse of good—shall we not be right in saying that all these are unnecessary?

Yes, certainly.

Suppose we select an example of either kind, in order that we may have a general notion of them?

Very good.

Will not the desire of eating, that is, of simple food and condiments, in so far as they are required for health and strength, be of the necessary class?

That is what I should suppose.

The pleasure of eating is necessary in two ways; it does us good

b   and it is essential to the continuance of life?

Yes.

But the condiments are only necessary in so far as they are good for health?

Certainly.

And the desire which goes beyond this, of more delicate food, or other luxuries, which might generally be got rid of, if controlled and trained in youth, and is hurtful to the body, and hurtful to the soul in the pursuit of wisdom and virtue, may be rightly called unnecessary?

Very true.

May we not say that these desires spend, and that the others make money because they conduce to production?   c

Certainly.

And of the pleasures of love, and all other pleasures, the same holds good?

True.

And the drone of whom we spoke was he who was glutted in pleasures and desires of this sort, and was the slave of the unnecessary desires, whereas he who was subject to the necessary only was miserly and oligarchical?

Very true.

Again, let us see how the democratical man grows out of the oligarchical: the following, as I suspect, is commonly the process.   d

What is the process?

When a young man who has been brought up as we were just now describing, in a vulgar and miserly way, has tasted drones' honey and has come to associate with fierce and crafty natures who are able to provide for him all sorts of refinements and varieties of pleasure—then, as you may imagine, the change will begin of the oligarchical principle within him into the democratical?

Inevitably.

And as in the city like was helping like, and the change was effected by an alliance from without assisting one division of the citizens, so too the young man is changed by a class of desires   e coming from without to assist the desires within him, that which is akin and alike again helping that which is akin and alike?

Certainly.

And if there be any ally which aids the oligarchical principle within him, whether the influence of a father or of kindred, advising or rebuking him, then there arises in his soul a faction and an opposite faction, and he goes to war with himself.

It must be so.

And there are times when the democratical principle gives way

560 to the oligarchical, and some of his desires die, and others are banished; a spirit of reverence enters into the young man's soul and order is restored.

Yes, he said, that sometimes happens.

And then, again, after the old desires have been driven out, fresh ones spring up, which are akin to them, and because he their father does not know how to educate them, wax fierce and numerous.

Yes, he said, that is apt to be the way.

b They draw him to his old associates, and holding secret intercourse with them, breed and multiply in him.

Very true.

At length they seize upon the citadel of the young man's soul, which they perceive to be void of all accomplishments and fair pursuits and true words, which make their abode in the minds of men who are dear to the gods, and are their best guardians and sentinels.

None better.

False and boastful conceits and phrases mount upwards and take their place.

They are certain to do so.

And so the young man returns into the country of the lotus-eaters,
c and takes up his dwelling there in the face of all men; and if any help be sent by his friends to the oligarchical part of him, the aforesaid vain conceits shut the gate of the king's fastness; and they will neither allow the embassy itself to enter, nor if private advisers offer the fatherly counsel of the aged will they listen to them or receive them. There is a battle and they gain the day, and then modesty, which they call silliness, is ignominiously thrust into exile by them, and temperance, which they nickname unmanliness, is trampled in the mire and cast forth; they persuade men that moderation and orderly expenditure are vulgarity and meanness, and so, by the help
d of a rabble of evil appetites, they drive them beyond the border.

Yes, with a will.

And when they have emptied and swept clean the soul of him who is now in their power and who is being initiated by them in great mysteries, the next thing is to bring back to their house insolence and anarchy and waste and impudence in bright array having garlands on their heads, and a great company with them, hymning their praises and calling them by sweet names; insolence
e they term breeding, and anarchy liberty, and waste magnificence, and impudence courage. And so the young man passes out of his original nature, which was trained in the school of necessity, into the freedom and libertinism of useless and unnecessary pleasures.

Yes, he said, the change in him is visible enough.

After this he lives on, spending his money and labour and time on unnecessary pleasures quite as much as on necessary ones; but if he be fortunate, and is not too much disordered in his wits, when years have elapsed, and the heyday of passion is over—supposing that he then re-admits into the city some part of the exiled virtues, and does not wholly give himself up to their successors—in that case he balances his pleasures and lives in a sort of equilibrium, putting the government of himself into the hands of the one which comes first and wins the turn; and when he has had enough of that, then into the hands of another; he despises none of them but encourages them all equally.

Very true, he said.

Neither does he receive or let pass into the fortress any true word of advice; if any one says to him that some pleasures are the satisfactions of good and noble desires, and others of evil desires, and that he ought to use and honour some and chastise and master the others—whenever this is repeated to him he shakes his head and says that they are all alike, and that one is as good as another.

Yes, he said; that is the way with him.

Yes, I said, he lives from day to day indulging the appetite of the hour; and sometimes he is lapped in drink and strains of the flute; then he becomes a water-drinker, and tries to get thin; then he takes a turn at gymnastics; sometimes idling and neglecting everything, then once more living the life of a philosopher; often he is busy with politics, and starts to his feet and says and does whatever comes into his head; and, if he is emulous of any one who is a warrior, off he is in that direction, or of men of business, once more in that. His life has neither law nor order; and this distracted existence he terms joy and bliss and freedom; and so he goes on.

Yes, he replied, he is all liberty and equality.

Yes, I said; his life is motley and manifold and an epitome of the lives of many;—he answers to the State which we described as fair and spangled. And many a man and many a woman will take him for their pattern, and many a constitution and many an example of manners is contained in him.

Just so.

Let him then be set over against democracy; he may truly be called the democratic man.

Let that be his place, he said.

Last of all comes the most beautiful of all, man and State alike, tyranny and the tyrant; these we have now to consider.

Quite true, he said.

Say then, my friend, In what manner does tyranny arise?—that it has a democratic origin is evident.

Clearly.

And does not tyranny spring from democracy in the same manner as democracy from oligarchy—I mean, after a sort?

How?

The good which oligarchy proposed to itself and the means by which it was maintained was excess of wealth—am I not right?

Yes.

And the insatiable desire of wealth and the neglect of all other things for the sake of money-getting was also the ruin of oligarchy?

True.

b   And democracy has her own good, of which the insatiable desire brings her to dissolution?

What good?

Freedom, I replied; which, as they tell you in a democracy, is the glory of the State—and that therefore in a democracy alone will the freeman of nature deign to dwell.

Yes; the saying is in every body's mouth.

I was going to observe, that the insatiable desire of this and the neglect of other things introduces the change in democracy, which occasions a demand for tyranny.

c   How so?

When a democracy which is thirsting for freedom has evil officials presiding over the feast, and has drunk too deeply of the strong wine of freedom, then, unless her rulers are very amenable and give a plentiful supply, she calls them to account and punishes them, and says that they are cursed oligarchs.

Yes, he replied, a very common occurrence.

Yes, I said; and loyal citizens are insultingly termed by her slaves

d   who hug their chains and men of no worth; she would have subjects who are like rulers, and rulers who are like subjects: these are men after her own heart, whom she praises and honours both in private and public. Now, in such a State, can liberty have any limit?

Certainly not.

By degrees the anarchy finds a way into private houses, and ends by getting among the animals and infecting them.

How do you mean?

I mean that the father grows accustomed to descend to the level

e   of his sons and to fear them, and the son is on a level with his father, he having no respect or reverence for either of his parents; and this is his freedom, and the metic is equal with the citizen and the citizen with the metic, and the stranger is quite as good as either.

Yes, he said, that is the way.

And these are not the only evils, I said—there are several lesser ones: In such a state of society the master fears and flatters his scholars, and the scholars despise their masters and tutors; young and old are all alike; and the young man is on a level with the old, and is ready to compete with him in word or deed; and old men condescend to the young and are full of pleasantry and gaiety; they are loth to be thought morose and authoritative, and therefore they adopt the manners of the young. 563

Quite true, he said.

The last extreme of popular liberty is when the slave bought with money, whether male or female, is just as free as his or her purchaser; nor must I forget to tell of the liberty and equality of the two sexes in relation to each other. b

Why not, as Aeschylus says, utter the word which rises to our lips?

That is what I am doing, I replied; and I must add that no one who does not know would believe, how much greater is the liberty which the animals who are under the dominion of man have in a democracy than in any other State: for truly, the she-dogs, as the proverb says, are as good as their she-mistresses, and the horses and asses have a way of marching along with all the rights and dignities of freemen; and they will run at any body who comes in their way if he does not leave the road clear for them: and all things are just ready to burst with liberty. c

When I take a country walk, he said, I often experience what you describe. You and I have dreamed the same thing. d

And above all, I said, and as the result of all, see how sensitive the citizens become; they chafe impatiently at the least touch of authority, and at length, as you know, they cease to care even for the laws, written or unwritten; they will have no one over them.

Yes, he said, I know it too well. e

Such, my friend, I said, is the fair and glorious beginning out of which springs tyranny.

THE TAKEOVER OF THE TYRANT FROM THE DEMOCRACY [563E-569C]

Glorious indeed, he said. But what is the next step?

The ruin of oligarchy is the ruin of democracy; the same disease magnified and intensified by liberty overmasters democracy—the truth being that the excessive increase of anything often causes a reaction in the opposite direction; and this is the case not only in the seasons and in vegetable and animal life, but above all in forms of government.

564

True.

The excess of liberty, whether in States or individuals, seems only to pass into excess of slavery.

Yes, the natural order.

And so tyranny naturally arises out of democracy, and the most aggravated form of tyranny and slavery out of the most extreme form of liberty?

As we might expect.

That, however, was not, as I believe, your question—you rather desired to know what is that disorder which is generated alike in oligarchy and democracy, and is the ruin of both?

b

Just so, he replied.

Well, I said, I meant to refer to the class of idle spendthrifts, of whom the more courageous are the leaders and the more timid the followers, the same whom we were comparing to drones, some stingless, and others having stings.

A very just comparison.

These two classes are the plagues of every city in which they are generated, being what phlegm and bile are to the body. And the good physician and lawgiver of the State ought, like the wise bee-master, to keep them at a distance and prevent, if possible, their ever coming in; and if they have anyhow found a way in, then he should have them and their cells cut out as speedily as possible.

c

Yes, by all means, he said.

Then, in order that we may see clearly what we are doing, let us imagine democracy to be divided, as indeed it is, into three classes; for in the first place freedom creates rather more drones in the democratic than there were in the oligarchical State.

d

That is true.

And in the democracy they are certainly more intensified.

How so?

Because in the oligarchical State they are disqualified and driven from office, and therefore they cannot train or gather strength; whereas in a democracy they are almost the entire ruling power, and while the keener sort speak and act, the rest keep buzzing about the podium and do not suffer a word to be said on the other side; hence in democracies almost everything is managed by the drones.

e

Very true, he said.

Then there is another class which is always being severed from the mass.

What is that?

They are the orderly class, which in a nation of traders is sure to be the richest.

Naturally so.

They are the most squeezable persons and yield the largest amount of honey to the drones.

Why, he said, there is little to be squeezed out of people who have little.

And this is called the wealthy class, and the drones feed upon them.

That is pretty much the case, he said.

The people are a third class, consisting of those who work with   565
their own hands; they are not politicians, and have not much to live upon. This, when assembled, is the largest and most powerful class in a democracy.

True, he said; but then the multitude is seldom willing to congregate unless they get a little honey.

And do they not share? I said. Do not their leaders deprive the rich of their estates and distribute them among the people; at the same time taking care to reserve the larger part for themselves?

Why, yes, he said, to that extent the people do share.   b

And the persons whose property is taken from them are compelled to defend themselves before the people as they best can?

What else can they do?

And then, although they may have no desire of change, the others charge them with plotting against the people and being friends of oligarchy?

True.

And the end is that when they see the people, not of their own accord, but through ignorance, and because they are deceived by informers, seeking to do them wrong, then at last they are forced to become oligarchs in reality; they do not wish to be, but the sting of   c
the drones torments them and breeds revolution in them.

That is exactly the truth.

Then come impeachments and judgments and trials of one another.

True.

The people have always some champion whom they set over them and nurse into greatness.

Yes, that is their way.

^d

This and no other is the root from which a tyrant springs; when he first appears above ground he is a protector.

Yes, that is quite clear.

How then does a protector begin to change into a tyrant? Clearly when he does what the man is said to do in the tale of the Arcadian temple of Lycaean Zeus.

What tale?

The tale is that he who has tasted the entrails of a single human victim minced up with the entrails of other victims is destined to become a wolf. Did you never hear it?

^e

Oh, yes.

And the protector of the people is like him; having a mob entirely at his disposal, he is not restrained from shedding the blood of kinsmen; by the favourite method of false accusation he brings them into court and murders them, making the life of man to disappear, and with unholy tongue and lips tasting the blood of his fellow citizens; some he kills and others he banishes, at the same time hinting at the abolition of debts and partition of lands: and after this, what will be his destiny? Must he not either perish at the hands of his enemies, or from being a man become a wolf—that is, a tyrant?

⁵⁶⁶

Inevitably.

This, I said, is he who begins to make a party against the rich?

The same.

After a while he is driven out, but comes back, in spite of his enemies, a tyrant full grown.

That is clear.

And if they are unable to expel him, or to get him condemned to death by a public accusation, they conspire to assassinate him.

^b

Yes, he said, that is their usual way.

Then comes the famous request for a body-guard, which is the device of all those who have got thus far in their tyrannical career— 'Let not the people's friend,' as they say, 'be lost to them.'

Exactly.

The people readily assent; all their fears are for him—they have none for themselves.

^c

Very true.

And when a man who is wealthy and is also accused of being an enemy of the people sees this, then, my friend, as the oracle said to Croesus,

'By pebbly Hermus' shore he flees and rests not, and is not ashamed to be a coward.'

And quite right too, said he, for if he were, he would never be ashamed again.

But if he is caught he dies.

Of course.

And he, the protector of whom we spoke, is to be seen, not   d
'larding the plain' with his bulk, but himself the overthrower of
many, standing up in the chariot of State with the reins in his hand,
no longer protector, but tyrant absolute.

No doubt, he said.

And now let us consider the happiness of the man, and also of the
State in which a creature like him is generated.

Yes, he said, let us consider that.

At first, in the early days of his power, he is full of smiles, and
he salutes every one whom he meets;—he to be called a tyrant, who   e
is making promises in public and also in private! liberating debtors,
and distributing land to the people and his followers, and wanting to
be so kind and good to every one!

Of course, he said.

But when he has disposed of foreign enemies by conquest or
treaty, and there is nothing to fear from them, then he is always
stirring up some war or other, in order that the people may require
a leader.

To be sure.

Has he not also another object, which is that they may be   567
impoverished by payment of taxes, and thus compelled to devote
themselves to their daily wants and therefore less likely to conspire
against him?

Clearly.

And if any of them are suspected by him of having notions of
freedom, and of resistance to his authority, he will have a good
pretext for destroying them by placing them at the mercy of the
enemy; and for all these reasons the tyrant must be always getting
up a war.

He must.

Now he begins to grow unpopular.

A necessary result.   b

Then some of those who joined in setting him up, and who are
in power, speak their minds to him and to one another, and the more
courageous of them cast in his teeth what is being done.

Yes, that may be expected.

And the tyrant, if he means to rule, must get rid of them; he
cannot stop while he has a friend or an enemy who is good for
anything.

He cannot.

And therefore he must look about him and see who is valiant, who is high-minded, who is wise, who is wealthy; happy man, he is the enemy of them all, and must seek occasion against them whether he will or no, until he has made a purgation of the State.

Yes, he said, and a rare purgation.

Yes, I said, not the sort of purgation which the physicians make of the body; for they take away the worse and leave the better part, but he does the reverse.

If he is to rule, I suppose that he cannot help himself.

What a blessed alternative, I said:—to be compelled to dwell only with the many bad, and to be by them hated, or not to live at all!

Yes, that is the alternative.

And the more detestable his actions are to the citizens the more satellites and the greater devotion in them will he require?

Certainly.

And who are the devoted band, and where will he procure them?

They will flock to him, he said, of their own accord, if he pays them.

By the dog! I said, here are more drones, of every sort and from every land.

Yes, he said, there are.

But will he not desire to get them on the spot?

How do you mean?

He will rob the citizens of their slaves; he will then set them free and enrol them in his body-guard.

To be sure, he said; and he will be able to trust them best of all.

What a blessed creature, I said, must this tyrant be; he has put to death the others and has these for his trusted friends.

Yes, he said; they are quite of his sort.

Yes, I said, and these are the new citizens whom he has called into existence, who admire him and are his companions, while the good hate and avoid him.

Of course.

Verily, then, tragedy is a wise thing and Euripides a great tragedian.

Why so?

Why, because he is the author of the pregnant saying,

'Tyrants are wise by living with the wise;'

and he clearly meant to say that they are the wise whom the tyrant makes his companions.

Yes, he said, and he also praises tyranny as godlike; and many other things of the same kind are said by him and by the other poets.

And therefore, I said, the tragic poets being wise men will forgive us and any others who live after our manner if we do not receive them into our State, because they are the eulogists of tyranny.

Yes, he said, those who have the wit will doubtless forgive us.   c

But they will continue to go to other cities and attract mobs, and hire voices fair and loud and persuasive, and draw the cities over to tyrannies and democracies.

Very true.

Moreover, they are paid for this and receive honour—the greatest honour, as might be expected, from tyrants, and the next greatest from democracies; but the higher they ascend our constitution hill, the more their reputation fails, and seems unable from shortness of breath to proceed further.   d

True.

But we are wandering from the subject: Let us therefore return and enquire how the tyrant will maintain that fair and numerous and various and ever-changing army of his.

If, he said, there are sacred treasures in the city, he will confiscate and spend them; and in so far as the fortunes of corrupt persons may suffice, he will be able to diminish the taxes which he would otherwise have to impose upon the people.

And when these fail?

Why, clearly, he said, then he and his boon companions, whether   e
male or female, will be maintained out of his father's estate.

You mean to say that the people, from whom he has derived his being, will maintain him and his companions?

Yes, he said; they cannot help themselves.

But what if the people fly into a passion, and aver that a grown-up son ought not to be supported by his father, but that the father should be supported by the son? The father did not bring him into being, or settle him in life, in order that when his son became a man he should himself be the servant of his own servants and should   569
support him and his rabble of slaves and companions; but that his son should protect him, and that by his help he might be emancipated from the government of the rich and aristocratic, as they are termed. And so he bids him and his companions depart, just as any other father might drive out of the house a riotous son and his undesirable associates.

By heaven, he said, then the parent will discover what a monster b he has been fostering in his bosom; and, when he wants to drive him out, he will find that he is weak and his son strong.

Why, you do not mean to say that the tyrant will use violence? What! beat his father if he opposes him?

Yes, he will, having first disarmed him.

Then he is a parricide, and a cruel guardian of an aged parent; and this is real tyranny, about which there can be no longer a mistake: as the saying is, the people who would escape the smoke which is the
c slavery of freemen, has fallen into the fire which is the tyranny of slaves. Thus liberty, getting out of all order and reason, passes into the harshest and bitterest form of slavery.

True, he said.

Very well; and may we not rightly say that we have sufficiently discussed the nature of tyranny, and the manner of the transition from democracy to tyranny?

Yes, quite enough, he said.

BOOK IX

TRANSITION TO BOOK IX [571A-575D]

571 Last of all comes the tyrannical man; about whom we have once more to ask, how is he formed out of the democratical? and how does he live, in happiness or in misery?

Yes, he said, he is the only one remaining.

There is, however, I said, a previous question which remains unanswered.

What question?

I do not think that we have adequately determined the nature and number of the appetites, and until this is accomplished the enquiry
b will always be confused.

Well, he said, it is not too late to supply the omission.

Very true, I said; and observe the point which I want to understand: Certain of the unnecessary pleasures and appetites I conceive to be unlawful; every one appears to have them, but in some persons they are controlled by the laws and by reason, and the better desires prevail over them—either they are wholly banished or they become few and weak; while in the case of others they are
c stronger, and there are more of them.

Which appetites do you mean?

I mean those which are awake when the reasoning and human and ruling power is asleep; then the wild beast within us, gorged with meat or drink, starts up and having shaken off sleep, goes forth to satisfy his desires; and there is no conceivable folly or crime— not excepting incest or any other unnatural union, or parricide, or the eating of forbidden food—which at such a time, when he has parted company with all shame and sense, a man may not be ready to commit.

Most true, he said.

But when a man's pulse is healthy and temperate, and when before going to sleep he has awakened his rational powers, and fed them on noble thoughts and enquiries, collecting himself in meditation; after having first indulged his appetites neither too much nor too little, but just enough to lay them to sleep, and prevent them and their enjoyments and pains from interfering with the higher principle—which he leaves in the solitude of pure abstraction, free to contemplate and aspire to the knowledge of the unknown, whether in past, present, or future: when again he has allayed the passionate element, if he has a quarrel against any one—I say, when, after pacifying the two irrational principles, he rouses up the third, which is reason, before he takes his rest, then, as you know, he attains truth most nearly, and is least likely to be the sport of fantastic and lawless visions.

I quite agree.

In saying this I have been running into a digression; but the point which I desire to note is that in all of us, even in good men, there is a lawless wild-beast nature, which peers out in sleep. Pray, consider whether I am right, and you agree with me.

Yes, I agree.

And now remember the character which we attributed to the democratic man. He was supposed from his youth upwards to have been trained under a miserly parent, who encouraged the saving appetites in him, but disapproved of the unnecessary, which aim only at amusement and ornament?

True.

And then he got into the company of a more refined, licentious sort of people, and taking to all their wanton ways rushed into the opposite extreme from an abhorrence of his father's meanness. At last, being a better man than his corruptors, he was drawn in both directions until he halted midway and led a life, not of vulgar and slavish passion, but of what he deemed moderate indulgence in various pleasures. After this manner the democrat was generated out of the oligarch?

Yes, he said; that was our view of him, and is so still.

And now, I said, years will have passed away, and you must conceive this man, such as he is, to have a son, who is brought up in his father's principles.

I can imagine him.

Then you must further imagine the same thing to happen to the son which has already happened to the father:—he is drawn into a perfectly lawless life, which by his seducers is termed perfect liberty; and his father and friends take part with his moderate desires, and the opposite party assist the opposite ones. As soon as these dire magicians and tyrant-makers find that they are losing their hold on him, they contrive to implant in him a master passion, to be lord over his idle and spendthrift lusts—a sort of monstrous winged drone—that is the only image which will adequately describe him.

Yes, he said, that is the only adequate image of him.

And when his other lusts, amid clouds of incense and perfumes and garlands and wines, and all the pleasures of a dissolute life, now let loose, come buzzing around him, nourishing to the utmost the sting of desire which they implant in his drone-like nature, then at last this lord of the soul, having Madness for the captain of his guard, breaks out into a frenzy: and if he finds in himself any good opinions or appetites in process of formation, and there is in him any sense of shame remaining, to these better principles he puts an end, and casts them forth until he has purged away temperance and brought in madness to the full.

Yes, he said, that is the way in which the tyrannical man is generated.

And is not this the reason why of old love has been called a tyrant?

I should not wonder.

Further, I said, has not a drunken man also the spirit of a tyrant?

He has.

And you know that a man who is deranged and not right in his mind, will fancy that he is able to rule, not only over men, but also over the gods?

That he will.

And the tyrannical man in the true sense of the word comes into being when, either under the influence of nature, or habit, or both, he becomes drunken, lustful, passionate? O my friend, is not that so?

Assuredly.

Such is the man and such is his origin. And next, how does he live?

Suppose, as people facetiously say, you were to tell me.

I imagine, I said, at the next step in his progress, that there will be   d
feasts and carousals and revellings and courtezans, and all that sort
of thing; Love is the lord of the house within him, and orders all the
concerns of his soul.

That is certain.

Yes; and every day and every night desires grow up many and
formidable, and their demands are many.

They are indeed, he said.

His revenues, if he has any, are soon spent.

True.

Then comes debt and the cutting down of his property.

Of course.   e

When he has nothing left, must not his desires, crowding in the
nest like young ravens, be crying aloud for food; and he, goaded
on by them, and especially by love himself, who is in a manner the
captain of them, is in a frenzy, and would fain discover whom he can
defraud or despoil of his property, in order that he may gratify them?

Yes, that is sure to be the case.   574

He must have money, no matter how, if he is to escape horrid
pains and pangs.

He must.

And as in himself there was a succession of pleasures, and the
new got the better of the old and took away their rights, so he being
younger will claim to have more than his father and his mother, and
if he has spent his own share of the property, he will take a slice of
theirs.

No doubt he will.

And if his parents will not give way, then he will try first of all to
cheat and deceive them.   b

Very true.

And if he fails, then he will use force and plunder them.

Yes, probably.

And if the old man and woman fight for their own, what then,
my friend? Will the creature feel any compunction at tyrannizing
over them?

Nay, he said, I should not feel at all comfortable about his parents.

But, O heavens! Adeimantus, on account of some new-fangled
love of a harlot, who is anything but a necessary connection, can
you believe that he would strike the mother who is his ancient friend
and necessary to his very existence, and would place her under the

authority of the other, when she is brought under the same roof with her; or that, under like circumstances, he would do the same to his withered old father, first and most indispensable of friends, for the sake of some newly-found blooming youth who is the reverse of indispensable?

Yes, indeed, he said; I believe that he would.

Truly, then, I said, a tyrannical son is a blessing to his father and mother.

He is indeed, he replied.

He first takes their property, and when that fails, and pleasures are beginning to swarm in the hive of his soul, then he breaks into a house, or steals the garments of some nightly wayfarer; next he proceeds to clear a temple. Meanwhile the old opinions which he had when a child, and which gave judgment about good and evil, are overthrown by those others which have just been emancipated, and are now the body-guard of love and share his empire. These in his democratic days, when he was still subject to the laws and to his father, were only let loose in the dreams of sleep. But now that he is under the dominion of love, he becomes always and in waking reality what he was then very rarely and in a dream only; he will commit the foulest murder, or eat forbidden food, or be guilty of any other horrid act. Love is his tyrant, and lives lordly in him and lawlessly, and being himself a king, leads him on, as a tyrant leads a State, to the performance of any reckless deed by which he can maintain himself and the rabble of his associates, whether those whom evil communications have brought in from without, or those whom he himself has allowed to break loose within him by reason of a similar evil nature in himself. Have we not here a picture of his way of life?

Yes, indeed, he said.

And if there are only a few of them in the State, and the rest of the people are well disposed, they go away and become the body-guard or mercenary soldiers of some other tyrant who may probably want them for a war; and if there is no war, they stay at home and do many little pieces of mischief in the city.

What sort of mischief?

For example, they are the thieves, burglars, cut-purses, foot-pads, robbers of temples, man-stealers of the community; or if they are able to speak they turn informers, and bear false witness, and take bribes.

You descibe a small catalogue of evils, even if the perpetrators of them are few in number.

Yes, I said; but small and great are comparative terms, and all these things, in the misery and evil which they inflict upon a State, do not come within a thousand miles of the tyrant; when this noxious class and their followers grow numerous and become conscious of their strength, assisted by the infatuation of the people, they choose from among themselves the one who has most of the tyrant in his own soul, and him they create their tyrant.

d

Yes, he said, and he will be the most fit to be a tyrant.

GLAUCON'S MASTER CLASS [575D-580D]

If the people yield, well and good; but if they resist him, as he began by beating his own father and mother, so now, if he has the power, he beats them, and will keep his dear old fatherland or motherland, as the Cretans say, in subjection to his young retainers whom he has introduced to be their rulers and masters. This is the end of his passions and desires.

Exactly.

e

When such men are only private individuals and before they get power, this is their character; they associate entirely with their own flatterers or ready tools; or if they want anything from anybody, they in their turn are equally ready to bow down before them: they profess every sort of affection for them; but when they have gained their point they know them no more.

576

Yes, truly.

They are always either the masters or servants and never the friends of anybody; the tyrant never tastes of true freedom or friendship.

Certainly not.

And may we not rightly call such men treacherous?

No question.

Also they are utterly unjust, if we were right in our notion of justice?

b

Yes, he said, and we were perfectly right.

Let us then sum up in a word, I said, the character of the worst man: he is the waking reality of what we dreamed.

Most true.

And this is he who being by nature most of a tyrant bears rule, and the longer he lives the more of a tyrant he becomes.

That is certain, said Glaucon, taking his turn to answer.

And will not he who has been shown to be the wickedest, be also the most miserable? and he who has tyrannized longest and most, c   most continually and truly miserable; although this may not be the opinion of men in general?

Yes, he said, inevitably.

And must not the tyrannical man be like the tyrannical State, and the democratical man like the democratical State; and the same of the others?

Certainly.

And as State is to State in virtue and happiness, so is man in relation to man?

To be sure.

d   Then comparing our original city, which was under a king, and the city which is under a tyrant, how do they stand as to virtue?

They are the opposite extremes, he said, for one is the very best and the other is the very worst.

There can be no mistake, I said, as to which is which, and therefore I will at once enquire whether you would arrive at a similar decision about their relative happiness and misery. And here we must not allow ourselves to be panic-stricken at the apparition of the tyrant, who is only a unit and may perhaps have a few retainers about him; but let us go as we ought into every corner of the city and look all

e   about, and then we will give our opinion.

A fair invitation, he replied; and I see, as every one must, that a tyranny is the wretchedest form of government, and the rule of a king the happiest.

And in estimating the men too, may I not fairly make a like request, that I should have a judge whose mind can enter into and see

577   through human nature? he must not be like a child who looks at the outside and is dazzled at the pompous aspect which the tyrannical nature assumes to the beholder, but let him be one who has a clear insight. May I suppose that the judgment is given in the hearing of us all by one who is able to judge, and has dwelt in the same place with him, and been present at his daily life and known him in his family relations, where he may be seen stripped of his tragedy attire,

b   and again in the hour of public danger—he shall tell us about the happiness and misery of the tyrant when compared with other men?

That again, he said, is a very fair proposal.

Shall I assume that we ourselves are able and experienced judges and have before now met with such a person? We shall then have some one who will answer our enquiries.

By all means.

c   Let me ask you not to forget the parallel of the individual and the State; bearing this in mind, and glancing in turn from one to the other of them, will you tell me their respective conditions?

What do you mean? he asked.

Beginning with the State, I replied, would you say that a city which is governed by a tyrant is free or enslaved?

No city, he said, can be more completely enslaved.

And yet, as you see, there are freemen as well as masters in such a State?

Yes, he said, I see that there are—a few; but the people, speaking generally, and the best of them are miserably degraded and enslaved.

Then if the man is like the State, I said, must not the same rule prevail? his soul is full of meanness and vulgarity—the best   d
elements in him are enslaved; and there is a small ruling part, which is also the worst and maddest.

Inevitably.

And would you say that the soul of such an one is the soul of a freeman, or of a slave?

He has the soul of a slave, in my opinion.

And the State which is enslaved under a tyrant is utterly incapable of acting voluntarily?

Utterly incapable.

And also the soul which is under a tyrant (I am speaking of the soul taken as a whole) is least capable of doing what she desires;   e
there is a gadfly which goads her, and she is full of trouble and remorse?

Certainly.

And is the city which is under a tyrant rich or poor?

Poor.

And the tyrannical soul must be always poor and insatiable?

True.   578

And must not such a State and such a man be always full of fear?

Yes, indeed.

Is there any State in which you will find more of lamentation and sorrow and groaning and pain?

Certainly not.

And is there any man in whom you will find more of this sort of misery than in the tyrannical man, who is in a fury of passions and desires?

Impossible.

Reflecting upon these and similar evils, you held the tyrannical State to be the most miserable of States?

And I was right, he said.

Certainly, I said. And when you see the same evils in the   b tyrannical man, what do you say of him?

I say that he is by far the most miserable of all men.

There, I said, I think that you are beginning to go wrong.

What do you mean?

I do not think that he has as yet reached the utmost extreme of misery.

Then who is more miserable?

One of whom I am about to speak.

Who is that?

c   He who is of a tyrannical nature, and instead of leading a private life has been cursed with the further misfortune of being a public tyrant.

From what has been said, I gather that you are right.

Yes, I replied, but in this high argument you should be a little more certain, and should not conjecture only; for of all questions, this respecting good and evil is the greatest.

Very true, he said.

d   Let me then offer you an illustration, which may, I think, throw a light upon this subject.

What is your illustration?

The case of rich individuals in cities who possess many slaves: from them you may form an idea of the tyrant's condition, for they both have slaves; the only difference is that he has more slaves.

Yes, that is the difference.

You know that they live securely and have nothing to apprehend from their servants?

What should they fear?

Nothing. But do you observe the reason of this?

Yes; the reason is, that the whole city is leagued together for the protection of each individual.

e   Very true, I said. But imagine one of these owners, the master say of some fifty slaves, together with his family and property and slaves, carried off by a god into the wilderness, where there are no freemen to help him—will he not be in an agony of fear lest he and his wife and children should be put to death by his slaves?

Yes, he said, he will be in the utmost fear.

The time has arrived when he will be compelled to flatter divers 579   of his slaves, and make many promises to them of freedom and other things, much against his will—he will have to cajole his own servants.

Yes, he said, that will be the only way of saving himself.

And suppose the same god, who carried him away, to surround

him with neighbours who will not suffer one man to be the master of another, and who, if they could catch the offender, would take his life?

His case will be still worse, if you suppose him to be everywhere surrounded and watched by enemies.

And is not this the sort of prison in which the tyrant will be bound—he who being by nature such as we have described, is full of all sorts of fears and lusts? His soul is dainty and greedy, and yet alone, of all men in the city, he is never allowed to go on a journey, or to see the things which other freemen desire to see, but he lives in his hole like a woman hidden in the house, and is jealous of any other citizen who goes into foreign parts and sees anything of interest.

Very true, he said.

And amid evils such as these will not he who is ill-governed in his own person—the tyrannical man, I mean—whom you just now decided to be the most miserable of all—will not he be yet more miserable when, instead of leading a private life, he is constrained by fortune to be a public tyrant? He has to be master of others when he is not master of himself: he is like a diseased or paralytic man who is compelled to pass his life, not in retirement, but fighting and combating with other men.

Yes, he said, the similitude is most exact.

Is not his case utterly miserable? and does not the actual tyrant lead a worse life than he whose life you determined to be the worst?

Certainly.

He who is the real tyrant, whatever men may think, is the real slave, and is obliged to practise the greatest adulation and servility, and to be the flatterer of the vilest of mankind. He has desires which he is utterly unable to satisfy, and has more wants than any one, and is truly poor, if you know how to inspect the whole soul of him: all his life long he is beset with fear and is full of convulsions and distractions, even as the State which he resembles: and surely the resemblance holds?

Very true, he said.

Moreover, as we were saying before, he grows worse from having power: he becomes and is of necessity more jealous, more faithless, more unjust, more friendless, more impious, than he was at first; he is the purveyor and cherisher of every sort of vice, and the consequence is that he is supremely miserable, and that he makes everybody else as miserable as himself.

No man of any sense will dispute your words.

b

Come then, I said, and as the general umpire in theatrical contests proclaims the result, do you also decide who in your opinion is first in the scale of happiness, and who second, and in what order the others follow: there are five of them in all—they are the royal, timocratical, oligarchical, democratical, tyrannical.

The decision will be easily given, he replied; they shall be choruses coming on the stage, and I must judge them in the order in which they enter, by the criterion of virtue and vice, happiness and misery.

Need we hire a herald, or shall I announce, that the son of Ariston (the best) has decided that the best and justest is also the happiest,

c

and that this is he who is the most royal man and king over himself; and that the worst and most unjust man is also the most miserable, and that this is he who being the greatest tyrant of himself is also the greatest tyrant of his State?

Make the proclamation yourself, he said.

And shall I add, 'whether seen or unseen by gods and men'?

Let the words be added.

RETURN TO THE TRIPARTITE SOUL [580D-585E]

d

Then this, I said, will be our first proof; and there is another, which may also have some weight.

What is that?

The second proof is derived from the nature of the soul: seeing that the individual soul, like the State, has been divided by us into three principles, the division may, I think, furnish a new demonstration.

Of what nature?

It seems to me that to these three principles three pleasures correspond; also three desires and governing powers.

How do you mean? he said.

There is one principle with which, as we were saying, a man learns, another with which he is angry; the third, having many forms, has no special name, but is denoted by the general term appetitive, from the extraordinary strength and vehemence of the desires of

e

eating and drinking and the other sensual appetites which are the main elements of it; also money-loving, because such desires are

581

generally satisfied by the help of money.

That is true, he said.

If we were to say that the loves and pleasures of this third part were concerned with gain, we should then be able to fall back on a single notion; and might truly and intelligibly describe this part of the soul as loving gain or money.

I agree with you.

Again, is not the passionate element wholly set on ruling and conquering and getting fame?

True.   b

Suppose we call it the contentious or ambitious—would the term be suitable?

Extremely suitable.

On the other hand, every one sees that the principle of knowledge is wholly directed to the truth, and cares less than either of the others for gain or fame.

Far less.

'Lover of wisdom,' 'lover of knowledge,' are titles which we may fitly apply to that part of the soul?

Certainly.

One principle prevails in the souls of one class of men, another in others, as may happen?

Yes.   c

Then we may begin by assuming that there are three classes of men—lovers of wisdom, lovers of honour, lovers of gain?

Exactly.

And there are three kinds of pleasure, which are their several objects?

Very true.

Now, if you examine the three classes of men, and ask of them in turn which of their lives is pleasantest, each will be found praising his own and depreciating that of others: the money-maker will contrast the vanity of honour or of learning if they bring no money with the solid advantages of gold and silver?   d

True, he said.

And the lover of honour—what will be his opinion? Will he not think that the pleasure of riches is vulgar, while the pleasure of learning, if it brings no distinction, is all smoke and nonsense to him?

Very true.

And are we to suppose, I said, that the philosopher sets any value   e
on other pleasures in comparison with the pleasure of knowing the truth, and in that pursuit abiding, ever learning, not so far indeed from the heaven of pleasure? Does he not call the other pleasures necessary, under the idea that if there were no necessity for them, he would rather not have them?

There can be no doubt of that, he replied.

582   Since, then, the pleasures of each class and the life of each are in dispute, and the question is not which life is more or less honourable, or better or worse, but which is the more pleasant or painless—how shall we know who speaks truly?

I cannot myself tell, he said.

Well, but what ought to be the criterion? Is any better than experience and wisdom and reason?

There cannot be a better, he said.

Then, I said, reflect. Of the three individuals, which has the greatest experience of all the pleasures which we enumerated? Has the lover of gain, in learning the nature of essential truth, greater experience of the pleasure of knowledge than the philosopher has of the pleasure of gain?

b   The philosopher, he replied, has greatly the advantage; for he has of necessity always known the taste of the other pleasures from his childhood upwards: but the lover of gain in all his experience has not of necessity tasted—or, I should rather say, even had he desired, could hardly have tasted—the sweetness of learning and knowing truth.

Then the lover of wisdom has a great advantage over the lover of gain, for he has a double experience?

c   Yes, very great.

Again, has he greater experience of the pleasures of honour, or the lover of honour of the pleasures of wisdom?

Nay, he said, all three are honoured in proportion as they attain their object; for the rich man and the brave man and the wise man alike have their crowd of admirers, and as they all receive honour they all have experience of the pleasures of honour; but the delight which is to be found in the knowledge of true being is known to the philosopher only.

His experience, then, will enable him to judge better than any one?

d   Far better.

And he is the only one who has wisdom as well as experience?

Certainly.

Further, the very faculty which is the instrument of judgment is not possessed by the covetous or ambitious man, but only by the philosopher?

What faculty?

Reason, with whom, as we were saying, the decision ought to rest.

Yes.

And reasoning is peculiarly his instrument?

Certainly.

If wealth and gain were the criterion, then the praise or blame of the lover of gain would surely be the most trustworthy?   e

Assuredly.

Or if honour or victory or courage, in that case the judgment of the ambitious or pugnacious would be the truest?

Clearly.

But since experience and wisdom and reason are the judges—

The only inference possible, he replied, is that pleasures which are approved by the lover of wisdom and reason are the truest.

And so we arrive at the result, that the pleasure of the intelligent   583 part of the soul is the pleasantest of the three, and that he of us in whom this is the ruling principle has the pleasantest life.

Unquestionably, he said, the wise man speaks with authority when he approves of his own life.

And what does the judge affirm to be the life which is next, and the pleasure which is next?

Clearly that of the soldier and lover of honour; who is nearer to himself than the money-maker.

Last comes the lover of gain?

Very true, he said.

Twice in succession, then, has the just man overthrown the unjust   b in this conflict; and now comes the third trial, which is dedicated to Olympian Zeus the saviour: a sage whispers in my ear that no pleasure except that of the wise is quite true and pure—all others are a shadow only; and surely this will prove the greatest and most decisive of falls?

Yes, the greatest; but will you explain yourself?

I will work out the subject and you shall answer my questions.   c

Proceed.

Say, then, is not pleasure opposed to pain?

True.

And there is a neutral state which is neither pleasure nor pain?

There is.

A state which is intermediate, and a sort of repose of the soul about either—that is what you mean?

Yes.

You remember what people say when they are sick?

What do they say?

That after all nothing is pleasanter than health. But then they never knew this to be the greatest of pleasures until they were ill.   d

Yes, I know, he said.

And when persons are suffering from acute pain, you must have heard them say that there is nothing pleasanter than to get rid of their pain?

I have.

And there are many other cases of suffering in which the mere rest and cessation of pain, and not any positive enjoyment, is extolled by them as the greatest pleasure?

Yes, he said; at the time they are pleased and well content to be at rest.

e

Again, when pleasure ceases, that sort of rest or cessation will be painful?

Doubtless, he said.

Then the intermediate state of rest will be pleasure and will also be pain?

So it would seem.

But can that which is neither become both?

I should say not.

And both pleasure and pain are motions of the soul, are they not?

Yes.

But that which is neither was just now shown to be rest and not motion, and in a mean between them?

584

Yes.

How, then, can we be right in supposing that the absence of pain is pleasure, or that the absence of pleasure is pain?

Impossible.

This then is an appearance only and not a reality; that is to say, the rest is pleasure at the moment and in comparison of what is painful, and painful in comparison of what is pleasant; but all these representations, when tried by the test of true pleasure, are not real but a sort of imposition?

That is the inference.

Look at the other class of pleasures which have no antecedent

b

pains and you will no longer suppose, as you perhaps may at present, that pleasure is only the cessation of pain, or pain of pleasure.

What are they, he said, and where shall I find them?

There are many of them: take as an example the pleasures of smell, which are very great and have no antecedent pains; they come in a moment, and when they depart leave no pain behind them.

Most true, he said.

Let us not, then, be induced to believe that pure pleasure is the

c

cessation of pain, or pain of pleasure.

No.

Still, the more numerous and violent pleasures which reach the soul through the body are generally of this sort—they are reliefs of pain.

That is true.

And the anticipations of future pleasures and pains are of a like nature?

Yes.

Shall I give you an illustration of them?   d

Let me hear.

You would allow, I said, that there is in nature an upper and lower and middle region?

I should.

And if a person were to go from the lower to the middle region, would he not imagine that he is going up; and he who is standing in the middle and sees whence he has come, would imagine that he is already in the upper region, if he has never seen the true upper world?

To be sure, he said; how can he think otherwise?

But if he were taken back again he would imagine, and truly   e imagine, that he was descending?

No doubt.

All that would arise out of his ignorance of the true upper and middle and lower regions?

Yes.

Then can you wonder that persons who are inexperienced in the truth, as they have wrong ideas about many other things, should also have wrong ideas about pleasure and pain and the intermediate state; so that when they are only being drawn towards the painful they feel   585 pain and think the pain which they experience to be real, and in like manner, when drawn away from pain to the neutral or intermediate state, they firmly believe that they have reached the goal of satiety and pleasure; they, not knowing pleasure, err in contrasting pain with the absence of pain, which is like contrasting black with grey instead of white—can you wonder, I say, at this?

No, indeed; I should be much more disposed to wonder at the opposite.

Look at the matter thus:—Hunger, thirst, and the like, are weaknesses of the bodily state?

Yes.   b

And ignorance and folly are weaknesses of the soul?

True.

And food and wisdom are the corresponding satisfactions of either?

Certainly.

And is the satisfaction derived from that which has less or from that which has more existence the truer?

Clearly, from that which has more.

What classes of things have a greater share of pure existence in your judgment—those of which food and drink and condiments and all kinds of sustenance are examples, or the class which contains true opinion and knowledge and mind and all the different kinds of virtue? Put the question in this way:—Which has a more pure being—that which is concerned with the invariable, the immortal, and the true, and is of such a nature, and is found in such natures; or that which is concerned with and found in the variable and mortal, and is itself variable and mortal?

Far purer, he replied, is the being of that which is concerned with the invariable.

And does the essence of the invariable partake of knowledge in the same degree as of essence?

Yes, of knowledge in the same degree.

And of truth in the same degree?

Yes.

And, conversely, that which has less of truth will also have less of essence?

Necessarily.

Then, in general, those kinds of things which are in the service of the body have less of truth and essence than those which are in the service of the soul?

Far less.

And has not the body itself less of truth and essence than the soul?

Yes.

What is filled with more real existence, and actually has a more real existence, is more really filled than that which is filled with less real existence and is less real?

Of course.

And if there be a pleasure in being filled with that which is according to nature, that which is more really filled with more real being will more really and truly enjoy true pleasure; whereas that which participates in less real being will be less truly and surely satisfied, and will participate in an illusory and less real pleasure?

Unquestionably.

STORMING THE CITADEL [586A-592B]

Those then who know not wisdom and virtue, and are always busy
with gluttony and sensuality, go down and up again as far as the
mean; and in this region they move at random throughout life, but
they never pass into the true upper world; thither they neither look,
nor do they ever find their way, neither are they truly filled with true
being, nor do they taste of pure and abiding pleasure. Like cattle,
with their eyes always looking down and their heads stooping to the
earth, that is, to the dining-table, they fatten and feed and breed, and,   b
in their excessive love of these delights, they kick and butt at one
another with horns and hoofs which are made of iron; and they kill
one another by reason of their insatiable lust. For they fill themselves
with that which is not substantial, and the part of themselves which
they fill is also unsubstantial and incontinent.

Verily, Socrates, said Glaucon, you describe the life of the many
like an oracle.

Their pleasures are mixed with pains—how can they be
otherwise? For they are mere shadows and pictures of the true,
and are coloured by contrast, which exaggerates both light and   c
shade, and so they implant in the minds of fools insane desires of
themselves; and they are fought about as Stesichorus says that the
Greeks fought about the shadow of Helen at Troy in ignorance of
the truth.

Something of that sort must inevitably happen.

And must not the like happen with the spirited or passionate
element of the soul? Will not the passionate man who carries his
passion into action, be in the like case, whether he is envious and
ambitious, or violent and contentious, or angry and discontented, if
he be seeking to attain honour and victory and the satisfaction of his   d
anger without reason or sense?

Yes, he said, the same will happen with the spirited element also.

Then may we not confidently assert that the lovers of money
and honour, when they seek their pleasures under the guidance and
in the company of reason and knowledge, and pursue after and
win the pleasures which wisdom shows them, will also have the
truest pleasures in the highest degree which is attainable to them,   e
inasmuch as they follow truth; and they will have the pleasures
which are natural to them, if that which is best for each one is also
most natural to him?

Yes, certainly; the best is the most natural.

587   And when the whole soul follows the philosophical principle, and there is no division, the several parts are just, and do each of them their own business, and enjoy severally the best and truest pleasures of which they are capable?

Exactly.

But when either of the two other principles prevails, it fails in attaining its own pleasure, and compels the rest to pursue after a pleasure which is a shadow only and which is not their own?

True.

And the greater the interval which separates them from philosophy and reason, the more strange and illusive will be the pleasure?

Yes.

And is not that farthest from reason which is at the greatest

b   distance from law and order?

Clearly.

And the lustful and tyrannical desires are, as we saw, at the greatest distance? Yes.

And the royal and orderly desires are nearest?

Yes.

Then the tyrant will live at the greatest distance from true or natural pleasure, and the king at the least?

Certainly.

But if so, the tyrant will live most unpleasantly, and the king most pleasantly?

Inevitably.

Would you know the measure of the interval which separates them?

Will you tell me?

There appear to be three pleasures, one genuine and two spurious: now the transgression of the tyrant reaches a point beyond the spurious; he has run away from the region of law and reason, and taken up his abode with certain slave pleasures which are his

c   satellites, and the measure of his inferiority can only be expressed in a figure.

How do you mean?

I assume, I said, that the tyrant is in the third place from the oligarch; the democrat was in the middle?

Yes.

And if there is truth in what has preceded, he will be wedded to an image of pleasure which is thrice removed as to truth from the pleasure of the oligarch?

He will.

And the oligarch is third from the royal; since we count as one   d
royal and aristocratical?

Yes, he is third.

Then the tyrant is removed from true pleasure by the space of a
number which is three times three?

Manifestly.

The shadow then of tyrannical pleasure determined by the
number of length will be a plane figure.

Certainly.

And if you raise the power and make the plane a solid, there is
no difficulty in seeing how vast is the interval by which the tyrant is
parted from the king.

Yes; the arithmetician will easily do the sum.

Or if some person begins at the other end and measures the   e
interval by which the king is parted from the tyrant in truth of
pleasure, he will find him, when the multiplication is completed,
living 729 times more pleasantly, and the tyrant more painfully by
this same interval.

What a wonderful calculation! And how enormous is the distance   588
which separates the just from the unjust in regard to pleasure and
pain!

Yet a true calculation, I said, and a number which nearly concerns
human life, if human beings are concerned with days and nights and
months and years. (729 NEARLY equals the number of days and
nights in the year.)

Yes, he said, human life is certainly concerned with them.

Then if the good and just man be thus superior in pleasure to the
evil and unjust, his superiority will be infinitely greater in propriety
of life and in beauty and virtue?

Immeasurably greater.

Well, I said, and now having arrived at this stage of the argument,
we may revert to the words which brought us hither: Was not some   b
one saying that injustice was a gain to the perfectly unjust who was
reputed to be just?

Yes, that was said.

Now then, having determined the power and quality of justice
and injustice, let us have a little conversation with him.

What shall we say to him?

Let us make an image of the soul, that he may have his own
words presented before his eyes.

Of what sort?

c   An ideal image of the soul, like the composite creations of ancient mythology, such as the Chimera or Scylla or Cerberus, and there are many others in which two or more different natures are said to grow into one.

There are said of have been such unions.

Then do you now model the form of a multitudinous, many-headed monster, having a ring of heads of all manner of beasts, tame and wild, which he is able to generate and metamorphose at will.

d   You suppose marvellous powers in the artist; but, as language is more pliable than wax or any similar substance, let there be such a model as you propose.

Suppose now that you make a second form as of a lion, and a third of a man, the second smaller than the first, and the third smaller than the second.

That, he said, is an easier task; and I have made them as you say.

And now join them, and let the three grow into one.

That has been accomplished.

Next fashion the outside of them into a single image, as of a man, so that he who is not able to look within, and sees only the outer hull, may believe the beast to be a single human creature.

e   I have done so, he said.

And now, to him who maintains that it is profitable for the human creature to be unjust, and unprofitable to be just, let us reply that, if he be right, it is profitable for this creature to feast the multitudinous monster and strengthen the lion and the lion-like qualities, but to starve and weaken the man, who is consequently liable to be dragged about at the mercy of either of the other two; and he is not to attempt to familiarize or harmonize them with one another—he ought rather to suffer them to fight and bite and devour one another.

589

Certainly, he said; that is what the approver of injustice says.

To him the supporter of justice makes answer that he should ever so speak and act as to give the man within him in some way or other the most complete mastery over the entire human creature.

b   He should watch over the many-headed monster like a good farmer, fostering and cultivating the gentle qualities, and preventing the wild ones from growing; he should be making the lion-heart his ally, and in common care of them all should be uniting the several parts with one another and with himself.

Yes, he said, that is quite what the maintainer of justice say.

And so from every point of view, whether of pleasure, honour, or advantage, the approver of justice is right and speaks the truth, and the disapprover is wrong and false and ignorant?

c

Yes, from every point of view.

Come, now, and let us gently reason with the unjust, who is not intentionally in error. 'Sweet Sir,' we will say to him, 'what do you think of things esteemed noble and ignoble? Is not the noble that which subjects the beast to the man, or rather to the god in man; and the ignoble that which subjects the man to the beast?' He can hardly avoid saying Yes—can he now?

d

Not if he has any regard for my opinion.

But, if he agree so far, we may ask him to answer another question: 'Then how would a man profit if he received gold and silver on the condition that he was to enslave the noblest part of him to the worst? Who can imagine that a man who sold his son or daughter into slavery for money, especially if he sold them into the hands of fierce and evil men, would be the gainer, however large might be the sum which he received? And will any one say that he is not a miserable friend who remorselessly sells his own divine being to that which is most godless and detestable? Eriphyle took the necklace as the price of her husband's life, but he is taking a bribe in order to foster a worse ruin.'

e

590

Yes, said Glaucon, far worse—I will answer for him.

Has not the intemperate been censured of old, because in him the huge multiform monster is allowed to be too much at large?

Clearly.

And men are blamed for pride and bad temper when the lion and serpent element in them disproportionately grows and gains strength?

b

Yes.

And luxury and softness are blamed, because they relax and weaken this same creature, and make a coward of him?

Very true.

And is not a man reproached for flattery and meanness who subordinates the spirited animal to the unruly monster, and, for the sake of money, of which he can never have enough, habituates him in the days of his youth to be trampled in the mire, and from being a lion to become a monkey?

True, he said.

c

And why are mean employments and manual arts a reproach? Only because they imply a natural weakness of the higher principle; the individual is unable to control the creatures within him, but has to court them, and his great study is how to flatter them.

Such appears to be the reason.

And therefore, being desirous of placing him under a rule like that of the best, we say that he ought to be the servant of the best, in whom the Divine rules; not, as Thrasymachus supposed, to the injury of the servant, but because every one had better be ruled by divine wisdom dwelling within him; or, if this be impossible, then by an external authority, in order that we may be all, as far as possible, under the same government, friends and equals.

True, he said.

And this is clearly seen to be the intention of the law, which is the ally of the whole city; and is seen also in the authority which we exercise over children, and the refusal to let them be free until we have established in them a principle analogous to the constitution of a state, and by cultivation of this higher element have set up in their hearts a guardian and ruler like our own, and when this is done they may go their ways.

Yes, he said, the purpose of the law is manifest.

From what point of view, then, and on what ground can we say that a man is profited by injustice or intemperance or other baseness, which will make him a worse man, even though he acquire money or power by his wickedness?

From no point of view at all.

What shall he profit, if his injustice be undetected and unpunished? He who is undetected only gets worse, whereas he who is detected and punished has the brutal part of his nature silenced and humanized; the gentler element in him is liberated, and his whole soul is perfected and ennobled by the acquirement of justice and temperance and wisdom, more than the body ever is by receiving gifts of beauty, strength and health, in proportion as the soul is more honourable than the body.

Certainly, he said.

To this nobler purpose the man of understanding will devote the energies of his life. And in the first place, he will honour studies which impress these qualities on his soul and will disregard others?

Clearly, he said.

In the next place, he will regulate his bodily habit and training, and so far will he be from yielding to brutal and irrational pleasures, that he will regard even health as quite a secondary matter; his first object will be not that he may be fair or strong or well, unless he is likely thereby to gain temperance, but he will always desire so to attemper the body as to preserve the harmony of the soul?

Certainly he will, if he has true music in him.

And in the acquisition of wealth there is a principle of order and harmony which he will also observe; he will not allow himself to be dazzled by the foolish applause of the world, and heap up riches to his own infinite harm?

Certainly not, he said.

He will look at the city which is within him, and take heed that   c
no disorder occur in it, such as might arise either from superfluity or from want; and upon this principle he will regulate his property and gain or spend according to his means.

Very true.

And, for the same reason, he will gladly accept and enjoy such   592
honours as he deems likely to make him a better man; but those, whether private or public, which are likely to disorder his life, he will avoid?

Then, if that is his motive, he will not be a statesman.

By the dog of Egypt, he will! in the city which is his own he certainly will, though in the land of his birth perhaps not, unless he have a divine call.

I understand; you mean that he will be a ruler in the city of which we are the founders, and which exists in idea only; for I do not believe that there is such an one anywhere on earth?   b

In heaven, I replied, there is laid up a pattern of it, methinks, which he who desires may behold, and beholding, may set his own house in order. But whether such an one exists, or ever will exist in fact, is no matter; for he will live after the manner of that city, having nothing to do with any other.

I think so, he said.

13

PHILOSOPHY AND POETRY

The culminating book of the *Republic* is about the triumph of philosophy over poetic expressions of the cosmos and the triumph of philosophy, with its apprehension of ideal truth and goodness over any materialistic or naturalistic notion of human success or glory.

At the end of Book IX, the deep contrast between the philosopher-king or Queen and the tyrant is made manifest. The secret desire of Glaucon to become a tyrant all the while masquerading as a king is finally vanquished, but now the question becomes: where on earth can Glaucon find a city-state like that invented in *Republic* Books IV-VI that he would be allowed to rule? The suggestion proffered in Book VII (541a) that all the children under ten be re-indoctrinated and the rest of the over-ten population exiled from the city is either a serious, if morally bankrupt, proposal or a concession that the city-in-speech is impossible to realize.

At the end of Book IX the question of what to do if one cannot find an Ideal State within to dwell or rule is raised and the answer is that a wise person will find such a regime within themselves and that makes one impervious to the imperfect culture in which one actually dwells. This clearly is the inspiration for Augustine of Hippo's (354-430 ACE) *The City of God* in which he contrasts the saintly citizens forced to dwell in the Stoic inspired City of Man under Roman domination.

In Book X, Plato sets out to challenge the Athenian's principle source of morality: the poetry of Homer and Hesiod. After trashing poetry, he ironically completes the dialogue with his own substitute poetic myth: the Myth of Er. In Plato's version of the afterlife, the gods do not punish wrongdoers and reward do-gooders once and for all. Rather the individual souls are caught up in cycles of punishment and reward, life and rebirth, which are the results of each soul's choice of lifestyles. It is demonstrated that only the philosopher can escape this cycle with the achievement of a harmonized psyche valuable in itself and indifferent to the external rewards and punishments meted out to her.

CRITIQUE OF POETRY [595A-608D]

Plato's critique of poetry in Book X is cringe-worthy until you recognize the cultural dominance   poetry had in Athens.   Poetry was inspired by Calliope, the muse of epic poetry and Polyhymnia, the muse of religious poetry. The closest modern analogy we might have to Athenian understanding of such divinely inspired poetry would be the respect that believers have of sacred scripture as a direct revelation of the divine kingdom, divine commandments and models of saintly behavior. Plato's critique of poetry is comparable to modern higher criticism of the bible. Plato may be responding to the Athenians' accusations and condemnation of Socrates' heterodoxy the way that liberal theologians respond to the reactions of religious fundamentalists today. Plato's pathetically philistine theory of art is somewhat forgivable if we put it in the context of popular Athenian beliefs that the poems of Homer and Hesiod were making factual claims about the cosmos, the gods and objective moral ideals.

Plato's main argument against the superiority of poetry to philosophy is that art, including poetry, is imitative. It took Western Civilization until the 19th century with the invention of photography to overcome this prejudice, so perhaps we can forgive Plato this colossal error. If art imitates life, and this attempt at realistic depiction is the source of its truth, then Plato has an easy time demolishing its claims. There is, in Plato's understanding, but one ideal Form of couch (an essence pre-existing any actual couch we could sit on). This couch-essence is universal, eternal, perfect couchness itself. The furniture maker appeals to this conceptual blueprint but doesn't invent it. Using wood, nails and upholstery he makes a copy of it, imitating the ideal as close as he can, but failing miserably because no material couch is perfect, at least not for long. The hapless artist imitates the material couch, basing his rendition in tempera on surface appearances at a particular time and place. Thus the painting is an imitation of an imitation. Now Plato completes his debunking of the truth of art by pointing out that the *telos* of a couch cannot be fulfilled by a painting, since you cannot sit, lounge or participate in a symposium on a painting.

We don't usually expect to sit on a painting, but Plato's point is that we can only understand the painting by referring to concrete couches; however, concrete couches are understood only through intellection of their universal Form and *telos* as lounging objects. The truth is obtained through ideation not by a copy of sensual appearances.

This only becomes a serious matter when one turns to poetry as a source of truth about the gods and morality. Socrates sets up the poet by asking Glaucon about a remarkable being who would be capable of making not only couches but animals, plants, stars, the whole cosmos. Then he asks him what he would think of someone who claimed to be such a Maker who merely held up a mirror to the animals, plants, etc. Glaucon says, he'd be a great charlatan. So too, implies Socrates, is the epic poet who describes the afterlife, heaven and the gods.

Socrates, who professes abashment for criticizing so revered a figure as Homer, still bashes him for portraying all the crafts and arts in the society without mastering any of them. Thus one would hardly consult Homer if one were in need of a physician, a pilot, a general or a magistrate. The social uselessness of the poet is juxtaposed against the social utility of the philosopher who knows the Forms and *Teli* of the crafts and arts. If only the public would recognize the philosopher's aptitudes, then he or she would be put in charge of the education of the youth.

Since the poet is concerned with how things appear (the shadows and images) rather than the real being of things (the Forms), all the doubts about the veracity of the senses illustrated by the existence of optical illusions are heaped upon the veracity of the poet. Objects of equal magnitude appear smaller at a distance than close, a straight stick appears bent in water, the moon is smaller at the zenith than on the horizon, etc. Homer speaks of the wine dark sea because, as has been suggested, he was colorblind.

The poet delights in portraying human emotions rather than celebrating reason. Here Plato turns to his basic reaction against the arts, especially poetry. The education of youth consisted largely of the communal singing of the epics of Homer. If Homer depicts the heroes and heroines, which Athenian youth are supposed to emulate, as emotionally distraught over losses and adversity, the youth imitate (an imitation of an imitation) that which is disreputable and unlawful.

Take, for example the behavior of Achilles in the *Iliad*. So petulantly angered by the loss of Brandissi, his mistress, to King Agamemnon, he refuses to fight for the Greeks. After the Trojan hero Hector kills Achilles' beloved Patroclus, Achilles goes berserk, calling out Hector and having killed him, drags his body round and round the walls of Troy; and then he shockingly refuses to cremate the body according to religious custom and command.

Odysseus also does not pass the moral test for Plato. The poet depicts heroes and gods as irrational and distraught whereas the law demands that a man publicly keep his emotions in check so that he may reasonably act in situations of loss and adversity.

Plato blames the entire educational system based on Homer of producing bad leaders and bad regimes.

He then accuses the poets of pandering to our taste for buffoonery and salacious sensuality. What we would be ashamed to do ourselves we love to experience vicariously through the arts. But our indulgences in art tempt us into indiscretions that degrade our characters and discredit our reputations. This latter assumption of Plato leads to the banishment of the poets and poetry from the Ideal State. Because of the charm of poetry, the philosopher kings and queens will readmit them so long as they conform to community standards.

Having challenged the poets and asserted superiority of philosophy in the description of the blessed, virtuous and happy man, Socrates now challenges the theological claims of poetry. Life is short, and the rewards and sufferings of life are finite; but the soul is immortal and the rewards and sufferings in the afterlife are long-lasting.

PROOF OF IMMORTALITY [608D-614A]

Distinguishing between alien forms of evil and evil proper to itself, Socrates shows that both bring dissolution and death to material bodies. Alien evil may include poison, bad air, bad water or rotten food which a body can ingest. Evil proper to an organism might include disease, ill health, wasting or dementia. Comparable afflictions of bodies include rotting, rusting, corrosion, erosion, etc. Now the soul endures alien evil in the form of temptresses, corrupt companions, false prophets; the evils proper to the soul include licentiousness, cowardice and ignorance. The alleged fact that the soul can endure all manner of moral corruption, vice and ruthlessness suggests to Socrates that, unlike the body, the soul must be eternal. Its internal evil doesn't kill it the way an infection kills a body.

This unconvincing but intriguing argument brings Socrates to discuss the rewards and punishments of justice in the afterlife. Having already shown that philosophy is superior to poetry in providing models of behavior in this life, Plato wants to compete with the poet's description of heaven and hell in an eschatological myth informed by philosophy; one that demonstrates that the wisdom of philosophy and its comprehension of justice as an intrinsic value can break through an endless cycle of reward and punishment and procure for the soul endless peace and happiness.

THE MYTH OF ER   [614B-621D]

Plato's foray into theology suggests that he thinks the poets were as inventive as they were revelatory in their depiction of the afterlife. Clearly he is offering the kind of cleaned-up, reformed poetry suitable for the Ideal State as an alternative to the morally flawed Homer, who depicted Odysseus' travels into Hades and his visitation with the exalted dead. Unlike the temporally linear view of everlasting life that Westerners of the Judeo-Christian traditions are used to, Plato depicts a more Eastern view of the afterlife that is cyclical and features souls going to and returning from heaven and Hades in a perpetual fashion.

Er is a warrior who dies in battle. His body does not putrefy even after twelve days. On his funeral pyre, he returns to life and relates what he learned of the afterlife.

He relates that he walked to a meadow where he saw two entrances into the earth and two entrances into the heavens. In the meadow were judges who decided where the souls that accompanied Er would go. The just were sent to the right and up through the entrance to heaven; the unjust were sent to the left and down to Hades. As these left, more souls emerged from the lower right entrance from Hades and other souls descended from heaven through the remaining upper left portal. These arriving souls commingled in the meadow and spoke of their thousand year journey. Those from Hades spoke of their misery and their agonizing punishments (tenfold for every injustice they committed in life). Those returning from heaven spoke of inconceivable beauty and bliss. It is reported that great tyrants never complete their punishment and remain forever in Hades.

Poetic Vision of the Cosmos

The returning souls then are sent on a four day journey after which they find a spot where they can take in the whole universe.

In the center is a column of light which holds everything together. Atop the shaft of light is the Spindle of Necessity. The spindle consists of eight concentric whorls. Here it is clear that Plato is describing the geo-centric cosmos with eight planets orbiting the earth in the order that appears to the spectator on earth unschooled in current astronomy: 8. Fixed stars (the constellations), 7. Chronos (Saturn); 6. Jove (Jupiter); 5. Ares (Mars); 4. Apollo (Sun); 3. Aphrodite (Venus); 2. Hermes (Mercury); 1. Artemis (Moon).

Interestingly from a poetic point of view, each of the planetary whorls exhibits a different color making a rainbow effect. On each circle sits a Siren who sings a single note. Together, all eight Sirens produce a harmonious chord: The music of the Spheres.

The Spindle of the planets revolving around the shaft of light turns in the lap of Necessity, a goddess. Around Necessity sit her three daughters: Lachesis, Fate in charge of the past; Clotho, Fate of the present; and Atropos,

Fate of the future. These fates literally have a hand in mechanically turning the planets in their orbits.

Life Choices

A guide shows up to offer the retuning souls a choice of a new earthly life. Out of the lap of Lachesis, the guide draws a huge number of patterns of possible lives: rich, poor, famous, ordinary, human and animal. Casting these patterns down from a high platform in an array before the returning souls, he enjoins them to pick their next go-round in the cycle of life and death. Not only will each choose his own life, but he will be also choosing the habits of the heart and mind that go with it. Thus he can choose the sort of life that leads to wisdom, courage and justice or one that is rife with vice. Nothing is imposed on the soul but once the soul chooses, there is no going back and his fate is sealed.

One can see here that Plato is culminating his dialogue on justice with the existential choice of character that is entirely the responsibility of the individual. As in the Myth of the Cave, it all depends on the good toward which the individual turns (either toward the shadows on the wall or the sun outside of the cave.) We will see as well that anyone bathed in fortune, as are those blessed with the beauty and bliss of heaven, are not necessarily gifted with wisdom. As noticed in Book I, even the gods can be fooled or bribed into favoring a pious conformist like the wealthy Cephalus who conforms to the laws out of selfish fear of punishment, either by municipal or divine authorities. Such a one, relieved of all fear, may well choose the life of the tyrant if they, like the dead in Plato's Myth, had that chance.

"Now here, my dear Glaucon, is the whole risk for a human being, as it seems."

Each of us must choose among the life choices and this requires a study of the soul most of all, including all the permutations of various circumstances (poverty, wealth, the experience of beauty, private or public life) that affect our soul and its fulfillment and health. In Book I, alarmed over Thrasymachus's immoralist position (344b), Socrates insisted that the Sophist stay and continue to dispute since he was proposing no small matter, but "a course of life on the basis of which each of us would have the most profitable existence."

If one chooses a life that ends in being sent to Hades, then one should choose one that protects him against the temptations and influences of the people there, lest he become more unjust and tyrannical meriting himself more suffering and punishment for the evils he commits. Today, one hopes that young people emerge from prison reformed and resolute rather than hardened, educated in criminality and embittered toward society. Socrates suggests that those who can avoid the extremes in life (for example between asceticism and sensualism or cowardice and rashness) may successfully navigate both this life and the next. Clearly the *eudaimon*, the fully flourishing virtuous person, is Socrates' champion, "for in this way a human being becomes happiest."

Once he lays out this happy prospect for happiness on earth, in heaven and in Hades, Socrates recounts what Er witnesses of the actual choices the retuned souls make:

Out of heaven, the first man chooses the life of a tyrant. Clearly heaven taught him nothing. One wonders what kind of life he previously had to merit him heaven in the first place. It fits the discussion of Cephalus in Book I that his justice and lawfulness were an external show which he maintained because of the external goods that come to the just in appearance. He may have craved the reputation that appearing just and generous in his public sacrifices gave him. Either that or he feared the law, either human or divine. Er relates that the soul from heaven now observed was good in his former life out of mindless conformity, for he lacked philosophy. Need we remind the reader that by this he means the love of wisdom? Moreover one needs a mentor who is wise to lead the lover to the beloved. Such a mentor is Socrates and Socrates is doing his best to teach us wisdom through the Myth of Er.

Offered the chance to quench his lust and rage with impunity this first soul picks the life of a tyrant. Once the lot is chosen there is no turning back and it is revealed to him that his future contains the cannibalization of his own children among other horrifying evil acts. Too late he bemoans his fate.

Er reports some amusing stories about the life choices of the returning souls.

1. Orpheus, who was ripped to shreds by the Meneads, chose the life of a swan to avoid being born of human women who he now hates.
2. Thanyras, a blind singer, chose the life of a nightingale.
3. Ajax, son of Telamon, hero of the Trojan War, who fell on his own sword after Odysseus was deemed more worthy of receiving Achilles' charmed armor, chose the life of an eagle out of hatred for mankind.
4. Atalanta, left for dead by a father who wanted a son, raised by a bear to fight and hunt, chose the life of a victorious male athlete.
5. Epeius, son of Panopeus, known as a coward, chose the life of an artisan woman.
6. Thersites, the buffoon, chose the life of an ape.
7. Finally Odysseus, made wise by his previous labors, chose the life of an ordinary private citizen, minding his business with skill and diligence.

Isn't it clear that with the possible exception of Odysseus each of these souls chose badly for themselves? They chose lives that are not those of fully flourishing human beings and the tragedy is that they are about to make the same mistakes of their first lives, facing the circumstances, travails and opportunities they encounter without the skills and habits of wisdom, temperance, courage and justice which would allow them to flourish humanly in the teeth of adversity.

Forgetting and Rebirth

Lachesis assigns a demon to each soul. The demon leads the soul to Clotho who spins the Spindle of Necessity sealing the fate of the soul. Then the demon leads the soul to Atropos who spins her planets making the fate irreversible. From there they go to Necessity's throne. All make their way through the burning plain of Lethe, finally coming to the bank of the river of Carelessness. Each drinks from the river and goes to sleep to awaken by birth into the new lives having forgotten his past.

Er was stopped from drinking the water and was sent back to his body to tell the tale.

The tale told to Glaucon is a cautionary tale for those who fail to heed the desire for wisdom that only philosophy can provide. Doomed to the eternal recurrence of heaven and Hades, the unlearned soul lurches from desire to desire, from one extreme to the other, from bestial lives to mindless conformity, from bliss to torture.

With a mentor like the martyred Socrates, however, the cycle can be broken, a knowledge of the right kind of life to choose, whether private or public, can be obtained. Such a habituated predisposition to the Good will avoid the pitfalls of extremism. It will courageously withstand even the miseries and adversity of Hades without loss of honor or happiness. It can choose the kind of life that could avoid the lower way of Hades and produce a happy life on earth that would consistently merit the upper way. But even after returning to the Cave after experiencing the bliss and magnificence of the Sun, the planets and the Forms, the philosopher can find the good in life, even in its most shadowy and murky regions. The sensate temptations of cruel exploitation, evil violations and the trappings of power cannot affect a soul whose own worth is impervious to degrading influences. "And so here and in the thousand year journey that we have described, we shall fare well."

Plato's *Republic* was never designed to merely present a philosophical theory. It has been from start to finish a text designed to change us. In this it fits a classical pattern of edifying texts, one that not only convinces us that the just life might be advantageous or may obtain for us a good social reputation. Rather it is a text that sets out to show us the value of actually being just. And *more so,* that, by the end of the text, we have become just (or at least, resolved to consistently act justly, so that eventually we might habitually behave justly). So this is not merely a text about justice but a transformative text…one that alters lives.

SUGGESTIONS FOR FURTHER READING

Annas, Julia. *An Introduction to Plato's* Republic. New York: Oxford, 1981. [335-354]

Asmis, Elizabeth. "Plato on Poetic Creativity." *The Cambridge Companion to Plato.* Ed. Richard Kraut. Cambridge: Cambridge University Press, 1992.

Bernadete, Seth. *Socrates' Second Sailing: On Plato's* Republic. Chicago: University of Chicago Press, 1989. [213-229]

Bloom, Allan. *The Republic of Plato.* New York: Harper Collins, 1968. [426-436]

Murdoch, Iris. *Fire and Sun: Why Plato Banished the Arts.* Oxford: Clarendon Press, 1977.

Pappas, Nickolas. *Plato and the Republic.* New York: Routledge, 1995. [209-216]

Rice, Daryl. *A Guide to Plato's Republic.* Oxford: Oxford University Press, 1998. [114-117]

Rosen, Stanley. *Plato's Republic: A Study.* New Haven: Yale University Press, 2005. [352-388]

Sayers, Sean. *Plato's Republic: An Introductiuon.* Edinburgh: Edinburgh University Press, 1999. [148-157]

Tate, J. "Imitation in Plato's *Republic.*" *Classical Quarterly* 22 (1928): 16-23.

—. "Plato and Imitation." *Classical Quarterly* 22 (1928): 16-23.

Urmson, James O. "Plato and the Poets." *Plato's Republic: Critical Essays.* Lanham, MD: Rowman and Littlefield, 1997. [223-234]

White, Nicholas P. *A Companion to Plato's Republic.* Indianapolis: Hackett, 1979. [246-266]

REPUBLIC 10.595A-621D

BOOK X

CRITIQUE OF POETRY [595A-608D]

595   Of the many excellences which I perceive in the order of our State, there is none which upon reflection pleases me better than the rule about poetry.

To what do you refer?

To the rejection of imitative poetry, which certainly ought not to be received; as I see far more clearly now that the parts of the soul
b   have been distinguished.

What do you mean?

Speaking in confidence, for I should not like to have my words repeated to the tragedians and the rest of the imitative tribe—but I do not mind saying to you, that all poetical imitations are ruinous to the understanding of the hearers, and that the knowledge of their true nature is the only antidote to them.

Explain the purport of your remark.

Well, I will tell you, although I have always from my earliest youth had an awe and love of Homer, which even now makes the
c   words falter on my lips, for he is the great captain and teacher of the whole of that charming tragic company; but a man is not to be reverenced more than the truth, and therefore I will speak out.

Very good, he said.

Listen to me then, or rather, answer me.

Put your question.

Can you tell me what imitation is? for I really do not know.

A likely thing, then, that I should know.

596   Why not? for the duller eye may often see a thing sooner than the keener.

Very true, he said; but in your presence, even if I had any faint notion, I could not muster courage to utter it. Will you enquire yourself?

Well then, shall we begin the enquiry in our usual manner:

Whenever a number of individuals have a common name, we assume them to have also a corresponding idea or form:—do you understand me?

I do.

Let us take any common instance; there are beds and tables in the world—plenty of them, are there not?

Yes.

But there are only two ideas or forms of them—one the idea of a bed, the other of a table.

True.

And the maker of either of them makes a bed or he makes a table for our use, in accordance with the idea—that is our way of speaking in this and similar instances—but no artificer makes the ideas themselves: how could he?

Impossible.

And there is another artist,—I should like to know what you would say of him.

Who is he?

One who is the maker of all the works of all other workmen.

What an extraordinary man!

Wait a little, and there will be more reason for your saying so. For this is he who is able to make not only vessels of every kind, but plants and animals, himself and all other things—the earth and heaven, and the things which are in heaven or under the earth; he makes the gods also.

He must be a wizard and no mistake.

Oh! you are incredulous, are you? Do you mean that there is no such maker or creator, or that in one sense there might be a maker of all these things but in another not? Do you see that there is a way in which you could make them all yourself?

What way?

An easy way enough; or rather, there are many ways in which the feat might be quickly and easily accomplished, none quicker than that of turning a mirror round and round—you would soon enough make the sun and the heavens, and the earth and yourself, and other animals and plants, and all the other things of which we were just now speaking, in the mirror.

Yes, he said; but they would be appearances only.

Very good, I said, you are coming to the point now. And the painter too is, as I conceive, just such another—a creator of appearances, is he not?

Of course.

But then I suppose you will say that what he creates is untrue. And yet there is a sense in which the painter also creates a bed?

Yes, he said, but not a real bed.

And what of the maker of the bed? were you not saying that he too makes, not the idea which, according to our view, is the essence of the bed, but only a particular bed?

Yes, I did.

Then if he does not make that which exists he cannot make true existence, but only some semblance of existence; and if any one were to say that the work of the maker of the bed, or of any other workman, has real existence, he could hardly be supposed to be speaking the truth.

At any rate, he replied, philosophers would say that he was not speaking the truth.

No wonder, then, that his work too is an indistinct expression of truth.

b   No wonder.

Suppose now that by the light of the examples just offered we enquire who this imitator is?

If you please.

Well then, here are three beds: one existing in nature, which is made by God, as I think that we may say—for no one else can be the maker?

No.

There is another which is the work of the carpenter?

Yes.

And the work of the painter is a third?

Yes.

Beds, then, are of three kinds, and there are three artists who superintend them: God, the maker of the bed, and the painter?

Yes, there are three of them.

c   God, whether from choice or from necessity, made one bed in nature and one only; two or more such ideal beds neither ever have been nor ever will be made by God.

Why is that?

Because even if He had made but two, a third would still appear behind them which both of them would have for their idea, and that would be the ideal bed and not the two others.

Very true, he said.

d   God knew this, and He desired to be the real maker of a real bed, not a particular maker of a particular bed, and therefore He created a bed which is essentially and by nature one only.

So we believe.

Shall we, then, speak of Him as the natural author or maker of the bed?

Yes, he replied; inasmuch as by the natural process of creation He is the author of this and of all other things.

And what shall we say of the carpenter—is not he also the maker of the bed?

Yes.

But would you call the painter a creator and maker?

Certainly not.

Yet if he is not the maker, what is he in relation to the bed?

I think, he said, that we may fairly designate him as the imitator of that which the others make.

Good, I said; then you call him who is third in the descent from nature an imitator?

Certainly, he said.

And the tragic poet is an imitator, and therefore, like all other imitators, he is thrice removed from the king and from the truth?

That appears to be so.

Then about the imitator we are agreed. And what about the painter?—I would like to know whether he may be thought to imitate that which originally exists in nature, or only the creations of artists?

The latter.

As they are or as they appear? you have still to determine this.

What do you mean?

I mean, that you may look at a bed from different points of view, obliquely or directly or from any other point of view, and the bed will appear different, but there is no difference in reality. And the same of all things.

Yes, he said, the difference is only apparent.

Now let me ask you another question: Which is the art of painting designed to be—an imitation of things as they are, or as they appear—of appearance or of reality?

Of appearance.

Then the imitator, I said, is a long way off the truth, and can do all things because he lightly touches on a small part of them, and that part an image. For example: A painter will paint a cobbler, carpenter, or any other artist, though he knows nothing of their arts; and, if he is a good artist, he may deceive children or simple persons, when he shows them his picture of a carpenter from a distance, and they will fancy that they are looking at a real carpenter.

Certainly.

And whenever any one informs us that he has found a man who knows all the arts, and all things else that anybody knows, and every single thing with a higher degree of accuracy than any other man—whoever tells us this, I think that we can only imagine him to be a simple creature who is likely to have been deceived by some wizard or actor whom he met, and whom he thought all-knowing, because he himself was unable to analyse the nature of knowledge and ignorance and imitation.

Most true.

And so, when we hear persons saying that the tragedians, and Homer, who is at their head, know all the arts and all things human, virtue as well as vice, and divine things too, for that the good poet cannot compose well unless he knows his subject, and that he who has not this knowledge can never be a poet, we ought to consider whether here also there may not be a similar illusion. Perhaps they may have come across imitators and been deceived by them; they may not have remembered when they saw their works that these were but imitations thrice removed from the truth, and could easily be made without any knowledge of the truth, because they are appearances only and not realities? Or, after all, they may be in the right, and poets do really know the things about which they seem to the many to speak so well?

The question, he said, should by all means be considered.

Now do you suppose that if a person were able to make the original as well as the image, he would seriously devote himself to the image-making branch? Would he allow imitation to be the ruling principle of his life, as if he had nothing higher in him?

I should say not.

The real artist, who knew what he was imitating, would be interested in realities and not in imitations; and would desire to leave as memorials of himself works many and fair; and, instead of being the author of tributes, he would prefer to be the theme of them.

Yes, he said, that would be to him a source of much greater honour and profit.

Then, I said, we must put a question to Homer; not about medicine, or any of the arts to which his poems only incidentally refer: we are not going to ask him, or any other poet, whether he has cured patients like Asclepius, or left behind him a school of medicine such as the Asclepiads were, or whether he only talks about medicine and other arts at second-hand; but we have a right to know respecting military tactics, politics, education, which are the chiefest and noblest subjects of his poems, and we may fairly ask him about them. 'Friend Homer,' then we say to him, 'if you are only in the second remove from truth in what you say of virtue, and not in the third—not an image maker or imitator—and if you are able to discern what pursuits make men better or worse in private or public life, tell us what State was ever better governed by your help? The good order of Lacedaemon is due to Lycurgus, and many other cities great and small have been similarly benefited by others; but who says that you have been a good legislator to them and have done them any good? Italy and Sicily boast of Charondas, and there is Solon who is renowned among us; but what city has anything to say about you?' Is there any city which he might name?

I think not, said Glaucon; not even the Homerids themselves pretend that he was a legislator.

Well, but is there any war on record which was carried on successfully by him, or aided by his counsels, when he was alive?

There is not.

Or is there any invention of his, applicable to the arts or to human life, such as Thales the Milesian or Anacharsis the Scythian, and other ingenious men have conceived, which is attributed to him?

There is absolutely nothing of the kind.

But, if Homer never did any public service, was he privately a guide or teacher of any? Had he in his lifetime friends who loved to associate with him, and who handed down to posterity an Homeric way of life, such as was established by Pythagoras who was so greatly beloved for his wisdom, and whose followers are to this day quite celebrated for the order which was named after him?

Nothing of the kind is recorded of him. For surely, Socrates, Creophylus, the companion of Homer, that child of flesh, whose name always makes us laugh, might be more justly ridiculed for his stupidity, if, as is said, Homer was greatly neglected by him and others in his own day when he was alive?

Yes, I replied, that is the tradition. But can you imagine, Glaucon, that if Homer had really been able to educate and improve mankind—if he had possessed knowledge and not been a mere imitator—can you imagine, I say, that he would not have had many followers, and been honoured and loved by them? Protagoras of Abdera, and Prodicus of Ceos, and a host of others, have only to whisper to their contemporaries: 'You will never be able to manage either your own house or your own State until you appoint us to be your ministers of education'—and this ingenious device of theirs has such an effect in making men love them that their companions all but carry them about on their shoulders. And is it conceivable that the contemporaries of Homer, or again of Hesiod, would have allowed either of them to go about as rhapsodists, if they had really been able to make mankind virtuous? Would they not have been as unwilling to part with them as with gold, and have compelled them to stay at home with them? Or, if the master would not stay, then the disciples would have followed him about everywhere, until they had got education enough?

Yes, Socrates, that, I think, is quite true.

Then must we not infer that all these poetical individuals, beginning with Homer, are only imitators; they copy images of virtue and the like, but the truth they never reach? The poet is like a painter who, as we have already observed, will make a likeness of a cobbler though he understands nothing of cobbling; and his picture is good enough for those who know no more than he does, and judge only by colours and figures.

Quite so.

In like manner the poet with his words and phrases may be said to lay on the colours of the several arts, himself understanding their nature only enough to imitate them; and other people, who are as ignorant as he is, and judge only from his words, imagine that if he speaks of cobbling, or of military tactics, or of anything else, in metre and harmony and rhythm, he speaks very well—such is the sweet influence which melody and rhythm by nature have. And I think that you must have observed again and again what a poor appearance the tales of poets make when stripped of the colours which music puts upon them, and recited in simple prose.

Yes, he said.

They are like faces which were never really beautiful, but only blooming; and now the bloom of youth has passed away from them?

Exactly.

Here is another point: The imitator or maker of the image knows nothing of true existence; he knows appearances only. Am I not right?

Yes.

Then let us have a clear understanding, and not be satisfied with half an explanation.

Proceed.

Of the painter we say that he will paint reins, and he will paint a bit?

Yes.

And the worker in leather and brass will make them?

Certainly.

But does the painter know the right form of the bit and reins? Nay, hardly even the workers in brass and leather who make them; only the horseman who knows how to use them—he knows their right form.

Most true.

And may we not say the same of all things?

What?

That there are three arts which are concerned with all things: one which uses, another which makes, a third which imitates them?

Yes.   d

And the excellence or beauty or truth of every structure, animate or inanimate, and of every action of man, is relative to the use for which nature or the artist has intended them.

True.

Then the user of them must have the greatest experience of them, and he must indicate to the maker the good or bad qualities which develop themselves in use; for example, the flute-player will tell the flute-maker which of his flutes is satisfactory to the performer; he will tell him how he ought to make them, and the other will attend to his instructions?

Of course.   e

The one knows and therefore speaks with authority about the goodness and badness of flutes, while the other, confiding in him, will do what he is told by him?

True.

The instrument is the same, but about the excellence or badness of it the maker will only attain to a correct belief; and this he will gain from him who knows, by talking to him and being compelled to hear what he has to say, whereas the user will have knowledge?

True.

But will the imitator have either? Will he know from use whether   602 or no his drawing is correct or beautiful? or will he have right opinion from being compelled to associate with another who knows and gives him instructions about what he should draw?

Neither.

Then he will no more have true opinion than he will have knowledge about the goodness or badness of his imitations?

I suppose not.

The imitative artist will be in a brilliant state of intelligence about his own creations?

Nay, very much the reverse.

And still he will go on imitating without knowing what makes a thing good or bad, and may be expected therefore to imitate only that which appears to be good to the ignorant multitude?

Just so.

Thus far then we are pretty well agreed that the imitator has no knowledge worth mentioning of what he imitates. Imitation is only a kind of play or sport, and the tragic poets, whether they write in Iambic or in Heroic verse, are imitators in the highest degree?

Very true.

And now tell me, I conjure you, has not imitation been shown by us to be concerned with that which is thrice removed from the truth?

Certainly.

And what is the faculty in man to which imitation is addressed?

What do you mean?

I will explain: The body which is large when seen near, appears small when seen at a distance?

True.

And the same object appears straight when looked at out of the water, and crooked when in the water; and the concave becomes convex, owing to the illusion about colours to which the sight is liable. Thus every sort of confusion is revealed within us; and this is that weakness of the human mind on which the art of conjuring and of deceiving by light and shadow and other ingenious devices imposes, having an effect upon us like magic.

True.

And the arts of measuring and numbering and weighing come to the rescue of the human understanding—there is the beauty of them—and the apparent greater or less, or more or heavier, no longer have the mastery over us, but give way before calculation and measure and weight?

Most true.

And this, surely, must be the work of the calculating and rational principle in the soul?

To be sure.

And when this principle measures and certifies that some things are equal, or that some are greater or less than others, there occurs an apparent contradiction?

True.

But were we not saying that such a contradiction is impossible— the same faculty cannot have contrary opinions at the same time about the same thing?

Very true.

Then that part of the soul which has an opinion contrary to measure is not the same with that which has an opinion in accordance with measure?

True.   603

And the better part of the soul is likely to be that which trusts to measure and calculation?

Certainly.

And that which is opposed to them is one of the inferior principles of the soul?

No doubt.

This was the conclusion at which I was seeking to arrive when I said that painting or drawing, and imitation in general, when doing their own proper work, are far removed from truth, and the companions and friends and associates of a principle within us which is equally removed from reason, and that they have no true or healthy aim.

Exactly.

The imitative art is an inferior who marries an inferior, and has   b
inferior offspring.

Very true.

And is this confined to the sight only, or does it extend to the hearing also, relating in fact to what we term poetry?

Probably the same would be true of poetry.

Do not rely, I said, on a probability derived from the analogy of painting; but let us examine further and see whether the faculty with which poetical imitation is concerned is good or bad.

By all means.

We may state the question thus:—Imitation imitates the actions of men, whether voluntary or involuntary, on which, as they   c
imagine, a good or bad result has ensued, and they rejoice or sorrow accordingly. Is there anything more?

No, there is nothing else.

But in all this variety of circumstances is the man at unity with himself—or rather, as in the instance of sight there was confusion and opposition in his opinions about the same things, so here also is there not strife and inconsistency in his life? Though I need hardly raise the question again, for I remember that all this has been   d
already admitted; and the soul has been acknowledged by us to be full of these and ten thousand similar oppositions occurring at the same moment?

And we were right, he said.

Yes, I said, thus far we were right; but there was an omission which must now be supplied.

What was the omission?

Were we not saying that a good man, who has the misfortune to lose his son or anything else which is most dear to him, will bear the loss with more equanimity than another?

Yes.

But will he have no sorrow, or shall we say that although he cannot help sorrowing, he will moderate his sorrow?

The latter, he said, is the truer statement.

Tell me: will he be more likely to struggle and hold out against his sorrow when he is seen by his equals, or when he is alone?

It will make a great difference whether he is seen or not.

When he is by himself he will not mind saying or doing many things which he would be ashamed of any one hearing or seeing him do?

True.

There is a principle of law and reason in him which bids him resist, as well as a feeling of his misfortune which is forcing him to indulge his sorrow?

True.

But when a man is drawn in two opposite directions, to and from the same object, this, as we affirm, necessarily implies two distinct principles in him?

Certainly.

One of them is ready to follow the guidance of the law?

How do you mean?

The law would say that to be patient under suffering is best, and that we should not give way to impatience, as there is no knowing whether such things are good or evil; and nothing is gained by impatience; also, because no human thing is of serious importance, and grief stands in the way of that which at the moment is most required.

What is most required? he asked.

That we should take counsel about what has happened, and when the dice have been thrown order our affairs in the way which reason deems best; not, like children who have had a fall, keeping hold of the part struck and wasting time in setting up a howl, but always accustoming the soul forthwith to apply a remedy, raising up that which is sickly and fallen, banishing the cry of sorrow by the healing art.

Yes, he said, that is the true way of meeting the attacks of fortune.

Yes, I said; and the higher principle is ready to follow this suggestion of reason?

Clearly.

And the other principle, which inclines us to recollection of our troubles and to lamentation, and can never have enough of them, we may call irrational, useless, and cowardly?

Indeed, we may.

And does not the latter—I mean the rebellious principle—furnish a great variety of materials for imitation? Whereas the wise and calm temperament, being always nearly at peace, is not easy to imitate or to appreciate when imitated, especially at a public festival when a debauched crowd is assembled in a theatre. For the feeling represented is one to which they are strangers.

Certainly.

Then the imitative poet who aims at being popular is not by nature made, nor is his art intended, to please or to affect the rational principle in the soul; but he will prefer the passionate and fitful temper, which is easily imitated?

Clearly.

And now we may fairly take him and place him by the side of the painter, for he is like him in two ways: first, inasmuch as his creations have an inferior degree of truth—in this, I say, he is like him; and he is also like him in being concerned with an inferior part of the soul; and therefore we shall be right in refusing to admit him into a well-ordered State, because he awakens and nourishes and strengthens the feelings and impairs the reason. As in a city when the evil are permitted to have authority and the good are put out of the way, so in the soul of man, as we maintain, the imitative poet implants an evil constitution, for he indulges the irrational nature which has no discernment of greater and less, but thinks the same thing at one time great and at another small—he is a manufacturer of images and is very far removed from the truth.

Exactly.

But we have not yet brought forward the heaviest count in our accusation:—the power which poetry has of harming even the good (and there are very few who are not harmed), is surely an awful thing?

Yes, certainly, if the effect is what you say.

Hear and judge: The best of us, as I conceive, when we listen to a passage of Homer, or one of the tragedians, in which he represents some pitiful hero who is drawling out his sorrows in a long oration, or weeping, and smiting his breast—the best of us, you know, delight in giving way to sympathy, and are in raptures at the excellence of the poet who stirs our feelings most.

d   Yes, of course I know.

But when any sorrow of our own happens to us, then you may observe that we pride ourselves on the opposite quality—we would willingly be quiet and patient; this is the manly part, and the other which delighted us in the recitation is now deemed to be the part of a woman.

Very true, he said.

Now can we be right in praising and admiring another who is doing that which any one of us would abominate and be ashamed of in his own person?

No, he said, that is certainly not reasonable.

Nay, I said, quite reasonable from one point of view.

What point of view?

If you consider, I said, that when in misfortune we feel a natural hunger and desire to relieve our sorrow by weeping and lamentation, and that this feeling which is kept under control in our own calamities is satisfied and delighted by the poets;—the better nature in each of us, not having been sufficiently trained by reason or habit, allows the sympathetic element to break loose because the sorrow is another's; and the spectator fancies that there can be no disgrace to himself in praising and pitying any one who comes telling him what a good man he is, and making a fuss about his troubles; he thinks that the pleasure is a gain, and why should he be too proud to lose this and the poem too? Few persons ever reflect, as I should imagine, that from the evil of other men something of evil is communicated to themselves. And so the feeling of sorrow which has gathered strength at the sight of the misfortunes of others is with difficulty repressed in our own.

How very true!

And does not the same hold also of the ridiculous? There are jests which you would be ashamed to make yourself, and yet on the comic stage, or indeed in private, when you hear them, you are greatly amused by them, and are not at all disgusted at their unseemliness;—the case of pity is repeated;—there is a principle in human nature which is disposed to raise a laugh, and this which you once restrained by reason, because you were afraid of being thought a buffoon, is now let out again; and having stimulated the comedic faculty at the theatre, you are betrayed unconsciously to yourself into playing the comic poet at home.

Quite true, he said.

And the same may be said of lust and anger and all the other affections, of desire and pain and pleasure, which are held to be inseparable from every action—in all of them poetry feeds and waters the passions instead of drying them up; she lets them rule, although they ought to be controlled, if mankind are ever to increase in happiness and virtue.

    d

    I cannot deny it.

    Therefore, Glaucon, I said, whenever you meet with any of the eulogists of Homer declaring that he has been the educator of Hellas, and that he is profitable for education and for the ordering of human things, and that you should take him up again and again and get to know him and regulate your whole life according to him, we may love and honour those who say these things—they are excellent people, as far as their lights extend; and we are ready to acknowledge that Homer is the greatest of poets and first of tragedy writers; but we must remain firm in our conviction that hymns to the gods and praises of famous men are the only poetry which ought to be admitted into our State. For if you go beyond this and allow the honeyed muse to enter, either in epic or lyric verse, not law and the reason of mankind, which by common consent have ever been deemed best, but pleasure and pain will be the rulers in our State.

    e

    607

    That is most true, he said.

    And now since we have reverted to the subject of poetry, let this our defence serve to show the reasonableness of our former judgment in sending away out of our State an art having the tendencies which we have described; for reason constrained us. But that she may not impute to us any harshness or want of politeness, let us tell her that there is an ancient quarrel between philosophy and poetry; of which there are many proofs, such as the saying of 'the yelping hound howling at her lord,' or of one 'mighty in the vain talk of fools,' and 'the mob of sages circumventing Zeus,' and the 'subtle thinkers who are beggars after all'; and there are innumerable other signs of ancient enmity between them. Notwithstanding this, let us assure our sweet friend and the sister arts of imitation, that if she will only prove her title to exist in a well-ordered State we shall be delighted to receive her—we are very conscious of her charms; but we may not on that account betray the truth. I dare say, Glaucon, that you are as much charmed by her as I am, especially when she appears in Homer?

    b

    c

    Yes, indeed, I am greatly charmed.

    Shall I propose, then, that she be allowed to return from exile, but upon this condition only—that she make a defence of herself in lyrical or some other metre?

    d

Certainly.

And we may further grant to those of her defenders who are lovers of poetry and yet not poets the permission to speak in prose on her behalf: let them show not only that she is pleasant but also useful to States and to human life, and we will listen in a kindly spirit; for if this can be proved we shall surely be the gainers—I mean, if there is a use in poetry as well as a delight?

Certainly, he said, we shall be the gainers.

If her defence fails, then, my dear friend, like other persons who are enamoured of something, but put a restraint upon themselves when they think their desires are opposed to their interests, so too must we after the manner of lovers give her up, though not without a struggle. We too are inspired by that love of poetry which the education of noble States has implanted in us, and therefore we would have her appear at her best and truest; but so long as she is unable to make good her defence, this argument of ours shall be a charm to us, which we will repeat to ourselves while we listen to her strains; that we may not fall away into the childish love of her which captivates the many. At all events we are well aware that poetry being such as we have described is not to be regarded seriously as attaining to the truth; and he who listens to her, fearing for the safety of the city which is within him, should be on his guard against her seductions and make our words his law.

Yes, he said, I quite agree with you.

Yes, I said, my dear Glaucon, for great is the issue at stake, greater than appears, whether a man is to be good or bad. And what will any one be profited if under the influence of honour or money or power, aye, or under the excitement of poetry, he neglect justice and virtue?

Yes, he said; I have been convinced by the argument, as I believe that any one else would have been.

And yet no mention has been made of the greatest prizes and rewards which await virtue.

What, are there any greater still? If there are, they must be of an inconceivable greatness.

Why, I said, what was ever great in a short time? The whole period of three score years and ten is surely but a little thing in comparison with eternity?

Say rather 'nothing,' he replied.

And should an immortal being seriously think of this little space rather than of the whole?

Of the whole, certainly. But why do you ask?

PROOF OF IMMORTALITY [608D-614A]

Are you not aware, I said, that the soul of man is immortal and   d
imperishable?

He looked at me in astonishment, and said: No, by heaven: And
are you really prepared to maintain this?

Yes, I said, I ought to be, and you too—there is no difficulty in
proving it.

I see a great difficulty; but I should like to hear you state this
argument of which you make so light.

Listen then.

I am attending.

There is a thing which you call good and another which you call
evil?

Yes, he replied.

Would you agree with me in thinking that the corrupting and
destroying element is the evil, and the saving and improving element   e
the good?

Yes.

And you admit that every thing has a good and also an evil; as
conjunctivitis is the evil of the eyes and disease of the whole body;
as mildew is of corn, and rot of timber, or rust of copper and iron:
in everything, or in almost everything, there is an inherent evil and   609
disease?

Yes, he said.

And anything which is infected by any of these evils is made
evil, and at last wholly dissolves and dies?

True.

The vice and evil which is inherent in each is the destruction
of each; and if this does not destroy them there is nothing else that
will; for good certainly will not destroy them, nor again, that which
is neither good nor evil.   b

Certainly not.

If, then, we find any nature which having this inherent corruption
cannot be dissolved or destroyed, we may be certain that of such a
nature there is no destruction?

That may be assumed.

Well, I said, and is there no evil which corrupts the soul?

Yes, he said, there are all the evils which we were just now passing
in review: unrighteousness, intemperance, cowardice, ignorance.   c

But does any of these dissolve or destroy her?—and here do not
let us fall into the error of supposing that the unjust and foolish man,

when he is detected, perishes through his own injustice, which is an evil of the soul. Take the analogy of the body: The evil of the body is a disease which wastes and reduces and annihilates the body; and all the things of which we were just now speaking come to annihilation through their own corruption attaching to them and inhering in them and so destroying them. Is not this true?

d

Yes.

Consider the soul in like manner. Does the injustice or other evil which exists in the soul waste and consume her? Do they by attaching to the soul and inhering in her at last bring her to death, and so separate her from the body?

Certainly not.

And yet, I said, it is unreasonable to suppose that anything can perish from without through affection of external evil which could not be destroyed from within by a corruption of its own?

It is, he replied.

Consider, I said, Glaucon, that even the badness of food, whether staleness, decomposition, or any other bad quality, when confined to the actual food, is not supposed to destroy the body; although, if the badness of food communicates corruption to the body, then we should say that the body has been destroyed by a corruption of itself, which is disease, brought on by this; but that the body, being one thing, can be destroyed by the badness of food, which is another, and which does not engender any natural infection—this we shall absolutely deny?

e

610

Very true.

And, on the same principle, unless some bodily evil can produce an evil of the soul, we must not suppose that the soul, which is one thing, can be dissolved by any merely external evil which belongs to another?

Yes, he said, there is reason in that.

Either, then, let us refute this conclusion, or, while it remains unrefuted, let us never say that fever, or any other disease, or the knife put to the throat, or even the cutting up of the whole body into the minutest pieces, can destroy the soul, until she herself is proved to become more unholy or unrighteous in consequence of these things being done to the body; but that the soul, or anything else if not destroyed by an internal evil, can be destroyed by an external one, is not to be affirmed by any man.

b

c

And surely, he replied, no one will ever prove that the souls of men become more unjust in consequence of death.

But if some one who would rather not admit the immortality of the soul boldly denies this, and says that the dying do really become more evil and unrighteous, then, if the speaker is right, I suppose that injustice, like disease, must be assumed to be fatal to the unjust, and that those who take this disorder die by the natural inherent power of destruction which evil has, and which kills them sooner or later, but in quite another way from that in which, at present, the wicked receive death at the hands of others as the penalty of their deeds?   d

No, he said, in that case injustice, if fatal to the unjust, will not be so very terrible to him, for he will be delivered from evil. But I rather suspect the opposite to be the truth, and that injustice which, if it have the power, will murder others, keeps the murderer alive—   e
yes, and well awake too; so far removed is her dwelling-place from being a house of death.

True, I said; if the inherent natural vice or evil of the soul is unable to kill or destroy her, hardly will that which is appointed to be the destruction of some other body, destroy a soul or anything else except that of which it was appointed to be the destruction.

Yes, that can hardly be.

But the soul which cannot be destroyed by an evil, whether inherent or external, must exist for ever, and if existing for ever,   611
must be immortal?

Certainly.

That is the conclusion, I said; and, if a true conclusion, then the souls must always be the same, for if none be destroyed they will not diminish in number. Neither will they increase, for the increase of the immortal natures must come from something mortal, and all things would thus end in immortality.

Very true.

But this we cannot believe—reason will not allow us—any more than we can believe the soul, in her truest nature, to be full of variety and difference and dissimilarity.   b

What do you mean? he said.

The soul, I said, being, as is now proven, immortal, must be the fairest of compositions and cannot be compounded of many elements?

Certainly not.

Her immortality is demonstrated by the previous argument, and there are many other proofs; but to see her as she really is, not as we now behold her, marred by communion with the body and other miseries, you must contemplate her with the eye of reason, in her original purity; and then her beauty will be revealed, and

c   justice and injustice and all the things which we have described
will be manifested more clearly. Thus far, we have spoken the truth
concerning her as she appears at present, but we must remember also
that we have seen her only in a condition which may be compared
to that of the sea-god Glaucus, whose original image can hardly be
discerned because his natural members are broken off and crushed
d   and damaged by the waves in all sorts of ways, and incrustations
have grown over them of seaweed and shells and stones, so that he
is more like some monster than he is to his own natural form. And
the soul which we behold is in a similar condition, disfigured by ten
thousand ills. But not there, Glaucon, not there must we look.

Where then?

At her love of wisdom. Let us see whom she affects, and what
e   society and converse she seeks in virtue of her near kindred with
the immortal and eternal and divine; also how different she would
become if wholly following this superior principle, and borne by a
divine impulse out of the ocean in which she now is, and disengaged
from the stones and shells and things of earth and rock which in wild
variety spring up around her because she feeds upon earth, and is
612   overgrown by the good things of this life as they are termed: then
you would see her as she is, and know whether she have one shape
only or many, or what her nature is. Of her affections and of the
forms which she takes in this present life I think that we have now
said enough.

True, he replied.

And thus, I said, we have fulfilled the conditions of the argument;
we have not introduced the rewards and glories of justice, which, as
b   you were saying, are to be found in Homer and Hesiod; but justice
in her own nature has been shown to be best for the soul in her own
nature. Let a man do what is just, whether he have the ring of Gyges
or not, and even if in addition to the ring of Gyges he put on the
helmet of Hades.

Very true.

And now, Glaucon, there will be no harm in further enumerating
how many and how great are the rewards which justice and the other
c   virtues procure to the soul from gods and men, both in life and after
death.

Certainly not, he said.

Will you repay me, then, what you borrowed in the argument?

What did I borrow?

The assumption that the just man should appear unjust and the
unjust just: for you were of opinion that even if the true state of the

case could not possibly escape the eyes of gods and men, still this admission ought to be made for the sake of the argument, in order that pure justice might be weighed against pure injustice. Do you remember?

I should be much to blame if I had forgotten.   d

Then, as the cause is decided, I demand on behalf of justice that the estimation in which she is held by gods and men and which we acknowledge to be her due should now be restored to her by us; since she has been shown to confer reality, and not to deceive those who truly possess her, let what has been taken from her be given back, that so she may win that palm of appearance which is hers also, and which she gives to her own.

The demand, he said, is just.

In the first place, I said—and this is the first thing which you will   e have to give back—the nature both of the just and unjust is truly known to the gods.

Granted.

And if they are both known to them, one must be the friend and the other the enemy of the gods, as we admitted from the beginning?

True.

And the friend of the gods may be supposed to receive from them all things at their best, excepting only such evil as is the necessary consequence of former sins?   613

Certainly.

Then this must be our notion of the just man, that even when he is in poverty or sickness, or any other seeming misfortune, all things will in the end work together for good to him in life and death: for the gods have a care of any one whose desire is to become just and to be like God, as far as man can attain the divine likeness, by the   b pursuit of virtue?

Yes, he said; if he is like God he will surely not be neglected by him.

And of the unjust may not the opposite be supposed?

Certainly.

Such, then, are the palms of victory which the gods give the just?

That is my conviction.

And what do they receive of men? Look at things as they really are, and you will see that the clever unjust are in the case of runners, who run well from the starting-place to the goal but not back again from the goal: they go off at a great pace, but in the end only look foolish, slinking away with their ears draggling on their shoulders, and without a crown; but the true runner comes to the finish and   c receives the prize and is crowned. And this is the way with the just; he who endures to the end of every action and occasion of his entire life has a good report and carries off the prize which men have to bestow.

True.

And now you must allow me to repeat of the just the blessings which you were attributing to the fortunate unjust. I shall say of them, what you were saying of the others, that as they grow older, they become rulers in their own city if they care to be; they marry whom they like and give in marriage to whom they will; all that you said of the others I now say of these. And, on the other hand, of the unjust I say that the greater number, even though they escape in their youth, are found out at last and look foolish at the end of their course, and when they come to be old and miserable are flouted alike by stranger and citizen; they are beaten and then come those things unfit for ears polite, as you truly term them; they will be racked and have their eyes burned out, as you were saying. And you may suppose that I have repeated the remainder of your tale of horrors. But will you let me assume, without reciting them, that these things are true?

Certainly, he said, what you say is true.

These, then, are the prizes and rewards and gifts which are bestowed upon the just by gods and men in this present life, in addition to the other good things which justice of herself provides.

Yes, he said; and they are fair and lasting.

And yet, I said, all these are as nothing either in number or greatness in comparison with those other recompenses which await both just and unjust after death. And you ought to hear them, and then both just and unjust will have received from us a full payment of the debt which the argument owes to them.

Speak, he said; there are few things which I would more gladly hear.

THE MYTH OF ER   [614B–621D]

Well, I said, I will tell you a tale; not one of the tales which Odysseus tells to the hero Alcinous, yet this too is a tale of a hero, Er the son of Armenius, a Pamphylian by birth. He was slain in battle, and ten days afterwards, when the bodies of the dead were taken up already in a state of corruption, his body was found unaffected by decay, and carried away home to be buried. And on the twelfth day, as he was lying on the funeral pile, he returned to life and told them what he had seen in the other world. He said that when his soul left the body he went on a journey with a great company, and that they came to a mysterious place at which there were two openings in the earth; they were near together, and over against them were two other openings in the heaven above. In the intermediate space there were judges seated, who commanded the just, after they had given judgment on them and had bound their sentences in front of them, to ascend by the heavenly way on the right hand; and in like manner the unjust were bidden by them to descend by the lower way on the left hand; these also bore the symbols of their deeds, but fastened on their backs. He drew near, and they told him that he was to be the messenger who would carry the report of the other world to men, and they bade him hear and see all that was to be heard and seen in that place. Then he beheld and saw on one side the souls departing at either opening of heaven and earth when sentence had been given on them; and at the two other openings other souls, some ascending out of the earth dusty and worn with travel, some descending out of heaven clean and bright. And arriving ever and anon they seemed to have come from a long journey, and they went forth with gladness into the meadow, where they encamped as at a festival; and those who knew one another embraced and conversed, the souls which came from earth curiously enquiring about the things above, and the souls which came from heaven about the things beneath. And they told one another of what had happened by the way, those from below weeping and sorrowing at the remembrance of the things which they had endured and seen in their journey beneath the earth (now the journey lasted a thousand years), while those from above were describing heavenly delights and visions of inconceivable beauty. The story, Glaucon, would take too long to tell; but the sum was this:—He said that for every wrong which they had done to any one they suffered tenfold; or once in a hundred years—such being reckoned to be the length of man's life, and the penalty being thus paid ten times in a thousand years. If, for example, there were any who had been the cause of many deaths, or had betrayed or enslaved cities or armies, or been guilty of any other evil behaviour, for each and all of their offences they received punishment ten times over, and the rewards of beneficence and justice and holiness were in the same proportion. I need hardly repeat what he said concerning young children dying almost as soon as they were born. Of piety and impiety to gods and parents, and of murderers, there were retributions other and greater far which he described. He mentioned that he was present when one of the spirits asked another,

'Where is Ardiaeus the Great?' (Now this Ardiaeus lived a thousand years before the time of Er: he had been the tyrant of some city of Pamphylia, and had murdered his aged father and his elder brother, and was said to have committed many other abominable crimes.) The answer of the other spirit was: 'He doesn't come here and will never come. And this,' said he, 'was one of the dreadful sights which we ourselves witnessed. We were at the mouth of the cavern, and, having completed all our experiences, were about to reascend, when of a sudden Ardiaeus appeared and several others, most of whom were tyrants; and there were also besides the tyrants private individuals who had been great criminals: they were just, as they fancied, about to return into the upper world, but the mouth, instead of admitting them, gave a roar, whenever any of these incurable sinners or some one who had not been sufficiently punished tried to ascend; and then wild men of fiery aspect, who were standing by and heard the sound, seized and carried them off; and Ardiaeus and others they bound head and foot and hand, and threw them down and flayed them with scourges, and dragged them along the road at the side, scraping them on thorns like wool carders, and declaring to the passers-by what were their crimes, and that they were being taken away to be cast into hell.' And of all the many terrors which they had endured, he said that there was none like the terror which each of them felt at that moment, lest they should hear the voice; and when there was silence, one by one they ascended with exceeding joy. These, said Er, were the penalties and retributions, and there were blessings as great.

Now when the spirits which were in the meadow had tarried seven days, on the eighth they were obliged to proceed on their journey, and, on the fourth day after, he said that they came to a place where they could see from above a line of light, straight as a column, extending right through the whole heaven and through the earth, in colour resembling the rainbow, only brighter and purer; another day's journey brought them to the place, and there, in the midst of the light, they saw the ends of the chains of heaven let down from above: for this light is the belt of heaven, and holds together the circle of the universe, like the under-girders of a trireme. From these ends is extended the spindle of Necessity, on which all the revolutions turn. The shaft and hook of this spindle are made of steel, and the whorl is made partly of steel and also partly of other materials. Now the whorl is in form like the whorl used on earth; and the description of it implied that there is one large hollow whorl which is quite scooped out, and into this is fitted another lesser one, and another, and another, and four others, making eight in all, like vessels which fit into one another; the whorls show their edges on the upper side, and on their lower side all together form one continuous whorl. This is pierced by the spindle, which is driven home through the centre of the eighth. The first and outermost whorl has the rim broadest, and the seven inner whorls are narrower, in the following proportions—the sixth is next to the first in size, the fourth next to the sixth; then comes the eighth; the seventh is fifth, the fifth is sixth, the third is seventh, last and eighth comes the second. The largest (or fixed stars) is spangled, and the seventh (or sun) is brightest; the eighth (or moon) coloured by the reflected light of the seventh; the second and fifth (Saturn and Mercury) are in colour like one another, and yellower than the preceding; the third (Venus) has the whitest light; the fourth (Mars) is reddish; the sixth (Jupiter) is in whiteness second. Now the whole spindle has the same motion; but, as the whole revolves in one direction, the seven inner circles move slowly in the other, and of these the swiftest is the eighth; next in swiftness are the seventh, sixth, and fifth, which move together; third in swiftness appeared to move according to the law of this reversed motion the fourth; the third appeared fourth and the second fifth. The spindle turns on the knees of Necessity; and on the upper surface of each circle is a siren, who goes round with them, hymning a single tone or note. The eight together form one harmony; and round about, at equal intervals, there is another band, three in number, each sitting upon her throne: these are the Fates, daughters of Necessity, who are clothed in white robes and have chaplets upon their heads, Lachesis and Clotho and Atropos, who accompany with their voices the harmony of the sirens—Lachesis singing of the past, Clotho of the present, Atropos of the future; Clotho from time to time assisting with a touch of her right hand the revolution of the outer circle of the whorl or spindle, and Atropos with her left hand touching and guiding the inner ones, and Lachesis laying hold of either in turn, first with one hand and then with the other.

When Er and the spirits arrived, their duty was to go at once to Lachesis; but first of all there came a prophet who arranged them in order; then he took from the knees of Lachesis lots and samples of lives, and having mounted a high pulpit, spoke as follows: 'Hear the word of Lachesis, the daughter of Necessity. Mortal souls, behold a new cycle of life and mortality. Your genius will not be allotted to you, but you will choose your genius; and let him who draws the first lot have the first choice, and the life which he chooses shall be his destiny. Virtue is free, and as a man honours or dishonours her he will have more or less of her; the responsibility is with the chooser—God is justified.' When the Interpreter had thus spoken he scattered lots indifferently among them all, and each of them took up the lot which fell near him, all but Er himself (he was not allowed), and each as he took his lot perceived the number which he had obtained. Then the Interpreter placed on the ground before them the samples of lives; and there were many more lives than the souls present, and they were of all sorts. There were lives of every animal and of man in every condition. And there were tyrannies among them, some lasting out the tyrant's life, others which broke off in the middle and came to an end in poverty and exile and beggary; and there were lives of famous men, some who were famous for their form and beauty as well as for their strength and success in games, or, again, for their birth and the qualities of their ancestors; and some who were the reverse of famous for the opposite qualities. And of women likewise; there was not, however, any definite character in them, because the soul, when choosing a new life, must of necessity become different. But there was every other quality, and the all mingled with one another, and also with elements of wealth and poverty, and disease and health; and there were mean states also. And here, my dear Glaucon, is the supreme peril of our human state; and therefore the utmost care should be taken. Let each one of us leave every other kind of knowledge and seek and follow one thing only, if possibly he may be able to learn and may find some one who will make him able to learn and discern between good and evil, and so to choose always and everywhere the better life as he has opportunity. He should consider the bearing of all these things which have been mentioned severally and collectively upon virtue; he should know what the effect of beauty is when combined with poverty or wealth in a particular soul, and what are the good and evil consequences of noble and humble birth, of private and public station, of strength and weakness, of cleverness and dullness, and of all the natural and acquired gifts of the soul, and the operation of them when conjoined; he will then look at the nature of the soul, and from the consideration of all these qualities he will be able to determine which is the better and which is the worse; and so he will choose, giving the name of evil to the life which will make his soul more unjust, and good to the life which will make his soul more just; all else he will disregard. For we have seen and know that this is the best choice both in life and after death. A man must take with him into the world below an unyielding faith in truth and right, that there too he may be undazzled by the desire of wealth or the other allurements of evil, lest, coming upon tyrannies and similar villainies, he do irremediable wrongs to others and suffer yet worse himself; but let him know how to choose the mean and avoid the extremes on either side, as far as possible, not only in this life but in all that which is to come. For this is the way of happiness.

And according to the report of the messenger from the other world this was what the prophet said at the time: 'Even for the last comer, if he chooses wisely and will live diligently, there is appointed a happy and not undesirable existence. Let not him who chooses first be careless, and let not the last despair.' And when he had spoken, he who had the first choice came forward and in a moment chose the greatest tyranny; his mind having been darkened by folly and sensuality, he had not thought out the whole matter before he chose, and did not at first sight perceive that he was fated, among other evils, to devour his own children. But when he had time to reflect, and saw what was in the lot, he began to beat his breast and lament over his choice, forgetting the proclamation of the prophet; for, instead of throwing the blame of his misfortune on himself, he accused chance and the gods, and everything rather than himself. Now he was one of those who came from heaven, and in a former life had dwelt in a well-ordered State, but his virtue was a matter of habit only, and he had no philosophy. And it was true of others who were similarly overtaken, that the greater number of them came from heaven and therefore they had never been schooled by trial, whereas the pilgrims who came from earth having themselves suffered and seen others suffer, were not in a hurry to choose. And owing to this inexperience of theirs, and also because the lot was a chance, many of the souls exchanged a good destiny for an evil or an evil for a good. For if a man had always on his arrival in this world dedicated himself from the first to sound philosophy, and had been moderately fortunate in the number of the lot, he might, as the messenger reported, be happy here, and also his journey to another life and return to this, instead of being rough and underground, would be smooth and heavenly. Most curious, he said, was the spectacle—sad and laughable and strange; for the choice of the souls was in most cases based on their experience of a previous life. There he saw the soul which had once been Orpheus choosing the life of a swan out of enmity to the race of women, hating to be born of a woman because they had been his murderers; he beheld also the soul of Thamyras choosing the life of a nightingale; birds, on the other hand, like the swan and other musicians, wanting to be

b

c

d

e

620

b   men. The soul which obtained the twentieth lot chose the life of a lion, and this was the soul of Ajax the son of Telamon, who would not be a man, remembering the injustice which was done him in the judgment about the arms. The next was Agamemnon, who took the life of an eagle, because, like Ajax, he hated human nature by reason of his sufferings. About the middle came the lot of Atalanta; she, seeing the great fame of an athlete, was unable to resist the temptation: and after her there followed the soul of Epeus the son of Panopeus passing into the nature of a woman cunning in the

c   arts; and far away among the last who chose, the soul of the jester Thersites was putting on the form of a monkey. There came also the soul of Odysseus having yet to make a choice, and his lot happened to be the last of them all. Now the recollection of former toils had disenchanted him of ambition, and he went about for a considerable time in search of the life of a private man who had no cares; he had

d   some difficulty in finding this, which was lying about and had been neglected by everybody else; and when he saw it, he said that he would have done the same had his lot been first instead of last, and that he was delighted to have it. And not only did men pass into animals, but I must also mention that there were animals tame and wild who changed into one another and into corresponding human natures—the good into the gentle and the evil into the savage, in all sorts of combinations.

    All the souls had now chosen their lives, and they went in the order of their choice to Lachesis, who sent with them the genius whom they had severally chosen, to be the guardian of their lives and the fulfiller of the choice: this genius led the souls first to Clotho,

e   and drew them within the revolution of the spindle impelled by her hand, thus ratifying the destiny of each; and then, when they were fastened to this, carried them to Atropos, who spun the threads and made them irreversible, whence without turning round they passed

621   beneath the throne of Necessity; and when they had all passed, they marched on in a scorching heat to the plain of Forgetfulness, which was a barren waste destitute of trees and verdure; and then towards evening they encamped by the river of Unmindfulness, whose water no vessel can hold; of this they were all obliged to drink a certain quantity, and those who were not saved by wisdom drank more than

b   was necessary; and each one as he drank forgot all things. Now after they had gone to rest, about the middle of the night there was a thunderstorm and earthquake, and then in an instant they were driven upwards in all manner of ways to their birth, like stars shooting. He himself was hindered from drinking the water. But in what manner or by what means he returned to the body he could not say; only, in the morning, awaking suddenly, he found himself lying on the pyre.   c

And thus, Glaucon, the tale has been saved and has not perished, and will save us if we are obedient to the word spoken; and we shall pass safely over the river of Forgetfulness and our soul will not be defiled. Wherefore my counsel is, that we hold fast ever to the heavenly way and follow after justice and virtue always, considering that the soul is immortal and able to endure every sort of good and every sort of evil. Thus shall we live dear to one another and to the gods, both while remaining here and when, like conquerors in the games who go round to gather gifts, we receive our reward. And   d it shall be well with us both in this life and in the pilgrimage of a thousand years which we have been describing.

SophiaOmni

Made in the USA
Monee, IL
09 November 2021

81723821R00229